# The Cold War
## A Military History

## JEREMY BLACK

Bloomsbury Academic
An imprint of Bloomsbury Publishing Plc

BLOOMSBURY
LONDON • NEW DELHI • NEW YORK • SYDNEY

**Bloomsbury Academic**

An imprint of Bloomsbury Publishing Plc

| | |
|---|---|
| 50 Bedford Square | 1385 Broadway |
| London | New York |
| WC1B 3DP | NY 10018 |
| UK | USA |

www.bloomsbury.com

First published 2015

**British Library Cataloguing-in-Publication Data**

A catalogue record for this book is available from the British Library.

ISBN: HB: 978-1-4742-1799-6
PB: 978-1-4742-1798-9
ePDF: 978-1-4742-1801-6
ePub: 978-1-4742-1800-9

**Library of Congress Cataloging-in-Publication Data**

Black, Jeremy, 1955-
The Cold War : a military history / Jeremy Black.
pages cm
Includes bibliographical references and index.
ISBN 978-1-4742-1799-6 (hardback)– ISBN 978-1-4742-1798-9 (paperback)– ISBN 978-1-4742-1801-6 (ePDF)– ISBN 978-1-4742-1800-9 (ePub) 1. Military history, Modern–20th century. 2. Cold War. 3. History, Modern–1945-1989. I. Title.
D842.2.B55 2015
355.009'045–dc23
2014034951

Typeset by Fakenham Prepress Solutions, Fakenham, Norfolk NR21 8NN
Printed and bound in India

*For*
*Pete Brown*

# CONTENTS

*Abbreviations* viii
*Preface* ix

**1** 1917–39 1
**2** 1939–45 27
**3** 1945–53 37
**4** 1953–68 81
**5** 1968–79 137
**6** 1979–85 171
**7** 1985–92 197

*Postscript* 219
*Selected Further Reading* 225
*Notes* 229
*Index* 253

# ABBREVIATIONS

CAB     Cabinet Office Papers
FO      Foreign Office Papers
NA      Kew, National Archives
NSC     National Security Council Report
WO      War Office

# PREFACE

This book adopts a particular focus on the Cold War, a focus that is thematic and chronological. The stress is on diplomatic and military confrontation and conflict, and the book begins in 1917. In practice, the Cold War has had many meanings and interpretations since the term was used by the British writer George Orwell, in an article, 'You and the Atomic Bomb', published in the magazine *Tribune* on 19 October 1945, to describe an unwelcome division of the world between the USA and the Soviet Union at the close of World War Two. The Cold War is commonly employed to describe the confrontation between the two powers and their respective alliance systems, from then until the demise of the Soviet Union in 1991 at the hands of its own politicians and citizens. The Cold War has also been employed to describe and, indeed, explain much else in the world in this period. The degree to which the Cold War led to the mobilisation of whole societies ensured that the term has been used to analyse everything and across the world; for example, from comics to pro-natalist policies,[1] and science fiction to gender politics. This range has great value, not least in capturing a potent sense of cultural challenge and the varied dimensions of ideological conflict. Yet, this range also poses problems, notably by diluting the focus on war of a certain type, and by exacerbating a lack of precision in the definition and analysis of Cold War.[2]

Such a lack of precision is helpful in one respect in that it captures the very different international, national and personal experiences and perceptions of the Cold War. This range owes much to the extent to which the term is frequently understood to relate to a period as a whole and, therefore, to much that happened in that period. At once, the Cold War was the global and militarised conflict that was the price to be paid for the 'long peace' from 1945 – the avoidance of the recurrence of a war at the scale of World War Two; and also the peace itself in so far as the avoidance of war was concerned. Moreover, even defined simply in terms of the confrontation mentioned in the first paragraph, there is much that can then be brought into this confrontation or considered in terms of it: the Cold War therefore becomes an economic, social, cultural and intellectual history, as well as a political one, in short a form of total history. Such an approach has great value. Indeed, the Cold War was ideological as well as strategic; and moreover, as the former, but also the latter, cultural in its manifestations. Economics was a linked sphere, one relating to military and diplomatic issues, but also to ideological considerations and to related cultural assumptions.

The different emphases offered in particular studies raise the question, within this wide prospectus, of the reasons for the stance adopted by individual commentators. The variety of approaches, indeed, reflect the extent to which there should be no formulaic narrative and analysis for the Cold War, and no single geographical focus. In particular, the tendency to centre the Cold War on a panoptic vision based on the American experience (or indeed that of any other individual state) is limited as an analysis of developments across much of the world. It was instructive that one American reader advising on a draft of this book noted that a chapter break at 1985 was 'curious for Americans' as it did not mark a change in presidency. This is despite the significance of Mikhail Gorbachev's coming to power in the Soviet Union that year. A similar point was made about 1979, which in practice saw an increase in tension with the Soviet invasion of Afghanistan. Furthermore, as an illustration of the range of other possible interpretations, the Cold War, at least in its origins, can be seen in terms largely unrelated to ideology, for example as a phase in a prolonged struggle over the Eurasian borderlands,[3] or, more cautiously, as an aspect of Russian expansionism and the resistance to it; resistance which, in turn, can be presented as Western expansionism.

As a military historian with a background in diplomatic history, I adopt a particular perspective that accords more with certain approaches than others. That, however, is not intended to suggest that there is only one appropriate way to discuss the Cold War. As an instance of other approaches, it is also possible to bring in the ramifications of policymaking debates, notably the inner-circle deliberations and personalities. First-rate scholarship has been devoted by specialists to these topics. However, the focus here is on outcomes, in particular, but not only, international rivalry and conflict, in large part for reasons of space.

Even focusing on the military and diplomatic confrontation, the extent to which the international relations of that period as a whole can be described in terms of the Cold War, or the Cold War as conventionally understood with regard to antagonism between the Communist bloc and the West, can be questioned. The thrust of most recent research on the Cold War, and, in fact, on global history in this period, is to emphasise multipolarity, and to move away from monocausal explanations of the Cold War. Indeed, the Cold War was a matter not only of superpower relationships, but also of the organic, dynamic interaction between the superpower confrontation on the one hand and complex regional and local situations on the other. At the same time, the latter wars outside Europe were part of the Cold War. These wars frequently involved the struggle over different ideas about modernity that is a key root of the Cold War.

To range even further chronologically may seem very unhelpful, but the argument here is for a long Cold War; namely that the Cold War began, not in 1945 in the aftermath of World War Two (1939–45), or even in the later stages of that war; but in 1917. In that year, the 7 November Revolution (25 October in the Julian or old style calendar used by the Russians then) brought Bolshevik (Soviet Communist) control of Russia. This seismic shift, indeed schism, in the World War One alliance of the Western powers and Russia created a crucial base for the spread of Communist activity. It was followed by an ideological rift that lasted until the fall of Soviet Communism, a rift that was the basis of the Cold War.

To discuss the period after 1945 without considering the earlier years is mistaken, not least because the later period in many respects witnessed a resumption and revival of earlier animosities and disputes after World War Two. The period was also seen in that light by many contemporaries, both east and west. A chronology beginning in 1917 has the further merit that it lessens the customary emphasis on the USA. The early Cold War had another protagonist against the Soviet Union: Britain, the leading imperial power and a prominent opponent of the Communists in the Russian Civil War that followed the Revolution. Moreover, to bridge the Cold War and the two world wars when thinking about geopolitics, strategy and global conflict is very important.

The chronological extension back to 1917 underlines the extent to which the Cold War was a complex and multi-faceted process. There were chronological variations, turning points, and contrasting national perspectives. The views from America and the Soviet Union were very different from those from and about weaker states. Similarly, the perspective centred on Europe was different from those centred on East Asia, the Middle East and Africa. In turn, each of these geographical regions can be differently considered not least as a result of being broken down into sub-regions. There were also the important perceptions, actions and experience of sub-state actors.[4] The Cold War is also open to very different retrospective reinterpretations. As an instance of the latter, the peaceful end of the Cold War in Europe in 1989 led to a tendency to underrate the extent to which preparation for conflict on an unprecedented scale was a key aspect of the Cold War.

Thinking about, and writing, this book has led me to reflect on visits to Communist countries during the Cold War. Living through part of the period of this book and visiting several Communist countries then, as well as sites of confrontation and negotiation, such as Berlin, Budapest, Havana, Helsinki, Kabul, Prague, Tehran and Yalta, has made thinking about this study particularly interesting for me. At the same time, this book is intended to be forward-looking as well as retrospective, not least in encouraging us to reflect on how much the character of the present world owes to the Cold War and in assessing the relevance of current claims about a new Cold War in international relations.

I have benefited from invitations to speak on this topic at the World Affairs Council, George Washington University, Mary Washington University, William Paterson University, the University of Rheims and the University of Naples. I would like to thank Gill Bennett, Pete Brown, Stan Carpenter, Richard Connell, Bill Gibson, Spencer Mawby, Sara Moore, Holger Nehring, Richard Toye, Ingo Trauschweizer, and five anonymous readers for commenting on all or part of earlier drafts. They are not responsible for any errors that remain. I am also grateful for Max Boot and Daniel Stone for their advice. I am again most grateful for the support of Kim Storry in helping see the book through the production process. It gives me considerable pleasure to dedicate this book to Pete Brown. Discussing both this subject and broader historical topics has provided great interest and Pete's insights have been of major value. That he is also good company is a great boon, and I value his friendship.

# CHAPTER ONE

# 1917–39

The Cold War stemmed from war, from the violence, fear and paranoia that conflict fostered, and from defeat and victory in two successive struggles, World War One and the Russian Civil War. Defeat at the hands of Germany and, even more, the social and political strain of conflict on an unprecedented scale in World War One (1914–18) led, in March 1917, to the fall of the Romanov dynasty in Russia and its replacement by a provisional, republican government.[1] The dynasty had responded more successfully to the challenge of the Thirteen Years' War with Poland in 1654–67, to the Great Northern War with Sweden in 1700–21, to wars with the Turks, Sweden and France between 1806 and 1815, and even to the brief French occupation of Moscow in 1812, than it was to do to war of a very different type with Germany. The same problems, of defeat at the hands of Germany, political division and social strain, weakened the Romanovs' republican Social Democratic replacement, and this weakness provided the opportunity for a Bolshevik (Soviet Communist) coup in Russia later in 1917. The victory of the Bolsheviks over domestic foes and foreign intervention in the subsequent Russian Civil War (1918–21) ensured that their regime would not be short-lived, as for example was Communist rule in Hungary in 1919. The victory also furthered the identification of the Soviet regime with struggle, as well as giving such struggle a specific character. The war provided the regime with a strong rationale for opposition to Western states, notably the leading European empires, Britain and France, as well as the USA and, indeed, Japan.

In many respects, the history of the following decades saw a working-out of themes from these years, whether the Soviet attempt to overthrow the British empire in Asia or to conquer Poland. In each of these cases, there was also a continuation with earlier pre-Soviet history. Russian rulers had struggled to control Poland and its outlier in Ukraine for centuries, notably from the late sixteenth century, culminating with Russia gaining the largest share in the three partitions of Poland from 1772–95, partitions that ended Polish independence until 1918 and that left Warsaw under Russian control

until German conquest in 1915, bar for a Napoleonic interlude. Britain and
Russia had had a geopolitical rivalry from the 1710s, as Russian forces, in
their overthrow of the Swedish empire, then operated as far west as modern
Denmark and Germany, and Britain sought by diplomatic and military
means to limit this expansion. This led, in 1720, to the prospect of war
in an attempt to get Russia to abandon its recent conquests of (modern)
Estonia, Finland and part of Latvia, only for Britain to back down when
faced by domestic problems as well as the determination of Tsar Peter the
Great of Russia (r. 1689–1725). In 1791, during the Ochakov Crisis, there
was a revival of this tendency in the first of a series of attempts to thwart
Russian expansion at the expense of the Ottoman (Turkish) empire. There
were ideological as well as geopolitical aspects to this rivalry during the
nineteenth century. In what became known as the Eastern Question, Britain
fought Russia during the Crimean War (1854–6), in an effort to limit
Russian territorial gains. In 1878, the British deployed forces in a further
effort to limit Russian expansion. This was nineteenth-century containment
in action.[2] In turn, the Soviet Union drew both on current ideological
contrasts and on older geopolitical rivalries. Soviet policymakers regarded
Britain as hostile and saw Poland as a reactionary power, largely carved out
of the former Russian empire, and willing and able to resist Soviet attempts
to influence developments further west.

The Russian Revolution and Soviet policy were seen by others, both at
the time and subsequently, in part in terms of earlier concerns. Sir Halford
Mackinder, Britain's leading geopolitician as well as a politician, was
British High Commissioner in South Russia during the Russian Civil War.
He pressed the Cabinet in January 1920 on the danger of 'a new Russian
Czardom of the Proletariat' and of 'Bolshevism, sweeping forward like a
prairie fire' towards India, the core of Britain's overseas empire, and 'lower
Asia'.[3] Such accounts presented Communism as giving renewed energy to
established geopolitical drives, notably the Russian threat to the British
empire in South Asia (the nineteenth century 'Great Game'), and to British
interests and influence in South-West Asia.

This theme has been given even longer-term resonance in some recent
scholarship. In offering a borderland perspective on the origins of the
Cold War, significantly after the latter was over, Alfred Rieber saw the
Cold War as 'a phase in a prolonged struggle over the Eurasian borderlands that stretches back to the early modern period, when the great
polyethnic, bureaucratic conquest empires began to reverse a thousand
years of nomadic military hegemony over sedentary cultures'.[4] More of the
literature looked for continuity between the Soviet Union and Romanov
Russia,[5] and notably with the expansionism of both, for example the search
for warm-water ports.

Yet, as with changes in other aspects of Russian life, for example the
countryside,[6] Communism provided, alongside elements of continuity, new
ideology and direction for geopolitical drives as well as renewed energy.

Communism ensured that there was a Leninist policy for international relations that was very different to the liberal internationalism supported by President Woodrow Wilson of the USA. Moreover, the resulting ideological divisions had major consequences for the practice, as well as content, of international relations.

As another instance of the working out of themes, the early years of the Russian Revolution and the revolutionary regime proved crucial in the developing attitudes and experience of individuals who were to play a key role in the post-1945 period, most notably Joseph Stalin, the Soviet dictator from 1924 until his death in 1953. Similarly, as British Secretary for War in 1918–20, Winston Churchill, later Prime Minister from 1940 to 1945 and 1951 to 1955, sought to strengthen and sustain the war effort against the Communists during the Russian Civil War.[7] This effort entailed British commitments to the new states of the area, such as Finland.

# Russian Civil War

The Russian Civil War is also instructive because the Cold War was quintessentially a military confrontation and a key episode in military history, as well as an ideological rift. Far from being contained short of conflict, the first challenge to the Soviet Union was a hot war involving armies and large-scale military campaigns. Moreover, the Russian Civil War underlined the extent to which, in international and military terms, the Cold War did not simply entail rivalry between leading militaries deploying high-spectrum weaponry, as was to be the case for the Soviet Union and the USA after World War Two, notably with atomic weaponry and missiles. Instead, as was to be seen in the classic 1945–89 period of the Cold War, particularly in Africa in the 1970s, the Russian Civil War involved a range of forces and methods, both military and non-military: regular operations, insurrectionary and counter-insurrectionary conflicts, propaganda, and economic and commercial elements among them.

In military history, the Russian Civil War is often brushed into a brief cul-de-sac, after a lengthy treatment of World War One, with the latter conventionally understood as the move into modern and total warfare. That approach is mistaken, not least because it fails to accept the military significance of the Russian Civil War and the modern and total war it represented, but also the degree to which the Soviet Union was born in the experience of civil war, and took on part of its character accordingly. This was a civil war that for long appeared to hang in the balance. For both sides, force was linked to fear in a sense of assault from linked threats, internal and external. The reaction on the part of the Communists[8] was one of unparalleled brutality, although, even without the civil war, the Communists would probably have conducted themselves pretty much the same. Much of the content and tone of the writings before the Russian Civil War of Vladimir Ilyich Lenin, the Communist leader, predicted what would happen. However, a dream of violence was superseded by a grimmer reality. Such a trajectory was more generally the case for the establishment of Communist regimes. Others were born in the experience of civil war, including Albania, Yugoslavia, China, Cuba, Vietnam and Ethiopia, and such a trajectory would also have been true for would-be Communist regimes. Moreover, as with the Soviet Union, such civil war frequently overlapped with international conflict. This was frequently presented in terms of revolutionary struggle with imperial and colonial powers.

Initially, the November Revolution in 1917 led to a coalition government in Russia. However, the Communists only ever tended to see such government as a means to their end of necessary absolute control as the exponents of the dictatorship of the proletariat. This was an attitude that frequently undermined attempts to create left-wing unity, notably in the form of a Popular Front. Other left-wing parties were regarded as rivals, and ones that were particularly dangerous because they encouraged 'false consciousness' on the part of the working class, in the sense of not supporting Communism. In the spring of 1918, the Communists launched a drive for power that led, by June, to a civil war. This was a struggle that was greater in scale and led to more casualties in Russia than World War One. The Communists were opposed by the (conservative and royalist) Whites, as well as by the Greens (Russia's peasant armies); by the forces of non-Russian peoples which had been brought under the sway of the Russian empire and now had separatist agendas of their own, for example Latvians and Ukrainians; and by foreign forces.

There was concern among Russia's former allies in World War One about the willingness of the Communists in 1918 to align with the Germans, as they in a sense did by signing the Treaty of Brest Litovsk, a separate peace with Germany. This peace enabled the Communists to focus on their opponents within Russia. Earlier, aside from enabling Lenin to return to Russia, Germany had provided the Communists with money. There was among the former allies anxiety about the far more remote possibility of active co-operation between Germany and Russia. Such co-operation would have prefigured, in a different context, the Nazi-Soviet Pact of 1939–41. This concern helped lead in 1918, in the last stage of World War One, to intervention in Russia by its former allies against Germany. This was notably true of Britain, the ally best placed, thanks to naval power and its position in the Middle East, to project force into European Russia. There was a determination to prevent Germany from seizing supplies and territory, and thus better pursuing World War One in the west with Britain, France and the USA. Moreover, after the close of World War One in November 1918, this concern was redefined as a wish to suppress Bolshevism as a force for instability and radicalism, and as a threat both to neighbouring, and nearby, states and interests and more generally.

Fourteen states sent troops and weaponry to help the Whites. British forces were dispatched to the Baltic, Black and Caspian Seas, and to Archangel and Murmansk in northern Russia; while the Americans and the Japanese deployed forces in Siberia, and the French in the Baltic and Black Seas and northern Russia. Other participants included Canadians, Italians, Serbs and Americans in northern Russia, former Czech prisoners of war in Siberia, and Finns, Latvians, Poles and Romanians on Russia's western borders. The victorious alliance that had finally defeated Germany in 1918 now had a new opponent, as well as new members. In part, this effort was part of the attempted re-creation of Eastern Europe in the aftermath of the war. As a result, there was considerable continuity between World War One and the outbreak of the conflicts between Communism and anti-Communism, as there was again to be after World War Two. In turn, Eastern Europe was to be transformed anew in 1989–91.

As far as conflict between Western liberal states and the Soviet Union was concerned, the Russian Civil War was far more bitter than anything seen before or anything that was to occur after 1945. There had been war between Britain and Russia in 1854–6 and rivalry for much of the period from 1790 to 1907. However, there was nothing to match the civilisational conflict between Britain and Soviet Communism that began in 1917. This was even more the case for the USA which had never hitherto fought Russia and was never again to send troops there to fight, but which was to see Soviet Communism as a fundamental threat. In one sense, the Cold War reached its height in the Russian Civil War and, thereafter, had a long after-life. Alternatively, if the Russian Civil War is seen as separate, the after-life was the Cold War. For example, in January 1974, the Philosophy Division in Moscow State University organised a gathering in which, after a display by banner-bearing troops, a general gave a bellicose speech in which he lingered over the Russian Civil War and American involvement in it.[9] This could be made relevant for an audience over half a century later. References to the Civil War, and specifically to Western intervention, were a frequent theme in the conversation of Communists. Given the significance of the Civil War for Soviet assumptions and attitudes thereafter, both before and after World War Two, it is most appropriate to begin the discussion of the Cold War with the Civil War. To do so underlines the importance of the longer term when considering the crises post-1945, and of seeing the deterioration of relations between the allies of World War Two, America, Britain and the Soviet Union, as a return to pre-war animosities, indeed a repetition, albeit in a very different fashion, of the collapse of the alliance between these powers in World War One. At the same time, it is necessary not to assume a static position, or mentality, for any of the powers. To do so for the Soviet Union, or its opponents, is a rather Cold War position.

The Russian Civil War was to be won by the Soviets and lost by their opponents. As with most struggles, it is possible to put the emphasis on either element: winning and losing. In practice, it is necessary to put it on both. The brutal tenacity of the Communists was a key element. Indeed, Soviet policy was in some respects a revival of the harsh military politics of internal conflict in the revolutionary France of the 1790s, and this harshness lent particular drive to the process by which, as in many other civil wars, military necessity led toward internal violence. This necessity stemmed from the requirement to create and sustain forces without the support of a clear-cut, coherent and uncontested governmental structure, or the possibility of eliciting consent through established political channels. These problems faced many other revolutionary movements, such as those in Latin America in the 1810s and 1820s, and they also took a violent turn. Within Russia, the Communists nationalised businesses, seized grain, and imposed a firm dictatorship, while opposition was brutally suppressed, frequently with considerable violence. The Communist mind-set was very much one of unconstrained struggle; a notion that was also to be seen in Fascist ideology. Analysis of Communist Party internal language indicates that, as with the French revolutionaries in the 1790s, their self-belief readily permitted, from the outset, a rationalisation of the use of force. This was not least in the absence of the mass support anticipated, or hoped for, because of the Communists' proclaimed role as vanguards of the people.[10] This stance looked toward the subsequent 'peacetime' policy of Stalinism in which those who followed, or could be alleged to follow, different social practices were regarded as enemies, irrespective of their degree of political activism.[11] 'Peace' propaganda was used to establish this form of mobilisation.

Communist tenacity in the Civil War was accompanied by the large-scale use of terror. In December 1917, Felix Dzerzhinskii, the head of the All-Russian Extraordinary Commission for Struggle Against Sabotage and Counter-Revolution, or Cheka, established that month, declared 'we are not in need of justice. It is war now – face to face, a fight to the finish'.[12] Lenin followed up in January 1918 by demanding extra-judicial executions against speculators and bandits causing food shortages. That September, the Cheka was ordered to shoot opponents summarily, launching a 'Red Terror'. Arbitrary imprisonment, concentration camps, large-scale torture, and the mass killings of those suspected, were all integral parts of the Revolution, and the Cheka was far more brutal and murderous than the Tsarist police had been, albeit in more difficult circumstances. The random, as well as large-scale, character of the killings reflected the wide and paranoid definition of the counter-revolutionaries supposedly plotting to overthrow the revolution. Despite the propaganda aimed against counter-revolutionaries on the Right, many of those slaughtered were rivals on the Left because no other interpretation of politics was permitted. Communist violence contributed to a general social and political fragmentation.[13] While the secret police helped maintain control, troops were employed to crush opposition within the Soviet-dominated zone. However, the ruthless Communist mobilisation of resources could also be counterproductive. For example, in 1918, the Cossack Don Army was able to raise troops against the Red Army because of the harsh nature of Bolshevik grain requisitioning.

Force and intimidation played a role in the raising of a large conscript force by the Communists in 1918. Numerical superiority over the Whites, as a result of this force, was of great importance on a number of occasions early in the struggle and, more generally, in the later stages of the war as the Whites were overcome and the Red Army advanced on widely-distant fronts. The Red Army grew rapidly, especially in early 1919, and heavily outnumbered the Whites in infantry and artillery, but not in cavalry. However, because of the degree to which much of the army was dedicated to food requisitioning and otherwise maintaining the remainder of the army in the field, and due to the impact of desertion, the effective size of the Red Army was not as large as total numbers might imply. Desertion, which was countered with considerable brutality, was an aspect of the chaos and disorder of Russia, including the Communist zone, disorder which the Communists sought to counter with surveillance, force and terror. The Communists' central position was crucial to their war effort, as they had control of the vital populous centres, the industrial areas, including key arms factories around Moscow, and of leading rail nodes, notably Moscow and St Petersburg. Arms supplies were a vital element. For example, foreign troops were sent to Archangel and eventually deployed along the Northern Dvina River to prevent the Communists from seizing the sizeable amount of Western armaments originally destined for the imperial Russian army. As was to be the case in World War Two, these arms had been shipped from Britain. In control of the major cities, the Communists were able to seize and make use of dominance of the telegraph, telephone and postal services. This situation was opposite to the geo-strategy of conflict seen with the Maoist theory of war and with the guerrilla operations that characterised most (but not all) of the conflicts in the Third World in the 1960s and 1970s. In these, the revolutionaries operated from marginal areas, while their opponents controlled the cities. However, in the Russian Civil War, in contrast to the Bolsheviks, the Whites lacked manufacturing capacity.

By retaining control of St Petersburg and Moscow, the Communists, in a traditional Russian response to attackers, could afford to trade space for time. They did so in what was very much a war of movement,[14] a character-istic of a conflict with a lower force density than that on the Western Front in World War One. Indeed, by October 1919, White forces were within 250 miles of Moscow, as well as close to St Petersburg. Nevertheless, the Communist ability to trade space for time, while benefiting from a central position, provided an opportunity to benefit from the failings of the anti-Communist forces. These failings owed much to their internal divisions and to their political and strategic mismanagement. Although, in combination, there was a formidable array of opponents, each of the anti-Communist forces had its own goals, and they sometimes took non-cooperation as far as conflict.

Foreign intervention was not central to the struggle in Russia, but acted as a catalyst for much of the conflict there, notably because of the signifiance of relying on assistance from external forces. This intervention, however, suggested some of the problems that might have affected later attempts at intervention had they been launched, most notably American action against the Communists in the Chinese Civil War (1946–9) after World War Two. There was a lack of agreed aims among the intervening powers. Most obviously, the Americans were suspicious of Japanese ambitions and far less willing than Japan to co-operate with the White regime of Alexander Kolchak in Siberia.[15] Foreign intervention was affected by a shortage of resolve. The forces actually committed were very small, which had much to do with the general unpopularity at home of intervention. Post-war demobilisation and the crippling financial burdens left by World War One placed obvious limits on interventionism. Commitments elsewhere were also significant, notably, for Japan in China and for Britain and France both in the Middle East, where they expanded, gaining parts of the Ottoman empire, and also in occupying part of Germany. Moreover, there was unrest within the British army and navy, which led the government to demobilise more rapidly than it had originally intended. There was also unrest and mutiny in the French navy in the Black Sea in 1919 with a refusal to intervene in the Russian Civil War. Back in Paris, worker militancy in part focused on opposition to this intervention.[16]

The weakness of foreign intervention was greatly exacerbated by the failure of the Whites, which owed much to their internal divisions and their political and strategic mismanagement. Their governments were selfish, greedy and incompetent, which helped to alienate support, especially from the peasantry. A British General Staff report of 22 July 1919 was pessimistic about the chances of Anton Denikin, the leading White general:

> Unless he can offer to the wretched inhabitants of the liberated districts … conditions of existence better than those which they suffered under the Bolshevik regime, he will in the course of time be faced with revolt and hostility in his rear just at the time when the Bolsheviks will be concentrating large numbers of troops for a counter-offensive.[17]

Success in the struggle between Communists and Whites depended in part on who was best able to avoid fighting the Greens and, even more, on who was able to win some of their support.[18] Civilian hostility to conscription and requisitioning undercut the White effort as well as that of the Red Army. The defeat of the Whites helped make foreign intervention redundant, although the Japanese supported the Whites in Siberia until 1922, which enabled the Japanese in the same period to control the Soviet Far East; just as they tried to hold onto the Shantung peninsula in China as a product of their intervention in World War One.

By mid-1921, the Red Army had overcome opposition in the Caucasus and Central Asia, although its invasion of Poland in 1920 was driven back. These conflicts were linked to rivalry between the great powers. The conflict in the Caucasus was in part an instance of the struggle between Britain and the Soviet Union. The British saw Armenia, Azerbaijan and Georgia, each of which briefly became independent in the Russian Civil War, as a buffer for their interests in Iraq, Persia (Iran)[19] and India; and as a source of raw materials, notably oil from Azerbaijan and access to oil from Georgia. In late 1918, the British landed troops in the Black Sea port of Batumi, the terminus of the railway to the oil-producing centre of Baku on the Caspian Sea. This was a commitment advocated by Mackinder. Torpedo-armed coastal motor boats were sent overland to the Caspian Sea. However, under pressure from too many commitments, the British withdrew their forces from late 1919. Benefiting from the divisions between the Caucasus republics, the Soviets advanced and took them over in 1920–1.

Soviet activity and expansionism rested on specific goals; but also on the belief that Communism was a global need and a worldwide movement, and that the legitimacy of the Russian Revolution lay in Russia transforming the world. Its transformation was treated as a necessary and inevitable result of the historical process as described by Karl Marx. Institutionally, this belief was expressed in the revolutionary Comintern, or Communist International, created in 1919. Leon Trotsky claimed of the formal mechanisms of foreign policy, that of the Ministries of Foreign Affairs that were the alternative to the Comintern, that it would be necessary only to 'issue a few revolutionary proclamations to the people and then shut up shop'.[20] In the situation of great flux that followed World War One and accompanied the Russian Civil War, major efforts were made to spread the revolution and to encourage revolutionary movements elsewhere. This was especially the case of Germany, which was seen as particularly susceptible to Communism. This was both because of Marx's view of the causal relationship between Germany's advanced socio-economic development and its propensity to revolution, and due to Germany's defeat in World War One and subsequent instability. There were also high hopes of parts of Eastern Europe, notably Bulgaria and Hungary. A series of Communist parties was founded, for example that of Yugoslavia in 1919. In March 1919, a Communist-led government under Béla Kun won power in Hungary and proclaimed it a Soviet republic. However, the Romanians, with Czech support, invaded in April. Meeting weak resistance, the Romanians entered the capital Budapest in August, helped by Conservatives who took power under Miklós Horthy. In turn, the latter were to be overthrown by the Soviet invasion of 1944–5. If, with hindsight, the idea of the Communist International might appear implausible, Soviet, and then also Chinese, power was to help enable a major expansion in Communist control from 1944 to 1954. Moreover, the Communists were following the approach taken by the French Revolutionaries in the 1790s, an example of which they were very conscious.

As a result of the Soviet hopes of world revolution or, at least, ideological expansion into Central Europe, the Polish victories near Warsaw between 16 and 25 August 1920 were a key incident in the Cold War. The Battle of Warsaw ended the drive west by the Soviets, a drive which had already led them to capture the cities of Minsk and Vilnius the previous month. Had the Soviets succeeded in 1920 and established a sister republic in Poland, on the model of the French Revolutionaries in Italy, Switzerland and the Netherlands, then Communism would have had an opportunity to become more strongly grounded. In this episode, as with the post-1945 conflicts more classically seen as part of the Cold War, the struggle between the Great Powers was indirect: even in the Korean War (1950–3), there was no declaration of war or full-scale conflict. In 1920, the French provided the Poles with useful supplies and military advice, but there was no commitment of troops. Instead, the Poles benefited from their ability to gain the initiative, and then defeat separately the Soviet forces whose coordination was handicapped by mutually-distrustful Communist generals and by lengthy supply lines. Advancing over a very wide front and reliant on long supply lines, the tired Soviet forces lacked depth and nearby reserves.[21] This was a very different situation to their successful fighting advance across this territory against the Germans in 1944. Prior to the Battle of Warsaw in 1920, Soviet strength seemed particularly potent and threatening, and it was unclear whether it would be possible for the Western powers to stop Soviet expansion short of full-scale war. What containment (to employ a later term) could mean in practice was unclear. In the event, after the battle, the Poles, in turn, advanced to within ninety miles of Kiev, before agreeing an armistice. The eventual Treaty of Riga, in March 1921, left Poland with some territory in modern Lithuania, Ukraine and Belarus, and with a frontier far to the east of modern Poland.[22] Similarly, in Finland, the Communists had been stopped, being defeated by anti-Bolshevik forces under Carl Gustav von Mannerheim in 1918; although a treaty accepting Finnish independence was not signed by the Soviets until October 1920. Thanks to the course of the Civil War, the Soviets did not conquer Tallinn, Riga and Vilnius until 1940 and, again, 1944, the year in which they also seized Warsaw. Earlier success would have made the Soviet Union a more formidable power and threat. Indeed, on 22 September 1920, Lenin, who had played a larger role in strategy from the summer of 1919, gave a speech to the Communist Party calling for the advance of the Red Army into Germany.

The failure of the Soviets to conquer Poland, Finland, and the Baltic Republics of Estonia, Latvia and Lithuania, owed something to containment by Britain and France, not least in the shape of the Royal Navy in the Baltic. It played a particularly important role in Estonia and Latvia. Containment, indeed, was to be a significant theme in the diplomacy and domestic policies of the 1920s and 1930s, with the prevention of 'infection' from the Soviet Union a major goal. The alignment and focus of this containment varied to that after 1945. A Soviet-American confrontation from 1945 was likely, due to the power vacuum in Central Europe caused by Germany's collapse[23] and due to the abutting occupation zones in Germany. In contrast, the powers in question in the 1920s were the Soviet Union on one hand, and Britain and France as supporters of the independence of Eastern European states on the other. Moreover, in the absence of occupation zones, there was no equivalent military confrontation to that from 1945.

In emphasising containment, however, there was a tendency, as after 1945, to underplay the role of local opinion, in the shape of the determination of the population not to be engulfed by the Soviets and their local Communist allies. This important element in the situation exemplified the more general role of consent in imperial expansion alongside overcoming local opposition. If there was only limited support for the Whites in Russia, the Communists, in turn, found in many areas into which they expanded, or sought to expand, notably Poland, Finland and Lithuania, even less support, in large part due to anti-Russian nationalism. In Poland and Lithuania, countries with an overwhelming Catholic majority, opposition to the anti-clerical and atheist Communists was also significant. The Latvian and Estonian Communists, in contrast, waged aggressive struggles and did enjoy some popular support. The Soviet defeat by Poland in 1920 left a deep enmity. This was to help lead, first, to the persecution of the Polish minority in the Soviet Union in the 1930s, notably with the murderous 'Polish Operation' of 1937–8, then to Soviet alliance with Nazi Germany in partitioning Poland out of existence in 1939, and to a marked hostility toward Polish nationalism as the Germans were driven back in 1944. In the case of Poland, the Soviet animus against the post-World War One settlement found particular focus.

## World Revolution?

From the outset in 1917, the Communists believed in a utopian ideology, extreme, organised violence, atheism, a redefined place of the individual that served to reject Enlightenment precepts, and the rejection of preceding Russian history. During the Civil War and the 1920s, the Orthodox Church was crushed, with the slaughter of tens of thousands of priests and monks, and the desecration and destruction of churches, monasteries and the tombs of saints. The real and spiritual landscapes of Russia and the psychological life of the people were transformed as a consequence. Communism in its own way therefore constituted a major civilisational challenge to the notion in Europe and North America of a 'Western Civilisation', whether or not articulated explicitly in this fashion. This civilisation owed much to

Christianity and placed considerable weight on liberalism and toleration. From this perspective, Communism, drawing both on a reconceptualisation of Russian authoritarianism and on a new, totalitarian ideology and practice,[24] posed a counter-civilisational challenge with its own precepts, aims, methods and anticipated outcomes. The chiliastic significance of Communist aspirations deserve emphasis. This significance was also to be seen in subsequent Communist revolutions. Moreover, aside from its hostility to the peace settlements following both World War One and the Russian Civil War, the very assumptions and core policies of the Soviet Union posed a major and continuing challenge to the international system. This was more serious, because the successor states established in Eastern Europe after World War One were relatively weak as well as divided by territorial aspirations. This created a volatile situation that was open to exploitation by aggressive states.[25]

If the admission of the Soviet Union to the international system by the other major powers was grudging, Soviet attitudes were also a problem, and, as a result of pro-Soviet activity, there was widespread concern about subversion. Paranoia about the Soviets was not the sole element. Soviet propaganda, a key element of mobilisation externally as well as internally, and the activities, known and suspected, of the Comintern and of Communist parties, went beyond the confines of acceptable diplomacy.[26] There was also much anti-Soviet propaganda. In practice, the hopes of world revolution, with Moscow as the centre and inspiration of the new power of progressive forces around the world, as well as the carrying forward of wartime methods in order to ensure Communist success,[27] were, as a result of painful experience, to be subordinated to the more pragmatic interests of the Soviet state. This was a process that had also been seen with the French Revolution in the 1790s. It proved necessary for the Russian revolutionaries both to accept a new international order[28] and to consolidate their position in a state that was to become the Soviet Union. As a result, in 1921, the People's Commissariat for Foreign Affairs (*Narkomindel*) became more important than the Comintern, and, that year, talented individuals were moved to it from the Comintern.

Diplomatic links, moreover, were developed with capitalist states as well as business interests. In March 1921, an Anglo-Soviet trade agreement was used by the Communists to affirm Russia's legitimate role as a state. An indignant Churchill, who was a fervent anti-Communist, complained that David Lloyd George, the Liberal Prime Minister who had held that post throughout the British intervention in the Russian Civil War, had grasped the 'hairy hand of the baboon' in welcoming the Soviet representative, Leonid Krassin, to his office at No. 10 Downing Street.[29] The British government hoped that engagement, in the shape of trade, would not only provide raw materials to assist European reconstruction while moderating the Communist regime, but would also be a way to dissolve Communism in Russia; but these hopes proved fruitless. The coercive nature of the authoritarian Communist state and the Soviet leader Lenin's mastery of *realpolitik* both helped consolidate the new regime. The *realpolitik* was seen in 1922 when the Treaty of Rapallo with Germany brought two states of very different political type, but both outcast nations, into alliance. This alliance served each as a way to try to overcome their diplomatic weakness, and exemplified a key geopolitical anxiety for both Britain and France, that of Russo-German alignment. This treaty greatly concerned British policy-makers and they accordingly sought to ease Franco-German relations.

The German question made Russian developments more of a challenge to the other European powers, both the Western powers and those in Eastern Europe. Germany was able to use Russia for military training that was forbidden under the 1919 Paris Peace Settlement, thus evading the Inter-Allied Military Control Commission in Germany. In 1922, the Turks bought for use against Greece 20 planes from Germany, which were supplied via Russia. There were also to be important economic links between Germany and Russia, links in part directed against Anglo-French interests. Germany helped in modernising the Soviet Union's armaments and industrial base.[30] Germany provided significant help for Stalin during the Depression. Germany was to play a key role throughout the Cold War. As a result of World War Two, most of Germany was located as part of the Western bloc and, if sometimes somewhat ambiguously so, less ambiguously than France. However, in contrast, prior to World War Two, Germany followed an independent course, not least as a power that rejected the primacy of the 1918 victors. This independent course has again been an element in German policies since the 1970s and, even more, 2000s.

Diplomacy served the Soviets in different ways. In 1923, in contrast to the Rapallo agreement between the two powers the previous year, the Soviets planned war with Germany. This was in support of a hoped-for Communist revolution in the country. At that time, diplomatic efforts were used to support this policy. Arrangements were sought with Poland and the Baltic Republics, whose territory separated Germany from the Soviet Union. In that crisis, there was no division between the realists of the People's Commissariat for Foreign Affairs and the 'bomb-throwers' – revolutionaries – of the Comintern; but, instead, there was excessive optimism at the prospects for revolution.[31] In any event, there was no revolution in Germany. The Soviet envoy had also failed to win Polish support for any Soviet intervention. The pressure in the Soviet Union for a *realpolitik* in international relations that represented the normalisation of relations with other states was not linked to the abandonment of the Communist cause, but, rather, to a focus on the pursuit of Socialism (ie. Communism) in one state (the Soviet Union). This was a course presented as leading to the strengthening of the cause. This emphasis was associated with Stalin who dominated the state after Lenin's death in 1924. However, Stalin was also interested in world revolution and committed to the spread of Communism. Thus, his difference with the more volatile Leon Trotsky's demand for permanent and global revolution was more one of tactics than goals, although that was still a highly significant difference. At a meeting of the Politburo in 1926, Trotsky accused his rival Stalin of becoming 'the gravedigger of the revolution'. Trotsky was to be forced into exile, first internal (1927), and then external (1929), by Stalin. A major element of Stalinist policy, both before and after World War Two, was suppressing those held to be Trotskyites. This was a rift that fed Stalinist paranoia and gave potent force to the idea of the enemy within. This idea was brutally enforced in Communist and allied movements abroad, as with the hunting down of those in the Republican camp considered suspect during the Spanish Civil War (1936–9). Sentenced to death in absentia in 1937, Trotsky himself was murdered in Mexico in 1940 in a plot by Soviet Intelligence, the NKVD.

Domestic politics did not only play a role in Cold War policy in the Soviet Union. In 1924, Britain's Labour government recognised the Soviet Union and negotiated a trade treaty, only for its Conservative successor, alleging Soviet support for subversion, to end the trade agreement and to break off diplomatic relations in 1927. The pro-Conservative press had made the same claim at the time of the October 1924 general election. It was claimed that a letter published on 25 October, supposedly by Grigory Zinoviev, a member of the Politburo, demonstrated that the Soviet government sought the overthrow of the established order in Britain, including in the army. Later an opponent of Stalin, Zinoviev was to be executed in 1936. The letter was probably forged by White Russian émigrés.[32] In September 1924, the Conservatives had tabled a motion of censure in the House of Commons after the Labour government had had a charge of inciting soldiers to disobedience, brought against a Communist journalist, R. J. Campbell, dropped. In 1926, a Soviet role in the unsuccessful General Strike in Britain was suspected, although, in practice, this was far from a revolutionary episode.

In the USA, concern about left-wing labour disorder led to planning for military action, notably, with Plan White, immediately after World War One. This concern remained an important theme into the late 1930s.[33] Moreover, in broader terms of strategy and policy, there was a marked defensive content and tone in America in the 1920s, especially with the legislation of 1920 and 1924 limiting immigration, which was associated with Bolshevism in the conservative mind-set of the period.

Alongside politicians and the press, writers of fiction picked up the theme of a sinister Communist threat, a theme that drew on the intelligence wars between the Soviet Union and the West.[34] John Buchan, a Scottish novelist who had served in intelligence during World War One before becoming an MP, saw the hidden hand of a Communist plot to take over the world. In her novel *The Big Four* (1927), Agatha Christie, a successful British novelist, referred to 'the world-wide unrest, the labour troubles that beset every nation, and the revolutions that break out in some'. The sense of menace played an important role in imaginative fiction. It took forward the pre-war strand of spy fiction, but added a theme of social disorder. There was also frequently a racial dimension, with a tendency to depict hostile figures as Slav and Jewish, frequently in league with sinister elements in British (or French or American) society. This theme drew on a broader hostility to Jews that was given renewed energy by the association of the Russian Revolution in hostile eyes with them. Russian émigrés spread this assessment.[35] In turn, there was similar material in the Soviet Union about Western plots to overthrow the Revolution, a theme that long continued.

Despite the rejection of Trotsky and the focus on the development of the Soviet Union, the pursuit of foreign policy by Stalin was still characterised by a willingness to expand Communist interests worldwide, while subversive means also played a role. Stalin did not trust decision-making to the Foreign Ministry, and, instead, used multiple sources of information, as well as a number of agents and institutions to implement policy.[36] His views, indeed, paranoia, were a reflection not only of his tortuous personality, but also of his experience of the revolutionary underground against Tsarist rule, and later of the Russian Civil War, as well as of his reading and reinterpretation of Marx.

The challenge posed to the stability of other states ensured that this was a Cold War and not simply a continuation of imperial tensions. This challenge helped lead Britain and China to cut off relations with the Soviet Union in 1927. Both powers blamed the Soviet Union for instability in China. The Soviet Trade Delegation in London, accused of espionage, was raided, as were the offices of the All-Russian Co-Operative Society. In 1927, Albert Sarraut, French Minister of the Interior, declared Communism 'the enemy'.[37] Two years later, relations with France were affected by the Soviet attempt to recruit French Communists to spy on French military and logistical capabilities.[38] There was a degree of substance to the fears about Soviet plans and intentions. They were more challenging than the other new republican regimes that had come to power in the 1910s and early 1920s, notably in China and Turkey.

Moreover, the dominance of ideological suppositions and long-term advantage in Soviet policy was seen in the early 1930s when the Soviet government regarded the rise of Hitler, a strident opponent of Communism, as a way to advance its interests, distracting France and radicalising Germany en route towards a proletarian revolution.[39] This approach was a serious misreading of the situation, indeed an aspect of what Communists called 'false consciousness'. However, the policy exemplified Stalin's emphasis on tactical opportunism in order to achieve long-term gains, and also looked toward the post-1945 treatment of East Germany.

At the same time, efforts were made by Western governments to improve relations with the Soviet Union. After Labour returned to power in Britain in 1929, diplomatic relations were resumed and a trade agreement negotiated. The USA did not grant the Soviet Union full diplomatic relations until

1933, when Franklin Delano Roosevelt, a Democrat President, succeeded a longstanding series of Republican Presidents (Warren Harding, Calvin Coolidge, Herbert Hoover), each of whom had been suspicious of Soviet intentions and policies. At the same time, the American insistence that the Soviet Union commit to repaying Tsarist debt was little different from the American insistence that Britain and France repay their wartime borrowing. Without an empire to protect, like that of Britain and France, the USA was less troubled by the Soviet Union than they were. This looked toward the situation immediately after World War Two, but contrasted with that thereafter. The focus of Republican presidents in the 1920s and early 1930s was on reducing government budgets, lowering taxes, raising tariffs, and seeking debt repayments from European nations.[40]

The diplomats sent by Roosevelt to the Soviet Union swiftly realised that it was a harsh tyranny. William C. Bullitt, the first ambassador, who had pressed for full diplomatic relations, reported that fear was a condition of Soviet life, with arbitrary arrests frequent. He soon saw little prospect of better relations between the two states. By the time of his departure in 1936, Bullitt had come to the view that the inherent character of the Soviet system made such relations impossible, an apt conclusion. In August 1935, Bullitt informed Roosevelt, with whom he had a private correspondence, that the emotions of the Comintern 'in deciding to cooperate with the Socialists and bourgeois Democrats in a fight against Fascism are, of course, on all fours with the emotions of the tiger when he went out for that historic ride with the young lady of Niger. The Communists feel sure they will come back from the ride with the Socialists and Democrats inside'.[41] This was an apt summary of Popular Front views. There was a parallel with the Nazi treatment of the rest of the Right in Germany.

## Anti-Imperialism

Soviet subversion targeted Western interests, notably the British empire, the world's largest. The USA, in contrast, had emerged from World War One as, by far, the most significant economic power, but without a global political presence or any intention to seek one. This was capitalism without imperialism, with the important exception of Central America and the Pacific in neither of which the Soviets sought or were able to achieve much. The USA appeared less important as a global force than Britain and less promising as a target.

Although for different reasons than Germany, China, a key area of Western 'informal empire', where British interests were particularly prominent from the 1830s, was also regarded by the Soviets as promising. The Chinese Revolution of 1911 led to the creation of a republic, but also to serious internal disunity. Sun Yat-sen, the leader of the Chinese Nationalists

(Guomindang), was sent a message declaring all unequal treaties null and void, a call that challenged the basis of the foreign political and commercial presence in China and that was intended, in particular, to hit Britain's position there. The Soviets became influential in China in the mid-1920s when they provided support to the Nationalists: advisers, weapons (from October 1924) and money, but not troops. In 1924, Soviet money funded the establishment of the Whampoa Military Academy near Guangzhou (Canton), the Nationalists' base. Designed to provide the basis of an army modelled on that of the Soviet Red Army, the academy was placed under Sun's major military aide, Jiang Jieshi. In 1924, Nationalist forces defeated the merchants' militia, a conservative group in Guangzhou that looked to the British. In 1926, the Northern Expedition, a drive north by the Nationalists' army under Jiang Jieshi, against the warlords who controlled central and northern China, benefited from Soviet advisers, money and equipment, including planes. However, the advisers were disparaging of the Chinese and provided help largely as part of a long-term plan to assist the Chinese Communists, who were then allied to the Nationalists as part of a united-front movement favoured by Stalin, although opposed by Trotsky who preferred revolutionary integrity.

In 1927, after capturing Shanghai and Nanjing, Jiang turned on the Communists, then largely urban-based. Suspicious of their intentions, he crushed the Communists in a bloody 'white purge' that enabled him to improve his relations with the warlords, whom he was seeking to lead and manipulate as well as coerce or defeat. This crushing of the Communists also made it easier for Britain to accept Jiang. In response, Stalin withdrew Soviet advisers and instructed the Chinese Communists to form a Red Army, embark on rural revolution, and try to take over the Nationalists. In 1927, the Communists began a rebellion, only to be swiftly defeated, notably at Nanchang, Shantou and Guangzhou.[42]

Mongolia was also an area of Soviet activity. In addition, ambitious to coordinate opposition to imperial rule, the Soviet Union, in 1920, held a Congress of Peoples of the East at Baku. More generally, the Soviets employed and deployed future Communist leaders. Soviet expansionism and influence, not only in China but, notably, into and in the Islamic world, including Turkey, Iraq, Persia (Iran) and Afghanistan, challenged British interests. The Soviet Union backed opposition to Britain in each country, and provided arms, particularly to Afghanistan, with which Britain fought a war in 1919, and to the nationalists in Turkey, who successfully defied Britain and British interests in 1920–3. Moreover, the failure of Allied intervention in the Russian Civil War encouraged Britain's opponents in these countries. The Soviet role was an element in the drawing in of British ambitions in the Islamic world in 1919–22, although nationalist opposition was more significant.

In January 1920, the Admiralty expressed concern that Soviet expansion into the Middle East threatened the oil supplies required by the Royal

Navy.[43] This threat focused on Persia (Iran) where, as after World War Two, Soviet pressure in northern Persia was seen as a challenge to Britain's position further south on the Gulf. In north-east Persia, the Soviets supported a key local figure, Kuchek Khan, the leader of a revolt in the province of Gilan from 1917. He had been forced by the British to stop his expansionism in 1918, but, in 1920, backed by the Soviets, he announced the foundation of an Iranian Soviet Socialist Republic, and Soviet troops arrived. The Soviets also backed a separatist movement in the Persian part of Azerbaijan, an area in which they were to pursue a comparable agenda after World War Two. However, in 1921, the Soviets found it expedient to negotiate a treaty with Persia, not least because its new government under Reza Khan was rejecting British influence, while Kuchek Khan had turned against the Communists. The Soviets then withdrew their troops. In Persia, as in China and Turkey, the Soviet Union benefited from, and sought to exploit and mould, nationalist opposition to Britain. This pattern was to recur after World War Two, when the Soviet Union was more powerful, but, again, it found it difficult to influence, let alone direct, nationalist states over a long timescale. The complex relationships between the Soviet Union, Britain, and the new nationalist regimes of Persia and Turkey after World War One led to concerns by British commentators about threats to the British empire, notably, but not only, to the British position in India.[44] The fear on the part of British ministers of Soviet subversion in India looked back to pre-Communist days. The Soviet-Turkish Treaty of Friendship signed in 1925 sustained these anxieties because Turkey and Britain had competing views over the oil-rich northern part of Iraq. As a result, Britain built up its military presence in the region, notably deploying air power.

Soviet attempts to exploit anti-imperialism in the 1920s were of limited success. This was the case for example in the Dutch East Indies (later Indonesia), and in Inner Mongolia (against Chinese rule), and, even more, in India (against British rule). Such attempts were to become far more important from the late 1940s as the Soviet Union, and later also China and Cuba, backed what could be defined as national liberation struggles. These were a new version of nineteenth-century nationalist struggles. Earlier in the Cold War, there was less success, and less focus on such activity. In China, in the brief Sino-Soviet War of 1929, the forces of the powerful Manchurian warlord, Zhang Xueliang, were trounced, with heavy casualties, indicating the Soviet Union's determination to maintain Russian interests in the Far East. However, this was scant compensation for the failure to maintain the alliance with the Nationalists or, from 1927, to overthrow them.

The tensions within Soviet foreign policy were to be seen in the 1930s when, alongside opposition to imperial interests, there was a downplaying of anti-colonialism, as part of an attempt to create popular fronts with non-Communist parties, especially in France. The interplay of ideology, strategic goals and tactical advantage seen in these, and other, episodes was scarcely unique to the Soviet Union. It was seen, albeit very differently, in the Anglo-French response to the rise of the Fascist dictators. This interplay underlines the difficulties contemporaries found in evaluating Soviet intentions and policy.

## Stalinist Control

Within the Soviet Union, the emphasis was on total state control. Rebellions were brutally suppressed, notably in Georgia in 1921–2 and 1924, as well as Islamic risings in Chechnya and Daghestan (both in the Russian part of the Caucasus) in 1924, 1928, 1929, 1936 and 1940.[45] These risings looked back to persistent opposition in the Caucasus region to Russian expansion in the nineteenth century, and forward to bitter post-Soviet hostilities in the 1990s and 2000s. This continuity indicates not only longstanding geopolitical rifts, but also the ready transference of ideological rivalries into new contexts as well as the related moulding of the latter by these rivalries. Meanwhile, under Stalin, the Soviet Union was taken into state ownership, the country was forced into centrally-directed industrialisation, and, in place of the willingness to allow peasants to trade in food under the New Economic Policy of 1921, collectivisation was imposed on the countryside. Already hit hard, the Orthodox Church was further devastated. Muslim courts and schools were suppressed.[46] The secret police were a crucial prop to the state. Surveillance was important to reshaping society.[47] The government's manipulation of public information, so that it served the purposes of propaganda, was linked to its control over the means of information. All lived in an information void, unsure of events. At the same time, the government found it difficult to gain reliable information and to direct associated systems, such as the registration of residency and control over movement.[48]

Terror and government-tolerated famine killed at least eleven million in Stalin's 'peacetime' years, warped the lives of the remainder of the population, and made casualties of faith, hope and truth. During the 1931–3 Soviet famine, about three to five million people died in Ukraine and two million in northern Kazakhstan and southern Russia. Soviet policies towards the Ukraine famine which was, to a degree, a result of deliberate policies, led to claims of genocide, both from within Ukraine and elsewhere, claims that were frequently expressed once Ukraine became independent in 1991. The Ukrainian term for this event is *Holodomor* [The Famine Epidemic]. The Soviet census of 1937, the first for eleven years, was suppressed, and the officials involved executed, probably because it revealed losses through famine earlier in the decade that, according to the government, had not occurred.[49] Similarly, in 1936, the project for the mapping of the population density of European Russia was abandoned.

Allowing for the multiple deceptions of Soviet propaganda, and for the disaster of rural collectivisation, there was also, however, important development in the Soviet economy, not least because there was continuing scope for recovery from war and revolution, as economic output in 1928 was still below that in 1913. There was a major expansion of the industrial sector and of electricity generation, albeit, as a result of the state-driven focus of resources on developing industry, at a heavy cost in terms of the everyday life of the population. The forced labour of those made to work in harsh, often fatal, conditions on these projects was another aspect of the more general pressure on living standards. However, the lives of those deemed enemies of the revolution were treated as valueless.

## Military Industrialisation

In a clear parallel with the Soviet situation after 1945, industrial capacity was regarded as a basis for warmaking, both offensive and defensive. The theme of mobilisation was a potent one. It linked Soviet ideology to a consistent fear, indeed paranoia, that was integral to the character of Communism. Stalin was particularly prone to this paranoia, albeit with a blind spot as far as Hitler was concerned. Stalin's perceptions of encirclement, capitalist crisis and inevitable, imminent war, generated his policies of breakneck modernisation. Frustrated by the persistent gap between intention and implementation, the regime in the 1930s adopted more radical and totalitarian impulses and initiatives. These led, in the purges, to the large-scale killing and imprisonment of those held to threaten the revolution or regarded as untrustworthy.

Military industry, the primary justification for the five-years' plans for economic development and priorities, was greatly expanded, due to its having a highly-placed patron, in the shape of the Red Army, to push for investment and resources. The shift in Communist military thought from the early idea of the people under arms, in the shape of a militia, to the recognition of the need for a strong regular military and for comprehensive peacetime organisation for war was also highly important.[50] Unlike in Western states, this focus on a military-industrial complex was a drive that was not restricted by meaningful pressures limiting investment, such as concern for consumer well-being. Military industry was encouraged by an ideology of hostility to foreign states and influences that characterised even Communist moderates. The extent to which Stalin's rise to power was supported by a military high command concerned by the efforts of the fiscally conservative Communist Right, such as Nicolay Bukharin (also an opponent of collectivisation), to resist the rise in military spending was also relevant. All these factors together contributed to and interacted with an extensive development of Soviet military industry. Stalin was eager to back the industrialisation necessary for large-scale mechanisation of the army. He regarded powerful military forces as a way to defend the Revolution against the allegedly implacably hostile capitalist states, especially Britain and Japan. Moreover, his support for Socialism in one state was not inherently pacific, as he used the idea of international crisis to press for an extension of state dominance, notably with the war scare of 1927, which he did not try to defuse.[51] Bukharin, a prominent member of the Politburo in 1924–9, was arrested in 1937. After a show-trial, he was shot in 1938.

A type of defence Keynesianism had a stimulating impact on the Soviet economy, although it also distorted it, not least by clearly limiting the investment possibilities for other sectors of the economy. This factor remained pertinent until the end of the Soviet Union, and provided a clear and important continuity from the pre-World War Two Cold War to its later decades. There were also harsh consequences from the military industrial build-up for living standards. The deadly 1931–3 famine owed much to the disruption linked to agrarian collectivisation, but can in part be blamed on grain stockpiling and railway diversion in preparation for war. However, such a liberal conception about living standards meant little within the authoritarian political parameters, and opportunistic and paranoid strategic culture, of Stalin's Soviet Union. Ideological mobilisation, through Socialism (ie. Communism) backed by terror, was a central feature in the new society.[52] In the purges of 1937–8, the political police used the details on everyone considered anti-Soviet that they had been building up from the early 1920s. The information was provided from outside, notably by denunciations, but also by the varied agencies and processes open to the political police, such as agents, informers, membership purges and verification procedures within the Communist Party. The gathering of data also threw up information on networks of acquaintances. In 1937, when the purges were launched, it proved easy to base them on these records and to link victims in supposed conspiracies. So also, when the purges were joined by 'mass operations' against groups in the population at large such as Poles. Both were linked to the belief that alleged dissidence within the Soviet Union was manipulated by hostile foreign forces.

At the same time, and more profoundly, the regime experienced grave problems in its capacity to govern. Indeed, to a degree, the totalitarian dynamic was the response of the Stalinist regime to the problems created by the nature of the political system itself. Belief in sedition directed against the system led to a search for supporting evidence, and to a treatment of information to the contrary as misleading. When information on sedition was not found, as was often the case, it was fabricated. Networks of spies and saboteurs were invented by the secret police, for example in the Kuzbass, a key industrial zone in western Siberia. Whereas, in its own eyes, Stalinism was a modern form of government, reliant on scientific planning and the expression of the direction of world history and human progress, in practice it was pre-modern and dependent on myth and faith. Combined with paranoia, this position left the system ripe for internal confusion and external manipulation, the very situation that was supposedly being guarded against.[53] Despite the rhetoric of modernisation, this pre-modern form of government remained a fundamental problem until the fall of the Soviet Union.

In the economy, there was a comparable situation, with a universal fabrication of data. Central planners set politically motivated targets, and factory managers lied about their available inputs and achievable outputs to maximise the former and minimise the latter, and then lied again when they failed to meet quotas. Then, regional Party and state bosses lied to cover up the lies of the big local factories. Industrial ministries, sensing that the information they were receiving from localities was false, lied so as to maintain a semblance of efficiency. All this misinformation was communicated back to the planning authorities, who lied to the political leadership about the fulfilment of Five Year Plans. And the regime, realising things were seriously wrong, lied to the population about their triumphs, and set even higher targets for next time. This system, which remained the case throughout the Communist period, did not provide an effective background for policy-making. The purges of 1937–8, in which many of the senior employees of economic commissariats and major industrial plants, project institutes and design bureaux, were sent to prison camps (some were shot), encouraged the avoidance of risk. Moreover, censorship, the 'need-to-know' principle, and restrictions on travel and communications, all made it difficult to relate work to advances elsewhere, and thus to ensure productive synergies.

Nevertheless, the defence Keynesianism, or stimulus through deficit spending, did bring important economic benefits, with the direction of resources leading to the major build-up of industrial, transport and energy infrastructure. These benefits were considered within an international and ideological context, seen as inherently competitive, in which the Soviet Union was perceived, as Marx and Lenin saw it, as a late developer having to try harder in order to catch up. This situation led to an all-encompassing approach, with the range of policies focused on catching up. Elements of a similar attitude could also be seen elsewhere, notably in Nationalist China and in Ataturk's Turkey, but in neither case was this attitude linked to an ideology of global revolution. Moreover, although there was considerable violence, the degree of internal transformation in China and Turkey in the 1920s and 1930s, once their civil wars had finished,[54] was less dependent on terror than in the Soviet case.

The catalyst for full Soviet militarisation was Japan's conquest of Manchuria in September 1931. Manchuria was the part of China where heavy industry was most developed, and this development was to be taken further by Japan, which also used Manchuria as an area for Japanese settlement. Seen as a strategic asset against the Soviet Union, Manchuria abutted the Soviet Far East as well as the rail route to it.[55] This conquest, which accentuated Soviet anxieties about the fate of the embattled revolution as a whole, brought forward concern about Japan as a strategic threat in the Far East, to the Soviet Union as well as China. This concern was greatly strengthened by Japan's success in its 1904–5 war with Russia and by Japan's large-scale intervention in the Russian Civil War. The Soviet Union had hitherto been the dominant power in north Manchuria, but, feeling vulnerable and wishing at this stage to avoid war, it proved willing to cede its interest before the Japanese advance.

Fears of Japan provoked a full-scale industrial mobilisation in the Soviet Union. This mobilisation included expanding bases and forces in the Far East. The TB-3, the world's first mass-produced four-engine, all-metal bomber, was intended as a deterrent against Japan. This was part of the build-up of what, for a while, became the largest air force in the world. The heart of Soviet heavy industry was retooled for armaments production. The cost was immense, but levels of production far ahead of anything else in the world were achieved, notably 4,000 tanks annually, instead of about 1,000 annually until the end of 1931. Under Stalin, there was never any meaningful retreat from that level of production.[56] Despite serious dislocation caused by major German conquest in 1941, and allowing for the important help provided in 1941–5 by the Western allies, this economic growth in the 1930s was to sustain a large-scale military effort in World War Two and to be the basis of Soviet military strength in the Cold War. The location of industrial development influenced Soviet strategic capability. Boosted in all regions, industry in the Urals and Siberia increased in the same proportion as elsewhere, but the already-strong metallurgical industry in the Urals served as the basis for an expansion of industrial production that proved to be beyond the range of German air attack. This productive capacity proved a key strategic asset during World War Two. Major new industrial capacity was also developed near Novosibirsk in south-west Siberia, while new plants were built in Soviet Central Asia.[57] This build-up of a large Soviet military-industrial complex was of major significance for the global arms race of the 1930s and for the development of the Soviet economy and system.

The focus was on the army which was intended to be able to fight Japan and in Europe. There was less success in building up a major navy, a significant failure in terms of the Soviet ability to project power, but this was not for want of effort. Moreover, plans for the Soviet navy are instructive, both because of what they indicate about Stalin's global intentions, at least insofar as military capability was concerned, and because they look toward the major Soviet naval build-up in the 1960s–80s. From 1937–8, Stalin abandoned the emphasis of the 'Young School' on submarines and torpedo boats, an emphasis focused on the defence of Soviet waters, notably the Gulf of Finland, particularly against British attack which had been the issue during the Russian Civil War. Instead, Stalin came to focus on big ships. In part, this was a response to the commitment to such ships by Britain, the USA, Germany and Japan. He planned a 59,000 ton battleship, the *Sovetskii Soiuz*, but was thwarted in his plans to order the world's largest battleship from an American yard.[58] By 1939, there were three battleships of this class under construction in the Soviet Union, as well as two 35,000 ton cruisers, but none was ever completed. World War Two was to reveal serious deficiencies with the Soviet navy, not least the large submarine force.

The purges of the military from 1937 reflected both the close linkage of force and politics in the Soviet Union and Stalin's determination to crush any potential form of dissidence. Claiming to discover a conspiracy between the Soviet and German armies, a belief fed by the German provision of forged information,[59] Stalin had the military heavily purged in 1937, the purges continuing until 1941. The claim by the Soviet leadership that there were plans for a military coup is not without some basis,[60] but also requires more evidence. In the purges, over half the generals, including the vast majority of corps and divisional commanders, were killed, as were thousands of officers. An alternative basis of political power was thus ruthlessly crushed, while the purge of the military encouraged a more general terror against perceived opponents of the Revolution. Moreover, Party control over the military was strengthened with the reintroduction, in 1937, of the system of dual control initially introduced in the Civil War. All military orders had to be countersigned by a political commissar. In 1938, military soviets, with a commander, a chief of staff and a commissar, were created to provide trusted leadership at army and corps level. The purges hit the effectiveness of the military hard. In the case of the navy, the purges greatly exacerbated the problems created by Stalin's unrealistic assumptions about naval construction. As with the air force, the flawed result of Stalin's major build-up of the navy also reflected the difficulty of developing capability and the requirement for more than resources.[61] Stalin's focus anyway remained on the army. For example, the purges, which also greatly affected the air force, were linked to a move for the air force from independent strategic capability to army support. Foreign governments assumed that the purges would greatly compromise Soviet military capability in any war. This affected attitudes to the possibility of the Soviet Union intervening effectively against Hitler during the Munich Crisis of 1938. His confidence about Soviet vulnerability, including when he launched Germany against the Soviet Union in June 1941, owed much to the purges. In this fashion, geopolitics were affected by attitudes and, in this case, these were linked to the perception of the consequences of Stalin's domestic policies.

# Conflict Begins

After the Civil War, the Red Army first faced conflict with a foreign military in 1938, and that as part of the escalating confrontation in East Asia. Throughout the twentieth century, indeed, East Asia was to be a central region of international confrontation and conflict. This preceded the Cold

War, notably with the Sino-Japanese War of 1894–5 and the Russo-Japanese War of 1904–5, but the Cold War cannot be understood unless related to the longstanding geopolitical and ideological rivalries of the region.[62] In December 1931, Japan had rejected a Soviet offer of a non-aggression pact. Subsequently, Japan came to look to Germany, where Hitler gained power in 1933, for a strategic partnership designed to counter both the hostility of Britain and the USA to Japanese expansion against China, and the challenge posed by the Soviet Union to both Japanese and German ambitions and ideologies. Soviet preparations in the Far East, and the more general build-up of the Red Army, were well covered by Japanese intelligence, not least the development, by the end of 1935, of a 170-strong long-range Soviet bomber force able to reach Japan. In turn, the Japanese army produced plans for an invasion of the Soviet Far East and eastern Siberia. The Soviet government saw the challenge it faced in ideological and geopolitical terms. Reports in late 1935 about an Anti-Comintern Pact, which Japan, in fact, was to sign with Germany on 25 November 1936, led Soviet strategists to fear a war on two fronts, as opposed to their previous confidence that they would be able to fight on one front at a time. This fear prefigured their concern in the 1970s and 1980s about conflict with both the USA and China. In January 1936, Marshal Mikhail Tukhachevsky, the commander of the Red Army (who was to be shot on the night of 12 June 1937), pressed the Central Committee of the Communist Party on the need to confront the danger of simultaneous war with Germany and Japan. Concern about Japanese intentions towards neighbouring Mongolia led the Soviet Union to sign a pact of mutual assistance with Mongolia and to warn Japan against expanding there. Moreover, signing a non-aggression pact with China on 21 August 1937, and supplying Jiang Jieshi with plentiful arms, including 297 planes flown by Soviet pilots, and over 3,000 advisers, were steps taken by Stalin to divert Japan into a new intractable commitment in China.[63] Full-scale war had broken out between Japan and China in July 1937, and Japan captured Beijing, Shanghai and the Chinese capital, Nanjing, that year.

In August 1938, at Changkufeng, the Red Army displayed its capability in a clash on the uncertain new frontier with Japan's expanding power. Stalin was ready to fight because he knew from military intelligence that, despite the bellicosity of the Japanese Kwantung Army's leadership in Manchuria, the Japanese government and military leadership in Tokyo did not want another conflict to add to the costly war in China. A limited war served Stalin's purposes. In August 1939, Soviet forces under General Georgi Zhukov were more successful in another border struggle, the Battle of Khalkhin Gol (Russian term) or Nomonhan (Japanese). The Japanese were seriously out-fought.[64] Like the smaller-scale clash between Soviet and Chinese forces on the Ussuri River in 1969 (see p. 134), this limited border war was an aspect of the diplomatic and political realignment of the period, one focused on the Molotov-Ribbentrop (Soviet-German) Pact of August 1939. The complexities and unpredictabilities of such international developments (unpredictabilities that encouraged espionage) were linked to more profound ideological and geopolitical rivalries. In part, the latter came to deadly fruition in World War Two, notably with the German attack on the Soviet Union in 1941, and that of the latter on Japan in 1945. Equally, in part, the alignments of that war witnessed simply a particular stage of those rivalries. This wartime stage, more correctly stages, did not end a deep rivalry between Communism and the West, nor the related struggles to control the fate of Europe, the Far East, and the Western empires. These remained a theme during the war, and became more important thereafter.

# CHAPTER TWO

# 1939–45

The military-industrial build-up of the 1930s was to help the Soviet Union greatly in war with Germany from 1941 to 1945. This was a traumatic conflict that subsequently became very important to the positioning of the Communist Party, and, for many years, of Stalin, as protectors of the country. This positioning still greatly affects Russian thinking, as Vladimir Putin's comments in the 2000s and 2010s have repeatedly indicated. Moreover, implicitly or explicitly, Soviet thinking located the subsequent confrontation with the USA from 1945 to 1989 in a continuum that looked back to the German attack on the Soviet Union in World War Two.

## Hitler and Stalin as Allies, 1939–41

Once Germany had attacked the Soviet Union on 22 June 1941, Soviet commentators emphasised the struggle between Fascism and Communism, and thus between Hitler's Germany and Stalin's Soviet Union. However, in practice, opposition to Britain and to liberal values was highly significant to the policies of Hitler and, even more, Stalin; and the latter's earlier accommodating response to Hitler in 1939–41 powerfully reflected his own animosity to Britain. In each case, there was hostility to Britain's political position, but also a rejection of its liberalism. This was a product not only of an opposition to liberal capitalism as a domestic agenda for liberty and freedom, but also hostility to it as an international agenda focused on resistance to dictatorial expansionism and, instead, on support for the independence of small states: Belgium in 1914 and Poland in 1939. Stalin's powerful hostility to Britain (and France) was also a legacy of the Russian Civil War. Both Stalin and Hitler supported policies of economic self-reliance or *autarky*, and were opposed to the international economic system of free-trade and foreign investment centred on Britain, whose banknotes the Comintern had considered forging. An incompatibility in long-term goals between Britain and the Soviet Union provided a key context for their diplomatic relations, as with the failure of naval armaments diplomacy in 1935–9.[1]

Hitler was a committed anti-Communist, frequently linking Communism with Jews and the fundamental menace to Germany he (inaccurately) claimed the latter posed. Hitler's treatment of German Communists was brutal. Moreover, Germany negotiated an Anti-Comintern Pact with Italy and Japan in 1936, while Germany and the Soviet Union had actively supported opposite sides in the Spanish Civil War (1936–9).[2] To some Spanish commentators today, this war was an aspect of World War Two. Alongside its crucial national dynamics, the Spanish Civil War can be located in the ideological rivalries of the Cold War. Germany and Italy supplied arms and men to the Nationalists, in total about 100,000 men, while Stalin provided arms, notably aircraft and tanks, to the Communists. In response to Soviet shipments, Italy began submarine attacks on Soviet shipping in 1937. At the same time, as a reminder that international priorities reflected geopolitics as well as ideology, the Soviet decision in July 1937 to send aid against Japan to the Nationalists in China greatly reduced the amount available to help Spain. The Cold War would have been much more difficult for the West if the Communists had won in Spain. After the civil war ended, a guerrilla movement fought the Franco regime until the 1950s, while, during World War Two, Franco sent the Blue Division of 'volunteers' to aid Hitler against the Soviet Union in a 'crusade' against Communism.

However, as a reminder of cross-currents, a shared interest in revisionism and opposition to democracy provided a basis for agreement, however insincere, between Hitler and Stalin in 1939. Both reacted strongly against Enlightenment, liberal and capitalist values, and Stalin was more than willing to subordinate the cause of international Communism, about which he was anyway dubious, to that of state expansion in concert with Germany. Each man was responsible for massive slaughter.[3] In the summer of 1938, Stalin planned to approach Hitler for an alliance. Moreover, later that year, the Czech crisis found the Soviets unwilling to give substance to their anti-Appeasement rhetoric even when given permission to transport troops and weaponry across Romania to help Czechoslovakia resist German pressure. Indeed, the Soviet Union may in 1938 have sought to help cause a war that would exhaust other powers but that it could then sit out,[4] rather as Stalin succeeded in doing with the Korean War in 1950–3.

Far from seeking to protect neutrals when Britain and France guaranteed Poland and Romania on 31 March 1939 after the German occupation of Bohemia and Moravia on 15 March, Stalin joined Hitler with the Ribbentrop-Molotov (Nazi-Soviet) Pact or Treaty of Non-Aggression of 23 August 1939. Stalin celebrated the Pact with a toast to 'the health of this great man', Hitler. The Pact divided Eastern Europe into German and Soviet spheres of influence and expansion, and freed Germany in 1939–40 from the risk of a two-front war comparable to that it faced in 1914–17 and 1941–5. German propagandists suggested a link in managing the Soviet Union between Hitler and the care to avoid conflict with Russia taken by Otto von Bismarck, the Prime Minister, then Chancellor of Prussia, then Germany, from 1862 to 1890, who had engineered the German Wars of Unification in 1864–71. The Pact also finally ended earlier Soviet fears of a Polish-Japanese alliance, a fear that had encouraged large-scale action against Polish and Japanese minorities.

Although crucial to the diplomacy and warfare of 1939–41, the German-Soviet Pact became an aspect of the propaganda of the Cold War. After 1941, the Pact was written out of the Soviet historical account and that of Communist parties and leaders who had praised it, such as Mao Zedong, part of a more general pattern of history by omission. Insofar as it was officially discussed, the Pact was presented as an opportunity to gain time and space to resist German attack, which was not, in fact, Stalin's intention. In contrast, the Pact was referred to by external and internal critics of the Soviet system. For example, the fortieth anniversary of the Pact in 1989 was marked by opponents in the Baltic Republics as it had provided the Soviet Union with the opportunity to seize Estonia, Latvia and Lithuania in 1940. The Pact has never had a comparable resonance in the West to the Munich agreement of 1938 between Germany, Italy, Britain and France. The highpoint of Appeasement, this agreement to settle the Czech crisis left Czechoslovakia totally vulnerable to future German attack. Appeasement has proven a more significant image and term in public debate than the Pact. However, far from being a Soviet tactical consequence of Appeasement, the Nazi-Soviet Pact showed much about the logic, as well as methods, of Soviet foreign policy. Moreover, there is no inherent reason why the Pact should be regarded as less significant than the Munich agreement, which did not last for as long.

On 17 September 1939, in accordance with the Nazi-Soviet Pact, Stalin joined in the German attack on Poland, although only after the Germans, who had invaded on 1 September, had already largely defeated the Poles in a conflict that absorbed the Polish military. Stalin therefore prefigured Mussolini's declaration of war on France and Britain in June 1940 once France had been defeated by its German invaders. Soviet policy over Poland demonstrated a habitual pattern, notably with Stalin, of allowing potential opponents to exhaust each other before deriving more direct benefit, a practice that helps to explain what might otherwise be referred to simply as caution. The Soviet Union claimed to be neutral and to be intervening in Poland to safeguard fellow Slavs: the Belarus and Ukrainian communities. The Poles, who were not able to mount much resistance, saw themselves as in a state of war with the Soviet Union, but Britain and France, which, in response to the invasion of Poland, had gone to war with Germany on 3 September, did not take this view and did not declare war on the Soviet Union.

As a result of this attack, the Soviets annexed eastern Poland, after fraudulent elections had led to the election of 'People's Assemblies'. The latter voted in favour of incorporation into the Soviet Union which thereby gained control of 77,500 square miles and 13 million people. The brutality of the Soviet system, and its treatment of all politics as social war, was seen in its occupation policy. In 1939–40, 1.17 million people, many from social categories deemed undesirable and reactionary, were deported from Soviet-occupied Poland to Soviet labour camps,[5] the *gulags*, which were similar to the German concentration (as opposed to extermination) camps. A large number died in the harsh conditions of the long journeys. Many others who were not deported were slaughtered, and, although the degree of co-ordination is unclear, the NKVD shared information about Poles with the Gestapo.[6] Those regarded as leaders of the community and as bourgeois were particular targets. The eastern Polish provinces were treated as an integral part of the Soviet Union and transferred to the local Soviet republics, Ukraine and Belarus. Nikita Khrushchev, a veteran of the Civil War, the First Secretary of the Ukrainian Communist Party from 1938 to 1947, played a major role in the resulting brutal transformation of government, society, business and culture. Later, he was to succeed Stalin, though to disavow his legacy and methods.

In 1939–41, the Soviet Union, moreover, provided significant levels of economic support for Germany, helping the latter to overcome the block-ading capability of British oceanic power. Thus, the Soviet Union, to a degree, counteracted Germany's exclusion from the global trading system. This realised the fears of Allied policymakers in 1918 when Germany made major territorial inroads into Russia and reached agreement with the Communist government. Grain and oil were among the supplies provided in 1939–41. As late as June 1941, Stalin permitted a huge transfer of goods into Germany. There was also some military co-operation.[7] As a result of the Soviet-German alignment, British hopes of winning through a long war in which the Germans would be exhausted by blockade appeared flawed. The Pact underlined the Western sense of threat from Communism. It led the French government to clamp down on the Communists, with its leadership arrested and the Party banned. The Pact also encouraged suspicion of the Communists across the British world, for example in Australasia.

In December 1939, the Soviet Union, which had entered the League of Nations in 1934, was expelled for invading Finland the previous month, an invasion that was a consequence of the Pact and the creation of zones of expansion. Initially unsuccessful, due to the Finns' proficiency in winter warfare, the Soviets finally won by focusing in February 1940 on smashing through the major Finnish defensive line, the Mannerheim Line, using large amounts of artillery to support the breakthrough. In addition, Helsinki was bombed. Britain was in no position to provide help to the Finns as it had done during the Russian Civil War. In the subsequent Treaty of Moscow of 12 March, the territory Finland had to cede, ten per cent of the country, included the province of Karelia which gave the Soviet Union strategic depth for the city of Leningrad. Most of the population of Karelia became refugees in Finland. Karelia was resettled by Russians and remained part of Russia after the collapse of the Soviet Union.

In June 1940, the Soviet Union pressed on to invade and, after fraudulent elections, annex the Baltic Republics, as well as to extort the regions of Bessarabia and Northern Bukovina from Romania. In each case, there was a brutal treatment of the population, with large-scale slaughter and the wholesale movement of people to labour camps. About 127,000 people were deported to the *gulags* from the Baltic States. This was part of the process by which Hitler and Stalin were each responsible for the slaughter of large numbers of people in Eastern Europe.[8] The repeated gain of territory revealed a determination to create and use opportunities to expand.[9]

## Germany and the Soviet Union Fight, 1941–5

The Nazi-Soviet alignment was destroyed by Operation Barbarossa, the German attack on the Soviet Union launched on 22 June 1941. This was launched to give effect to Hitler's determination to destroy Communism and Jews and to create a greater Germany.[10] The defeat of the Soviet Union was also designed to put pressure on Britain. As a result of this surprise attack, an alliance of shared enmity to Germany replaced the earlier hostility between the Soviet Union and Britain. The system expanded in December 1941 to include the USA when Hitler declared war on the latter after the Japanese attack on Pearl Harbor, an attack that challenged America's ability to oppose German interests. Already, prior to this, Stalin had accepted Roosevelt's offer to extend lend-lease to the Soviet Union, although Harry Truman, then a relatively obscure Senator, remarked that, if it appeared that the Soviet Union was winning, America should aid Germany and vice versa. In December 1941, the USA and Britain agreed, in the 'Germany First' policy, to focus on war with Germany, rather than Japan. In contrast, the Soviet Union, which had lost much territory to the German invasion, did not go to war with Japan until August 1945. This delay enabled the Japanese to concentrate on conflict with the USA, China, Britain and Australia. The Soviets, assured of Japanese priorities by their effective spy Richard Sorge, the Press Attaché of the German embassy,[11] were freed from the problems of a two-front war. Troops could be transferred from Siberia where they were deployed against the Japanese in order to fight the Germans in the battle of Moscow in late 1941.

Although the point was neglected by the Soviets, the Allied focus on Germany, not Japan, greatly helped the Soviet Union by diverting German resources to resist Anglo-American attacks and the potential of such attacks. Nevertheless, less help was provided to the Soviet Union by this factor than the Americans imagined. As much in fear of a repeat of the Russian collapse of 1917 as anything else, Winston Churchill, British Prime Minister from 1940 to 1945, told the American Congress on 19 May 1943, 'we must do everything in our power that is sensible and practicable to take more of the weight off Russia in 1943'. At the Casablanca Conference that January, the British and Americans agreed on the Combined Bomber Offensive against Germany, which was seen as a way, in the face of pressure to invade Western Europe, to show Stalin that the Western Allies were doing their utmost to weaken Hitler, and thus to aid Soviet operations. The commitment at Casablanca to unconditional surrender by the Axis Powers as a war goal was designed to reassure Stalin. There was much talk among the Allies of unity against Hitler. Stalin, who was humanised as 'Uncle Joe' in Britain, assisted by abolishing the Comintern in 1943, a decision taken by its Executive Committee on 15 May and formally accomplished on 8 June. This decision was explained in terms of the need for Communist parties to serve within anti-Fascist coalitions. Moreover, the Communist Party of the United States of America eased its tone. There was much pro-Soviet coverage in the West. Joseph E. Davies, a multi-millionaire who had served as American envoy to Moscow, produced a sympathetic book, *Mission to Moscow* (1943), that was turned, at the behest of the Office of War Information, into a propaganda film of the same name designed to promote American-Soviet relations. After the war, Davies was to be rejected, with reason, as a dupe. Several of those involved in making the film were in trouble during the post-war McCarthyite attack on real or supposed Communists.[12]

Meanwhile, the paranoid Stalin was suspicious about the failure of Britain and the USA to launch a large-scale ground attack on Germany by opening a Second Front in Western Europe; second to the first, that of German-Soviet conflict. In particular, Stalin who, throughout, played down the Anglo-American war effort, exaggerated British commitment to the cause of hostility to Communism, just as he had, earlier, neglected British warnings about likely German attack, as well as those from his own agents, notably Sorge. When, in May 1941, Rudolf Hess, Hitler's deputy, flew to Britain on an unauthorised, uninvited and unsuccessful attempt to settle Anglo-German differences, this mission was seen by Stalin as a possible means of negotiation designed to isolate the Soviet Union. This may, indeed, have been the intention, but was certainly not Churchill's response.[13] Again, in the autumn of 1942, Stalin discussed whether Churchill wanted a separate peace with Germany so as to leave the latter free to oppose the Soviet Union.[14] Moreover, when probing the possibility of a separate peace with Germany, the Soviets mentioned their suspicion of the Anglo-American failure to open a Second Front in Western Europe. These probings led to a Soviet peace offer to Germany in September 1943. The Germans had lost tremendously in their failed offensive against the Soviets that led to the battle of Kursk (5–13 July), and Stalin sent out feelers for peace negotiations, with the intent of having the Germans withdraw from the Soviet Union and of ending the war between the two powers. Hitler was not interested in pursuing the offer. Maxim Litvinov, a Jew who had headed the Commissariat for Foreign Affairs from 1930, before being dismissed in early 1939 as an aspect of the Soviet *rapprochement* with Germany, was in part reinstated in December 1941, becoming envoy to the USA that December. However, his replacement as People's Commissar of Foreign Affairs in May 1939, Vyacheslav Molotov, an ideologue, was a pliant vehicle for Stalin's views,[15] which were focused on a distrust of the West. The net result was a hostility while wartime allies that helped sustain, and then entrench, the Cold War. While allies, the Soviets mounted a major intelligence offensive against Britain and the USA, one that laid the basis for the acquisition of American nuclear secrets,[16] and that was greater in scale and more hostile than equivalent British and American activities against the Soviet Union.

## Planning the Post-War World

German defeat at Kursk in July 1943 was followed by a series of Soviet offensives. These became increasingly effective in 1944. The margin of superiority was not that marked for some Soviet operations, but the knowledge of how to use their forces effectively, specifically in echelon formations, was crucial. Moreover, because there was no one-campaign end to the war, it had an attritional character. This accorded with the authoritarian nature of the Stalinist regime and its focus on the production of military resources.[17]

Stalin was convinced that capitalism was doomed. His assumption that the wartime Grand Alliance could not be sustained after the war, itself almost the definition of a self-fulfilling prophecy, left him determined to extend the Soviet sphere of influence, as well as to obtain direct territorial control through annexations. The latter would show that Stalin could reverse the losses Lenin had had to accept in 1918, and then again in 1920–1. Stalin saw such expansion as a way to limit the risks from any later sudden attack comparable to the German invasion of 1941. Thus, Soviet expansionism was in part defensive in ethos and intention, although other elements were involved, including acquiring strategic points from which further gains could be pursued.[18] The Soviets now (not the French as against the Soviets after World War One) were the ones seeking to create an Eastern European *cordon sanitaire*. That *cordon* was their first barrier. The second were the Soviet non-Russian union republics arced around the western and southern frontiers of that part of the Russian Federal Soviet Socialist Republic west of the Ural Mountains.

In response to Soviet expansionism, Churchill, who mistakenly hoped that personal links with Stalin would be beneficial,[19] nevertheless sought to direct Anglo-American strategy in order to ensure that the scope of the eventual Soviet advance against Germany and its allies was limited by Anglo-American moves into the Balkans, especially, he hoped, Yugoslavia and Greece. Churchill also aimed to restrict Soviet control in parts of Eastern Europe that could not be reached by Western forces, notably by winning Hungary over from the Germans. The focus was Poland, its government, and the extent to which the Soviets were to be able to annex eastern Poland anew, as they had done in 1939. British concern about Soviet intentions affected wartime strategy and planning for the post-war world. Already, in mid-1944, planners for the British Chiefs of Staff were suggesting a post-war reform of Germany and Japan so that they could play a role against the Soviet Union. Such concern was not simply directed against the Soviet Union. Fears about Nationalist (Guomindang) China seeking to dominate Tibet led to interest in strengthening Britain's position north of India. There was a common anxiety about post-war volatility. At the same time, this anxiety was most strongly felt about the Soviet Union. Indeed, in 1945, there were not only angry expostulations, as the Germans were defeated, about the need now to fight the Soviet Union,[20] but also the preparation of plans for World War Three. In May 1945, considering the possibility of war between the Soviet Union and an Anglo-American alliance, the British Joint Planning Staff anticipated that Soviet resilience would prevent a speedy end, and that the conflict could only be waged as a total war, entailing a fully-mobilised American war economy, as well as German support.[21]

However, as contrary pressures on their planning, the British were determined not only to keep the Soviet Union in the war, but also to ensure that the USA sustained the peace settlement, unlike after World War One when it had refused to join the League of Nations. Moreover, Roosevelt wanted to make certain that Stalin was committed, in the short term, to conflict with Japan, which posed a formidable military challenge, and, in the long term, to the eventual peace settlement.[22] Suspicious of Churchill's warnings, Roosevelt was also naive to a degree about Stalin's intentions, as when he assured Pope Pius XII in September 1941 that the Soviet Union would act responsibly after the war. Churchill proved more prescient. Nevertheless, Britain's role in the formulation of Allied policy was eroded by the greater economic strength and military power of its allies, as well, notably in 1944, as by Soviet successes in Eastern Europe and by American advances in the Pacific. Whatever the views of Western leaders, the central role of the Red Army in destroying the German army ensured that the Soviet Union would play the dominant part in Eastern Europe, as it had sought, without success, to do in 1920. The reality of the Soviet advance to a considerable extent vitiated subsequent claims that Roosevelt and Churchill sold out Eastern Europe to Stalin at the Yalta conference of 4–11 February 1945. In practice, Poland was already occupied by Soviet forces, and eastern Germany soon would be.[23] Warsaw in 1944, and Berlin, Prague, Vienna and Budapest in

1945, all fell to Soviet forces, and not to their American or British counter-parts. At the inaugural meeting of the United Nations in San Francisco in April–June 1945, the Polish seat was left vacant, as the USA was unwilling to accept the Soviet claim that the Moscow-supported Polish government was independent.

As in 1814–15, when the future of the European world was negotiated at the Congress of Vienna in the aftermath of Napoleon's defeat, Russian/Soviet power and success were key factors that could not be wished away from the negotiating table. Similarly, on 14 March 1946, the British embassy in Moscow asked if the world was now 'faced with the danger of the modern equivalent of the religious wars of the sixteenth century', with Soviet Communism battling against Western social democracy and American capitalism for 'domination of the world'. Yet, no historical episode is repeated exactly. In 1945 there was a strong sense, not seen in 1815, that Soviet success against Germany and, to a far lesser extent, Japan was part of an expansionism, both strategic and ideological, that was inexo-rable in intention. This sense helped ensure that 1945 saw conflict change character, and not cease, as World War Two was swiftly replaced by the Cold War. The Soviet Union in 1945, as in 1917, was badly battered in the aftermath of war. However, in 1945, unlike 1917, it was victorious. Soviet troops were in Berlin, Vienna and, after the rapid defeat of Japanese forces in August 1945, Manchuria, northern Korea, Southern Sakhalin and the Kurile Islands. At least in theory, these were ideologically engaged troops. By July 1945, 47% of Soviet military personnel were members or candidate members of the Communist Party or its Youth League, the Komsomol.[24] Leadership, violence, will-power, and improvisation had all played a role in Soviet success;[25] as had the mistakes and weaknesses of other powers, notably Hitler's Germany but also his Eastern European allies, such as Romania and Hungary. The extent to which the basis of Soviet success was sound and would be lasting, however, was unclear, and this was to affect the perception, indeed course, of the Cold War.

# CHAPTER THREE

# 1945–53

*A foreign bogey and the fear of foreign aggression must be held before them to stimulate their efforts for the new Five-Year Plan, and to persuade them that a large proportion of these efforts must be devoted not to improving the lot of the Soviet people … the Soviet Union although confident in its ultimate strength, is nothing like so strong at present as the Western democratic world, and knows it.*

FRANK ROBERTS, BRITISH DIPLOMAT IN MOSCOW, 1946.[1]

## Breakdown in Europe

The Cold War that followed World War Two was not a formal nor a frontal conflict, but a period of sustained hostility involving a protracted arms race, as well as numerous proxy conflicts in which the major powers intervened in other struggles. In turn, the latter sustained attitudes of animosity among the major powers, exacerbated fears, and contributed to a high level of military preparedness. Just as nineteenth-century theorists of international relations had focused on military conflict, so, notably in developing and applying realist theories, their Cold War successors concentrated on confrontation rather than conciliation, affecting both the public and political and military leaders.

Wartime alliances frequently do not survive peace, and this was especially true of World War Two because of the ideological division between the Soviet Union and the Western Allies. Moreover, this division was central to the polarisation of politics that helped link World War Two to the Cold War. There were also links in terms of the material and ideological resources the different parties were drawing on. Arguably, the wartime alliance scarcely survived the war itself. Ideological and geopolitical tensions revived in its closing stages. By 1944, differences over the fate of Eastern Europe were readily apparent, especially over Poland, which Stalin was determined to dominate. Political rivalries within Eastern Europe, and between the allies, fed into the revival of the Cold War.[2]

Fighting broke out in Greece, where German evacuation in 1944 led to an accentuation of the conflict between left-wing and right-wing guerrilla groups seen across much of Europe, notably in Yugoslavia. In Greece, as in Yugoslavia, northern Italy and China, there was a similar pattern: cruel occupation, a growing popularity (of sorts) of a Communist Party, and the outbreak of civil war between non-Communists and Communists once the occupiers (Germans and Japanese) left or were expelled. Greece and Italy both were small, had semi-peninsular locations, and were confronted by powerful seaborne British or American forces that could bring their weight to bear. The situation was very different in Yugoslavia and China. In Greece, in order to thwart a left-wing takeover, conflict between Communists and Royalists was followed by military intervention by the British in support of the latter. Having arrived in October 1944, the British were fighting the Communist National Popular Liberation Army (ELAS) on behalf of the returned exile government two months later.

After World War Two ended, the Soviet Union initially lacked the atom bomb, which had been used by the Americans against Japan in August 1945. The previous month, Churchill, who was convinced of the value of atom bombs, had reacted to the American atomic test by arguing that Soviet dominance could now be redressed.[3] However, helped by the startlingly fast demobilisation of American combat forces in 1945–6 as soldiers returned to civilian society, the Soviet army was apparently well placed to overrun Western Europe. It seemed that the Soviet army could only, in that event, be stopped by the West's use of nuclear weaponry. In reality, had it advanced, the Red Army's logistical base probably would not have permitted it to have gone farther than the Rhine. The Red Army was renamed the Soviet Army in early 1946 as Stalin wanted a more uplifting name than the Workers'-Peasants' Red Army to accord with the Soviet Union's new world status. Nevertheless, once Truman, who became President in 1945, revoked wartime Lend Lease aid, the Soviets were no longer receiving spare parts for their military motor transport, which was composed overwhelmingly of Ford and Studebaker trucks supplied by the Americans during the war. The equipment for routine tune-ups, such as spark plugs and distributors, and for oil changes, as well as other material, such as batteries, tyres, inner tubes for tyres, oil and air filters, were no longer available. Nor were axles, drive shafts, gearboxes and engine blocks. Tanks alone rolling ahead would not have been enough, and the horses sequestered during the war for Red Army transportation had to be returned home as Soviet agriculture was in very poor shape. Meanwhile, during any invasion, American and British bombers, escorted by their better fighter planes and better fighter pilots, would have been bombing the opposing army, front and rear. Although they were poorly understood in the West, the Soviets were aware of their weaknesses.

From 1945, despite such limitations, each side increasingly felt threatened, and seriously so, by the other, militarily and ideologically. This sense of threat helped define and strengthen the sides. The escalation of the conflict owed much to a clear sense of asymmetry in strengths, weaknesses, ideologies and fears. Fear, indeed, was a driving element in the escalation of the Cold War, while also being a unifier of state and society, or, at least, a would-be unifier from the perspective of governments and commentators. Growing tension between, and within, states represented a failure of the hopes that it would be possible to use the United Nations to ensure a new peaceful world order. In 1943, the USA, the Soviet Union, Britain and (Nationalist) China had agreed the Moscow Declaration on General Security including the establishment of 'a general international organisation, based on the principle of sovereign equality'. The resulting United Nations was established in 1945, but it proved the setting, not the solution, for growing East–West tensions.

In addition, the Soviet victory over Nazi Germany and its allies had ensured a territorial and political settlement in which the Soviet Union affirmed its power. On 10 January 1945, Averell Harriman, the American ambassador in Moscow, reported that, in occupied areas of Eastern Europe, the Soviet Union was trying to establish pliant regimes and that no distinction was drawn between former enemy states, such as Romania, and others, notably Poland. He added 'the overriding consideration in Soviet foreign policy is the preoccupation with "security", as Moscow sees it ... the Soviet conception of "security" does not appear cognizant of the similar needs or rights of other countries and of Russia's obligation to accept the restraints as well as the benefits of an international security system'.[4] This point was to be more generally true of Soviet attitudes and policy. Communism played a role in the equation. So did a sense of natural pre-eminence in what was regarded as 'its region'. This attitude was also to be seen with Communist China and, indeed, with the USA in Latin America. Thus, the combination of realist and idealist factors that determined the policies of states and, notably, empires, was apparent with the protagonists in the Cold War. American intervention, puppet regimes, and economic direction in Central America and the Caribbean was similar, up to a point, to Soviet activity in Eastern Europe.

Post-war, the Soviet Union retained all of the gains it had obtained in 1939–40 (from Poland, Romania and Finland, as well as the Baltic Republics in their entirety). Thus, most of Lenin's losses were reversed. The Soviet Union also added part of Czechoslovakia that had been annexed by Hungary in 1939, which was called Carpatho-Ukraine, as well as the northern part of the German province of East Prussia. The (southern) remainder of East Prussia went to Poland, which also gained

German territories on its western frontier: Silesia and Eastern Pomerania. Poland, in turn, lost more extensive territories, about 48 per cent of pre-war Poland, on its eastern frontier, to the Soviet Union. This was an outcome, reversing the Polish gains in 1920–1, that was rejected by the exiled Polish government. Now, as a result of the disintegration of the latter in 1991, these territories are parts of Belarus, Ukraine and Lithuania. Poland, in effect, thus moved westwards as a country as a result of the post-war territorial settlement. Territories and cities were renamed accordingly. Thus, the German city of Breslau, where a long resistance to attacking Soviet forces had been mounted in 1945, became the Polish city of Wroclaw. Significantly, the city of Königsberg, the capital of East Prussia, and in the part that went to the Soviet Union, was renamed Kaliningrad, the first a German name marking royal power replaced by a Russian one honouring Mikhail Kalinin (1875–1946). He had been formal head of state, first as President of the Soviet Central Executive Committee (1919–38) and then of the Praesidium of the Supreme Soviet (1938–46). As an aspect of his fearful loyalty to Stalin, Kalinin signed the death warrant of his wife.

Territorial changes in Europe were not on the scale of changes in 1918–23, but were still significant. Moreover, there was a large-scale movement of people. In 1945–6, nine million Germans fled or were driven west from the territories acquired by the Soviet Union, but, even more, from pre-1939 Czechoslovakia, Poland and other countries. This flight was an aspect of the widespread displacement that the war had brought and that continued after its end. For example, Poles were moved out of the territories gained by the Soviet Union in the western Ukraine and were resettled in lands cleared of Germans. As a consequence of such movements, cities changed. The replacement of Poles, following on the German slaughter of Jews, made Lvov, Odessa and Vilnius each Soviet cities. This displacement was part of the large-scale disruption that continued after World War Two, notably, but not only, in Eastern Europe.[5] Whereas the population movements within Europe in the 1950s and 1960s were primarily of labour (with families sometimes following), for example Italians to work in German factories, those in the 1940s were mostly of entire families as an aspect of what would later be termed 'ethnic cleansing'. Violence was involved in 'ethnic cleansing', but not genocide. Thus, the outset of the revived Cold War proved to have a pronounced demographic dimension and one that contributed greatly to the social strain, if not breakdown, associated with Soviet control and Communist dominance in Eastern Europe. However, as in Czechoslovakia and Poland, nationalists who were not Communist also supported these displacements. There was a determination to avoid the post-World War One situation of sizeable ethnic minorities within the new nation states. Japanese settlers were expelled from China and Korea or imprisoned for use as forced labour. The violent nature of the population moves exacerbated tensions well past the immediate post-war years. Dreams and fears of revenge and recovery contributed to Cold War politics among and about the defeated (West Germany, Japan), as well as the successful.

Ideology was an important factor in Soviet policy as, differently, in the American determination to create both a new world order and an Atlantic community, each described in terms of *the* (not *a*) 'Free World'.[6] However, it is easy to understand why the British diplomat Frank Roberts and some other commentators focused on geopolitics as well, not least as it enabled them to assert a degree of continuity in Russian/Soviet policy. Roberts, who was later to be influential in the British Foreign Office, reported from Moscow in March 1946:

> There is one fundamental factor affecting Soviet policy dating back to the small beginnings of the Muscovite state. This is the constant striving for security of a state with no natural frontiers and surrounded by enemies. In this all-important respect the rulers and people of Russia are united by a common fear, deeply rooted in Russian policy, which explains much of the high-handed behaviour of the Kremlin and many of the suspicions genuinely held there concerning the outside world ... the fears aroused by foreign intervention after 1917 cannot yet have been eradicated from that of Western leaders, who, nevertheless, co-operated with the Soviet Union during the war.[7]

Concern about outside pressure was greatly accentuated by the war. For the Soviets, Eastern Europe served not only as an economic resource and an ideological bridgehead, but also as a strategic glacis. The Soviet determination to dominate Eastern Europe was a key cause of tension, both local and international, not least because domination meant the imposition, through force and manipulation, of Communist governments. The Soviets were not satisfied by the nuances of influence. The 1946 Polish elections in which the Communists did well were fraudulent. Force played an important role in the extension of Communist control. For example, King Michael of Romania abdicated on 30 December 1947 after the royal palace in the capital, Bucharest, was surrounded by troops of the Romanian division raised in the Soviet Union.[8]

The drive of Soviet policy appeared threatening. The Soviets abandoned co-operation over occupied Germany, which, like Austria, had been divided into Soviet, American, British and French occupation zones. They also imposed Communist governments in Eastern Europe, culminating with a coup in Prague in 1948. These moves vindicated Churchill's claim on 5 March 1946, in Fulton, Missouri in the USA, that an 'Iron Curtain' was descending from the Baltic to the Adriatic. Truman had invited Churchill, from 1945 to 1951 head of the Conservative opposition in Britain, to visit his home state of Missouri and to give this speech. It was a response to Stalin's speech in Moscow on the occasion of electing delegates to the

Supreme Soviet, a speech, given on 9 February 1946, in which Stalin spoke of the 'inevitability of war with the West'.

1948, when Stalin also forcefully clamped down on what he called 'nationalist-deviationist' Communist leaders, notably Josip Tito in Yugoslavia, was the bellwether year. This situation led to growing pressure for a Western reply. The coup in Prague in 1948 had a particular impact due to the rejection, in public discussion in the West, of the pre-war Appeasement policy that had delivered Czechoslovakia to German control in 1938–9 and the view that this had simply encouraged renewed German expansionism. The democratic background of Czech politics was also relevant, as was Czechoslovakia's location as the most westerly of the countries that received a Communist government in the 1940s, and one that threatened the security of the American occupation zone in neighbouring Bavaria. Thus, idealist and realist factors combined to make the Prague coup appear particularly sinister.

Soviet dominance of Eastern Europe was matched by an apparent threat to Western Europe. The extent of the threat is controversial, and there is debate about how serious it was, and how serious it was believed to be.[9] Nevertheless, there were scares, contributing to a culture of distrust.[10] Walter Bedell Smith, the American ambassador in Moscow, claimed in September 1947 that the Kremlin felt it could safely create war scares as it knew that the USA did not want war and would not be the aggressor.[11]

Concerns in Western Europe led to the investigation of defence co-operation. There was interest in the idea of a Western European Third Force independent of the USA and the Soviet Union, and Britain and France accordingly signed the Treaty of Dunkirk in 1947. This agreement was directed against Soviet expansionism, although fear of a resurgent Germany also played a role. However, in response to fears about Soviet plans, an American alliance, and commitment to Europe, appeared essential. In February 1947, the British, heavily indebted by World War Two, acknowledged that they could no longer provide the military and economic aid deemed necessary to keep Greece and Turkey out of Communist hands, an urgent issue in light of the Greek Civil War and of Soviet pressure on Turkey. Instead, the British successfully sought American intervention, which was a key development in this stage of the Cold War.

In both Britain and France, a sense of weakness in Europe that owed much to exhaustion due to the war was linked to concerns about their empires. Initially, there were wartime plans for the extension of British power. As Prime Minister from 1940 to 1945, Churchill was interested not only in extending British power in the former Italian colonies of Libya and Somalia, where, after conquering them in 1941–2, Britain was the leading occupying power. He also considered acquiring the Kra Isthmus in Thailand, and thus linking the colonies of Burma (Myanmar) and Malaya. Thailand had aligned with Japan for much of the war. In 1946, Sir Francis Tucker, Head of Eastern Command in India, was concerned about threats to India from the north and proposed a British protectorate over what he termed Mongol territory from Nepal to Butan. Sir Claude Auchinleck, Commander-in-Chief, India, had to explain that the idea was not realistic; and this was also true of ideas about extending British influence in Tibet and Xinjiang.

In the face of near bankruptcy, and of changing political and public attitudes in Britain, these hopes were indeed misplaced. Instead, there was a major retreat from the empire, a retreat encouraged by the USA which believed that newly-independent countries could be encouraged to be pro-Western. India and Pakistan were given independence in 1947, Burma (Myanmar), Ceylon (Sri Lanka), and Palestine following in 1948. The Labour government of 1945–51 wished to keep the empire going, notably in Africa, in part to provide economic help for Britain, but it supported an independence for India that greatly lessened the military strength of the empire.

In the long-term, the British retreat from empire was to cause problems for the USA and to be closely linked to the Cold War. Indeed, across much of the world, and notably in the Middle East and South Asia, the Cold War took on the character of the War of the British Succession, as Britain's imperial inheritance was contested. Similarly, after World War One and notably until 1927, challenging British imperial power had been a major theme. For example, in 1948, the breakout of war over the newly-formed state of Israel, as the British Mandate in Palestine ended, provided Stalin with an opportunity. He offered weapons both to Israel and to one of its opponents, Egypt, via Czechoslovakia. This was intended to give the Soviet Union a way into the Middle East, where Britain was the major power. However, despite providing significant amounts of supplies there, especially to Israel, no alliances resulted.[12]

Similar points can be made about France, with the focus here being France's enforced withdrawal from Indochina (Vietnam, Cambodia, Laos) in 1954 after defeat at the hands of a Communist nationalist movement supported by the Communist great powers. The Cold War there took on the character of the War of the French Succession. France, and to some extent Britain, tried to steer American policy toward intervention in Indochina from about 1948, at least in part for financial reasons. Within France, the Communists were kept from power, while their power in the trade unions was seen as a strategic, political and economic threat. The focus on the fate of Western empires approach is less valid for Eastern Europe and Latin America, both prior to World War Two and subsequently; although in sub-Saharan Africa in the 1960s and 1970s the fate of the Belgian and, still more, Portuguese empires played a major role in the Cold War.

# Germany

In the shorter term, the fate of Europe was far more urgent than that of trans-oceanic European empires as an issue for American and Soviet leaders, politicians and commentators in the late 1940s, and, indeed, for most of their British counterparts. The American position was crucial as far as Germany was concerned. In contrast with Britain and France, America was the occupying power best able, thanks to its economic strength, to resist Soviet schemes. The geopolitical map of Europe was in place after the Yalta agreement in 1945, but the result required confirming and defending. This need sat alongside American concerns about the situation outside Europe, notably, initially, in Iran where the Soviets proved reluctant to withdraw troops that had intervened at the same time as the British in 1941.[13] Moreover, the Chinese Civil War (1946–9) became a key root for a hardening of relations between the USA and the Soviet Union.

French plans for undoing Germany's unification in 1866–71 by the transformation of Germany into autonomous states, a bolder version of the interest shown in 1919, in the aftermath of World War One, in an independent Rhineland, had been rejected in favour of a joint occupation by the victorious powers of a thus still unified Germany. However, it proved impossible to sustain this policy, not least because of Stalin's pressure for control. Reparations payments proved a key element, with the Soviets demanding reparations (compensation for war damage) from the occupation zones of the Western powers, as well as a four-power supervision of the key industrial region of the Ruhr which was in the British zone. Such demands challenged Western plans for the regeneration of the German economy, and for the management of their zones, as well as crystalising a growing concern to limit the westward penetration of Soviet power and influence.

The Soviets sought to foster the Communist Party in Germany, and, to that end, forcibly merged the Social Democrats (SPD), the alternative left-wing party, in their zone with the Communists. This was a policy rejected by the SPD in the Western zones. Indeed, Soviet occupation policies in Eastern Europe alienated German public and political opinion in the Western zones. This alienation, which was an important aspect of the fear of Communism in Western Europe, influenced the occupation authorities, not least as they sought to develop a democratic political system. Similarly, in Poland, the Polish Socialist Party was merged with the Polish Communist Party to produce the new ruling party, the United Polish Workers' Party.

# The American Response: Containment and the Marshall Plan

Concerned about Communism on the global level, and about the stability of Europe and the future of Germany, the Americans, both government and public, did not intend to repeat their interwar isolationism when they had not responded to the expansion of Nazi Germany and, without getting the blame, had, in practice, been prominent among the appeasers. Containment as a concept that was to be applied in American political and military strategy received its intellectual rationale in 1947 from George Kennan, the acting head of the American diplomatic mission in Moscow. The emphasis on inherent Soviet antagonism under Stalin in Kennan's 'long telegram' of 22 February 1946 had an impact in Washington and elsewhere. Kennan's thesis was understood as advocating containment, a view also taken by the Canadian Escott Reid. Kennan followed up with a 'Mr X' article, drawing on the 'long telegram', in *Foreign Affairs* in April 1947, an article that made much use of the word containment. In 1947, Kennan, who argued that the division of Europe was reversible, became Director of Policy Planning in the State Department.[14] The concept of containment was developed with the Truman government advancing the idea of America's perimeter of vital interests. The perimeter was to be consolidated by the establishment of regional security pacts, notably the North Atlantic Treaty Organisation (NATO), created in 1949.

The American economy had expanded greatly during the war, both in absolute and in relative terms. America had the manufacturing capacity, organisational capability, and fiscal resources to meet the costs of post-war military commitments. These strengths underpinned the American effort to resist the Communist advance. This effort was economic and political as well as military. In June 1947, the Americans offered Marshall Plan Aid, an economic aid policy to help recovery and to avoid a return to the beggar-my-neighbour devaluations of the 1930s. It was named after George Marshall, the Secretary of State from 1947 to 1949. The Marshall Plan committed the USA to European recovery, and recovery in terms of promoting a specific model of productivity as well as economies dominated by welfare states. The Marshall Plan enabled the economies of Western Europe to overcome their dollar shortage and thus to finance trade and investment. This ensured that American-style technologies could be adopted and also that free trade would benefit at the expense of protectionism. The greater integration of the Western economy was an important consequence, and the Marshall Plan led to the European Payments Union, which encouraged the ready convertibility of currency, and looked toward the establishment of the European Economic Community.[15] Marshall Plan Aid was rejected by the Soviet Union as a form of economic imperialism. This aid certainly represented a demonstration of American strength that could serve to create links. This rejection created a new boundary line: between the areas that received such aid and those that did not.

The Soviets, meanwhile, alongside establishing and monitoring Communist governments in individual states, moved to consolidate their bloc and to advance its interests. One step was the creation, in September 1947, of the Cominform, the Communist Information Bureau, a recrudescence of the Comintern, which brought together European Communist parties under Soviet guidance. The existence of 'two camps' was announced by Andrei Zhdanov, Stalin's key ideological adviser, who chaired the first meeting.

# Yugoslavia

Stalin's assertiveness and determination to control helped lead to defeats for his plans, both in Yugoslavia and in Berlin. In 1948, as a result of Stalin's quest for ideological conformity and for control over policy, the governing Yugoslav Communist Party under Josip Tito, its wartime leader, was accused of abandoning Communist principles and of failing to follow Moscow's lead on foreign policy. The second was a key element, but Stalin's determination to control Communism was also crucial. The Yugoslav Party was expelled from Cominform in June and Tito's removal was called for. The Soviet Union continued by organising an economic blockade of Yugoslavia, beginning a propaganda offensive, and starting small-scale armed attacks. The offensive failed, however, in large part because the wartime Communist movement in Yugoslavia, notably the Communist-led People's Liberation Movement, had both been less dependent on the Soviet Union than those elsewhere in Eastern Europe (with the exception of Albania), and because (as with Albania and Bulgaria) the liberation from German control had not been dependent on Soviet forces. Moreover, Yugoslavia had no common border with the Soviet Union. First Secretary of the Yugoslav Communist Party from 1937, Tito was also Prime Minister, and President, of post-war Yugoslavia until his death in 1980.

The turn against Tito helped to poison the political atmosphere in the Soviet bloc as a whole. From 1949, there were attacks, particularly show trials, across the bloc, and notably in Czechoslovakia, on politicians and others deemed 'Titoists' and accused of nationalist deviationism. They joined the list already occupied by Trotskyites. Anti-Semitism played a prominent role in some of these attacks, notably in Czechoslovakia with the Slánský trial in 1952. The murderous pursuit of alleged internal dissidents weakened the Communist movement and lessened popular support for it, with tensions within Communism now coming more clearly to the fore. The Yugoslav crisis and the subsequent show trials showed that the Communist bloc was not going to be able to act as a united bloc in a comparable way to that of the less ideologically coherent West, because the emphasis on uniformity turned difference into disobedience or dissent. As a result, although the Warsaw Pact and COMECON, the Council for Mutual Economic Assistance established in 1955 and 1949 respectively, were to function as military and economic unions, the effectiveness of the Communist bloc was limited, and the same problem was replicated at the level of individual states. The nature of Communist political culture and government reduced flexibility in crises. This was a situation seen repeatedly in Eastern Europe down to the final Communist collapse in 1989, and was also an element in the divisions within the Chinese leadership, such as with the Cultural Revolution in the late 1960s and the 1975 Two Line Struggle against Deng Xiaoping, in the North Vietnamese leadership, notably in 1959, and in the Afghan leadership in 1979.

# The Berlin Crisis

Isolated within the Soviet occupation zone, Berlin, the former capital of Germany, was itself divided (like Vienna) between the four powers that also had occupation zones in Germany. This appeared to challenge the Soviet position, not least as it was possible for people to move within the city between the zones. Berlin also provided an apparently vulnerable target for Soviet attack. In the Berlin Crisis, the Soviets blockaded West Berlin (the American, British and French zones) from 24 June 1948 to 11 May 1949. This was met by an impressive and successful Anglo-American airlift of supplies into the city, with nearly 200,000 flights supplying 1.5 million tons of supplies. The crisis appeared to bring war near. However, the standoff went on too long for Stalin's liking, while the crisis led to the stationing in Britain of American B-29 bombers which were intended to bomb the Soviet Union in the event of war. The threat of the use of the atom bomb helped bring a solution to the crisis. The Soviets dropped the attempt to take over the city.

The Berlin Crisis had a symbolic as well as a real importance. The crisis convinced Western opinion of the threatening nature of Soviet power, and also provided a convincing demonstration both of Western unity, with Britain and France backing the USA, and of German popular opposition to Soviet expansion. American military commitment in, and to, Western Europe was greatly increased. The American bombers remained in Britain, and Brendan Bracken, a Conservative MP and the manager of the *Financial Times*, wrote in 1950:

> What a wonderful thought it is that President Truman can ring a bell and give an order that American aircraft can load their bombs and fly from London to Moscow. The interest of their visit will not be returned

on Washington, it will be returned on poor old London. All this talk about not giving up national sovereignty doesn't mean much when the President of the United States of America can use England as an aircraft carrier without the knowledge of the ship's company.[16]

At the same time, it is important not to deny agency to the people on the ground. In Berlin, the population played a key role in the blockade, not only because they were determined not to give in to the Soviets but also because they played a major role in obtaining and distributing goods.[17]

# Greece

Meanwhile, fighting was in progress in Greece: attempts to reach a compromise there had failed, leading to a second stage of the civil war in 1946–9. This was a conflict which was to be exacerbated by the developing Cold War. The Communists' inability to achieve their goals by political means led them to turn to a guerrilla insurrection, and, in this, they were backed by the newly-established neighbouring Communist governments of Bulgaria, Yugoslavia and Albania. In response, the Greek army became more militarily effective as a consequence of its abandonment, in 1948, of a policy of static defence, and, instead, its introduction of an offensive policy with a systematic clearance of guerrilla forces out of particular areas. The Greek army was also helped by the extent to which much of the population supported the government, as well as by the Communists' adoption of more conventional methods of fighting. This adoption was a political decision, taken in 1947, and rested on the belief that, by establishing a Communist government in parts of northern Greece near the Communist states, it would be possible to secure Soviet aid to counteract that from the USA for the Greek government. However, it proved impossible for the Communists to recruit the manpower anticipated, the Soviets did not provide the heavy weaponry that was sought, let alone intervene, and the Communists' reliance on position warfare led to their defeat. The Communists were driven back to their strongholds in Western Macedonia, and were finally defeated there. Both sides killed prisoners and civilians deemed hostile.

Foreign intervention had been important, particularly the provision of American military and economic aid (but not troops) to the government. This aid was provided under the so-called Truman doctrine proclaimed on 12 March 1947, when President Truman sought Congressional support for assistance to Greece and Turkey and announced that the USA would oppose the spread of totalitarianism. This doctrine was crucial to the formulation of containment as American policy in 1947.[18] The following year, General James Van Fleet was selected by Truman to train and revive the Greek army. The USA devoted about $1 billion to supporting the Greek government. Moreover, British assistance to the Greek army played a role in the evolution of British experience with counter-insurgency operations. Nevertheless, the key achievement was that by the Greek government and army as part of a multi-faceted counter-insurgency strategy that included military, social and economic drives.[19]

The eventual limitation of foreign aid to the Communists, especially after the Tito-Stalin breach of 1948 brought the first major division between Communist states, was also highly significant. By supporting Stalin, the Greek Communists wrecked their relations with Yugoslavia, which cut off the border, stopping the movement of military supplies.[20] In contrast, Communist victory in China in 1949 greatly helped the Viet Minh in Vietnam.

The Communist defeat in Greece in 1949 was not to be followed by Western 'roll-back' of Communism further north in the Balkans, despite Anglo-American efforts to support the overthrow of the Hoxha regime in Albania by encouraging a local resistance movement. However, the defeat in Greece did ensure that the Communist presence in the Mediterranean and near the Middle East was weaker than it would otherwise have been. Had Greece become Communist, there would have been the option to deploy Soviet warships in Crete (part of Greece), threatening Turkey, Israel and Egypt, or in the Ionian Islands (part of Greece), threatening Italy. Success against the Greek Communists was seen as a crucial success for containment, and was to be anchored when Greece joined NATO in 1952. This was a development that did not match the initial Atlanticist assumptions underlying the alliance, but that accorded with the concept of containment. Without Greek entry, that of Turkey in 1952 would have been less plausible.

## The Use of Force

Anti-Communist nationalist guerrilla movements in Albania, the Baltic Republics (the Forest Brethren), Bulgaria, Poland, Romania, Ukraine and Yugoslavia, some of which were based on earlier resistance opposition to the Germans, were all brutally suppressed by the Communist governments.[21] This resistance and its suppression reflected the highly divisive legacy of wartime German occupation and of resulting political differences over collaboration and resistance. Despite efforts by the USA and Britain, particularly in Albania, Poland, Romania and Ukraine, the guerrillas received little effective support from the West.[22] Indeed, Kim Philby, a well-placed traitor in British intelligence, betrayed the operation in Albania. Nevertheless, Western efforts to provide support contributed to Soviet paranoia, encouraging Stalin toward a more aggressive posture, not least with his approval for the invasion of South Korea in 1950. This was an important aspect of the way in which Western covert action played a role akin to its Soviet counterpart in exacerbating insecurity and sustaining hostility.[23] However, the Soviet atomic bomb test of 1949 was more significant in influencing Stalin toward a more aggressive posture.

Some of the conflicts in Eastern Europe involved substantial forces and heavy casualties, although many are still relatively obscure; this is true, for example, of Soviet campaigns in the Baltic republics and Ukraine in the late 1940s. It has been suggested that the Soviets lost 20,000 men in suppressing opposition in Lithuania alone. Such figures are a reminder both that the Soviet Union was continuing to use a policy of throwing manpower at conflicts and of the importance of non-conventional warfare in the late 1940s and early 1950s. The latter was also seen in the Korean conflict, which, from 1948, had a strong guerrilla war aspect at first, with left-wing uprisings against the government in South Korea. The use of troops to suppress opposition in the Soviet Union and Eastern Europe was part of a continuum there in which terror, violence and force were routinely employed to maintain control and to implement policies. Terror was not the sum total of rule, and there was a process of 'negotiation' at the local level through which the diktats of the system were implemented. Indeed, concern about public opinion was an important aspect of the insistent surveillance by government. Yet, this surveillance was designed to achieve control, for Stalinism worked in large part by creating an all-pervasive sense of surveillance and fear. Disorientated by the killing and seizure of activists, opposition was demoralised and worn down, notably in Poland in the late 1940s. Armed resistance in Eastern Europe lasted until the 1950s, but it was discouraged by a lack of appreciable Western support and failed.[24] The last resistance to the Soviets in west Ukraine was in 1957.

Terror thrived on ignorance, notably on the ungraspable nature and undefined scope of the oppressor and on the extent of co-operation with the oppressor's secret force. The *Stasi*, the East German secret police, rose to a size of 91,000 full-time officers and 173,000 informants in 1989, becoming the largest secret police organisation in global history and one capable of blanket surveillance of all the population. This surveillance created a sense of pervasive scrutiny, encouraging co-operation with the state, including in its demands for information.[25] For this reason, Communist states controlled information and made major efforts to block radio transmissions from the West. These efforts provided another aspect of conflict, for anti-Communist radio stations, such as Radio Free Europe and Radio Liberty, were sponsored by Western governments. Once the Communists had triumphed in the Chinese Civil War, Soviet organisers played a major role in the establishment of security agencies in China. Real and alleged foreign agents were targets as, in a context of arbitrary justice, terror and widespread violence, were 'saboteurs' and other 'bad elements'.[26]

# The War of Ideas

Soviet propaganda was propagated in the Soviet Union and further afield by every possible means. Thus, Frank Roberts forwarded details of a Soviet election campaign lecture he had heard in Moscow on Christmas Day 1945: 'Reference was made to American economic imperialism and to the disastrous economic situation likely to arise in USA as the result of mass unemployment', which did not in fact occur. Moreover, the lecturer expressed the view that no international question could be decided without Soviet participation. The summary of the reports in London by Christopher Warren noted that, 'by resurrecting the bogey of foreign aggression, and by completely distorting the information about the outside world which reaches the Soviet peoples and also by their intensive measures to indoctrinate them with the Marxist-Leninist religion', the Soviet government could affect popular views.[27]

In 1946, the Central Committee of the Communist Party decided to free Soviet culture from what it termed 'servility before the West'. Cosmopolitanism and Westernism were attacked, while Russian origins were found for Western inventions and scientific theories. This campaign, which was particularly associated with Andrei Zhdanov, the Party Secretary, who died in 1948, continued until Stalin's death in 1953. Jews were presented as unpatriotic cosmopolitans, the wartime Jewish Anti Fascist Committee was suppressed in 1948, and its leaders were executed in 1952. The satellite states followed suit. In 1953, Soviet Jewish doctors were denounced in *Pravda* as a 'Zionist terrorist gang', anti-Semitic attacks occurred, and it is possible that this campaign would have led to the deportation of Soviet Jews to Siberia, but Stalin's death cut short the idea.[28]

Science was also in the front line. The official adoption of Lysenkoism in 1948 was part of the war of ideas, as well as a major aspect of public policy. Lysenkoism reflected the Soviet ideological commitment to the dominance of environmental factors and to improving the human lot by understanding and bettering the physical and human environments. This ideology was advanced in conscious rivalry with genetical theories that were dismissed as bourgeois and were criticised as linked to racism. Trofim Lysenko (1898–1976), Director of the Institute of Genetics of the Soviet Academy of Sciences from 1940 to 1965, rejected the accepted theory derived from Gregor Mendel, and, instead, drew on the thesis of Ivan Michurin that acquired characteristics were inheritable. Indicating close interest and personal commitment, Stalin edited Lysenko's key speech himself. Lysenko's argument that environmental determinants could be changed was conducive to Soviet plans to expand arable production greatly in areas not hitherto under the plough, notably to the drier south and southeast of the existing cultivated area: for example, in Kazakhstan. In the event, Lysenkoism proved a serious mistake and hopes of greater arable production were not fulfilled.[29] This failure was serious not only because of an eventual need for Western grain imports, but also because the Soviets had hoped that grain exports would win influence in the Third World, for example in Egypt.

In the USA, meanwhile, the willingness of Hollywood to confront social problems, as in *The Grapes of Wrath* (1940), the film of the 1939 John Steinbeck novel about dispossessed dirt-farmers, slackened. This change reflected political pressure not to criticise America, but, instead, to resist Communist 'subversion'. This pressure was orchestrated by the House of Representatives' Committee on Un-American Activities as part of a battle over national identity and interests,[30] a battle that owed its origins to resistance to the New Deal, but that gathered pace after World War Two as opposition to Communism made it possible to discredit progressive ideas. Those in Hollywood with Communist associations were blacklisted from 1947. Moreover, anti-Communist films were produced, for example *The Red Menace* (1949) and *I Was a Communist for the FBI* (1951).[31] These films spread images of the USA around the world. Film was tremendously important to the practice and currency of myth, symbolisation and characterisation that were central to the imagining of people, country and world. Anti-Communism was both cause and device. It was directed against alternative views of a more egalitarian America which were presented, instead, as causes and reflections of internal division in the shape of class conflict and radicalism. Eric Johnston, President of the Motion Picture Association, a committed anti-Communist, told script writers to act accordingly, and was supported by Ronald Reagan, President of the Screen Actors Guild, who linked radicals and strikers to foreign Communists. The nature of the American consensus was redefined from the 1940s, with important political, social and intellectual effects.[32] Left-wing ideas were castigated as was cultural relativism. Instead, there was pressure for support of a conservative view of American culture.[33] The failed attempt by Henry Wallace, a New Dealer who had been Vice-President in 1941–5, to challenge Truman by running for President in 1948 as a candidate of the new Progressive Party, reflected not only the divisive impact of taking a relatively pro-Soviet foreign policy line, but also the popular preference of, and for, Truman. He had dismissed Wallace as Secretary of Commerce in 1946 for opposing American foreign policy as overly anti-Soviet.[34]

Attempts to influence opinion and mould domestic developments were less forceful in the USA and Western Europe than in the Soviet Union, but were also insistent. These attempts reflected concern about public opinion in the context of a politics of insecurity, but also the claim, of anti-Communists and Communists alike, to represent and advance universal values. For both Communists and anti-Communists, successive advances for Communism created the prospect that more would follow, and that everything that appeared stable was probably ripe for revolution. In the 1 April 1946 issue of *Time*, the leading American news magazine, R. M. Chapin produced a map entitled 'Communist Contagion', which dramatised the strength and threat of the Soviet Union. These were enhanced by a split-spherical presentation of Europe and Asia, making the Soviet Union more potent as a result of the break in the centre of the map. Communist expansion was emphasised in the map by presenting the Soviet Union as a vivid red, the colour of danger, and by categorising neighbouring states with regard to the risk of contagion, employing the language of disease: states were referred to as quarantined, infected or exposed. Such maps were an aspect of the visualisation of international relationships, a visualisation that lent itself to an assessment in terms of rivalry, if not conflict. Indeed, the Cold War was a conflict that played out through popular culture. People came to think about, understand (or misunderstand), engage with, debate and discuss the Cold War through maps, films and radio programmes, as well as through leaflets, flyers and information films that required citizens to participate in emergency preparedness routines or which asked them to be vigilant. The public came to be enrolled in a struggle for global destiny, a process greatly eased by the mass mobilisation and incessant propaganda that had been part of the experience of World War Two.

In the USA, anti-Communism was given energy and focus by the Communist victory in the Chinese Civil War (1946–9) and the development of the Soviet atomic bomb (1949). Liberal Democrats were criticised for being soft on Communism, and there was a hunt for traitors and spies, a hunt that owed much to revelations, from 1947 on, about Soviet espionage in the USA.[35] A series of arrests and trials, and surrounding reports and speculation, kept the atmosphere frenetic. Alger Hiss was tried twice, in 1949–50 for perjury, a case based on his passing information to the Soviet Union while working for the State Department. The case made the reputation of Richard Nixon as a 'Red-baiter' or anti-Communist. Klaus Fuch, a German émigré who worked in Britain and had worked in the USA on atomic weaponry, admitted in 1950 to spying for the Soviet Union, and Ethel and Julius Rosenberg, who worked for the American atomic programme, were executed in 1950 for spying.

This process reached its spectacular apogee in the claims about Communist influence made by Senator Joseph McCarthy, who searched anywhere and everywhere for Communists in government. In February 1950, McCarthy, hitherto a minor Republican political figure, announced in a speech that he had a list of 'card-carrying Communists' in the State Department. An investigative committee dismissed the allegation, but his claims gathered pace and gained publicity. At the 1952 Republican Convention, McCarthy referred to 'twenty years of treason' under the Democratic Party. He gave his name to a process of public legislative inquisition known as McCarthyism, which was very much a Korean War phenomenon and which drew on the potential of television. As Chairman of the Permanent Subcommittee on Investigations of the Senate Committee on Government Operations from 1953 to 1955, McCarthy launched numerous investigations which contributed to a sense of crisis. McCarthy overreached himself with his criticism, from 1954, of the army, a focus for patriotic values, and he was discredited in the Army hearings by his methods and extremism. President Eisenhower and the other Senators finally had had enough.[36] However, although McCarthy greatly exaggerated its scale, there was, indeed, Soviet penetration and Communist influence in the USA. Moreover, American Communists had an influence in organising the Philippine Communist Party which came to dominate the Huk insurrection in the Philippines. The lasting effects of McCarthyism on American political culture remain poorly understood. There was a rather uncomfortable McCarthyite legacy in some of the notions of John F. Kennedy's 'new frontiersmen'. Robert Kennedy's role on McCarthy's staff in the early 1950s can be seen in conjunction with his later vigour in directing anti-Castro operations for John F. Kennedy. There was also a shared Catholicism.

Alongside the demagogy of McCarthyism, anti-Communism was wide-ranging and insistent in the USA. The McCarren Internal Security Act, passed in 1950 over Truman's veto, established a Subversive Activities Control Board and required the registration of all Communist organi-sations and individuals, prohibited the employment of Communists in defence work, and denied entry to the USA to anyone who had belonged to a Communist or Fascist organisation. The McCarren-Walter Act (1952), again passed over Truman's veto, gave the Attorney-General powers to refuse admission to any 'subversive' and to deport any member of a 'Communist or Communist-front organization' even after they had become citizens. Such activity was duplicated at the regional and institutional levels. Universities were affected by speaker bans and loyalty oaths.

Anti-Communism contributed to the conservative ethos of the 1950s, an ethos which was reflected in the Republican Eisenhower presidency of 1953–61, as well as in the Menzies administration in Australia (1949–66), and government by conservative parties in Britain (1951–64), Japan (from the end of occupation in 1952 throughout the Cold War) and West Germany (1949–69). The Eisenhower presidency did not simply draw on this ethos. There was also a process of domestic propaganda to secure public support for what were presented as American values and to limit the development of attitudes that might be conducive for Communist propa-ganda.[37] A sense of vulnerability was important to both government and public in America, and helped give force and commitment to American policy. If such a sense has been a characteristic of all American crises,[38] that does not make the concern that developed and was encouraged from the late 1940s less notable. This concern was to be taken forward as a result of the Korean War (1950–3) in which the American army did not perform that well and was thwarted by Chinese intervention. The strategic situation in the 1950s was poor for the USA because of the Sino-Soviet alliance that followed Communist victory in the Chinese Civil War. The Eurasian land mass was overwhelmingly under the domain of the hostile other side. Once the Soviet Union and China publicly split in the 1960s, then the American strategic situation much improved.

In Western Europe as in the USA, there was a vitalist concern about the health of society. Anti-Communism, and related anxieties about the possibilities for revolution and subversion, played a role in the consideration and discussion of a wide range of social problems and policies, notably employment, but also housing, education and health. Anti-Communism encouraged the post-war maintenance of conscription, which, again, led to anxiety about the health of society. In West Germany, where a disavowal of militarism owed much to the rejection of the Nazi legacy and that of World War Two, the Cold War was to lead to the re-establishment of the German military. The key concern in Western Europe, by both right-wing and Social Democratic parties, was to prevent a disaffected working class from turning to the Communists. This concern contributed greatly to full-employment policies and to Keynesianism, or deficit financing, in order to ensure investment and economic activity. There was a linked determination to limit Communist infiltration of the trade unions and the Social Democratic parties. In a parallel with Soviet policy in Eastern Europe, the Americans took an active role against Communist trade unions in France and Italy. In 1947, 'Wild Bill' Donovan, the former head of the OSS, the American Office of Strategic Services, the forerunner of the CIA, helped persuade the American government to fund anti-Communists in the French trade unions that, he claimed, were a Communist fifth column.

This theme was to be the basis of Ian Fleming's first James Bond novel, *Casino Royale* (1953), as the villain was paymaster of the Communist-controlled trade union in the heavy and transport industries of Alsace, the most vulnerable part of France to Soviet attack. This trade union was presented as an important fifth column in the event of war with the Soviet Union. The early novels depicted SMERSH (*Smert' shpionam*, Death to Spies), a branch of the GRU (Main Intelligence Directorate), which was under the control of the Soviet Ministry of Defence, as the prime threat to the West. In practice, SMERSH was not actually involved in foreign intelligence, which was the function of the GRU in differing capacities and of the KGB. There was, indeed, considerable sensitivity in Britain about the extent of Communist influence in the trade unions. In 1949, the Labour government sent in troops to deal with a London dock strike that it blamed on Communists. The following year, Hugh Gaitskell, the Minister for Fuel and Power, and leader of the Labour Party from 1955 to 1962, claimed that a strike in the power stations was instigated by Communist shop stewards and served for them as a rehearsal for future confrontation. Critics argued that these views reflected Cold War paranoia, but the belief that Communists were encouraging agitation in the trade unions and the British empire was widespread and well-grounded. As a reminder of the multiple links between politics and culture, Fleming both contributed to such attitudes and derived benefit from their popularity. Gaitskell, who was to be the lover of Fleming's wife, Ann, died in 1962 after having tea at the Soviet embassy. It was claimed that he had been poisoned in order to leave the way clear for the more left-wing and less pro-American Harold Wilson who, as Prime Minister from 1964 to 1970, rejected American pressure for Britain to take part in the Vietnam War.

On 13 April 1948, the British Cabinet had discussed the need for propaganda against Communism, specifically activity by the Labour Party, the Co-operative and trade union movements, and the churches, to help anti-Communist Socialist tendencies. British achievements were to be emphasised to give confidence to Social Democratic parties in Europe. The Cabinet also decided that the BBC should be pressed about the speakers it asked to appear on the Brains Trust and the Friday Forum, leading radio programmes. On 1 June, the Cabinet returned to these themes, and it was argued: 'that the BBC should not afford facilities to enable sectional interests to continue to express their opposition to an Act which had been passed'.[39] The pro-Western policies of Clement Attlee's Labour government (1945–51) were supported by the vast majority of the Labour Party and trade union movement. Communist and Soviet sympathisers within both were isolated, and the Communist Party was kept at a distance. This helped prevent the development of a strong radical Left, and was linked to the alliance between labour and capital that was to be important in the post-war mixed economy in Britain; although the emphasis on state control and regulation was damaging to entrepreneurial ethos. The Attlee government also decided by January 1947 to develop a British nuclear bomb. This policy was regarded as necessary for Britain's independent security and independence. Throughout, the British government sought to play more than a secondary role to the USA. As a result, at considerable cost, Britain became the third nuclear power: the bomb was ready by 1952.

As an aspect of the Cold War, the struggle in Europe in the 1920s and 1930s between Leninist-Marxist (Communist) parties and various shades of non-Marxist liberal-democratic parties and groups intensified in the late 1940s and 1950s. In Italy, for example, Carlo Rosselli's teachings, denounced in the 1930s by the Italian Communist Party (ICP) as revisionist, became an inspiration for Italians of the centre and non-Marxist left after 1945 and helped blunt the appeal of the highly-popular ICP. The later move of the ICP by the late 1960s and early 1970s into Eurocommunism was one outcome, as was its commitment to parliamentary working. No such change occurred among the more left-wing French and Portuguese Communist parties. The major concern for the Americans and British was Germany. Nobody wanted a return to the factious Weimar politics of 1919–33 with their hyper-multi-party system. It was appreciated that the bitter fighting among the Communists (KPD) and Social Democrats (SPD), that had played a major role in enabling Hitler to rise to power in 1933, could not be repeated. The Americans and British did not want to face an alliance between the KPD and the SPD. Instead, an inspiration or even model, notably for the SPD, was the coming to power of the Labour Party in Britain in 1945. The SPD's two major policy declarations, the 1951 Frankfurt Declaration and the 1959 Godesberg Programme, removed Leninist thinking and Marxist class warfare from SPD doctrine. Thus, the late 1940s and 1950s proved a formative era for the later evolution of the SPD, which proved a major force for stability in West Germany. So also did the high rate of economic growth under the Christian Democratic Adenaeur government. The West German concept of the social market contrasted with the nationalisation and state control seen in Britain and France, as well as with East German Communism and American economic liberalism.[40] East Germany solved the political as well as the economic issue differently. The Communist leaders, Walter Ulbricht and Wilhelm Pieck, and a SPD leader, Wilhelm Grotewohl, merged the Communists and a SPD Splinter group to form the SED (*Sozialistische Einheitspartei Deutschlands*, or Socialist Unity Party) in 1946. This was to be the governing party until 1989. The Poles followed the same path in 1946.

## Chinese Civil War

Meanwhile, the broader geopolitical situation in East Asia and further afield had altered with the success of Communism in China. The small, urban-based Chinese Communist Party had been largely destroyed in the 1927 Autumn Harvest Uprising and other episodes elsewhere, after which control over the Party was increasingly taken by agrarian agitators under Mao Zedong who pressed for a rural revolution. Despite a series of large-scale offensives from 1930 to 1934, the forces of the Nationalist government were unable to destroy the Communists, although they did bring damaging pressure to bear. Again, as another instance of a 'Cold War' that involved much warfare, this was a struggle, between Communism and its opponent, that was scarcely non-violent. Jiang Jieshi deployed about 400,000 troops in the 1932 offensive.[41] Separately, the Nationalist position was increasingly challenged by Japanese aggression, with full-scale war breaking out in July 1937. Once Japan overran China's coasts and river valleys, destroying the Nationalists' urban power bases, capturing Shanghai and Nanjing in 1937, and Canton in 1938, the Communists were able to make a greater impact in many (not all) rural areas, where the Nationalists had less interest and control.

In opposition to the Nationalists, Mao had developed a three-stage revolutionary war model. During World War Two, he was able to use a combination of clandestine political-social organisation (Stage 1) and guerrilla warfare (Stage 2), in order to advance the Communist position, but was unable to move successfully into the conventional realm (Stage 3) until after the Japanese withdrawal.[42] The Nationalist government under Jiang Jieshi was gravely weakened by the long war with Japan, with key military units destroyed in 1937, the major cities lost and great damage to the economy and the social fabric. Moreover, there was no recovery in the latter half of the war. Instead, the Nationalists were particularly hard hit by large-scale Japanese advances in 1944 and 1945 which overran much of southern China.

Despite American support, the Nationalists were defeated anew after World War Two: by the Communists in the Chinese Civil War. This defeat would have been less likely, bar for the war. Prior to the Japanese attack on China, the Communists had been in a vulnerable position in their conflict with the Nationalists. As a result of repeated and increasingly successful Nationalist attacks from 1930, the Communists, in 1934, had abandoned their base in Jiangxi and, in the Long March, had moved in 1935 to a more remote rural power base in northern Shanxi. Funded and provided with arms by Stalin, Mao had become a factor in the complicated negotiations of power in China.[43] Following the Japanese attack, the Communists benefited from having become, during the late 1930s and early 1940s, the dominant anti-Japanese force in northern China and from the war having weakened the Nationalists.[44]

The Chinese Civil War was the largest conflict, in terms of number of combatants and area fought over, since World War Two, and it proves an instructive counterpoint to the latter, indicating the difficulty of drawing clear lessons from the conflicts of the 1940s. Nevertheless, there has been far less scholarship on the Chinese Civil War, and much of the work published on it has reflected ideological bias, notably being used to support the legitimacy of the Communist regime. In China, technology and the quantity of *matériel* did not triumph, as the Communists were inferior to the Nationalists in weaponry, and, in particular, lacked air and sea power. However, their strategic conceptions, operational planning and execution, army morale, and political leadership, proved superior, and they were able to make the transfer from guerrilla warfare to large-scale conventional operations; from denying their opponents control over territory to seizing and securing it. Mao's party and army possessed unitary command and lacked a multi-party consensus model. The Nationalist cause, in contrast, was weakened by poor and highly divided leadership, inept strategy, and, as the war went badly, poor morale. In addition, corruption and inflation greatly affected civilian support. Indeed, the *China White Paper* published by the State Department in 1950 blamed the Nationalists' failure on their own incompetence and corruption.

Nevertheless, the classic treatment of the war, as a Communist victory of 'hearts and minds' that allegedly indicated the superior virtues of Communism over the Nationalists, as well as the strength of the People's Liberation Army and its brave peasant fighters, has been qualified in scholarship over the last two decades by a greater emphasis on the importance of what actually happened in the fighting.[45] Until 1948, the Nationalists largely held their own. When the American use of atomic bombs led to

Japan's sudden surrender in August 1945, the Communists liberated much of the north of China from Japanese forces, capturing large quantities of weaponry. The Soviets also handed over captured Japanese weapons from their successful August 1945 invasion of Manchuria. Other than that, the Soviets largely stayed out of the Chinese Civil War. Negotiations between the Nationalists and the Communists were actively sponsored by the USA, which sought a unity government for China. However, the negotiations broke down, as the Communists were determined to retain control of the north; and the cease-fire agreement that was negotiated did not apply in Manchuria. In 1946, the Nationalist troops transported north by the American navy, occupied the major cities in Manchuria, China's industrial heartland, but most of the rest of the region was held by the Communists. The following year, Communist guerrilla tactics had an increasing impact in isolating Nationalist garrisons in the north, although, further south, the Nationalists overran the Communist-dominated province of Shensi.

There was strong pressure in the USA to intervene on the Nationalist side, particularly from the Republicans, who repeatedly raised the charge of weakness toward Communism. Longstanding American interest in China had been strengthened in World War Two, not least with a large-scale expansion of the economy of the Pacific states.[46] Moreover, the south and west became more important in economic and demographic terms during the post-war 'baby boom' and there was to be a cultural shift toward the Pacific coast. All these factors contributed to enhanced interest in East Asia. Nevertheless, the Truman government decided not to intervene in China. It took a lesser role than in the Greek Civil War, which was a more containable conflict and one more propitious for Western intervention. There was also great distrust of Jiang Jieshi, the Nationalist leader. As a result, the Republicans organised a witch hunt of those who had allegedly betrayed China.

In 1948, as the Communists switched to conventional, but mobile, operations, the Nationalist forces in Manchuria were isolated and then destroyed, and the Communists regained Shensi and conquered much of China north of the Yellow River. Communist victory in Manchuria led to a crucial shift in advantage, and was followed by the rapid collapse of the Nationalists the following year. The Communists made major gains of *matériel* in Manchuria, and it also served as a base for raising supplies for operations elsewhere.[47] After overrunning Manchuria, the Communists focused on the large Nationalist concentration in the Suchow-Kaifeng region. In the Huai Hai campaign, beginning on 6 November 1948, each side committed about 600,000 men. The Nationalists suffered from poor generalship, including insufficient coordination of units, and inadequate use of air support, and were also hit by defections. An important factor in many civil wars, defections from the Nationalists proved highly significant in the latter stages of the Chinese Civil War. Much of the Nationalist force was encircled thanks to effective Communist envelopment methods, and, in December 1948 and January 1949, it collapsed due to defections and combat losses.

Jiang Jieshi resigned as President on 21 January 1949, and the Communists captured Beijing the following day. They responded to the new President's offer of negotiation by demanding unconditional surrender, and the war continued. The Communist victories that winter had opened the way to advances further south, not least by enabling them to build up resources. The Communists crossed the Yangzi River on 20 April 1949, and the rapid overrunning of much of southern China over the following six months testified not only to the potential speed of operations, but also to the impact of success in winning over support. Nanjing fell on 22 April, and Shanghai on 27 May, and the Communists pressed on to capture rapidly the other major centres. Fleeing the mainland, Jiang Jieshi took refuge on the island of Formosa (Taiwan), which China had regained from Japan after the end of World War Two. It was protected by the limited aerial and naval capability of the Communists and, eventually, by American naval power. However, until he intervened in Korea in 1950, Mao Zedong prepared for an invasion of Formosa, creating an air force to that end.[48] Jiang, in turn, used Formosa and the other offshore islands he still controlled as a base for raids on the mainland. Meanwhile, in the spring of 1950, the island of Hainan and, in 1950–1, Tibet were conquered by the Communists, the capital of Tibet, Lhasa, being occupied on 7 October 1950. The CIA subsequently backed rebellion in Tibet, notably by Khampa rebels. The new strategic order in Asia was underlined in January 1950 when China and the Soviet Union signed a mutual security agreement. Mao was in Moscow for two weeks, an unheard of amount of time for a head of state: Stalin would not see Mao for a while, insulting him. Tension between the two regimes was there from the start.

The Chinese Civil War was not a simple struggle between Communists and anti-Communists. It drew on a number of strands in Chinese history, including regional rivalries and the issues of military control. Moreover, the success of the Nationalists' Northern Campaign in the late 1920s, when, from a base in the south, they gained control over all the country bar Manchuria, indicated that Communism was not itself necessary to deliver such a military verdict. Nevertheless, the Communist success in 1946–50 was more complete, not only because it included Manchuria and Tibet, but also because it was not dependent, as that of the Nationalists (or indeed the Manchu in the 1640s–50s) had been, on co-operation with warlords. Moreover, as a result of Mao, the nationalism and nation-state building seen in China earlier in the century was linked to the Cold War.

# South-East Asia

A separate set of conflicts arose from the reimposition of colonial control after the defeat of Japan in World War Two. The Dutch proved unable, in the face of nationalist opposition, to sustain their attempt to regain control of the East Indies, which became Indonesia in 1949. The Americans pressed the Dutch to withdraw because they regarded their opponents as nationalists rather than Communists.[49]

The French also faced a growing insurrection in Indochina. There, Ho Chi Minh, the Communist head of the nationalist Viet Minh, exploited the vacuum of power left by the Japanese surrender, and seized power across Vietnam in August 1945, proclaiming national independence and the foundation of the Democratic Republic of Vietnam on 2 September. The French, however, refused to accept the loss of colonial control, and, on 22 September 1945, French troops landed in Saigon. The following month saw both guerrilla operations, against the French in the south, and negotiations. After the latter, which went on into 1946, failed, in great part due to fighting, large-scale conflict broke out that December. The Viet Minh was unsuccessful in conventional conflict and resorted to guerrilla operations, with the French gaining and retaining control of the major urban centres. However, just as the Soviets, once they had conquered Manchuria in 1945, had transferred arms to the Chinese Communists, so the latter, victorious in 1949, provided arms to the Viet Minh, not least because they did not wish to see a European colonial presence on their southern border. Links between China and the Viet Minh developed from early 1950. Links between the Soviet Union and the Viet Minh also developed. The availability of these arms and of a secure neighbouring base in China helped the Viet Minh greatly. The conflict was internationalised and became a major part of the wider Cold War.

In 1954, the French were to be defeated at Dien Bien Phu, which they had developed as an advanced base. This became a location for a decisive battle that bore no relation to the limited inherent strategic significance of the site. The outnumbered French there proved vulnerable to Chinese-supplied artillery as well as to determined, but costly, frontal attacks by the Viet Minh, and to their superior engineering and novel tactics. The French positions were overrun.[50] The French still held all the major cities, but this defeat was followed by the French decision to abandon Indochina. France had portrayed the war as an internal issue until 1947–8, and then started advertising it to Washington as a Cold War conflict. The Americans took on much of the financial cost of the struggle for France, and had pressed in 1953–4 for a decisive military outcome, but were unwilling to commit ground troops and air attacks to that end, or after the French lost at Dien Bien Phu. John Foster Dulles, the American Secretary of State, wanted American interventionism as part of an internationalised war, but, first the British and then Australia and New Zealand refused to participate.

Moreover, President Eisenhower did not wish to restart the Korean War in Vietnam. While negotiations continued in Geneva, the French suffered fresh defeats in Central Vietnam. With the French determined to withdraw, Vietnam was then partitioned on the 17th parallel, between a Communist north and a pro-Western south.[51] The Viet Minh had not wanted this outcome and had made significant gains south of that parallel, but it was agreed at the level of the major powers, and China and the Soviet Union then pressed the Viet Minh to agree.

# NATO

In 1949, the foundation of the North Atlantic Treaty Organization (NATO) had created a security framework for Western Europe. Such a framework appeared necessary because of an increasingly threatening international situation. Communist success in China apparently increased Soviet options, while, in 1949, the first successful Soviet nuclear test seemed to remove the deterrent and intimidatory power of the American nuclear armoury. Meanwhile, the breaking of the Soviet blockade of West Berlin in 1949 fostered the Western commitment to Germany. Totally abandoning its pre-war tradition of isolationism, the USA played a crucial role in the formation of the new alliance, and was thus anchored to the defence of Western Europe. An analysis of World War Two that attributed the war, and Hitler's initial successes, to Appeasement in the 1930s led to a determination to contain the Soviet Union. In 1949, the Senate ratified the North Atlantic Treaty establishing NATO by 82 votes to 13, which was a clear contrast with its failure to support the League of Nations after World War One. The opposition to interventionism of many Republicans was not matched across the party as a whole.

In terms of attitudes and means, there was a marked degree of continuity from World War Two to the hostility seen by the end of the 1940s. World War Two had left the Soviets suspicious of attack by allies, as had occurred in 1941, while it led the Americans to construct a new international order which they now saw as threatened by Soviet expansionism. Moreover, the war had left both the USA and the Soviet Union with substantial militaries, and with the conviction that it was appropriate to address threats by the response to force. In the USA and the Soviet Union, war had become more significant for both state and nation; the two, moreover, closely linked in this significance. The state acquired purpose and legitimacy by assuaging the nation's anxiety in a context of international and ideological competition. Although the USA and Soviet Union had both reached this situation, they came at it with different traditions and convictions. The USA had no real prior experience in managing the foreign commitments it now would implement in response. From 1950, as a consequence of this new commitment to an anti-hegemonic policy towards Eurasia directed against the Soviet Union, substantial American land, sea and air forces were stationed in Europe.[52] This greatly increased the American commitment to the region. That December, Dwight Eisenhower, who had been the American commander in the European theatre during World War Two before being an American Army Chief of Staff (1945–8), was appointed head of NATO's forces as Supreme Allied Commander Europe. The establishment of NATO, which was part of the spread of the American logistical system,[53] was followed by the creation of a military structure, including a central command, by the provision of American munitions and surplus commodities, such as fuel, to NATO allies, and, eventually, by West German rearmament which owed a lot to American pressure and support.

The original members of NATO, the USA, Canada, Norway, Denmark, the UK, Netherlands, Belgium, France, Luxembourg, Italy and Portugal, were joined by Greece and Turkey in 1952, in an important eastward extension of NATO and a transformation of it from being an Atlantic body.[54] The extension greatly increased the frontier between NATO and Communist states, strengthened NATO's position in the Mediterranean, offered the major addition of the large Turkish army, and took NATO into the Black Sea. Moreover, from Cyprus, British bombers could overfly Turkey, and thus threaten industrial cities in Ukraine. The global architecture of the Cold War was made more apparent by this extension of NATO, as was NATO's position as a subordinate part of this American-directed system. Turkey's active participation in the Korean War (1950–3) as part of the American-led coalition was an important part of the equation, both politically and strategically.

## The Korean War, 1950–3

Leading NATO powers were tested not in Europe but in distant Korea where there was a major war that was far greater in scale and consequence than being simply an Asian counterpoint to the Greek Civil War.[55] The Communists had overwhelmingly won in the Chinese Civil War, but the Americans were determined that they should not be allowed further gains in East Asia. Sometimes a client kingdom of China, Korea had been conquered by Japan and become its colony in 1910. At the close of World War Two, Korea, a hitherto united territory, had been partitioned: northern Korea had been occupied by Soviet forces and southern Korea by the Americans. In the context of the difficulties posed by Korean political divisions, and growing American-Soviet distrust, both of which sapped attempts to create a united Korea, they each, in 1948, established authoritarian regimes: under Syngman Rhee in South Korea and Kim Il-Sung in North Korea. There was no historical foundation for this division, each regime had supporters across Korea, and both wished to govern the entire peninsula.

The regime in North Korea, whose military build-up was helped by the Soviet Union, was convinced that its counterpart in the South was weak and could be overthrown, and was likely to be denied American support. The South Korean army, indeed, lacked military experience and adequate equipment, while the Korean Military Assistance Group provided by the USA was only 500–strong. Moreover, in the late 1940s, with Communism triumphing in China, and in Eastern Europe bar Greece, the situation appeared propitious for expansion elsewhere. In December 1949, General Douglas MacArthur, American Commander in Chief Far East, told a visiting British journalist that the American defence line in the western Pacific specifically excluded South Korea and Taiwan, while specifically including Japan and the Philippines. The following month, Dean Acheson, the Secretary of State from 1949 to 1953, reiterated a similar view at the National Press Club.

The bitter rivalry between the two Korean states, as each sought to destabilise the other, included, from 1948, guerrilla operations in South Korea supported by the Communist North. This rivalry led to full-scale conflict, on 25 June 1950, when the North launched a surprise invasion of South Korea. It attacked with about 135,000 troops, and using T-34 tanks and Yak aeroplanes provided by the Soviets that gave them an advantage over their lightly-armed opponents. The South Korean army had no anti-tank weaponry, while the American infantry had the obsolete 2.5 inches bazooka which was useless against the T-34s in North Korean hands.

As elsewhere in the Cold War, there was a significant linkage between international and local factors. In February 1950, Stalin had agreed to provide heavy guns to North Korea, in contrast to his position in March and September 1949 when he had rejected Kim Il-Sung's suggestion that an attack be mounted. In March–April 1950, Stalin moved further toward Kim Il-Sung's position, telling him that the Soviet explosion of an atomic device on 29 August 1949 and the treaty of alliance between China and the Soviet Union had made the situation more propitious. Kim Il-Sung promised a quick victory in the 'Fatherland Liberation War'. Stalin made agreement, however, conditional on Chinese support and said that, if the Americans intervened, he would not send troops, which increased North Korea's reliance on Chinese backing. Given Stalin's position, Mao agreed, although he needed to consolidate his position in China and would have preferred an emphasis on gaining Taiwan rather than invading South Korea. Indeed, the Korean War helped save Taiwan from a Communist takeover, both by postponing a possible Chinese attack and by greatly increasing America's willingness to help Taiwan.

In June 1950, the South Koreans were pushed back by the invading North Koreans, the capital, Seoul, falling on 28 June. However, enough units fought sufficiently well in their delaying actions during their retreat south to give time for the arrival of American troops. As with the later Vietnam War, this was a conflict in which America's local ally played a

key role. American forces entered combat in Korea from 30 June as the
North Korean invasion led to intervention by an American-led United
Nations coalition. This wide-ranging coalition was determined to maintain
policies of collective security and containment, and was concerned that
a successful invasion of South Korea would be followed by Communist
pressure elsewhere, possibly on West Berlin, or on Taiwan, but, equally, at
any other point that might appear opportune. After the South Koreans, the
leading United Nations contingent was American, and the second largest
was British. Among the large number of international participants, the
Canadians and Turks were prominent. At the same time, some American
allies did not participate. Angered by American arms supplies to Argentina,
Brazil, unlike in World War Two, refused to send troops. The Americans
also provided most of the air and naval power, as well as the commander,
General Douglas MacArthur, their Commander in Chief Far East. The
UN forces benefited from the backing of a relatively stable South Korean
civilian government and from a unified command: MacArthur's position as
Supreme Commander of United Nations forces in Korea ensured control
over all military forces, including the South Korean army, and provided a
coherence that was to be lacking in the Vietnam War. American capability
was enhanced by the presence of their occupation forces in Japan, and
by the logistical infrastructure and support services provided by Japanese
facilities and resources.

Allied assistance was important in restricting criticism within the USA
of the role of other powers. On 2 August 1950, the Chancery at the British
Embassy at Washington, forwarding a report by Strafford Barff, the Director
of British Information Services in Chicago, noted: 'the cynical comments
about America being left alone to do the fighting are mainly confined to the
light-weight and lunatic newspapers and have not been indulged in by the
more responsible press which understands the implications on a world-wide
basis of Soviet strategy'. Barff on 31 July reported both press comment that
European countries, including Britain, were psychologically unfit to wage
war and that 'an increasing number of people believe that Korea is the
prelude to World War III and that it will follow soon'.[56]

Thanks to their major role in World War Two, the Americans were better
able than they would have been in the 1930s to fight in Korea. Nevertheless,
since 1945, due to post-war demobilisation as the 'peace dividend' was
taken, there had been a dramatic decline of available manpower and
matériel. The number of amphibious ships had fallen from 610 in 1945
to 81 in 1950, there was a grave shortage of artillery units, and, in 1949,
the American army only contained one armoured division. American
fighting effectiveness had also declined, as was shown by the experience
of some American units in the first year of the Korean War. The American
occupation forces sent from Japan to South Korea in late 1950 were out
of shape and performed poorly in July. Many of the National Guard units
dispatched were inadequately trained and equipped. Barff had noted on 31

July: 'The inadequacy of American arms and reported inefficiency of some officers and men have come as a great shock'.[57] The Americans were almost driven into the sea at the end of the peninsula in the first North Korean onslaught, but, once reinforced, managed to hold the Pusan perimeter there against attack. The situation was rescued by Operation Chromite, a daring and unrehearsed landing in very difficult tidal conditions on the Korean west coast at Inchon on 15 September 1950. This landing applied American force at a decisive point. Carried out far behind the front, and with very limited information about the conditions, physical and military, that they would encounter, about 83,000 troops were successfully landed. They pressed on to capture nearby Seoul.

This success wrecked both the coherence of North Korean forces and their supply system, which had anyway been put under great strain by the advance towards Pusan; and also achieved a major American psychological victory that was not to be matched in the Vietnam War. The capture of Seoul enabled the American forces in the Pusan area to move north. The North Koreans were driven back into their own half of the peninsula. On 7 October 1950, American forces crossed the 38° North parallel dividing North and South Korea. They moved north toward the Chinese frontier, advancing across a broad front against only limited resistance. However, the UN advance was affected by serious logistical problems that owed much to a lack of adequate harbours, but even more to the poor nature of ground routes, especially in the difficult mountainous interior. In addition, MacArthur's insistence on a landing on the east coast at Wonsan, as well as on the west coast, robbed Eighth Army's advance on the North Korean capital, Pyongyang, of logistical support, was delayed anyway until 25 October by the extensive mining of the harbour, and, as had been predicted by American staff officers, was rendered superfluous because South Korean troops advancing up the east coast had already seized the town on 11 October. Thus, much as Operation Chromite had been a success, the double envelopment failed to achieve its goals, not least of cutting off large numbers of North Koreans before they could fall back.

The UN advance was not welcome to the Chinese, who suddenly inter-vened in October 1950, exploiting the over-confidence of the Americans, notably, but not only, MacArthur. From July, the Chinese appear to have begun preparing for intervention, and certainly built up large forces near the border. Communist success in the Chinese Civil War had encouraged Mao to believe that technological advantages, especially in airpower which the Americans dominated, could be countered, not least by determination. However, as also by the Japanese in World War Two, American resilience, resources and fighting quality were under-estimated by the Chinese, in this the sole war between any of the world's leading military powers since 1945. Mao felt that UN support for Korean unification threatened China and might lead to a Nationalist (Guomindang) *revanche*, saw American support for Taiwan as provocative, and was also keen to present China as a major force, while Stalin, to whom Mao appealed for help, wanted to see China committed against the USA. This was the price for meeting Chinese requirements for assistance with military modernisation. Stalin promised help in the event of the Americans invading China as a result. It was not only the Western powers that faced problems in adjusting to the major changes in the international system. Indeed, under Stalin, there was a reluctance to see other Communist powers as more than clients, and notably in the case of Asian states. Mao's China was a key recipient of this patronage and attempted direction. Thus, the Soviet Union was reluctant to return to China the major warm-water Manchurian ports of Port Arthur and Dalian which it had taken from Japan in 1945. Despite Mao wanting the ports returned, the Soviet Union not do so while Stalin remained in power. This stance represented an important continuation from pre-Communist Russian interest in Manchuria: Port Arthur had been used as a naval base then.

Chinese intervention had not been anticipated by MacArthur, who had believed that, by maintaining the pace of the offensive and advancing to the Korean-Chinese frontier at the Yalu River, he would end the war. This advance had been authorised by the Joint Chiefs of Staff, and there was encouragement from CIA reports that direct intervention by China and the Soviet Union was unlikely. Despite a Chinese warning on 3 October 1950, via the Indian envoy in Beijing, of action if the UN forces advanced into North Korea, it was believed that the Communist leadership was intent on strengthening its position within China and that China lacked the resources for intervention abroad. MacArthur ignored the more cautious approach taken by Truman and his Secretary of State, Dean Acheson. Concerned about the Chinese response, Truman instructed MacArthur to use only South Korean forces close to the Chinese border, but MacArthur was insistent that American troops be employed. MacArthur told Truman that it was too late in the year for the Chinese to act in strength, and, after they initially intervened from 19 October in fairly small numbers, he neglected evidence of Chinese troops in Korea, not least of Chinese prisoners. The operational success MacArthur had shown in the Inchon operation was not matched by adequate strategic assessment on his part. Although his hubris was partly responsible, there were also serious weaknesses in American command and control reflecting the improvised way in which the conflict was being fought. In addition, the belief that airpower could isolate the battlefield led to misplaced confidence. These points throw suggestive light on the extent to which the theory, doctrine and infrastructure of nuclear deterrence might later have not worked had there been conflict between the major powers. The miscalculation shown in Korea in 1950, by the Americans, and also earlier by Communist planners who did not anticipate an American intervention in South Korea, did not provide an encouraging instance of the effectiveness of deterrence.

Attacking in force in November 1950, against the over-extended and, because of an advance on different axes, poorly-coordinated UN forces, the Chinese drove them out of North Korea in late 1950, pressing on to capture Seoul in January 1951. The Chinese, nominally Chinese People's Volunteers, not regulars, but, in practice, regular army units, proved better able to take advantage of the terrain, and outmanoeuvred the UN forces, who were more closely tied to their road links. The Americans lacked equipment appropriate for the harsh Korean winter. Valley envelopment became a Chinese speciality, first used to destroy an American battalion in late October 1950. The fighting quality and heroism of some retreating units, including American Marines and British forces, limited the scale of the defeat, but, nevertheless, it was a serious one. Thanks to control of the sea, however, it was possible to evacuate by sea units that had been cut off by the Communist advance, especially the 1st Marine Division from Hungnam, thus limiting the losses. The naval dimension was an important element in the conflict, and the Americans were able to deploy and apply a formidable amount of naval strength. The firepower of naval ordnance from Task Force 95 and from the carrier aircraft of Task Force 77 was of operational and tactical value, not least for ground support,[58] while naval control permitted easy resupply from Japan. Concerned to limit the war, the Soviet Union did not attack the American naval supply routes, not that they would have been able to do so successfully, and the small North Korean and Chinese navies were in no position to do so: in the Chinese Civil War, the Nationalists, not the Communists, had controlled Chinese naval power. Equally, there was no American or United Nations blockade of China, let alone amphibious attack, and the Chinese forces deployed in coastal regions that appeared threatened with an American invasion, for example near Tianjin, were not tested in battle.

Unlike at sea, the Korean War involved much conflict in the air as the Americans encountered resistance in the air space over North Korea. The Chinese, who had only created an air force in November 1949, and whose Soviet-trained pilots lacked adequate training, and were equipped with out-of-date Soviet planes, were supported, however, by the advanced MIG-15 fighters of the Manchurian-based Soviet 'Group 64', and the war saw the earliest dogfights between jet aircraft, with MIG-15s fighting American F-86 Sabres. Thus, the Americans were fighting another leading military power. Using more effective tactics, the Americans inflicted heavier casualties and were able to dominate the skies. Several hundred Soviet pilots were involved. The kill ratio was greatly in favour of the Americans, but against the Chinese and North Korean pilots, the F-86/MIG-15 kill ratio was even more in favour of them. The American victory in the air had serious consequences for respective ground support; although the absence of adequate command integration limited the American exploitation of this advantage. The Soviet refusal to heed Chinese pressure for Soviet air support of Chinese ground forces was a major advantage for the Americans, as well as helping limit the potential extension of the conflict.[59]

During the war, the Chinese made a full transition to a conventional army, with tanks, heavy artillery, and aircraft, thus continuing the process started during the latter stages of the Chinese Civil War. The UN forces, however, were now a more formidable opponent than when the war started. The Chinese were fought to a standstill in mid-February 1951, as UN supply lines shortened thanks to the retreat of UN forces, and as Chinese human-wave frontal attacks fell victim to American firepower, particularly in the 'Wŏnju Shoot' on 14 February.

MacArthur was relieved on 11 April 1951 for insubordination. MacArthur had requested an expansion of the war to include a blockade of China; as well as permission to pursue opposing aircraft into Manchuria and to attack their bases there; to bomb bridges along the Yalu River, hitting Chinese logistics; and to employ Nationalist Chinese troops against the Chinese coast (as a second front) or in Korea. These proposals were rejected by the Joint Chiefs of Staff as likely to lead to an escalation of the war, with the possibility, in particular, of direct Soviet entry. Truman's patience with the arrogant MacArthur was exhausted.[60] Truman was also under pressure from his allies, including Clement Attlee, the British Prime Minister, about the general's views; although, on the whole, the Americans tended to make decisions without much, or any, consultation, a situation that was to be repeated during the Vietnam War. Soviet entry into the Korean War was seen as a threat to Western Europe, which was regarded as particularly vulnerable to invasion. Had the Soviets attacked there, there would, indeed, have been no American reinforcements to spare for Korea.[61]

American restraint therefore helped ensure that the conflict did not become World War Three, or a nuclear war, and the Korean War served as an important introduction for American politicians to the complexities of limited warfare. More positively, containment – both by UN forces of the Communists, and of the nature of the war – prevented the risk of escalation. Aside from the decision not to use atomic bombs in Korea, which the British warned in December 1950 would probably lead to a totally unwanted all-out war with China,[62] USAF (United States Air Force) suggestions, in 1950, of the firebombing of the major industrial cities in North Korea were not initially implemented. Once the Chinese had entered the war, major incendiary attacks were launched on North Korea, creating, over several years of heavy bombing, much devastation and heavy casualties. However, there was no hot pursuit of Communist aircraft into China and no use of atomic weaponry.[63] In turn, Stalin, with his marked preference for exploiting advantages rather than facing risks, did not wish to take the chance of formal Soviet entry into the conflict.

The defence benefited from the appointment of Lieutenant-General Matthew Ridgway to head the UN forces in Korea. He was an able commander, better than possible alternatives: James Van Fleet, let alone Mark Clark. Without Ridgway, who, as commander of Eighth Army, had stabilised the front south of Seoul in February 1951, the Communist forces might have continued driving south, and the American public would have become disillusioned with the war, whereupon the USA would have had less prestige and possibility to guide events in East and South-East Asia. Seoul itself was recaptured by UN forces on 14 March.

The Chinese Fifth Offensive, that of 22–30 April 1951, which pushed the UN forces back toward Seoul, suffered very heavy casualties. The Communists tended to expose Nationalist troops who had defected in 1949 to the most risky tasks. Mao wished to get rid of these troops. Heavy Chinese and North Korean losses of men (about 160,000 casualties in April and May 1951) and equipment, including the surrender of large numbers of soldiers, the arrival of American reinforcements, and the deployment of American firepower, led the Chinese commander, P'eng The-huai, to abandon the attack in late May after his forces had again been fought to a standstill north of Seoul. Aside from the strength of the UN defence, the Chinese were affected because their advance had greatly increased the logistical burden of supporting China's large commitment of troops.

Thereafter, the war became far more static, with the front pushed back by a UN offensive between 20 May and 24 June 1951 to near the 38th Parallel. The attritional conflict that MacArthur had sought to avoid by Operation Chromite now prevailed. The advantage given to the defence by Korea's mountainous terrain, which was reminiscent of that in Italy in 1943–5 during World War Two, was accentuated by the politics of the conflict. Operational intensity and casualties both fell, and lengthy negotiations became more important, with offensives tied to their course. As trench replaced manoeuvre warfare, the role of artillery became more important, while, as the defences on both sides became stronger, the tendency for a more fixed front line was accentuated. With the Americans seeking an exit strategy from the war in the shape of the territorial *status quo* and a ceasefire, there was no attempt on their part to move forward from stalemate. On 10 July 1951, ceasefire talks began at Kaesong on the 38th Parallel. The Americans and Chinese both no longer felt they could take the casualties and risks of fighting on for a unification that was extremely unlikely. Nevertheless, there were still costly clashes. For example, in August-September 1951, American and South Korean forces captured the Bloody Ridge group of hills in order to prevent its use as an observation base for artillery fire. In September and October, they pressed on, with French support, to take Heartbreak Ridge to the north, in a series of assaults that recalled the methods of World War One trench warfare. UN forces suffered 60,000 casualties from July until November 1951, their opponents about 234,000, a sustained rate of loss that exceeded that seen for most of the Vietnam War. This was the last major UN offensive of the war, and, after October 1951, the front line changed little. Casualty rates were too high to justify the continuation of the UN advance. During the static line phase of the war, there was still prolonged, nasty fighting. The Chinese would scout out where the joining lines were between the American and South Korean units and then attack at that point. The South Koreans would tend to fall back, thereby exposing the American flank and causing problems for the Americans. The Chinese would sometimes drug their soldiers before launching attacks.

It was difficult to end the conflict, the goal of Eisenhower, who was elected American President in November 1952. Mao, convinced that his opponents lacked the necessary willpower to persist, and unwilling himself to accept failure, felt it appropriate to fight on. However, Mao was weakened by a shift in Soviet policy after Stalin died in March 1953. This shift was accentuated by anti-government riots in East Germany and Poland. Moreover, there was a more general uncertainty over Soviet intentions. Mao was also affected by the serious strain that the war was placing on the Chinese military. This strain did not prevent repeated Chinese attacks from 23 March to 16 July in the Battle of Porkchop Hill, attacks mounted in order to win advantage in the closing stages of the war. The Chinese made territorial gains, but only at the cost of very heavy casualties. Pressure on Mao was increased because Eisenhower, who visited South Korea soon after being elected, threatened to use atomic weaponry in order to bring the war to an end. This threat was enhanced because the Americans had first tested a hydrogen bomb in November 1952. Moreover, the Chinese knew that the Americans had tested atomic artillery in early 1953. The North Koreans responded to the Chinese lead and a settlement was reached. The eventual armistice, signed on 27 July 1953 by UN, North Korean and Chinese representations, left a military demarcation line along the 38th Parallel with an unfortified demilitarised zone two kilometres deep on either side.[64] At that stage, the largest UN contingent was South Korean (509,911), followed by the American (302,483), British (14,198) and Canadian (6,146) contingents.

By the time the fighting ended, with over three million dead (of whom 33,741 were classified as American battle deaths, with 2,835 non-battle deaths), the pattern of the Communist–Western confrontation known as the Cold War was set. The majority of casualties were Korean, prefiguring the situation with the Vietnam War, and for Korea the war was very far from limited, the South Korean military alone losing 415,000 killed. Over a million civilians were killed. The war closed with the partition of the peninsula between two hostile states well-entrenched and with this hostility unlanced. Indeed, the conflict had seen many of the symptoms of civil war, not least with the harsh treatment of civilians regarded as opponents by advancing Korean forces, both North and South Korean. 1953 saw an armistice agreement, not a peace treaty; and tensions, exacerbated by the war, remained high in Korea. Although Chinese forces were withdrawn from North Korea, a process completed in 1958, the USA, under the 1953 Mutual Defence Treaty, built up the South Korean army, and still retains a strong military presence in South Korea in order to deter North Korea from invading. In Korea, the Cold War remains a major presence. It certainly did not end there in 1989–91, as it did in Europe.[65]

# The Impact of the Korean War

Outside Korea, there was a process of radicalisation in the early 1950s that helped entrench ideological and political differences. Thus, Mao used conflict with the USA in order to consolidate the position of the Communist Party within China, and to push through land seizure, killing very large numbers in the process. Mao ruled by means of an iron fist and sheer terror. Those punished as landowners were frequently simply peasants who owned a little land. Whoever the victim, the 'people's justice' supposedly on show was vicious, bloody and destructive. This radicalisation of the Chinese Revolution, which would probably have happened anyway, was accompanied by a markedly hostile stance toward the USA which greatly furthered Stalin's goals. There had been little chance of a *rapprochement* between Mao and the USA, but Stalin was well-used to abrupt changes of policy, and Chinese entry into the Korean War made such a change highly unlikely. In China, the conflict is known to the present as the 'American War'. Indeed, a Sino-American *rapprochement* was postponed for over two decades, which provided the Soviet Union with a key element of strength for much of the Cold War. Moreover, the Korean War left the USA engaged in an area that was of scant strategic concern to the Soviet Union. Conversely, however, the conflict gave Mao a stronger sense of China's importance, which was to cause problems for the Soviet government, particularly after Stalin died. In addition, the war involved heavy costs for the Soviets, as they provided support for China and North Korea during it, while also having, in a developing arms race, to meet the consequences of greater military expenditure by the wealthier USA and its allies.

The war, which was in some respects a substitute for World War Three, led to a process of militarisation and a major increase in military expenditure, especially in the West. Soviet expenditure was already at a high rate. The Korean War, a hot war within the Cold War, propelled the Cold War American arms build-up. In the USA, military expenditure rose, both in absolute terms and as a percentage of total expenditure by the federal government. A large military-industrial complex came to play a greater role in the American economy and governmental structure, eventually to the publicly-proclaimed concern of Eisenhower.[66] Conscription was revived, and the size of the American armed forces greatly expanded. This increase rested on a degree of social support, indeed mobilisation, for the Cold War that made the policies of the American government readily viable. The Americans also put pressure on their allies to build-up their military and, more clearly, called for West German rearmament, a policy criticised by Soviet propaganda. The Korean War helped ensure that NATO was transformed into an effective alliance. In Canada, which played an active role in NATO and also sent troops to Korea, defence spending rose from $196 million in 1947 to $1.5 billion in 1951. Under American pressure, because it needed allies, Britain embarked in 1950 on a costly rearmament programme. This programme undid recent economic gains and strengthened the military commitment that was to be such a heavy post-war economic burden for Britain; and disproportionately so compared to West Germany, which became a more successful economic rival. At the same time, the war encouraged the expenditure of American wealth and the use of American credit, which led to a boom in demand that helped economic growth in Japan and Western Europe, particularly in West Germany. Having benefited greatly from economic growth during World War Two, and from a subsequent economic primacy in part based on the wartime devastation of other economies, the Americans were now spending part of the proceeds on military expenditure.

Similarly, the Korean War accentuated the already dominant stress on heavy industry in the Communist economies. From 1945 to 1955, during the Fourth and Fifth Five Year Plans, the emphasis within the Soviet Union was on rebuilding the country. Consumer concerns did not bother Soviet planners. Stalin never gave much concern at all to light industry, which is what helps create a standard of living. With Communist control, the five year plan model of heavy industry had also been laid upon Eastern Europe. In the early 1950s, the strength and brutality of its governments was such that they had scant reason to fear any demand for consumer goods, a demand which remained repressed. To argue that therefore the Soviet Union would have been better off had there been no Korean War, and had it been able to provide consumer goods, is to miss the point that both this war and the nature and content of economic planning were in accordance with Communist notions of world revolution, as well as with Stalin's determination to seize advantages. However, unrest in East Germany, Bulgaria, and Czechoslovakia, especially in the first, led to violence in 1953, and, once the workers rose in rebellion, this created a serious problem for the Communist bloc.

The Korean War greatly increased already significant American sensitivity to developments and threats in East Asia.[67] It led to an extension of the containment policy towards the Communist powers, which began with China and rapidly expanded to include North Korea and the Communists in North Vietnam. American aid to the governmental opposition to Communist insurgents in the Philippines was stepped up in 1950. In 1946–7, the conservative government had failed to defeat an insurrection by the Communist-led Hukbalahap movement. From 1948, the US-run Joint Military Advisory Group had received more American military assistance. The Americans financed and equipped the Philippines Army so that it was able to take the war to the Huks, and this policy was powerfully supported by land reform. The rebellion ended in 1954. The Korean War also resulted in the maintenance of American army, navy and air power in Japan, where important bases were preserved after the American occupation was ended as a result of peace and security treaties in 1952. Furthermore, the Korean War was responsible for a growing American commitment to the Nationalist Chinese in Taiwan, a marked shift from the position prior to the war when Truman had considered accepting a Communist invasion of the island. The outbreak of the war, and China's subsequent intervention, instead led to a major increase in aid to the Nationalists and, in June 1950, to the move of the powerful American Seventh Fleet into the Taiwan Strait. The American military presence in the region was fostered precisely because it could serve a variety of purposes, countering North Korea, China and the Soviet Union, but also providing an important element in relations with Japan. Concern about China also led to greater American interest in India as offering the West a democratic alternative as an Asian power, a view outlined by Secretary of State John Foster Dulles in June 1953,[68] and one that was to be revived in the 2000s and 2010s. In 1951, the USA entered into a defence pact with Australia and New Zealand.

More generally, a sense that the situation might slip out of control through what was later called a 'Domino Effect', as the fall of one country in Asia to Communism led to that of others, an image that was easy to communicate to politicians and public, encouraged the American government to take a greater interest in the course and consequences of the Western retreat from empire. This was especially so in Indochina where the French were under great pressure and where Chinese-backed expansion appeared to demonstrate this 'effect'. From 1950, assistance to the French in Indochina was increased, and, by 1953, the USA was supporting most of the financial burden of the war there. This commitment to the European colonial powers, however, was unwise from the perspective of America's wish to win Third World support. So also were some of the American interventions in the Third World. Notably so in 1953, when a CIA-instigated coup led to the fall of the Iranian nationalist President, Mohammed Mosaddeq. In the short term, this coup aligned British and American interests and stabilised the position of the Shah, Reza Pahlavi, who returned from exile. He was a pro-Western figure, important, particularly, from 1958, in offsetting the consequences of Soviet influence in Iraq and in being willing to co-operate with Israel. In the long-term, however, the coup encouraged Iranian popular hostility to the West. The coup was in part designed to limit populist nationalism and was also motivated by a drive to control Third World resources and strategic locations, such as Iranian oil.[69] The significance of these resources and locations for American strategy against the Soviet Union was more clearly understood. In 1954, a foreign consortium was given effective control over Iranian oil. Nationalist movements throughout the Third World were to be increasingly viewed by the Americans in their perspective of the struggle with Communism. The *realpolitik* of international relations was perceived in ideological terms by both the USA and its Communist opponents, helping to ensure that tensions between the two sides remained high, and encouraging not only competitive diplomacy but also the development of covert operations.

Western policy was fully militarised by 1953, America had become a national security state, and the division of Europe had been cemented. However, such remarks pay insufficient attention both to the threatening character of Stalin's policy and to the extent to which Western preparedness as a result of the Korean War may well have limited the possibility that the Soviet Union would subsequently risk war by aggressive action. In other words, containment worked, although it was costly and also meant that Communist control of its bloc was entrenched. This was a clear consequence of the partition of Korea, and the latter suggested that the partition of Germany would be a lasting one.

## The Intelligence War

The threat from the Soviet Union was also crucial to the development of Western intelligence agencies and of the practice of surveillance against both domestic and foreign opponents. In the USA, where the decryption, from 1946, of cables from American-based Soviet agents and authorities in Moscow increased concerns about Soviet penetration,[70] the Central Intelligence Agency was created under the National Security Act of 1947. This Act was crucial to the emergence of the national-security state and, to a lesser extent, to the militarisation of American policy, preceding the Korean War in the latter respect. Intelligence operations involved conflict, as with the use of covert operations. Like traditional Republicans, Eisenhower wished to reduce government spending and to focus American strength on the key theatre, which to him was Europe. As a result, he allowed the CIA to take a major role outside Europe, as in Iran in 1953 and Guatemala in 1954. This looked toward its planning for operations against Cuba in 1961 and its significant role in strategy and operations in South-East Asia. Conflict was also involved in attempts to intercept aerial reconnaissance missions. These included the Soviet shooting down near Sverdlovsk of the U-2 high-altitude photo-reconnaissance spy plane flown by Gary Powers on 1 May 1960.[71]

In turn, there were persistent efforts by both sides to penetrate opposing intelligence agencies. These increased tension between, and anxiety within, the competing blocs. Thus, American concern over the British spy system rose greatly after the defections of Guy Burgess and Donald Maclean to the Soviet Union in 1951. The Americans firmly, and correctly, believed that Kim Philby, the Secret Service's liaison officer in Washington, was a traitor, and in 1952 the Director of the CIA insisted that he not return to Washington. Evidence of Soviet penetration of Western intelligence agencies encouraged a fear of large-scale Soviet activity. Soviet defectors, notably Anatoly Golitsyn, suggested that there were high-level traitors everywhere, that other defectors were KGB plants, and that the Kremlin was aiming at world dominance. James Angleton, the CIA's head of counter-intelligence, believed this view. In November 1962, Harold Macmillan, the British Prime Minister, told the House of Commons that 'hostile intrigue and espionage are being relentlessly maintained on a very large scale'. Earlier that year, Yuri Nosenko, a KGB officer, had revealed the identity of an American, a Briton and a Canadian spying for the Soviets.

British intelligence activities were directed against both the Soviet Union and dissidence within the empire. The two could readily be linked.[72] However, much of the struggle with Soviet intelligence was not focused on the empire, but related to attempts to protect the details of high-spectrum British weaponry designed for any conflict with the Soviets.[73]

## Soviet Militarisation

In the Soviet Union, militarisation was already well-established at the time of the Korean War, thanks not only to World War Two, but also to the pre-war language and practice of state-directed national mobilisation: Soviet militarisation went back to 1917. The late 1940s saw a Sovietisation of the militaries of Eastern Europe. This process involved the armies of Romania and Bulgaria which had fought alongside Germany in World War Two before changing sides; but Sovietisation was also seen in Hungary, whose forces had largely disintegrated under Soviet attack in 1944; and in Poland and Czechoslovakia, where the military was based on units that had fought the Germans with Soviet support. In contrast, the Soviets disbanded the non-Communist Polish Home Army and persecuted many of the members of this former resistance organisation. Soviet officers were appointed to the Eastern European forces: Marshal Konstantin Rokossovsky, a Pole by birth, having been Commander of the Second Byelorussian Front and then, in 1945–9, commander of Soviet occupation forces in Poland, became Deputy Chairman of the Polish Council of Ministers and, later, Polish Minister of Defence and Marshal of Poland. The Sovietisation of the militaries rested on a broader pattern of political and economic control and, in particular, of a dominance of the security dimension. The various incarnations of the Soviet security apparatus (NKVD, MVD, KGB) sought to develop and direct its allies' intelligence services. Thus, Bulgarian agents were used for assassination missions.

## German Rearmament

The threat of Soviet attack in Europe while the Americans were committed in Korea, led, from 1950, to strong American pressure for German rearmament. Concerns about this threat were not restricted to the Americans. The British Chiefs of Staff who, in June 1950, had argued that the Soviets were essentially cautious and opportunistic, were more worried about their attitudes and plans a year later. West Germany was finally admitted to NATO in 1955, when the Allied High Commission came to an end, laying the basis for German rearmament within an alliance system. This rearmament was seen as necessary in order to provide the forces required to defend Western Europe, not least because of the heavy imperial commitments of British and French forces.[74] This rearmament was a key step in West Germany's integration into the Western alliance, although that integration did not extend to supporting the acquisition of nuclear arms.

The rival Warsaw Pact was formed on 14 May 1955, ten days after West Germany joined NATO, and the inclusion of the East German National People's Army in the Warsaw Pact forces (formally in 1958) sealed the international division of Germany. From the late 1940s, the Soviet Union had had bilateral defence treaties with all of its Eastern European puppet governments. However, West German rearmament helped drive the process further forward. It played a major role in Soviet propaganda, being treated as a threat to the Communist bloc and as a revival of German aggression. These themes were important within the Soviet Union where World War Two played a key role in the collective memory.[75] Anxiety about German rearmament was also used in Soviet propaganda for foreign audiences, notably in Eastern Europe.

# American Strategy

There had been major differences among American policymakers and politicians in the late 1940s over the strategy that should be followed, not least the degree to which there would be a policy of global containment of Communism and a reliance on nuclear weaponry. By the early 1950s, however, the requirement and strategy for atomic defence and war were in place: the American forces in Western Europe, a crucial expression of the new definition of the American national interest, had to be protected, and the same was true for South Korea and Japan. In April 1950, the National Security Council's NSC-68 document reflected the strong geopolitical sense of American strategy in the face of what was presented as a threat from the Soviet Union and China to American civilisation. The Soviet atomic test and Mao's conquest of China had transformed the parameters for American strategy. The document was a prime instance of fear driving policy or, at least, of fear as a selling point, within government and towards the population.

Whereas, initially, the American Joint Chiefs of Staff had assumed that the defence of Western Europe would be the responsibility of the Europeans, with the Americans providing help from the Strategic Air Command, and being most concerned about its air bases in Britain, membership in NATO

led to a full-scale American ground commitment to the defence of Western
Europe, and notably the inter-German border between West and East
Germany.[76] On 18 December 1950, the NATO Council agreed to a strategy
of forward defence which meant holding West Germany.[77] This strategy,
which was politically necessary rather than militarily realistic, affected
American, British and French planning and force requirements. Particularly
after the Communist takeover in Czechoslovakia in 1948, which considerably extended the frontier between Communism and West Germany, the
linear defence of the latter was a formidable and costly[78] task across a very
broad front. NATO, conversely, did not cover European colonies. Despite
French arguments, the exclusion extended to Algeria, which, legally, was
part of metropolitan France. However, the anti-colonial revolutionary
movement that was to develop in Algeria in the mid-1950s could not be
comfortably located in terms of Cold War tensions alone, although they
indeed played a role in the Algerian war.[79]

A clear front line was in place across Europe by 1953. The Communists
had been defeated in Greece, while, thanks to its anti-Communism, Franco's
Spain, a Fascist dictatorship, was eventually brought into the Western
alliance. Portugal, another authoritarian right-wing dictatorship, had been
a member of NATO from the outset, in large part because the American
air bases established in 1943 in the Azores, Portuguese possessions in the
Atlantic, were regarded as important to America's global strategy. Air
bases were also at issue with Spain. In 1953, the USA and Spain signed
an agreement giving the Americans rights to establish air bases, although
Spain did not join NATO until 1983, by which time it was a democracy. Air
bases were crucial both to the re-supply of American forces in NATO and
in providing strategic depth in the event of a Soviet advance overrunning
much territory.

Behind the front line of containment, the Americans encouraged political,
economic and cultural measures also focused on containment. Limiting
support for Communism was presented as a crucial aspect of defence. In
Western Europe, the period of the Korean War was a very important one
for the consolidation of NATO, one in which NATO policies to that end
combined with aggressive Soviet ones that helped ensure governmental and
political support for NATO. More generally, notions of development and
modernisation provided the US with a sense of superiority and necessary
leadership, and with an agenda of attitudes and policies that could be
applied to challenge Communism. There was an inherent preference for
democracy, but, across much of the world, American distrust of populism
and of left-wing politicians led to alliance with authoritarian élites.
Thus, containment in Iran, Portuguese Africa and South Vietnam meant
supporting these regimes' resistance to liberal tendencies, although the
opposition to these regimes in each case included markedly anti-liberal
movements. This was not so much a 'dark side' to the Cold War as its
integral character in many areas.[80] Increased support for European colonial

rule was also an aspect of American opposition to Communism. Resistance to Communism was a significant facet of this rule, one that bridged the world war. At the same time, policies designed to ensure economic development and a measure of self-government were also aspects of this rule.[81]

# Conclusion

The American emphasis was on a global struggle because, for those concerned with opposition to Communism, individual states took on meaning in these terms, rather than having important issues of their own, including specific geographical and political concerns and characters. This approach captured a key aspect of the international situation. At the same time, the emphasis on a global struggle underplayed the extent to which much could not be readily expressed in terms of the dichotomy of the Cold War. Moreover, the global approach minimised the autonomy of states and other agents within the respective blocs. Linked to this, the primacy of geostrategic concerns meant that the geopolitics of containment was more concerned with territory and strength than with values.[82] Values were understood by the USA and the Soviet Union in terms of their own concerns and with a tendency to neglect or underplay the priorities in other countries. Containment gave the Americans a new strategic vision and ramped up the Cold War. It did so not as a consequence of American aggression, but in response to a serious external development because the Korean War was the first time that the Soviet Union had, through proxies, launched a war against a country (South Korea) supported by a major adversary. This was quite different from the November 1939 Soviet invasion of Finland. Over Berlin, the Soviets had backed down without using force. The situation was very different in Korea, again indicating the volatility of East Asian power politics. This volatility contributed to a strong sense of unpredictability. The Korean War was also another instance of the willingness of Communist regimes to sacrifice large amounts of manpower to achieve their goals, and of the coerced supineness of the populations involved who went along with this. The Communist bloc had greatly expanded from 1939 to 1949, taking over much of Eurasia. This advance posed a serious challenge to Western interests and Western civilisation.

# CHAPTER FOUR

# 1953-68

NATO and the rival Soviet-led Warsaw Pact, established in 1949 and 1955 respectively, prepared and planned for conflict with each other. These preparations and plans were a key component of the Cold War, one that linked to other aspects of the confrontation, and that also encouraged an atmosphere of fear and anxiety. On the part of the Soviet Union, there was a strong, indeed paranoid, sense of vulnerability. This stemmed from Communist ideology and dated from the Russian Civil War, but also owed much to World War Two and the experience of being attacked then by an ally, Germany. Moreover, with his strong sense of ideological commitment and his emphasis on conflict, Stalin believed in the inevitability of war between what he saw as the capitalist and socialist countries. Nikita Khrushchev was to remark that foreign policy for Stalin meant keeping anti-aircraft batteries around Moscow on 24-hour alert. This sense of vulnerability encouraged a major emphasis on military expenditure in the Soviet Union, although the unreliable nature of Soviet statistics make precise figures difficult to establish. There was also a strong, indeed acute, sense of vulnerability in the West.

A feeling of uncertainty on both sides, and of the fragility of military strength, international links, political orders and ideological convictions, accentuated a sense of threat, a sense that was both general and related to particulars. This sense fuelled an arms race that was central to the Cold War, just as others had preceded the two world wars.[1] Both sides claimed to be strong, but declared they required an advantage in military capability to be secure. This approach represented the inherent instability of the arms race. Only the mutually assured destruction (MAD) threatened by massive nuclear stockpiles eventually brought a measure of stability. MAD gave substance to the use of the terms deterrent and deterrence, with the defensive mind-set they suggested. Aside from the competition between the USA and the Soviet Union to produce and deploy more and better weapons, there was also persistent rivalry between the various services of the American armed forces, and comparable arms races between the military services of other countries. These contributed to the general sense of threat. In the USA, the newly-formed United States Air Force (USAF) commanded much of the public relations publicity and money. In the Soviet Union, the army was stronger within the armed forces than in the USA.

The leading powers of the Cold War also tried to ensure that their allies were militarily effective, while the provision of arms helped to consolidate military co-operation, making command and control, training, and joint exercises easier. In Eastern Europe, the forces received Soviet equipment, uniforms and training, while assistance was also provided more broadly. Thus, in 1950, the Soviet Naval Advisory Mission to China was established: Soviet training, supplies and ship designs were important in the development of the Chinese navy.[2]

The outbreak of war in Korea in 1950 had helped increase tension elsewhere, not least because it was seen as a stage in Soviet expansion. In particular, it was assumed that this war, which did not involve the Soviet army, would be a prelude to an invasion of Western Europe by it. Such an invasion had not come, but the premises behind Western planning remained the need to repel Soviet attacks and to resist Soviet advances across the world. Nevertheless, there were variations in the intensity of confrontation. The Soviets did apparently consider attacks on Western Europe in the early 1950s, particularly in 1951. However, Stalin's death in 1953 led to a relaxation of tension and to advances toward the West for better relations. The relaxation of tension was notably apparent in the withdrawal of Soviet forces from their occupation zone in eastern Austria in 1955 as a consequence of the Austria State Treaty of 15 May 1955. Under this treaty signed by the four occupying powers – the Soviet Union, the USA, Britain and France, the Austrian Republic was formally recognised and it was agreed that occupation forces would withdraw within five months. The Soviet Union agreed to do so in return for reparation payments and strict neutrality on the part of Austria. Nikita Khrushchev, the Party First Secretary from 1953 to 1964, supported this measure as part of the demilitarisation of the Cold War he sought in order to cut expenditure on the armed forces. More specifically, Khrushchev hoped that the neutralisation of Austria could be followed by that of Germany. Already, a Soviet Note of 10 March 1952 had proposed free elections for Germany and reunification.[3] However, whereas Austria became a neutral buffer zone, outside NATO, the situation, despite discussion in the early 1950s about the possibility of German unification, was very different for Germany. There, based in the former occupation zones, the forces of NATO and the Warsaw Pact continued to be in close and hostile proximity.

The Austrian State Treaty was followed in July 1955 by the Geneva Summit, the first meeting of the leaders of the USA, the Soviet Union and Britain since 1945, and one that saw an attempt to take disarmament, or at least confidence-building, forward. Similarly, there were variations in the intensity of confrontation with China, with aggressive Chinese moves in the

Taiwan Strait area in 1954 and 1958 leading to serious crises. In contrast, neither the Soviet Union nor China protested in 1956 when the all-Vietnam elections agreed under the 1954 Geneva Agreement were not held.

## Nuclear Confrontation

Overhanging all else was the threat posed by nuclear weapons. In January 1946, Major-General Leslie Groves, the head of the American atomic bomb project, had warned: 'Either we must have a hard-boiled, realistic, enforceable, world-agreement ensuring the outlawing of atomic weapons or we and our dependable allies must have an exclusive supremacy in the field, which means that no other nation can be permitted to have atomic weapons'.[4] However, America's nuclear monopoly, which appeared to offer a means to coerce the Soviet Union, had lasted only until 1949. Then, thanks to successful spying on Western nuclear technology, the Soviet Union, at least two years before the CIA predicted,[5] completed its development of an effective bomb that was very similar to the American one. This development had required a formidable effort, as the Soviet Union was devastated by the impact of World War Two, and it was pursued because Stalin believed that only a position of nuclear equivalence would permit the Soviet Union to protect and advance its interests. However, such a policy was ruinous financially, seriously harmful to the economy, as it led to the distortion of research and investment choices, and militarily questionable, as resources were used that might otherwise have developed conventional military capability. Great cruelty was involved in the Soviet programme, part of which was located in the labour camps (gulags), and drew on their coerced slave labour. Although the Communist governments that followed Stalin, after he died in 1953, introduced changes in some aspects of policy, they did not break free from his legacy of nuclear competition.[6]

Even when America alone had had the atomic bomb, the value of the weapon was limited. Its potential use was restricted because the delivery systems were not as well developed as they were later. Moreover, the atom bomb was insufficiently flexible (in terms of military and political application or acceptance of its use) to meet challenges other than that of full-scale war. Thus, the Americans did not use the atom bomb (of which they then indeed had very few) to help their Nationalist Chinese allies in the Chinese Civil War. Similarly, American possession of the bomb did not deter the Soviets from trying to intimidate the West during the Berlin Crisis of 1948–9. Nevertheless, the availability of the bomb encouraged American reliance on a nuclear deterrent, which made it possible to hasten the demobilisation that accorded with the public mood after World War Two. This policy left the USA more vulnerable when the Korean War broke out in 1950.[7] In turn, the Soviet atomic bomb test in August 1949 encouraged Stalin to egg on the North Korean attack on South Korea.

The nuclear duopoly did not last long. Britain, France, China, India and Pakistan followed with their own atomic weapons in 1952, 1960, 1964, 1974 and 1988 respectively. Israel, South Africa and North Korea also developed a nuclear capability, although South Africa gave its up. Conversely, neither West Germany nor Japan developed such technology. In part, this reflected the absence of any policy of *revanche* on the part of the post-war leaderships that gained control after Western occupation ceased, which spoke well of the post-war Allied rebuilding effort. Nevertheless, West Germany wished to develop its own nuclear weapons as they were seen as a marker of state sovereignty. Although they did not admit this in public, Konrad Adenauer, the Chancellor from 1949 to 1963, and, especially Franz Josef Strauss, the Minister of Defence from 1956 to 1962, were keen on the idea. However, the lack of West German and Japanese atomic forces accorded with American-directed Western security policies.[8] It proved an important as well as lasting aspect of the strategic and geopolitical landscapes. Had either West Germany or Japan sought to develop atomic forces, as opposed to the peaceful generation of atomic energy, then this would have contributed greatly to tension with the Soviet Union and China.

The destructive power of nuclear weapons vastly increased when the atomic bomb was followed by the hydrogen bomb. The latter employed a nuclear explosion to heat hydrogen isotopes sufficiently to fuse them into helium atoms, a transformation that released an enormous amount of destructive energy. Work on this bomb had been carried out unsuccessfully during World War Two, but was stepped up after the Soviet atomic test of August 1949 as the Americans sought to reconfirm their nuclear superiority. Moreover, the Korean War spurred American activity. Termed the superbomb, the American hydrogen bomb (at that stage a device that had not yet been weaponised) was first tested on 1 November 1952, producing an explosive yield of ten megatons. In less than a decade, the destructive force released in 1945 had been made to seem limited. Whereas the bomb dropped on Hiroshima had 13.5 kilotons of TNT equivalent, the USA in 1954 tested one with 15 megatons of TNT equivalent, over 1,000 times more powerful. This was a level of lethality that proved difficult to comprehend and that certainly shocked contemporaries, both politicians and the public, giving rise to a range of ethical concerns and practical issues. Thus, the early Eisenhower years saw both heightened tensions and initiatives to lessen these tensions, notably the 1955 Geneva Summit. Alongside the lethality of the hydrogen bomb, came a rapid closure of the capability gap. Indeed, in what appeared a salutary warning to the Americans, the gap in the case of the hydrogen bomb proved far less than that with the atomic bomb. The Soviet Union tested an intermediate type of hydrogen bomb in August 1953, and, in November 1955, conducted a test showing it possessed the knowledge to build a hydrogen bomb. Britain followed in 1957, China in 1967, and France in 1969.[9]

The consequences of the new destructiveness was rapidly understood by American and Soviet leaders; and their shared assessment of the situation was important in the development of deterrence. In his inaugural address in 1953, Eisenhower referred to the risk of ending human life as a whole while, the following year, Georgy Malenkov, Chairman of the Council of Ministers from Stalin's death in 1953 to 1955, warned about the possible end of world civilisation. British Prime Minister again from 1951 to 1955, Churchill wanted to negotiate a reduction in Cold War tensions and, after Stalin's death, had proposed a summit of Soviet, American and British leaders, only to be rejected by Eisenhower. This division helped ensure that Soviet advances after Stalin's death were not reciprocated. The Soviet leadership, moreover, did not believe that Britain could do much to restrain the USA.[10] American policy changed after Churchill retired in April 1955, and that July, at Geneva, Soviet, American and British leaders met for the first time since Potsdam in 1945. Eisenhower emphasised that any nuclear war would, due to the windborne spread of radioactivity, end life in the northern hemisphere, and thus ensure that, whichever power launched a nuclear attack, would be destroyed by this very attack. This was a globalisation and globalism that was unprecedented, one that required an international effort towards disarmament and looked toward later international interest in environmental issues. No significant agreement stemmed from the Geneva summit, but the leaders became aware that their fellow nuclear-controllers were well-informed of the destructiveness, indeed unacceptability, of nuclear war. This confidence-building knowledge served as the basis of deterrence and also helped ensure that nuclear weaponry was seen as different to other weaponry. Preventive war, an idea expressed by some senior American officers earlier in the decade when considering destroying Soviet offensive capability, now seemed completely implausible, as did any 'roll-back' of the Soviets in Eastern Europe. During the 1952 elections, the Republicans had rejected 'containment' as too passive, called for 'rolling back Communism', and spoke of 'captive nations' in Eastern Europe. Radio Liberty and Radio Free Europe were used to beam supposedly honest news to Eastern Europe and to encourage opposition there. However, the reality, in American policy, was of enforced caution. The path from Geneva in 1955 to the very muted Western response towards the brutal Soviet suppression of Hungarian liberalism the following year was apparent. However, that path was not clearly understood by contemporaries. They preferred to put an emphasis on the consequences of the Suez Crisis of 1956 in explaining why NATO and the USA did not act over Hungary, and to argue that the West had betrayed the Hungarians.

Delivery systems for nuclear weapons had, in the meantime, changed radically. In the late 1940s and early 1950s, the Soviet Union had been within range of American bombers based in Britain, but the USA had been out of range of Soviet nuclear attack. American strategy and doctrine focused on massive nuclear retaliation in response to any Soviet use of their larger non-nuclear forces in Europe or elsewhere, and the dropping of the atom bombs in 1945 ensured that there was a new thrust to air power, one provided by the apparent ability of a small number of bombs to make a decisive difference. In the early 1930s, the most powerful American weapon was the battleship with 14-inch guns. The situation was now radically different. The major role of atomic attack in American strategy[11] was linked to the creation, in 1947, of an independent air service in the USA, with the United States Air Force (USAF). In order to justify and fulfil its independent role, and to take the leading part in the Cold War, American air force thinking was dominated by strategic nuclear bombing. The ability to strike at Soviet centres was seen as an effective deterrent, indeed as the sole counter to Soviet conventional strength, the Sino-Soviet alliance, and the vulnerability of America's allies and interests; as a war-winning capability; and as the essential purpose of American air power. This emphasis was given added force by the role of officers from Strategic Air Command in the senior ranks of the Air Staff; by a fascination with aerial self-sufficiency and big bombers; and by the absence of a powerful drive for integrated warfare, which would have encouraged the development, instead, of doctrines for co-operation with the army and navy, and for planes designed accordingly.[12]

The expansion of its nuclear arsenal was America's first major experience of leading in a peacetime arms race. This expansion was a response to the major change in military capability and to the American sense of the tenuousness of victory in World War Two. In the aftermath of the disaster year of 1942, which was still felt strongly, few in the USA in the early and mid-1950s believed in the inevitability of Axis defeat during the war. If the development of America's nuclear weapons spoke to its strategic weaknesses as much as its economic strengths, there was also a more specific problem with American military technology that encouraged an emphasis on nuclear weaponry. In particular, American bombers were obsolete. The propeller-driven B-29 was shot down with ease during the Korean War, and the B-50, which appeared in 1947, was only a modification, albeit with some significant changes, notably a greater bomb load capacity and larger engines. The B-50 had one large bomb bay, for carrying atomic bombs, instead of the two on the B-29. The B-50 was also designed to be refuelled in the air, which the B-29 could not be. In the late 1940s, B-50s flew reconnaissance missions above the Soviet Polar North, sometimes dipping into Soviet air space. However, the introduction of the M-15 jet interceptor provided the Soviets with the ceiling that the B-50 had. The Convair B-36 had near-intercontinental range, had a payload of 43 tons, was designed specifically to carry the A-bomb from the start, and was somewhat faster and capable of higher altitudes than the B-29. However, the B-36 was still basically a propeller plane and almost as vulnerable on that account. The six-jet B-47 'Stratojet' was intermediate, not long-range. The situation did not change until the B-52 'Stratofortress' entered service in 1955. It had a true intercontinental capacity.

Strategic nuclear bombing also played a major role in British air planning. The relevant air bases were in eastern England for bombing Leningrad (St Petersburg) and Moscow, and in northern Iraq, for bombing industrial sites in Ukraine and southern Russia.[13] In both the USA and Britain, the legacy of inter-war air doctrine and of the 'strategic' (i.e. war winning) bombing campaigns of World War Two, played a major role. In contrast, the value of close air support shown by Allied air operations in 1944–5, for example in Normandy and at Okinawa, was neglected. In the USA, the Tactical Air Command that was founded in 1948 as an equal to Strategic Air Command was rapidly downgraded and swiftly lost most of its aircraft.[14] This situation helped weaken the American military in the Vietnam War, and also looked toward the emphasis on air power as a stand-alone tool in the two Gulf Wars and the Kosovo War; an emphasis that was to be proved of limited value when dealing with insurrection in Iraq from 2003. In assessing the role of military considerations in the Cold War, it is necessary to give due weight not only to the impact of political considerations on military tasking, but also to the autonomous dynamics of military institutions and doctrine, and the consequences these had for influencing tasking. Furthermore, air power, and, even more, rocketry gave America a degree of independence from its allies. Inter-continental rockets could be based in the USA.

During the Cold War, the crucial strategic zone was defined as the North European Plain, and the Soviet Union had a great superiority in conventional forces there, notably in tanks and artillery. This superiority was enhanced as Soviet forces were modernised and as the military effectiveness of their Eastern European allies was enhanced. Soviet strength led to a series of responses in NATO planning (which was very much dominated by the USA), each of which focused on the degree to which nuclear weaponry would be involved, and when. The Korean War demonstrated the problems that conventional forces would face in stemming the tide. Moreover, it would take a long time to move significant reinforcements to Western Europe. The essential stages in this series were: first, an immediate nuclear response to a conventional Soviet assault; secondly, the massive nuclear retaliation outlined in 1954 by John Foster Dulles, the American Secretary of State; thirdly, the Flexible Response theory, outlined in 1962 under the Kennedy administration, which was capable of many interpretations; and, eventually, American stress on an enhanced conventional response, albeit with the potential backing of strategic and tactical nuclear weaponry.

In the early 1950s, it was feared that the Korean War might be the first stage of World War Three, and/or that Western Europe might receive similar treatment to South Korea. This prospect had seemed distant when, in the aftermath of the 'loss' of China, American strategy was outlined in April 1950 in 'United States Objectives and Programs for National Security' (NSC 68), but appeared much more imminent once the outbreak of the Korean War that June breached the threshold of a resort to full-scale conventional hostilities. Such hostilities had been seen in China with the civil war, but not in international conflict (although that was not how the North Koreans viewed an advance into South Korea), and not involving Western forces. In response to the threat of attack, NATO developed as a defensive system, supporting its plans with the creation of airfields, radar stations, telecommunications, and an oil pipeline system, as well as with the preparation of resistance networks able to operate if the Soviets occupied territory. The establishment of these networks provided a new role for the CIA and also led, notably in Italy, to a close relationship with right-wing political groups similar to that in Latin America.

There was also a major effort to develop opposition in the Soviet bloc in order to lessen the military value of Eastern Europe in the event of war. Aside from support for resistance groups, the development of émigré forces, and a major propaganda offensive, notably by radio, there was a growing interest in trying to exploit divisions between the Soviet Union and its satellite regimes. This interest led to attempts to woo Tito's Yugoslavia, from 1948, and to support for Romania when, from the 1960s, it took an independent stance in the Communist bloc. In practice, this policy resulted in Western backing for Nicolae Ceauşescu, a brutally authoritarian dictator.

Meanwhile, in military terms, as NATO countries were unable to match the build-up their military planners called for, there was a growing stress, especially from 1952, on the possibilities of nuclear weaponry both as a deterrent and, in the event of war, as a counterweight to Soviet conventional superiority.[15] The nuclearisation of NATO strategy was a response. The stationing of nuclear weapons in West Germany was an aspect of this nuclearisation, as well as a reaction to the slow build-up of the conventional German army. Nuclear strength was regarded as a condition of conventional warfare in defence of West Germany. Indeed, deterrence was a strategic shift to the defensive. The rapidly rising cost of the defence budget also encouraged an emphasis on nuclear preparedness in both the USA and Britain. Eisenhower advanced a 'New Look' national security policy in the 'Basic National Security Policy' (NSC 162/2), adopted on 30 October 1953. Arguing that a Soviet attack was unlikely soon, which was a reasonable response to the state of Soviet politics and to Eastern bloc uncertainty after the death of Stalin earlier in the year, the policy document suggested that the build-up in nuclear weaponry would lead to a stalemate of deterrence in which long-term economic strength was crucial to national success. As a result, there should be only limited investment in conventional forces, which were expensive, and, instead, a stress on nuclear strength and 'massive retaliation' which would deter Soviet bloc attacks.

The emphasis on deterrence reflected need, practicality, and also the stress, in the culture of planning, on restraint, caution and sobriety in judgment. The very idea of a Cold War presupposed restraint, with both sides avoiding direct and large-scale conflict that might have apocalyptic consequences. Such restraint characterised American policy. Preventive air-strikes against Soviet nuclear capabilities were seriously considered, only to be discarded.[16] The strategic vocabulary of the Cold War had become that of mutual vulnerability, bipolar balance and stability,[17] one that led both to the quest for individual advantage and to mutual arms control.

The stress on nuclear deterrence was seen with the deployment of tactical nuclear weapons to Europe and elsewhere, with the development of a cutting-edge strategic capability, with intercontinental ballistic missiles, submarine-launched ballistic missiles, and reconnaissance satellites, and with the massive expansion of the American nuclear stockpile, from 369 weapons in 1950 to over 27,000 in 1962. Prior to the development of intercontinental missiles, the Soviet Union was more vulnerable to attack than the USA, as the USA had a far larger strategic bomber force, as well as nearby bases, for example in East Anglia, and aircraft carriers. The Soviets had no such bases, nor carriers, which helped underline the shock caused for the Americans when Soviet missiles were deployed to Cuba in 1962.

Atomic weaponry was not employed during the Korean War, despite plans to do so and pressure from General MacArthur for its use to counteract Chinese numerical superiority. Instead, the war was fought with a strengthened conventional military; although, in 1953, the use of the atom bomb was threatened by the Americans in order to secure an end to the conflict. This threat encouraged the view that nuclear strategy had a major role to play in future confrontations, as indeed did the heavy cost of fighting the Korean War, and the extent to which it had revealed deficiencies and limitations in the American military.[18] However, the war also caused a revival in the American army and led to its growing concern with 'readiness', while in 1951 Congress's concern that the navy should maintain a cutting-edge warfare capability led it to authorise the building of the USS Forrestal, a 'supercarrier' able to handle heavy, fast jets. Launched in 1954 and put into service in 1955, this was the first American carrier to have an angled deck, which permitted two jets on two catapults to take off simultaneously. The Forrestal was the largest carrier yet built by the Americans, and their first to have steam catapults. The Forrestal could carry and launch jet aircraft armed with atomic bombs, even large ones. The Douglas A-3 Skywarrior introduced on 1956 was a two-seater, two-jet engined bomber carrying atomic bombs.[19] Similarly, the Korean War led the United States Air Force to develop a new generation of fighters and fighter-bombers.

The need to respond to Soviet conventional superiority on land and in the air, at least in terms of numbers, encouraged an interest both in tactical nuclear weaponry and in the atom bomb as a weapon of first resort. The tactical nuclear weapons that were developed by the Americans and British, such as bazookas firing atomic warheads with a range of one mile, were treated as a form of field artillery. The use of the atom bomb as a weapon of first resort was pushed by Eisenhower, who was SACEUR, NATO's first Supreme Allied Commander, from December 1950 until 1952, and US President from 1953 until 1961. Aware of NATO's vulnerability, he felt that strength must underpin diplomacy for it to be credible. In December 1955, the NATO Council authorised the employment of atomic weaponry in the event of war with the Warsaw Pact, even if the latter did not use such weaponry.

The heavy cost of raising conventional military capability was a factor in encouraging a reliance on atomic weaponry, as were the manpower implications in a period of very low unemployment, and, more specifically, the particular vulnerability of Western forces to Soviet attack in Western Europe. Thus, nuclear weaponry appeared less expensive and therefore politically more acceptable, as it would leave more money available for personal consumption or, in Britain, social welfare. Nuclear weaponry also appeared militarily more effective, either as a deterrent or, in the event of deterrence failing, as a decisive combat weapon. Building up nuclear strength seemed the best way to increase the capability in both respects. Charles Bohlen, who had been ambassador to the Soviet Union, told the Senate Foreign Relations Committee in May 1957 that: 'the Soviet rulers have become very acutely aware of what is involved in nuclear warfare, and I think they would have to have a very high margin of certain victory before they would be disposed consciously and as a matter of cold policy to unleash a nuclear war'.[20]

Building up American nuclear strength led both to the 'New Look' strategy[21] and to the enhancement of the American Strategic Air Command, which resulted in the USAF receiving much more money in defence allocations than either the army or the navy. About 45 per cent of annual military spending from 1952 to 1960 went on the Air Force. Already, in 1949, the American navy had found its programme rejected, and its major construction projects cancelled, in favour of the USAF's plans for strategic bombing. With the emphasis on asymmetric containment in the 'New Look', the number of divisions in the army fell from 18 in June 1956 to 14 by that December, and the number of naval vessels from 973 to 812.[22] Eisenhower described the reliance on the nuclear arsenal as 'more bang for the buck'. The Department of Defense expenditure fell from $43.4 billion in 1953 to $30.4 billion in 1954. The decline in conventional capability, which was resisted within the military,[23] affected the USA at the time of the Vietnam War, and further ensured a reliance in planning on nuclear weaponry. There was a comparable decline and reliance in Britain.[24] The USA committed the equivalent of seven army divisions, one marine division, several air groups, and several carrier attack groups to Vietnam. However, this commitment posed a challenge to America's ability to respond to attacks in Europe, the Mediterranean and South Korea. As a result, there was to be a reliance on draftees that caused public disquiet to grow.

America's allies were faced with difficult policy choices. Both in Western Europe and in the Far East, they relied on the American nuclear umbrella, but this reliance made them heavily dependent on American policy choices. Indeed, part of the rationale behind the development of independent nuclear deterrents by Britain and France was the doubt that the USA would use its atomic weaponry if Europe alone was attacked. Such anxieties about the strongest partner were, and are, normal in alliances. There was also concern that the 'New Look' strategy might lead to a diminished commitment to Europe. Only an air force capable of dropping nuclear bombs seemed to offer a deterrent, but, as with the USA, the emphasis on this development affected conventional capability. In 1958, Earl Mountbatten, the British First Lord of the Admiralty, observed, 'there certainly isn't going to be enough money for a very large independent deterrent which can inflict unacceptable damage on Russia as well as having the 88 [ship] Navy and the all-Regular Army with adequate equipment',[25] the last a reference to the cost involved in dispensing with conscription. There was also a debate about whether conscription could be maintained in a peacetime society. In Britain, the answer was no, and this helped provide the rationale for nuclear deterrence in the 1957 Defence White Paper.

British Cold War strategy was not only focused on Europe, nor only reliant on the independent nuclear deterrent. Instead, the defence of empire and of related interests was seen as an aspect of the containment of Communism. Thus, in 1955, Britain supported the creation of the Baghdad Pact, an attempt to create a northern layer of states in the Middle East opposed to southward expansion by the Soviet Union. Turkey, Iraq, Pakistan and Iran were the other members. The pact exaggerated British power, but was part of an assertive British policy in the Middle East, directed against the Soviets and against Arab nationalism, which culminated with the unsuccessful Suez invasion of Egypt in November 1956. Further east, the Baghdad Pact was matched by the South-East Asia Treaty Organisation (SEATO), a defensive alliance established in 1955 by Australia, Britain, New Zealand, Thailand, the Philippines, Pakistan, France and the USA to resist Soviet expansion in Asia. The Korean War was an important encouragement to these structures designed for containment.

As a reminder that Cold War weaponry fitted into a number of distinctive national political, strategic and military narratives, France's determination to develop an independent nuclear capability represented a significant shift from the emphasis on colonial defence. From the NATO perspective, the most worrying feature of French policy in the late 1950s was that, after the Indochina conflict, much of the army was concentrated in Algeria where it was resisting a left-wing, Arabist, nationalist movement. Under Charles de Gaulle, who became President in 1958, the emphasis on the nuclear *Force de Frappe* helped distract French military leaders from any challenge to civilian authority in the *metropole* and lured them away from their psychologically debilitating experiences of colonial defeats, with promises, instead, of a more prestigious and independent role in European and world affairs for France's armed forces. De Gaulle portrayed nuclear energy more generally as a symbol for the modernity of post-war France.

American focus on strategic air power encouraged concern about the Soviet counterpart, and, in 1954–5, there was fear in the USA of a 'bomber gap', with Soviet intercontinental bombers able to drop atomic weapons on North America. Driving into New York in *Live and Let Die* (1954), James Bond notes: 'the Civil Defence warnings: IN CASE OF ENEMY ATTACK – KEEP MOVING – GET OFF BRIDGE' and he tells his American escort 'this must be the fattest atomic-bomb target on the whole face of the globe'. Later in the novel, a Soviet threat to Caribbean bauxite supplies was discussed. Bauxite was necessary for the manufacture of aluminium, a strategic metal, not least for the aircraft industry.

Contingency planning played a major role for the military on both sides. The Soviet introduction of planes designed to attack American carriers was stepped up from 1954 when intelligence confirmed the presence on these carriers of nuclear weapons (bombs and Regulus missiles), as well as of planes able to deliver them.[26] The American fear of Soviet bombers led to a stepping up of the American bomber programme, to secret aerial reconnaissance of the Soviet Union, and, in a new strategic geography, to construction of early-warning radar systems in Canada designed to warn of Soviet attacks over the North Pole: the Pinetree Network in 1954, and the Distant Early Warning (DEW) and Mid-Canada Lines, both in 1957. The North American Air Defense Command, established in 1958, was important to the development of joint air-defence systems involving the USA and Canada. In order to attack over the North Pole, the USA had constructed a base at Thule in northwest Greenland in 1951–2, able to stage and refuel American bombers. The SAGE (Semi-Automatic-Ground Environment) Air Defense system, launched in 1958 was a part of the investment in air defence. It involved the largest computers ever built and enabled the predicting of the trajectory of aircraft and missiles. SAGE was an aspect of the key part of the Cold War in the development of American computer systems, with IBM and the Department of Defense playing central roles. The Internet was to be developed and funded by the Defense Department's Defense Advanced Research Projects Agency (DARPA) in order to help scientists using large computers to communicate with each other.[27] DARPA also developed a Strategic Computing Initiative that was responsible for advances in technologies such as computing vision and recognition, and the parallel processing useful for code-breaking.

The deployment of B-52 'Stratofortress' heavy bombers in 1955 upgraded American delivery capability, and a small number of aircraft appeared able, and rapidly, to achieve more than the far larger Allied bomber force had done against Germany in 1942–5. Equipped with eight Pratt and Whitney J57-P-1W turbojets, the B-52 could cruise at 525 miles per hour, had a combat range of 3,600 miles, a payload of 30 tons of bombs, and a service ceiling of 47,000 feet. These capabilities, which were to be enhanced by aerial refuelling, transformed the bombing threat. Begun in 1958, constant airborne alert flights continued until 1968, when a B-52 carrying four thermonuclear bombs crashed in Greenland, although without any nuclear detonation. Thus, deterrence seemed both realistic and affordable. It was hoped that these bombers would serve to deter both Soviet conventional and atomic attack, although doubts were expressed about the former. The B-52s were complemented by the four super-carriers built in 1954–8, as some of their planes could carry nuclear bombs.

# After Stalin

While the major powers developed thermo-nuclear forces, there were attempts after Stalin's death in 1953 to ease Cold War tensions, notably by ending the Korean War and by negotiating over Austria. These attempts at the international level also reflected changes within the Soviet bloc, as a form of unspoken social contract led to a relaxation in efforts to control society. These efforts took their lead from developments in the Soviet Union, but were not only seen there.[28] Although shot through with the rivalries, contradictions, ambiguities and secrecies of Kremlin politics, there was a significant reaction against Stalinism. Aside from with changes in personnel and the struggle between factions, this reaction focused on a wish, alongside maintaining military effectiveness, to shift some expenditure from military to domestic purposes including the consumer goods that would secure domestic support. The Soviet Union and Eastern Europe enjoyed appreciable growth during the global 'Long Boom' from World War Two, although there is room for considerable scepticism about the growth figures. In part, growth was a consequence of recovery from the war, but agricultural mechanisation, industrial modernisation, and the large-scale transfer of labour from agriculture to industry were all significant. However, the emphasis was on heavy industry which diverted resources and goods from consumers. In Hungary, for example, there was an attempt to create 'a country of iron and steel'.

Communist state control and planning was an attempt at modernisation, in a period of competing modernisations.[29] Nevertheless, despite considerable propaganda to the contrary, this state control and planning, and the wiping out of the pre-existing economic systems that went with it, were to prove unsuccessful and widely unpopular. Moreover, the ruthless exploitation of Eastern Europe for Soviet economic goals under Stalin further greatly compromised the popularity of Eastern European Communist governments. The inappropriate superimposition of control systems, structured round an ideology of Communism, state control and planning, on already existing social and economic systems that did not lend themselves to these means of direction, created serious problems and made it difficult to respond adequately to new possibilities. A key instance was provided by cybernetics, a term coined in the USA in 1947 to mean the study of control and communications. Military needs in the Cold War spread the new practice of systems thinking.[30] Cybernetics was deployed in the Soviet Union in the 1950s as an aspect, during the period of de-Stalinisation from 1953, of the attempt to lessen Marxist-Leninist ideas. In the 1960s, the Scientific-Technological Revolution (NTR) was meant to cure all the ills of the Soviet Union. It was hoped that computers might help with central planning and thus realise the great promise of Communist progress. However, the possibility of new analogies and unauthorised answers offered by cybernetics led to its bureaucratic stifling in the Soviet Union, not least because of a determination to restrict the unpredictable element of computers. This apparent triumph of dialectical materialism therefore was to be short-lived,[31] and the resulting lack of engagement with the possibilities offered by computers was to be regarded as a major weakness of the Soviet economy, notably so by the mid-1980s.

A sense of instability and flux after Stalin's death arose from uneasiness among the Communist élite as political links were tested and new policies suggested. Lavrentii Beria, the head of the Soviet security systems, failed in an attempt to take over the leadership, in part due to the opposition of Marshal Zhukov, the Deputy Minister of Defence. Beria was imprisoned and shot. There were survivals from the old Stalinist system, not least Lazar Kaganovich, and the continuation, as Foreign Minister, of Vyacheslav Molotov, and his effort to create a unified, neutral Germany. This was an attempt that ignored both West Germany's commitment to the Western bloc and the commitment of this bloc to West Germany. Georgy Malenkov, the Chairman of the Soviet Council of Ministers, in contrast, was more conciliatory to the West and, indeed, partly as a result, fell in 1955. He lost a power struggle with Nikita Khrushchev, the Party First Secretary from 1953 to 1964. Khrushchev's headship of the Party apparatus gave him a key advantage. A committed Communist who advanced Soviet interests in the Third World, notably through arms sales to Egypt, Khrushchev sought to achieve Soviet goals in Europe by demilitarising the Cold War and making Communist rule more attractive. Under Khrushchev, the military enjoyed less favour than had been the case under Stalin.

The 1955 creation of the Warsaw Pact gave Khrushchev leeway for the withdrawal from Austria. In 1955, he began articulating the doctrine of 'peaceful existence', an expression drawn from Lenin's canonical writings. This was a major change from the Stalinist doctrine of the inevitability of war between socialism and capitalism, a doctrine that had helped lead to the Korean War. What Lenin and Khrushchev both meant was that, while the ultimate outcome of the fourth stage of history in terms of the success of Communism was never in doubt, that did not preclude peaceful relations between the two blocs. In the West, this approach was seen as duplicitous.

Once Malenkov had fallen, Khrushchev tried to strengthen the Communist bloc itself through de-Stalinisation. Economic growth was to safeguard living conditions, and thus enhance popular support for Communism. Labour heroism was important to Khrushchev's vision, and labour was to be encouraged and rewarded. Far more than admonitions were to be on offer. There was to be a 'guaranteed tomorrow', as well as an equality of living space and income, and a modest standard of living. Khrushchev's 'Thaw' influenced a generation of people in their late teens, twenties and thirties, who, in the mid and late 1980s were to press change much further. However, Khrushchev was a devoted Communist. The central-planning system and the collective farms were Stalinist and remained unchanged until well into the Gorbachev period in the late 1980s when they both began to fall apart.

The Twentieth Congress of the CPSU (Communist Party of the Soviet Union) in February 1956 saw a denunciation by Khrushchev of the crimes committed by Stalin, and of the personality cult around him, but not of the basis of the Soviet system. Khrushchev argued that the party had deviated from its 'historic course' due to Stalin. The secret speech was selectively leaked.[32] This denunciation weakened his rivals, notably Kaganovich and Molotov, who were far more compromised by their role in Stalin's purges, although Khrushchev himself had actively supported them. Thousands of political prisoners were released in the 'Thaw'. As a major aspect of the break from Stalin, there had already been an attempt at reconciliation with Yugoslavia, leading, on 2 June 1955, to the Belgrade Declaration in which the Soviet Union accepted that relations with other Communist states should be guided by the principle of equality. In June 1956, Tito visited Moscow, and Party relations were officially normalised, although Tito refused to return to the fold of following Moscow's lead.

Meanwhile, de-Stalinisation in the Communist bloc was essentially left to the leadership of the individual states. In East Germany, Czechoslovakia and Romania, the authoritarian governments self-servedly argued that they had already introduced changes since 1953 and needed to do little more. In Bulgaria, Vulko Chervenkov, First Secretary from 1946 to 1953 and Premier from 1950, was displaced in 1956, although the country remained quite repressive well into the 1980s.

In Poland and Hungary, Khrushchev's speech triggered discontent within both the ruling Polish and Hungarian Party apparatuses. This discontent spread to the respective publics unhappy over miserable living standards and repression. There was greater pressure for change, because civil society displayed both considerable independence and also the unpopularity of Communist rule. Radio Free Europe and, to a lesser extent, Radio Free Liberty, encouraged this unpopularity. It was clear that there was demand for more than the limited de-Stalinisation that was on offer in the Khrushchev model. This process was to be repeated in the Gorbachev years in the late 1980s. Both the 1950s and the 1980s indicated the fragility of the Communist system and its vulnerability to reform attempts, indeed change. China after Mao died in 1976 offered a significant contrast.

Increasingly, volatility in Eastern Europe in 1953–6 led to criticism and a sense of instability. In Poland, the crisis arose with an armed workers' rising in the major industrial city of Poznán on 28 June 1956: a large-scale demonstration for better living conditions became a rebellion against the state, with arms seized from the police headquarters, prisons stormed, and the state security headquarters attacked, before troops and state security forces suppressed the rising. Seventy-three civilians and eight members of the armed forces were killed. This rising resulted in widespread pressure for change, and the Polish Party responded by replacing some Stalinist officials and by appointing Wladyslaw Gomulka as First Secretary. The one-time First Secretary of the Party (1945–8), Gomulka, a nationalist Communist, had been accused of nationalism and hostility to the Soviet Union. He was arrested and imprisoned in 1951. Gomulka's return to office as First Secretary in 1956 was enthusiastically received in Poland.

The Soviet Union had not been consulted, an unprecedented act that threatened the coherence of the Communist system. Visiting Warsaw on 19 October 1956, Khrushchev prepared to use the Soviet army to reassert Soviet dominance. It was well capable of doing so, not least because there were plentiful units in East Germany, as well as in nearby areas of the Soviet Union. Soviet action against Poland in 1956 is one of the might-have-beens of the Cold War. These counterfactuals repay consideration as they serve to underline the extent to which developments were far from inevitable, an approach that contrasts with the historical materialism of Communist thought. In the event, Gomulka persuaded Khrushchev that the changes in Poland could be acceptable to the Soviet Union, by promising that he would respect the unity of the Communist bloc and maintain Communist control in Poland. The avoidance of a deeper crisis was warmly applauded in Poland, where Gomulka was seen as defining a national Communism separate from, and thus opposed to, the Soviet path. This, indeed, was precisely what the Soviet leadership feared: Poland as another Yugoslavia. At the same time, prefiguring General Jaruzelski's suppression of the Solidarity movement in 1981, Gomulka had kept Poland within the Communist bloc without any use of Soviet force and this served Soviet interests. Moreover, Poland was not to become another Yugoslavia, in large part because of greater caution among both Polish and Soviet policymakers.

## Hungary, 1956

Had the Red Army been required for action in Poland, then it would have been much harder for it to have intervened in Hungary. There, a conflation of nationalism, popular pressure for change, and élite liberalisation led to a forceful response to the nature, and, increasingly, fact of Communist control. In a fashion typical of its inaccurate paranoia, the KGB presented nationalist activism as ideological sabotage actively sponsored by Western intelligence agencies; and this sabotage was seen as a threat to the continuation of Communism. Without being accused of deviationist sympathies, it was difficult to challenge such assessments. This situation provided a key instance of the weakness of this authoritarian system. Pressures for reform and freedom in Hungary became an armed rising in Budapest on 23 October 1956. The Hungarian leadership called for support from the Soviet forces in Hungary, and the Soviet government agreed, only to find that providing support greatly increased the scale and ambition of popular action, with the revolution becoming nationwide and the Party completely losing control.

Imre Nagy, the reforming Prime Minister from 1953, who had been dismissed in April 1955, was reappointed Prime Minister on 24 October 1956 in order to try to control the situation. Nagy pressed the Soviets to allow the Hungarian Communist Party to lead the nationwide demand for change, so as to achieve stability. The Soviet government initially agreed and, on 29 October, began to withdraw troops from Budapest. This step was presented by the Soviet government as the basis for a new international order within the Communist bloc, one based on equality and non-interference in domestic matters. The Soviet leadership saw this solution as an equivalent to the situation in Poland, and their requirements were similar: reformed Communism meant staying in the Communist bloc. However, on 31 October 1956, the Soviet leadership changed policy, deciding to resort to force in response to reports of the collapse of Communist control in Hungary that suggested that Soviet requirements would not be met. It was feared that Hungarian developments would be seen as an American triumph. In response to reports of Soviet military moves, the Hungarian government, on 1 November, withdrew from the Warsaw Pact and proclaimed neutrality. Nagy also appealed to the United Nations for help with the defence of Hungarian neutrality.

These steps did not deter Soviet action. Russian troops had crushed Hungarian nationalism in 1849 and had conquered Hungary in 1944–5. Now, on 4 November 1956, a full-scale invasion was launched. In Operation Whirlwind, the determined Soviet use of armour, notably JV Stalin III tanks, supported by air attacks and helicopters, crushed opposition. In response, the Hungarians attacked tanks with Molotov cocktails (petrol bombs) and sniped at Soviet troops. Heavily outnumbered and out-resourced, the resistance was brutally crushed, with about 2,700 people killed and 200,000 going into exile. Soviet *Spetsnaz* special forces went door to door and sniffed the hands of the men they detained. If they found traces of gunpowder, they shot the men on the spot. Scenes of people fleeing across the frontier, and the establishment of large refugee camps in Austria, testified anew to the fragility of peace in Europe. The flight is now a major theme in the Hungarian discussion of recent history and has attracted cultural attention, for example in Andrew Vajna's film *Children of Glory* (2008). Nagy and his close associates were detained, being executed in 1958.[33] The principle of peaceful coexistence trumpeted at the Twentieth Congress of the CPSU earlier in 1956 had been spectacularly breached, and there were some resignations from Communist parties in the West. Many in the West lost faith in the Soviet experiment: Communist intellectuals in the West found themselves in a particularly difficult situation.

The Americans were unwilling to intervene in Hungary for a number of reasons including United Nations' reluctance to act; the simultaneous Suez Crisis that divided the NATO powers, particularly the USA and Canada from Britain and France; the absence, due to Austrian neutrality, of direct NATO land access to Hungary; the fear of touching off a general war that would have involved nuclear devastation; the defensive military posture of NATO; and a lack of reliable information about options. Moreover, to deter American intervention, the Soviet army deployed troops along the Austrian frontier. The crisis suggested that there would be no 'roll-back' of Communism by Western action. Indeed, Hungary in 1956 was the most significant episode of violent opposition within a Communist state hitherto, and the absence of NATO action disheartened those who hoped to see a more active stance. There were comparisons with the failure to act in defence of Czechoslovakia in 1938 and 1948, in other words the Appeasement of Hitler and the situation before NATO was established respectively. Yet, as Allen Dulles, the Director of the CIA, told the Senate Foreign Relations Committee on 12 November 1956, although spreading education challenged Communist control in the Soviet Union, there was no chance of an uprising there as the army was firmly behind the government.[34] Paradoxically, indeed, the Soviet Union was to educate its élite to pursue a degree of change that helped lead to its fall.

Meanwhile, public awareness of the espionage aspect of the Cold War had risen in April 1956 when the Soviets broke into the American tunnel built to intercept their cable traffic in Berlin and publicised the episode. The same month, Commander Crabb's unsuccessful and fatal attempt, on behalf of MI6, the British spy system, to study the hull of a Soviet cruiser then in Portsmouth led to Soviet complaints, press discussion, and the replacement of the head of MI6.

# Missiles

In his James Bond novel *Moonraker* (1955), Ian Fleming had the Soviets provide the atomic warhead and missile expert for a missile designed to destroy London, but this missile was to be fired by Nazis based in nearby Kent. The military situation instead changed on 4 October 1957, when the Soviet Union launched a missile that carried Sputnik I, the first satellite, into orbit where it circled the world at 18,000 miles per hour. The launch did not mean that the Soviets had intercontinental ballistic missiles able to carry atomic bombs, but it meant that such missiles might soon be close. Intercontinental missiles would bring the entire world within striking range, and thus make the USA vulnerable to Soviet attack, both from first-strike and from counter-strike. In strategic terms, missiles threatened to give effect to the doctrine of air power advanced in the 1920s and 1930s. At the same time, although, into the early 1960s, the B-52s' guidance system was considered more accurate than those mounted on missiles, missiles soon rendered obsolescent the nuclear capability of the American Strategic Air Command, a capability which was already challenged by Soviet air defences. The development of ablative shields, made from composites, was important to the success of these missiles. Many test firings of the wartime German V-2 had proved unsuccessful because the missile broke up on re-entry, probably due to a combination of instability, vibration, pressure and heat. It was not until the 1950s that the ablative heat shield was devised, dealing with the need to protect a nuclear warhead from burning up in the atmosphere when it re-entered.

The deployment of intercontinental missiles altered the parameters of vulnerability, and ensured that space was even more seen in terms of straight lines between launching site and target. As the major targets were in the USA and the Soviet Union, this situation led to concern with axes of attack via the North Pole, and the consequent mapping of these shorter routes. The threat to the USA from Soviet attack was highlighted by the November 1957 secret report from the Gaither Committee.[35] The strategic possibilities offered by nuclear-tipped long-range ballistic missiles made investment in expensive missile technology seem an essential course of action, since they could go so much faster and further than planes and, unlike them, could not be shot down. This altered the character of both anti-nuclear defence and nuclear deterrence, as the latter now apparently required an enhanced level of military readiness. Vulnerability to missiles accentuated the already strong sense of concern in the face of nuclear weapons. Indeed, *Defence: Outline of Future Policy*, the British Defence White Paper of April 1957, noted: 'It must be frankly recognised that there is at present no means of providing adequate protection for the people of this country against the consequences of an attack with nuclear weapons'. The public response was one of considerable concern. There was a political dimension, as fear and anger about the likely devastation of nuclear war encouraged popular activism in favour of nuclear disarmament. This was more pronounced in Western Europe than in the USA. In turn, responding to this activism, whether by encouraging it or by opposing it, became an aspect of the Cold War.[36]

## Sputnik and the Soviet Age

The wider significance of Sputnik was not restricted to military strategy. It also appeared to prove Soviet claims that it was overtaking the USA and Western Europe, not simply in military hardware, but also in technological capability, as well as in standards of living. Indeed, the Cold War was, in one respect, a battle over technological modernity. Competition over living standards reflected the increasing sense in the late 1950s that the Cold War was a battle for the hearts and minds of consumers on the home front as much as of armed forces. A spirit of can-do optimism was propagated in the Soviet Union. However, the public relations coup created round Sputnik was totally misleading, in part because Soviet economic statistics were manipulated, but also because of a systemic Soviet failure to ensure that accurate figures were obtained and that proper balance sheets were produced. For example, in Uzbekistan (a republic in the Soviet Union) under Sharav Rashidov (1959–83), the figures for cotton production were persistently grossly inaccurate. Nevertheless, Western concern about Soviet economic growth lent added point to anxiety about its apparent expansionism and military capability. Moreover, Soviet growth was important in the propaganda war which increasingly focused in the late 1950s on the living standards of consumers. If the Soviet system could provide better outcomes, then surely, it was believed on the Soviet side and feared in the West, workers around the world would opt for it, as would newly-independent Third World states such as Egypt. This approach represented a challenge to capitalism, but also to the Socialist parties that the Communists presented as tarnished by their willingness to compromise with capitalism. In short, the Soviet project was relaunched on the competitive world stage in a fashion very different to its earlier versions in the early years of the Revolution and the successive attempts under Stalin. The Soviet modernity under offer was part of a new political struggle. Peaceful co-existence was to be won by the Soviet Union.[37]

Khrushchev had won the struggle to dominate the Soviet regime. Having compromised his rivals with his anti-Stalinism campaign in 1956, Khrushchev faced their counter-attack in June 1957 when the 'anti-Party group', led by Malenkov, Molotov, Kaganovich and Dimitry Shepilov, gained a majority in the Politburo for his dismissal. However, allied to Georgi Zhukov, the Minister of Defence, and to the KGB, Khrushchev insisted that the decision be ratified by the plenary session of the Central Committee. That overturned the Politburo's decision. Khrushchev then removed his opponents, sending Molotov to be ambassador in Mongolia, Malenkov to manage a hydroelectric plant, and Kaganovich to run an asbestos factory. Zhukov was dismissed in order to strengthen Khrushchev's position. Shepilov, who had replaced Molotov as Foreign Minister in June 1956, was replaced by Andrey Gromyko.

Competition with the USA was to the fore under Khrushchev as it represented the capitalist dream. Khrushchev saw 'a race to see who could do the best job at supplying the ordinary fellow on the beach with his cold drink'. Impressed by American consumerism, Khrushchev regarded it as the challenge now that the Western colonial empires were fading: 'The Americans got it. They understood that if ordinary people were to live the way the kings and merchants of old had lived, what would be required was a new kind of luxury, an ordinary luxury built up from goods turned out by the million so that everybody could have one'.[38] In the event, however, the Americans could deliver rockets and consumerism while the Soviets found the latter an impossible goal, in large part because of the serious deficiencies of a Communist-controlled economy.[39]

There was a long tradition of using Western visitors to showcase Soviet achievements.[40] In July 1959, Richard Nixon, the Vice-President, and Khrushchev significantly squared off in a kitchen in the American National Exhibition in Sololniki Park, Moscow, to debate the virtues of the two systems, Nixon boasting about colour television. Khrushchev criticised the 'gadgets' of the capitalist American home, but set out to ensure consumer satisfaction, although the Socialist consumerism that was to be on offer in the East, for example sensible 'Socialist fashions', suffered from a serious lack of understanding of the populism and market mechanisms of consumerism. Meanwhile, Americanisation was an ideological and institutional process, drawing on new consumer demands linked to mass production. Capitalism around the non-Communist world became more integrated and more organised on American models.[41] Television and film helped make American consumerism appear more attractive. When I visited Dresden in East Germany in 1980, I noticed that Hollywood films, such as *Kramer versus Kramer*, were on show. They provided striking indications of Western living standards and extended the impact of West German television.

In a parallel with Khruschchev's endorsement of Soviet modernism, American policy under Eisenhower (1953–61) took forward New Deal themes and led, in particular, to advances with Civil Rights, notably desegregation. There was a concern to minimise the possibility of Communist influence in the Civil Rights movement. In the effort to defeat the Communists, 'Americans of both parties discarded traditional fears of a centralised state and came together to enact national principles and purpose through a strong government'.[42] In 1958, in response to Sputnik, the USA passed the National Defense Education Act, which was designed to enhance technical training. That year, the National Air and Space Administration (NASA) was established in order to develop a space programme. Defence-related federal contracts led to university expansion.

## Nuclear Retaliation

Aside from high Western economic growth rates, the American army and air force (somewhat separately) had been developing long-range ballistic missiles after World War Two, using captured German V-2 scientists and equipment. Indeed, the rhetoric of the 'missile gap' of 1959–60 reflected more on domestic American politics than on the true situation. In his James Bond novel *Dr No* (1958), the villain, in partnership with the Soviets, who train his men, threatens the American missile tests based on the British Caribbean colony of Turks Island. From 1957, there was a twofold Western response to the enhanced Soviet missile capability and to the crucial uncertainty about further developments. Notions of graduated nuclear retaliation, through the use of 'tactical' (short-range) nuclear weapons in association with conventional forces, based in Western Europe, were complemented by a policy of developing an effective intercontinental retaliatory second-strike capability, in order to make it dangerous to risk attack on the USA. This attempt to give force to the notion of massive nuclear retaliation[43] entailed replacing vulnerable manned bombers with less vulnerable submarines equipped with Polaris missiles and, also, with land-based missiles located in reinforced concrete silos. The invulnerability of American nuclear weaponry was thus enhanced. The smaller, limited-range submarine-launched missiles, designed to hit the 'soft targets', i.e. cities, complemented, but did not replace, land-based rockets. With the latter, the Americans made the transition from vulnerable, time-consuming, liquid-fuel rockets to the instantaneous launch on command, solid fuel missiles. They were intended to destroy the silos holding Soviet underground missiles. The Soviets, in contrast, faced major problems in developing solid fuel propellants.

In a major regional impact of the Cold War, part of a pattern by which there were many specific regional and local manifestations of the more general process of military preparedness, part of the Upper Great Plains was covered in 1961–7 by a network of 1,000 missile silos, each containing an intercontinental ballistic missile, the LGM-30A Minuteman-1, armed with a 1.2 megaton nuclear warhead, and by their control bunkers.[44] A far less happy product of the build-up in nuclear arms was the radioactive contamination involved in their manufacture, notably in the plutonium towns, for example Hanford.[45] Another regional manifestation was the aircraft manufacture concentrated in Los Angeles County, notably with Convair, Lockheed and Douglas factories. Military facilities and the extension of the military-industrial complex led to the spread of Cold War values to particular communities, thence influencing state politics.[46]

The Americans had fired their first nuclear missile from a submarine in 1952. The capability of these missiles rapidly increased. The Americans fired their first intercontinental ballistic missile in 1958, and, in July 1960, off Cape Canaveral, the USS *George Washington* was responsible for the first successful underwater firing of a Polaris missile. The following year, the Americans commissioned the USS *Ethan Allen*, the first true fleet missile-firing submarine. Submarines could be based near the coast of target states, and were highly mobile and hard to detect. They represented a major shift in force structure, away from the bombers of the American air force and towards the navy, which argued that its invulnerable submarines could launch carefully controlled strikes, permitting a more sophisticated management of deterrence and retaliation. From 1964, ballistic-missile submarines went on patrol on a regular basis. The American navy was the largest and most developed in the world. The capability of submarines had been enhanced by the development of nuclear power plants as a means of propulsion. By enabling submarines to remain submerged for far longer, this increased their range and lessened their vulnerability. The first nuclear-powered submarine, the USS *Nautilus*, was launched in 1952. Other states followed. The first British Polaris test missile was fired from a submarine in 1968, while the French commissioned their first ballistic missile submarine in 1969.

The inhibiting effect of the destructive potential of intercontinental nuclear weaponry served as much to enhance the possibility of a nuclear war, by increasing interest in defining a sphere for tactical nuclear weapons and in planning an effective strategic nuclear first strike, as it did to lessen the chance of a great power war, or to increase the probability that such a conflict would be essentially conventional. The risk of nuclear destructiveness, nevertheless, made it important to prevent escalation to full-scale war, and thus encouraged interest in defining forms of warfare that could exist short of such escalation. American critics of Eisenhower argued that his emphasis on massive nuclear retaliation closed the necessary option of limited wars. This argument influenced policy under the following Kennedy administration (1961–3), by encouraging interest in limited nuclear war as well as in conventional conflict.

In the early 1960s, American concern about the nuclear balance increased. On 18 January 1960, Allen Dulles, still Director of the CIA, told the Senate Foreign Relations Committee that 'one of the key factors behind Soviet diplomacy lies in their view of their increasing power in the military field, particularly missiles'.[47] Later that year, John F. Kennedy fought the 1960 presidential election against Richard Nixon in part on the misleading platform that the Republican administration under Eisenhower, in which Nixon had been Vice-President from 1953, had failed to maintain America's defences, an argument employed to present the administration as tired.[48] In fact, Defense expenditure had risen from $30.4 billion in 1954 to $41.4 billion in 1960. Kennedy pressed for a more vigorous prosecution of the Cold War and a more robust presentation of American values. Concerned to provide for a range of American capabilities, Kennedy, once President in 1961–3, sought to build up both conventional and nuclear forces. He aimed for a strategic superiority over the Soviet Union and considerably increased defence spending. The race to the Moon was an aspect of this drive for superiority. In 1961, Kennedy committed the USA to sending a man to the Moon, a task completed on 20 July 1969 with the *Apollo 11* mission. The cost was enormous; about $100 billion for the *Apollo* missions.[49]

## Berlin Crisis, 1961

At the same time, international tensions increased as a consequence of Soviet pressure. The building of the Berlin Wall from early August 1961 provided an apt symbol of the lack of freedom to which Communist government gave rise. The open border between East and West Berlin had offered an easy means for fleeing from East Germany, and, by building the wall, the Communists abandoned any suggestion that their system was more popular. Their division of the city was initially with barbed wire, but later with a concrete wall supported by frontier troops trained to shoot would-be escapees, and ready to do so. This division was a breach of the agreements between the occupying powers that permitted the citizens of Berlin to move freely through the whole city. This challenge to the Western powers, which was part of a Soviet plan for the signing of a peace treaty with East Germany designed to end Allied occupation rights in Berlin, indicated the extent to which Khrushchev's goal of the Eastern bloc 'stabilisation' of interests was, in practice, destabilising at the international level. Berlin dominated Kennedy's attention in the summer of 1961 and contributed to a sense of his being under pressure. The Bay of Pigs failure in Cuba (see p. 105) contributed to this sense.

The crisis escalated when the Soviet Union resumed nuclear testing on 1 September 1961, and, secretly, with Soviet preparations for a military exercise designed to counter any Western response over Berlin.[50] The Americans meanwhile mobilised National Guardsmen and Reservists and sent additional troops to West Germany, moving them overland in order to assert access rights through East Germany. On 28 October, American and Soviet tanks were involved in a dangerous standoff. This standoff made both Kennedy and Khrushchev recognise that it was better to tolerate the status quo in Berlin. In the event, there was no war, and the Soviet Union backed away from the idea of an East German peace treaty. Khrushchev's caution may have reflected his concern about the American response, but the extent to which his bitter dispute with Mao came into the open in March 1960 at the Bucharest International Communist Party Congress may have been a factor. In October 1961, at the 22nd Soviet Communist Party Congress, Khrushchev and others criticised the Chinese. The Cold War rarely involved developments only on one front, but the consequences of broader interactions were, and are, frequently difficult to gauge. The dispute with Mao was not simply geopolitical. The contrasting origins of the different Soviet and Chinese Communist Parties were an issue, as were ideological factors, cultural differences, the temperaments of leaders, military competition, and concerns about status. The dispute also raised questions among Communist commentators of the fundamental legitimacy of particular Communist states, and thus potentially threatened Khrushchev's position in the Soviet Union.

The end result of the Berlin crisis was a Berlin Wall that left the city as a powerful testimony to hostility. The wall was also a declaration that East Berlin was in the Soviet zone,[51] and thus a guarantee of separate developments in the two parts of the city, however much they might in some respects be linked in a symbiotic fashion.[52] Kennedy's declaration 'Ich bin ein Berliner', on a visit to Berlin on 23 June 1963, served publicly to link the USA and West Germany, and to focus an idea of free citizenship on

Berlin. This looked back to Cicero's *Civis Romanus sum*, an affirmation of rights and protection. In contrast, Khrushchev's declaration two days later, 'I love the Wall', offered a grim ideology.[53] With the option of fleeing to the West removed, East Germany introduced conscription in 1962. The Berlin Wall suggested that German reunification was far distant. Indeed, while Western support clearly protected West Berlin, it could not bring German reunification, nor ease relations between West and East Germany. This situation was to be important to the *Ostpolitik* that developed later in the decade, for that represented a West German attempt to find a means to ease relations. The Berlin Wall also became a powerful and repeated subject and motif in fiction and film, for example the Len Deighton novel *Funeral in Berlin* (1965), which was turned into a film (1966). Novels and films make the Cold War vivid for readers and audiences around the world: not least as the subject was repeated in numerous languages.

## The Cuban Missile Crisis, 1962

Soviet pressure on Western interests became more frequent under Khrushchev in the early 1960s, reflecting in part his misplaced determination, while preserving peace, to gain success, in and by, pressing the West. On 6 January 1961, while stating that 'wars of liberation' against Western colonial control must not become wars between states, Khrushchev praised the former. Thus, in 1961–2, the Soviet Union, leapfrogging the containment ring, pursued plans for a naval base in Egypt, which was a challenge to the NATO position in the Mediterranean, sought to profit from the protracted civil war in the Congo (Zaire) that followed the end of Belgian colonial rule in 1960, and decided to help Fidel Castro counter American pressure on Cuba, pressure which included the use of covert force. The 1959 revolution in Cuba seemed to Soviet commentators to bring the revolution of 1917 to life again and was treated with great enthusiasm in the Soviet bloc.[54] Khrushchev was to follow revolutionary initiatives in other areas, backing with military aid Egypt's intervention in Yemen from 1962.[55]

Initially, Kennedy seriously mishandled the situation by supporting an invasion of Cuba on 17 April 1961 by 1,300 CIA-trained anti-Communist exiles, and then refusing to provide the necessary air support. The total failure of this badly-led invasion at the Bay of Pigs in the absence of a popular revolution and in the face of stiff opposition, was followed by the authorisation of Operation Mongoose, which involved covert American operations including sabotage. In an extrapolation of earlier fears about China and East Asia, the Americans, underestimating the strength of anti-American nationalism in Cuba, feared that the country would serve as the base for subversion across Latin America. This was more accurate as an account of the intentions of Castro's lieutenant, Che Guevara, than of the realities on the ground, as Che's total failure in Bolivia in 1967 revealed.

Believing, in part due to American naval exercises, reports that an American invasion of Cuba was imminent in 1962, and, indeed, it is possible that some such action was intended, not least in order to help produce a show of force before the American mid-term elections, Khrushchev decided to send nuclear missiles to Cuba. The plans entailed secretly dispatching 230,000 tons of *matériel* and sending 42,000 military personnel, but secrecy was lost due to American aerial surveillance. On 4 September 1962, the Americans warned the Soviets against deploying any significant offensive capability in Cuba. Far from dropping his plans, however, Khrushchev continued. He aimed to install strategic missiles that brought Washington within range, and also tactical nuclear weapons, while jet bombers capable of carrying nuclear weapons were shipped to Cuba. Khrushchev hoped that these missiles and bombers would not only protect Cuba but would also strengthen the overall Soviet position. This position was challenged by the American and NATO build-up in Western Europe. For Khrushchev, Cuba was an issue not only as far as the West was concerned but also with regard to China which had criticised him for failing to stand up to the West.

On 14 October 1962, a U-2 spy plane obtained proof that medium-range nuclear missile sites were under construction in Cuba, a breach of Khrushchev's assurance that he would not send offensive or nuclear weapons there. American decision makers agreed on the need for a response to get the missiles out, but were divided as to how best to do so, not least over whether to launch a pre-emptive military strike. This was the policy advocated by General Curtis LeMay, the bellicose Air Force Chief of Staff, who was to be George Wallace's Vice-Presidential running mate in the 1968 election. In the event, Kennedy determined on a blockade designed to stop the shipment of missiles. He was understandably concerned that an attack on Cuba might not be completely successful, and would lead to a damaging Soviet reaction against America from Cuba, or action elsewhere, for example an attack on Berlin.

Tension meanwhile rose when, in response to an Indian attempt to seize a border area in the Himalayas, China launched an offensive on 20 October, defeating and driving the Indians back. The Indian army units were not as accustomed to the high altitudes as the Chinese and had dated weaponry. This defeat resulted in the supply of American weaponry and the airlift of help to India. The Soviet Union did not openly support the Indians, but behind the scenes they did, while the Soviets irritated the Chinese by refusing to back them diplomatically. This episode led toward later Soviet-Indian military and commercial co-operation. Having revealed that the Indians would be unable to defend Assam, the Chinese declared a unilateral ceasefire on 21 November 1962, and withdrew their troops.

On 22 October 1962, Kennedy addressed the American people and announced a 'strict quarantine on all offensive military equipment under shipment to Cuba' (ie blockade), using the argument that 1930s'

Appeasement must not be repeated. He also made clear that Cuba could prove the trigger for Armageddon, as any nuclear attack on the Americans from Cuba would be seen as requiring a full-scale nuclear attack on the Soviet Union. The threat led to military preparations by both sides. The Americans prepared for air attacks on Cuba and an invasion, as well as for nuclear strikes against the Soviet Union. In the habitual manner of making public statements in order to affect the political economy of mutual perception, Khrushchev threatened 'catastrophic consequences' if the American blockade took effect, but turned down the idea of ordering a Soviet blockade round Berlin. On 25 October, the American blockade, that was intended to stop the transport of offensive military hardware, took effect, and, instead of pressing on, the Soviet ships carrying such material to Cuba stopped. Having decided not to escalate the crisis, Khrushchev sought to settle the matter so as to protect Cuba from invasion. In return for such an assurance, he was willing not only not to test the American blockade but also to dismantle the missile sites on Cuba.

On the American side, there was continued interest in an invasion, not least because Soviet approaches were inconsistent and included the demand that any withdrawal of missiles from Cuba be matched by that of American missiles from Turkey.[56] The divisions among the American policymakers can be followed with some ease. Kennedy urged caution, not least when a Soviet ground-to-air missile brought down a U-2 over Cuba, killing the pilot. In turn, American anti-submarine forces, dropping warning depth charges, forced three Soviet submarines to the surface. Concerned about the risk that differences over Cuba would lead to war, either by an American invasion or due to Castro's irresponsible belligerence, Khrushchev agreed to remove the missiles, in return for an American promise not to invade. In contrast, Kennedy's secret concession over the missiles in Turkey did not sway Khrushchev. Despite the bellicose Castro blocking on-site inspections of the missile sites, the American blockade ended on 20 November and the nuclear weapons were removed by the Soviets. The crisis had revealed the importance of restraint by the leaders, Kennedy and Khrushchev, but also suggested the risk that conflict could have resulted from unforeseen circumstances, notably clashes between armed units. Failures to obey orders, either due to breakdowns in communications or as a result of deliberate action, were a contributory risk. The problems of maintaining communications with nuclear-armed submarines posed a particular difficulty during the crisis and subsequently during the Cold War.

Kennedy came out of the 1962 crisis with his reputation for leadership much enhanced. The response was more positive than had been the case over the Bay of Pigs and Berlin in 1961. In part, this positive response was well-deserved, although the unpredictable nature of the favourable outcome has to be emphasised. Khrushchev, in contrast, was compromised by the crisis, being perceived as erratic by his Politburo colleagues. He had to hold them at bay by reputation; there was no equivalent to the role of terror and fear in the maintenance of Stalin's position. In addition, the deal between the two powers was criticised by Castro and Mao. They saw it as a 'Soviet Munich', a reference to the appeasement of Hitler in 1938. This response helped explain the difficulties the Americans encountered later in the decade: whereas American-Soviet relations were eased by the restraint Khrushchev learned, notably in 1962, the Americans proved mistaken in their conviction that they could use similar pressure to force other Communist powers to back down. Indeed, Ho Chi Minh, the North Vietnamese leader, was not to do so.[57] Thus, the Cuban crisis was followed by stability in Europe, but not elsewhere.

Khrushchev tried to build on the Cuban settlement in order to reach a broader agreement with the USA, suggesting talks on arms limitations and disarmament. The Partial Test-Ban Treaty signed in August 1963 banned nuclear testing in the atmosphere, outer space and under water. The direct telephone line between the White House and the Kremlin agreed in April 1963 reflected an effort to make diplomacy more central. However, there was no major improvement in relations. This (relative) failure compromised Khrushchev's position, as did the inability that year of attempts to settle the dispute with China, and the disappointing grain harvest which obliged the Soviet Union to import grain from the West. Grain supplies proved a persistent problem for the Soviet Union, notably again in the 1980s. These difficulties reflected both the unpredictability of the rainfall in central Eurasia and the failure of the Soviet economic model. Despite much effort and propaganda, hopes of greater agricultural production could not be realised. Trofim Lysenko (see p. 51) was dismissed in 1965. This failure ensured a need for engagement with the West. The requirement in 1964 to buy grain from Canada was a major event in Soviet history, for it revealed that the country could not feed itself unless it bought grain from the despised, degenerate, capitalist West.

When Khrushchev was removed from office by the Central Committee on 14 October 1964, being accused of risking war over Berlin and Cuba, collective leadership took power. The main figure, until his death in 1982, was Leonid Brezhnev, the Party leader, a protégé of Khrushchev. Brezhnev was determined to avoid war, in part because of his experience of World War Two as an army commissar. With the international system now, after Cuba and Berlin, seen in terms of risk as much as opportunity, and with class conflict not at the forefront of Soviet thought on the topic, it became easier to think in terms of the co-existence outlined in 1955. This represented an important stage in the Cold War, one that helped encourage a focus on rivalry in Asia, where China was more prominent, while other themes came to the fore in Europe.

Meanwhile, Kennedy had been assassinated in Dallas on 22 November 1963. It was believed by many that the KGB had been involved, not least because Lee Harvey Oswald had spent time in the Soviet Union. In February 1964, Yuri Nosenko defected and reported that the KGB had rejected Oswald, which is, indeed, probable as he was felt to be unreliable. However, Nosenko's veracity was questioned. President Johnson did not use the issue in order to cause a crisis in relations with the Soviet Union.

# Nuclear Deterrence

During the Berlin Crisis of 1961, Kennedy had reaffirmed the willingness of America to use atomic weaponry even if the Soviets did not, because West Berlin, an isolated position, was particularly vulnerable to Soviet conventional attack. Kennedy, nevertheless, sought to move from the idea of 'massive retaliation' with nuclear weaponry to a policy that did not automatically assume escalation to nuclear war. This move was an aspect of a more general strategy of 'Flexible Response' adopted in 1962, in part as an answer to Communist 'wars of national liberation', which, in the aftermath of the Soviets' backing down over Cuba, were perceived in the USA as posing a greater threat than full-scale conventional conflict. Proposing a symmetrical posture and strategy, 'Flexible Response' postulated a spectrum of conflict, from nuclear deterrence and conventional warfare at one end, to guerrilla combat and non-military applications of national power at the other, with the possibility of the careful escalation of forces as an aspect of the response. Whatever the language, as it was unlikely that any conventional conflict between the two blocs would be anything less than devastating, and would rapidly become nuclear, the deterrent helped prevent the devastation of high-tech conventional warfare between well-resourced alliances.

The increase in American defence spending in the early 1960s, the rise in the number of American nuclear warheads, the Soviet climbdown during the Cuban crisis, and the prospect of massive American nuclear retaliation, apparently lessened the Soviet threat in Europe. However, American preparations encouraged the KGB to report, inaccurately, that the USA was planning a nuclear first strike. Moreover, the Soviets responded to the Cuban missile crisis by expanding their intercontinental missile force, so as to lessen their vulnerability. With Khrushchev's fall, Soviet military leaders became more prominent. Nevertheless, in 1965, Robert McNamara, the American Secretary of Defense, felt able to state that the USA could rely on the threat of 'assured destruction' of about one-third of the Soviet population to deter a Soviet assault. Submarine-launched missiles provided the Americans with a secure second strike, as part of a triad that included bombers, ground-based missiles and sea-launched missiles.

Such strength did not, however, prevent further attempts by the nuclear powers to enhance their nuclear attack and defence capabilities, for the logic of deterrence required matching any advance in the techniques of nuclear weaponry. For example, having decided, in 1967, to proceed with the development of multiple independently-targeted re-entry vehicles (MIRVs), which were first tested in 1968, the Americans deployed Minuteman III missiles equipped with MIRVs, in 1970, thus ensuring that the strike capacity of an individual rocket or 'airbus' was greatly enhanced. As a consequence, warhead numbers, and thus the potential destructiveness of a nuclear exchange, rose greatly.[58] Moreover, the Americans increased the response time of their land-based intercontinental missiles by developing the Titan II, which had storable liquid propellants enabling in-silo launches and cutting the launch-time. This reduced the vulnerability of the missiles to a Soviet first-strike if the warning was sufficiently rapid, and improved the reaction time of the American missiles in a nuclear conflict.[59] Submarine-launched nuclear missiles became more powerful. Whereas the Polaris A-1 missile had a range of 1,400 miles, the Polaris A-3 (first test-fired in 1962) and Poseidon missiles had ranges of up to 2,800 miles. The deployment of A-3s across the board from 1964, especially in the Mediterranean posed a serious threat to the Soviet Union. Moreover, the Americans developed large missile-firing submarines (the *Los Angeles* class of the early 1970s and the *Ohio* class of the mid-1970s) capable of firing large numbers of missiles.

# Third World Struggles

Problems over Berlin, Cuba and relations with Khrushchev encouraged Kennedy to turn to Vietnam to project strength. Alongside a determination to show that America was robust militarily and able to resist any Soviet attack, the Kennedy administration was resolved to oppose the Communist advance in the Third World and to be seen to do so. Although nationalism was crucial to anti-colonial 'liberation struggles', they were also characterised by Communist exploitation, as the Soviet Union and China sought to challenge the USA indirectly, by encouraging supporters to attack America's allies. These attacks brought together notions of popular warfare, nationalism and revolutionary Communism, in a programme of revolutionary struggle in which success was believed to be inevitable. Thus, the Soviets supported President Gamal Abdel Nasser's nationalisation of the Suez Canal Company on 26 July 1956. They saw this as threatening the West's supplies of Middle Eastern oil. When, later in the year, Britain, France and Israel attacked Egypt in the Suez Crisis, the Soviet government threatened to send troops. There was a determined effort to use Nasser to win over Arab nationalism to the Soviet cause.

Western governments repeatedly feared that Third World anti-colonial movements and nationalism were crypto-Communist and would be exploited by the Communist powers. This fear encouraged a view that the West's front line ran round the world, and that Communism had to be contained in order for it not to spread. In March 1955, John Foster Dulles, the Secretary of State, told the Senate Foreign Relations Committee that, in South-East Asia, he regarded 'the subversive problem [as] ... a greater menace than the open military menace of the activities of the Communists'.[60] For political as well as military reasons, the USA was determined to keep the front line not only away from the Western hemisphere, but also as close to the Communist bloc as possible, the latter a key element of containment. Eisenhower also believed in collective-security alliances, which helps explain his efforts in establishing the Baghdad Pact (later called CENTO), and SEATO. In the 1950s, the Americans could concentrate their land forces in only two areas outside the USA, Europe and South Korea, and did not want to establish them elsewhere because they did not have the resources to do so. Thus, other methods had to be used for containment.

The cross-currents involved were seen in the case of Egypt. The Eisenhower administration courted Nasser hoping that Egypt would join up with the West against the Eastern Bloc. Nasser, however, would not join the Baghdad Pact, was not overly moved by American fears of the Soviets, and was unduly preoccupied, for American tastes, with the Israelis. The USA became disenchanted with Nasser before 1956, but Eisenhower was angry to be kept in the dark by Britain, France and Israel, and felt the invasion stupid.[61]

Containment was subsequently expanded as a consequence of Castro's success in Cuba. American policymakers became more anxious about the West Indies and Latin America. In 1965, the USA sent 23,000 troops into the Dominican Republic in order to thwart a left-wing movement from seizing power to reverse a coup of two years earlier.[62]

The fear of popular nationalism was seen in Congo which became independent from Belgium in 1960, a year in which the rising pace of imperial collapse was providing new fuel for Cold War rivalries.[63] The USA was hostile to the Congolese National Movement which was headed by Patrice Lumumba. Regarding him as pro-Soviet, the USA unsuccessfully sought to prevent his election. Comprising many ethnic groups and lacking a practice of united central government under African control, Congo fragmented. Lumumba sought UN support, but the fear that he might turn to the Soviet Union led the USA to support the seizure of power by the Congolese military under General Joseph Mobutu in 1960. Lumumba was assassinated in 1961, leading to massive protest demonstrations in the Eastern Bloc. The People's Friendship University established in Moscow in 1960 in order to teach Third World students was renamed Lumumba University in 1961. Mobuto's vicious policies increased opposition, and, in response, the CIA paid for and organised a campaign in eastern Congo in 1964–5, with CIA aircraft being particularly important. Waged by Western mercenaries and Mobuto's troops, this campaign enforced a very brutal settlement.

In practice, the attempt to shape world politics in terms of a geopolitical and ideological competition directed by the great powers was challenged by independent initiatives. Some were really or ostensibly linked to the ideological dynamic of the Cold War, but many were not, or not in the way that the USA and the Soviet Union sought. The cross-currents of other views and interests played a role, from the anti-imperial non-aligned movement[64] to more nationally specific elements. Repeatedly, the military were particularly significant. For example, in Egypt, Syria and Iraq, the army staged what were presented as progressive coups, while, in Indonesia and Turkey, the army turned against the Left in the 1960s and 1970s respectively.[65] The Americans saw a friendly military as a force for stability and, as outlined in Kennedy's National Security Memorandum of 18 December 1961, for development, and sought to influence and support them accordingly. This was successful in South Korea[66] and Indonesia,[67] but scarcely in South Vietnam, where independent initiatives by the Communists were matched by a politics of self-interest on the part of the army leadership. In Latin America, America frequently linked their perception of stability and development to backing the military, notably in Bolivia, where fear of Communism encouraged a linkage of aid and of alliance with the armed forces.[68] Other security agencies also attracted the interest of American agencies such as the Office of Public Safety established in 1962.[69] In Brazil, the army seized power in 1964 with American encouragement.

## Vietnam

American views about containment brought them to Vietnam, which had been partitioned under the Geneva Agreement as part of the withdrawal of the French in 1954. The Communist Viet Minh were left in control of North Vietnam, and an American-supported government was established in South Vietnam. Under the Geneva terms, all-Vietnam elections were supposed to be held in 1956, but they were not, in large part due to the opposition of the South Vietnamese government, which, led from 1954 to 1963 by Ngo Dinh Diem, was brutal, corrupt and unpopular. The government had won the 1956 election in South Vietnam using fraud, and it represented best the landowning élite that composed it. The Catholic identity of the regime further compromised its popularity in what was a largely Buddhist country, and the use of a divide and rule policy undermined stability.[70]

From 1957, South Vietnam faced a Communist rebellion by the Viet Cong, which resulted in more overt and widespread American intervention. The Viet Cong offered a programme of socio-economic transformation, including land reform. This offered opportunities for the young, who suffered from the mismatch between a rising population and the combination of limited additional labour demands in agriculture and a lack of factory industry to soak up rural surplus labour. Going into the Viet Cong or into the South Vietnamese army was a way out. Possibly partly due to this factor and possibly due to successful violent intimidation including assassinations and massacres, the Viet Cong won considerable support, providing a basis for military action. From 1959, forces from North Vietnam were infiltrated into South Vietnam in support of the Viet Cong, who were linked to the North Vietnamese Politburo. A struggle for control within the North Vietnamese government from 1955 had been won by 'South Firsters', those led by Le Duan, who became leader of the Vietnam Workers' Party in 1959. Although they did not seek open confrontation with the USA, they supported large-scale intervention in the South, rather than focusing on developing North Vietnam, the policy of the 'North Firsters'.[71]

As a prime instance of the 'Domino Theory', the Americans were concerned that a failure to support South Vietnam and to neutralise Laos, would lead to the further spread of Communism in South-East Asia. In response, the commitment of American 'advisers' to South Vietnam from the late 1950s, including the foundation in February 1962 of Military Assistance Command, Vietnam, encouraged pressure for further support, as the Americans, although not the colonial power, in effect increasingly adopted the earlier role of the French. By 1963, when Diem was assassinated by key elements of the South Vietnamese military with American connivance because he was insufficiently accommodating, there were 16,000 American advisers. American intervention helped limit Viet Cong advances in 1962. However, the combination of the lack of fighting quality of much of the South Vietnamese army (which grew in size from 150,000 men in 1960 to 250,000 in 1964), and flawed advice from the Americans, in particular an emphasis on firepower, failed to win victory.[72]

Invalidating notions, supported by France in particular, that South Vietnam could have been neutralised through negotiation (as Laos was in theory in 1960), the North Vietnamese were determined to maintain the struggle. In doing so, they benefited from the extent to which the Soviet Union did not control Communist countries: no more than with the West, there was no united bloc, and the Sino-Soviet split exacerbated divisions. The North Vietnamese regime had close relations with China, and marginalised politicians and officers trained in the Soviet Union and other moderates. Military Security and the Ministry of Public Security became key elements of a harshly authoritarian state. Whereas China had restrained Vietnamese military ambition in 1954–7, this was no longer the case. Meeting in December 1963, the ninth plenary session of their Communist Party's Central Committee criticised the Soviet notion of 'peaceful existence', decided to step up the war in South Vietnam, and pushed forward more militant politicians. North Vietnamese offensives in 1964–5, designed to bring victory before there was large-scale American intervention, in turn encouraged the Americans to build-up their forces.[73]

Meanwhile, an attack on the USS destroyer *Maddox* by the North Vietnamese in the Gulf of Tonkin off Vietnam on 2 August 1964 was followed by an alleged attack on 4 August. These attacks were provoked

by American support for South Vietnamese commando raids on the coast
of North Vietnam, but the situation was doctored by the American administration. The attacks, which resulted in American carrier strikes on 5
August, led Congress on 7 August to pass overwhelmingly a resolution,
the so-called Tonkin Gulf Resolution, permitting President Lyndon B.
Johnson 'to take all necessary measures to repel any armed attack against
the forces of the United States and to prevent further aggression', in short to
wage war without proclaiming it. This was the preferred American option
because Johnson wanted to avoid an explicit choice between war and disengagement, as well as to apply more easily the strategic concept of graduated
pressure. In practice, Johnson, an adroit Congressional deal-maker, was an
incompetent strategist. His incrementalist strategy was the opposite of what
the Americans did in Korea, and led to the dispatch and deployment of
insufficient troops to accomplish the task. In a general sense, the credibility
of American power appeared at issue, notably to Johnson who, as he put
it in July 1965, did not want to 'be the architect of surrender'. There was
a belief in Washington that the line against further Communist expansion
had to be drawn somewhere, and that this was it. The Americans were
concerned about the impact of developments in South Vietnam for those
elsewhere in Indochina, especially Laos, where Communist moves greatly
concerned its neighbour Thailand and where Kennedy had sought to
oppose Communist expansion.

The Americans were also concerned about the more general implications
of developments in Indochina for the situation throughout South Asia and
the West Pacific. Thus, the Vietnam struggle could be put not only with Laos
but also alongside China's successful 1962 war with India and Indonesian
attacks on Malaysia (from 1963, Sukarno, the President of Indonesia, was
close to China), to indicate a widespread Communist threat as part of a
crisis that America could respond to and affect by acting in South Vietnam.
The USA provided India with arms in 1962. The power in the USA of the
'China Lobby', i.e. the supporters of Taiwan, was also significant in encouraging an active military stance in South Vietnam. Whereas the Soviet Union
appeared to threaten expansionism in Europe, Communist expansionism
actually seemed to be in progress in East Asia. There, a theme of continued
threat could be used to link Chinese intervention in the Korean War in
1950, Chinese pressure on Taiwan, China's victory over India in 1962, and
Chinese and Soviet support for North Vietnam. These anxieties conflated
American concern about the ideological challenge from Communism with
the longstanding instability of the region that looked back to the 1890s,
and, in part, to the 1830s in China and the 1850s in Japan. This instability
owed much to the interaction of external pressures with the consequences
of drives for modernisation in particular states; and the Cold War appeared
to be another episode of this process. The USA had played a major role
from the 1850s, first in leading to change in Japan, and, subsequently, in
taking a major role in the future of China.

The 'Domino Theory' of incremental Communist advance, a concept that enjoyed powerful traction, not least because it could be readily explained in public, appeared to require a vigorous commitment in South Vietnam. At the same time, the easing of the issues that had brought the USA and the Soviet Union close to war in 1961–2 provided an opportunity for the Americans to focus on South Vietnam. This was not the priority Kennedy's successor, Lyndon Johnson, had sought, but it came to dominate his administration (1963–9), and with toxic effects. Seeing himself as another Franklin Delano Roosevelt, whom he idolised, Johnson would have preferred to concentrate on his Great Society reform programme at home. He also made efforts to find accommodation with the Soviet Union and China, but the American role in South Vietnam foiled these goals and Johnson ignored the opportunity to talk with Beijing and Hanoi in 1964. Instead, that year, he backed the coup that brought Major-General Nguyen Khanh to power in the South. Johnson believed it necessary to display firmness over South Vietnam in order to show determination, both to the American people and to the rest of the world. The personal dimension was important to Johnson, but so also was his conviction that America had a worthwhile purpose in the world and must heed its calling. To Johnson, this global mission was linked to his policies at home, and was not a separate add-on, nor a diversion. State-building was also to take place in South Vietnam.[74]

In late 1964, regular units of the North Vietnamese army were sent south in strength as the North Vietnamese sought an early victory, and, by 1965, the South Vietnamese army was on the verge of collapse.[75] These units were a potent threat to the South Vietnamese forces that the Americans had trained and this encouraged the build-up of American ground troops. The American response was encouraged by Johnson's wish to appear tough on Communism and thus thwart criticism by the Republican presidential candidate in November 1964, Barry Goldwater. In turn, defeating Goldwater, who was more extreme, enabled Johnson to follow his limited war, incrementalist strategy. By the end of 1964, American forces in South Vietnam had reached 23,000; they shot up to 181,000 in 1965, with the first combat battalions landing on 8 March, to 385,000 in 1966, and peaked at 543,000 in April 1969, only a minority of whom were combat infantry. The attack on the American air base at Pleïku in February 1965 was a major catalyst for American escalation, but there was also a lack of efficient and effective political oversight over the military dynamics for the escalation.

Aside from the important contribution by the South Vietnamese, massive American involvement was supplemented by troops from South Korea, the second largest international contingent with 48,000 troops,[76] and from Australia, New Zealand, Thailand and the Philippines. The South Koreans were largely paid for by the USA, which regarded them as good troops who cost less than Americans. The war effort was less international than the Americans had wished, and than had been the case in the

Korean War, with Harold Wilson, the Labour Prime Minister of Britain, preferring to get involved as a would-be (and unsuccessful) negotiator rather than as a combatant. If this was a major contrast with the position of the Labour government when the Korean War began in 1950, there was, unlike over Korea, no United Nations mandate for action. Nevertheless, the effort made by a number of states reflected a widespread concern about the strategic position in South-East Asia and the Communist advance, as well as a need to support the USA. Thus, Australia, which kept troops in Vietnam until 1972, was anxious to secure American support in the event of confrontation with Indonesia. Aligning with the USA had become more significant for Australia and New Zealand as a result of World War Two, notably American help against the Japanese threat in 1942, and, even more, as a consequence of Britain's retreat from empire and withdrawal from east of Suez. However, the risk of confrontation was greatly lessened after Sukarno was undermined and then overthrown in 1965–6 by Indonesian generals encouraged by the CIA. This was a key development that was accompanied by the large-scale massacre of Communists with possibly over half a million slaughtered. The failed coup in October 1965 that was blamed on the Communists led the army to slaughter the Communists as well as to gain effective power by the following March. This outcome permitted in August 1966 a settlement of the border struggle between Indonesia and Malaysia that had begun in 1963, with Malaysia supported by Britain and other Commonwealth states. A friendship treaty between Japan and South Korea, signed in 1965, further consolidated the pro-American bloc.

In North Vietnam, the Communists were well led and organised, and their political system and culture enabled them to mobilise and direct resources and to maintain a persistent effort. American involvement permitted the North to promote the war as a national crusade against Western imperialism. Military struggle and political indoctrination were seen to act in symbiosis, and the North Vietnamese and Viet Cong were more willing to suffer losses than the Americans, certainly so at the level of military organisations. Limited War theory was (and is) a Western concept that was not shared by the Vietnamese, and American strategy was wrongly based on the assumption that unacceptable losses could be inflicted on the North Vietnamese in the way that they could be on the Americans.[77] The Americans had largely forgotten their experience in World War Two of war with Japan, an opponent willing to fight to the end. Westmoreland, commander of the US Military Assistance Command, Vietnam, had served in Europe during that war. In the case of Vietnam:

Early in the war, U.S. policymakers opted for a war of attrition based in part on an imperfect understanding and unrealistic expectations of the ability of American firepower to send a persuasive message. The Communist forces never did crack, despite the ever-increasing levels of destruction. In the end it came down to a classic Clausewitzian test of wills and national resolve.[78]

In the face of North Vietnamese and Viet Cong determination and morale, the Americans cracked first, after attrition had apparently led to stalemate. Looked at differently, the Americans came to appreciate the consequences of Limited War: that it could lead to failure, and did so rapidly once their initial hopes for success had been thwarted. Subsequent debate as to whether total war, which, with the technology of the period, would have encompassed nuclear weapons, could have led to American victory can only go so far, as the intention was not to fight such a war. Whether there was an option in between is unclear.

The political context had a direct impact on American grand strategy. Concern that China might intervene, as in 1950 during the Korean War, discouraged any American invasion of North Vietnam, and thus dramatically reduced the options available to the Americans. In August 1965, when American jets pursued two North Vietnamese planes into China air space near to Hainan Island in China, Chou En-Lai, the Chinese Foreign Minister, warned the Americans not to do it again, and the Americans backed down. It can be debated whether the risk of invading North Vietnam was exaggerated, notably in light of the Sino-Soviet split, which contrasted with the situation during the Korean War, and also because of the turmoil in China during the Cultural Revolution launched by Mao Zedong. However, Chinese intervention in Korea in 1950 encouraged American caution, as did the marked stridency and volatility of China during the Cultural Revolution. Although unwilling to fight America, Mao was keen to support revolution in Indochina and provided North Vietnam with large quantities of *matériel* and substantial numbers (eventually 320,000 men) of support troops.[79] Competing for influence, the Soviet Union also provided aid. Soviet SAM surface-to-air missiles were particularly important in increasing the cost of using American air power.

Despite an initial thaw after Khrushchev's fall, Sino-Soviet relations remained poor. Although ready to take part in diplomatic signalling in order to keep the war limited,[80] the Chinese were particularly intransigent toward efforts to negotiate an agreement to the Vietnam conflict, notably in May 1965, when the Soviets were initially more accommodating.[81] Similarly, in 1967–71, the Chinese pressed the North Vietnamese not to accept a compromise solution suggested by the 'revisionist' Soviets. Thus, the Vietnam War, to the modern Vietnamese the American War, served China and the Soviet Union as an opportunity to pursue and test their rivalry alongside their goal of weakening the USA.[82] This rivalry provided North Vietnam with considerable opportunities for independent manoeuvre. This element underlined the extent to which, throughout the Cold War, local and regional powers pulled in and manipulated the superpowers for their own ends. The extent of the Sino-Soviet rift, combined with the lack of any

invasion of North Vietnam, meant that North Vietnam had more opportunity to do so than North Korea.

The role of the Communist great powers led American policymakers to
conclude that it was necessary to demonstrate that these powers could not
succeed by means of such a proxy war. Thus, Vietnam became the place
to show that America could and would act, and, because it was this place,
became the country where America must act. This issue took precedence
over the political possibilities for an acceptable settlement in Vietnam,
for, in practice, the Americans were committed in South Vietnam to an
unpopular, corrupt and unimpressive system. There had been rapid changes
of government in the year following Diem's assassination. Moreover, the
American quest to demonstrate credibility helped lead to a failure to understand the military situation in Vietnam. Looked at more harshly, there was
an unwillingness on the part of Johnson and his advisers, both political and
military, to admit that they might be wrong, and a reluctance to develop
new plans.[83]

The Americans failed to translate outputs, notably holding territory
and killing opponents, into outcome, a successful result accepted by both
sides, which is the central goal of military activity. They failed because Viet
Cong and North Vietnamese morale, or, at least, endurance were sustained
despite heavy casualties. This morale and endurance, which owed much to
coercion and indoctrination, extended throughout the army: the soldiers
who built the Ho Chi Minh Trail, down which supplies moved from North
Vietnam to Communist forces in the South, were inferior troops in military
terms, but they believed that they could attain status by doing these menial
tasks. They were also taught to believe that if they died – as most did – their
descendants would be rewarded, for instance in the distribution of land, a
key issue in Vietnamese society. In contrast, American morale suffered once
success proved elusive, and serious drug-use and indiscipline grew, affecting
unit cohesion and operations.

When the Americans intervened in Vietnam in force in 1965, their
opponents were already operating in sizeable units, and this situation
led, in 1965–8, to battles that were won by the Americans. Initially, the
Americans focused on defending coastal areas that were the centres of
South Vietnamese power and the areas of American deployment, but,
having prevented South Vietnam from being defeated in 1965, they then
moved into the interior. They were able to advance into parts of South
Vietnam which had been outside the control of Saigon, and to inflict serious
blows on the Viet Cong in the Mekong delta. In addition, direct mass Viet
Cong attacks on American positions were generally repulsed with heavy
casualties, for example at the siege of Plei Me in the Central Highlands
in 1965. Under General William Westmoreland the Americans sought to
attack throughout South Vietnam, establishing firebases from which operations would be mounted, in order to inflict casualties on their opponents
and wear down their strength. The helicopter played a major role in this

extension of activity, particularly with the use of the new 1st Cavalry Division (Airmobile).

Yet, the activity only brought so much advantage. Although heavy casualties were inflicted, opposing numbers rose, as North Vietnam responded to the American build-up by sending troops down the Ho Chi Minh Trail, thus vitiating American attempts to win by escalation and, instead, consigning them to stalemate. Furthermore, for the Americans, there was no concentration of opposing power that could be rapidly fixed and readily destroyed as, in very different circumstances, the Israelis were to do successfully against Egypt, Jordan and Syria in the Six Day War in 1967. American advantages and advances concealed the extent to which they shared the initiative with their opponents. Moreover, the need to devote so much strength to building up forces, logistics and security limited American combat strength. By the end of 1967, the situation, nevertheless, appeared promising, and Westmoreland felt that he was winning. He was committed to what he termed 'cross over', an attritional practice focused on killing or capturing more of his opponents than they could add. With the Viet Cong's momentum stopped, there appeared to be an opportunity for pacification. Under the aegis of Civil Operations and Revolutionary Development Support (CORDS), the Americans sought to win popular backing for the South Vietnamese government, a version of nation-building.

Westmoreland's perception of the situation proved deeply flawed.[84] The Tet offensive of 1968, which involved Viet Cong and North Vietnamese attacks on cities and military bases across South Vietnam, indicated the resilience of the opposition. Furthermore, however misleadingly, the offensive contributed greatly, within the USA, in its alliance system and, more widely, to a sense of crisis in the American world order, a crisis that suggested that the USA was losing the Cold War, and certainly the initiative. In geopolitical and international terms, this offensive was apparently the key event of 1968. The North Vietnamese and Viet Cong attacks, mounted under cover of the Lunar New Year celebrations of Tet, were launched in the belief that they would engender a popular uprising, but none followed, and the assaults were beaten off with heavy losses, hitting Viet Cong morale. The US benefited from a pre-Tet decision to move some combat units back from near the North Vietnamese border, where they had been concentrated. This decision, taken on 10 January 1968, was in response to indications that Viet Cong and North Vietnamese forces were being built up near the cities. However, the Americans failed to anticipate the timing and, more particularly, scale and character of the attack: over-optimistic assumptions about enemy casualties in the border battles of late 1967 were matched by an inability to believe that a full-scale attack on the cities would be mounted.

About 85,000 Viet Cong and North Vietnamese forces attacked from 30 January 1968, with 36 of the 44 South Vietnamese provincial capitals and five of the six autonomous cities being among the targets. Assaults also on

23 airfields were one testimony to the role of American air power, as well as to its apparent vulnerability. Over two divisions were used for the attacks in and close to Saigon, but these attacks were largely contained and overcome within several days. The most serious and longest battle was waged for control of the city of Hué, the former imperial capital, which was located in northern South Vietnam, close to the border with North Vietnam. Much of Hué fell to the Viet Cong on 31 January. The city, a natural defensive position, was not regained until 25 February, after both difficult house-to-house struggles within its walls and an eventually successful cutting off of supply routes into the city. The Americans lost 216 dead, the South Vietnamese forces 384 dead, and their opponents over 5,000. Part of the nature of the conflict, as well as its brutality, were shown by the slaughter or 'disappearance' of about 5,000 South Vietnamese civilians by the Viet Cong during their occupation: their crime was that they came from social categories judged unacceptable in the Maoist society that the Communists were trying to create. The massive use of air and artillery power by the Americans during the recapture of Hué destroyed about half of the city, making over 100,000 people homeless. Such an outcome was an aspect of the social dissolution that resulted from the war, a dissolution that gave a powerful advantage to the Communists who had a clear vision of the new society they sought to create and enforce. By the end of February 1968, however, it was clear that the North Vietnamese/Viet Cong Tet Offensive had failed to achieve its goals. There was no popular uprising, and the Americans and South Vietnamese had not been defeated, although their losses were heavier than in earlier battles.

More generally, the Tet Offensive epitomised a situation in which, while the Americans could repel mass attacks on their strong points, and drop thousands of bombs from a great height without opposition, their will for the war was worn down by its continuation, while they could not deny control of the countryside to their opponents. American units suffered from a lack of accurate intelligence, and this lack helped to lead them into ambushes. General Vo Nguyen Giap, the North Vietnamese commander and a student of Napoleon's campaigns, was an effective leader who developed logistical capability to give effect to his strategy of denying his opponents (first France, and then South Vietnam and the USA) control over territory while maintaining operational pressure on them. Giap was less successful when he turned to positional warfare and to mass attacks against opposing forces in reasonable positions, as in 1951 against the French, and in 1968 and 1972 against the South Vietnamese and Americans. However, his military strategy and also the political determination of the North Vietnamese government did not depend on continual success, which was an important key to their effectiveness.

In more specific terms, the jungle nature of the Vietnamese terrain limited the options for American airpower, which was applied for strategic, opera-tional and tactical goals. The tactical use of air power played an important role in helping army and marine units under attack, as at Khe Sanh in 1968, complementing artillery support in this valuable role. Over half the $200 billion the USA spent on the war, a sum far greater than that spent by other Western powers on decolonisation struggles, went on air operations, and nearly eight million tons of bombs were dropped on Vietnam, Laos and Cambodia; South Vietnam became the most heavily bombed country in the history of warfare. There were also major American bombing offensives against North Vietnam, which were designed both to limit Northern support for the war in the South and to affect policy in the North by driving the North Vietnamese to negotiate. These attacks faced serious opposition from Soviet SAM surface-to-air missiles, supplied from April 1965, as well as from Soviet MIG-17 and MIG-21 aircraft. American use of electronic jamming in order to limit attacks by missiles and radar-controlled guns had considerable success, but the North Vietnamese learned, in part, to counter this by aiming at the jamming signals.[85] Prisoners taken from American planes that were shot down gave the North Vietnamese a valuable negotiating card that they also used in their struggle to influence American domestic opinion, a struggle that critics of the war within America also waged. More seriously in operational terms, the failure of the Marines and the Navy to accept Air Force pressure for operational co-operation in the shape of a single airpower manager, a turf issue, had major consequences. This failure not only inhibited a consistent level of attack and thus maximising American capabilities, but also prevented the sharing of lessons. This instance was but part of a more general failure of American preparedness which encompassed inappropriate doctrine and aircraft, as well as inadequate command, command and training.[86]

As an instance of the difficulty of assessing military history, controversy continues over the extent to which, among other options,[87] a more determined (less reluctant and restricted) and persistent air campaign would have ensured American victory. American policymakers seeking to contain the struggle were reluctant to use an all-out non-nuclear air attack with unrestricted targeting and were affected by the idea that, by means of gradual escalation, they could send appropriate messages and affect their opponents' decisions.[88] This view was not to be vindicated by the Vietnam War. Writing to an American correspondent in July 1965, the distinguished British military theorist J. F. C. Fuller argued: 'Today your government and its military advisors appear to have accepted the concept that the way to defeat Communism in Vietnam is by bombing when clearly the precepts garnered from World War Two should have told them that ideas cannot be dislodged by bombs'.[89] There were also the terrible human consequences. Widespread napalm bombing alongside free-fire artillery zones caused appalling casualties and created enormous uncertainty and stress for South Vietnamese civilians. Conversely, the proponents of airpower claim that, had Operation Rolling Thunder (the restricted bombing of the North) continued (instead of ending in 1968), it would have led the North to yield.

However, Rolling Thunder had certainly not stopped the Tet Offensive.[90] Alternatively, a drive west of the Demilitarized Zone between North and South Vietnam to cut the Ho Chi Minh Trail, a policy rejected during the war, has also been hotly debated subsequently. So also has a 'northern' hook landing (similar to Inchon in 1950) around the port of Vinh in North Vietnam and west into the entrances to the Trail. It is also unclear why Johnson was unwilling to mine the port of Haiphong, through which the Soviet Union was supplying North Vietnam. This was a step Nixon was to take in 1972. Given that Soviet assistance was playing a role in challenging the situation in South Vietnam, it is unclear why Johnson did not take a symmetrical step. He appears to have been led by his fears.

At any rate, airpower played a major role in the unsuccessful attempt to block Viet Cong supply routes, as well as the more successful endeavour to provide tactical and supply support for American troops on the ground. Tactical air-support led to the use of slow-flying gunships able to apply massive firepower, although the Viet Cong were proficient in entrenching in order to minimise their losses. Moreover, helicopters were extensively employed, not least in supplying positions and in applying the doctrine of airmobility: airlifted troops brought mobility and helped take the war to the enemy. As an instance of the scale of conflict, the Americans flew about 36,125,000 helicopter sorties during the war, including 7,547,000 assault sorties, in which machine-guns and rockets were used, plus 3,932,000 attack sorties. Over 2,000 helicopters were lost to hostile causes (and many others to accidents), but heavier losses had been anticipated. Helicopters had become more reliable, more powerful, and faster than in the 1950s, and their use helped to overcome the serious challenge of guerrilla methods to land supply and communication routes. The French had made extensive and effective use of them in Algeria; and the Portuguese did so in their African colonies, although the effectiveness of the latter was affected in the 1970s by the Soviet provision of surface-to-air missiles to the anti-Portuguese insurrectionary movements.

The Americans had to adapt to fight in difficult and unfamiliar circumstances in Vietnam, including dense jungle and rice paddies. The jungle nature of much of the terrain gave the Viet Cong ideal cover, and ensured that superior American technology had little to aim at. Partly as a result, both Westmoreland's quest for battle, in which American firepower could be applied in order to ensure successful attrition, and the search-and-destroy operations, pursued until 1968 in order to build up a 'body count' of dead Viet Cong, were each of limited effectiveness, not least because it was difficult to 'fix' the Viet Cong. The Americans lacked adequate intelligence of their opponents' moves. Instead, the Viet Cong tended to control the tempo of much of the fighting, mounting ambushes that caused heavy casualties, and then ambushing relief units in their turn. The problems of pursuing conventional warfare had been noted in 1959 by Allen Dulles, the Director of the CIA. He had explained to the Senate Foreign Relations

Committee that in Cuba 'what you need against guerrillas are guerrillas ... It is rough country, and there is no use sending tanks and heavy artillery up there'.[91]

As with the air offensive against Viet Cong supply lines, the Americans displayed a preference for seeing the Viet Cong as a regular force that could be beaten by conventional means, in short, existing American equipment and doctrine; rather than seeking an understanding of Viet Cong doctrine and operational methods. Furthermore, the creation of a political organisation by the Viet Cong, ensured that more than the defeat of the guerrillas was required. The American army, however, bereft of an adequate counter-insurgency doctrine,[92] and lacking a reliable political base in South Vietnam, preferred to seek a military solution, and to emphasise big-unit operations, not pacification. Analysis that was unwelcome was ignored, while other findings were manipulated.[93] In practice, without pacification, American operations were of limited value and, instead, alienated civilian support. Many Americans found it difficult to try to understand the nature of the war they were engaged in, and to appreciate the extent to which their opponents, by refusing to fight on American terms, nullified American advantages, and thus multiplied the difficulties that the terrain posed for the Americans. The Americans failed to appreciate that, although they had more firepower and mobility than the French had done in Vietnam, they were faced with the same problems of Communist determination, and that, even if it was achieved, victory in battle would not change this.[94]

Creighton Abrams, who became American commander (of Military Assistance Command, Vietnam) in June 1968, preferred to rely on small-scale patrols and ambushes, which, he argued, provided less of a target for his opponents than large-scale sweeps. Some recent scholarship has queried the conventional contrast between Westmoreland and Abrams, and has argued, instead, that the former had a more subtle approach than one based on firepower. It has been suggested that, while both men believed in the use of American firepower to defeat Communist main force units, equally both men understood the need for the pacification of the countryside and for building up the South Vietnamese military which, however, lacked the reliability and fighting effectiveness of the South Korean army during the Korean War. In this account, Westmoreland had to employ particular tactics to confront an opposing field army that was backing a popular insurrection. Abrams, in contrast, appears to follow a different generalship, but in practice that was largely due to a switch in Viet Cong strategy after the Tet Offensive, towards guerrilla warfare.

An impressive commander, Abrams set out to contest the village-level support the Viet Cong enjoyed and to counter the impact of Tet, which had led to a regrouping of American and South Vietnamese troops as units were pulled back to defend the cities. The Americans also tried to lure the Communists onto killing grounds by establishing 'fire bases': positions supported by artillery and infantry. In 1969, the Americans inflicted serious blows on the Viet Cong, whose capability had already been badly compromised by the failure of the Tet Offensive in which the Viet Cong and the North Vietnamese had lost close to half the troops used. Viet Cong attacks in 1969 suffered heavy casualties and achieved little.[95] Conversely, the Communists came to rely in the 1970s more heavily on conventional operations mounted by the North Vietnamese. This was a consequence not only of the casualties and damage that Tet had inflicted on the Viet Cong, but also of the inability of Rolling Thunder, the bombing of North Vietnam launched in March 1965, to destroy the war-supporting capability of North Vietnam, and of the failure of the air offensives launched against the Ho Chi Minh Trail. The latter was crucial to North Vietnamese logistics, and the unwillingness and inability to cut it on the ground was a major limitation in American war making. Although American and South Vietnamese counter-insurgency policies worked in some parts of Vietnam, they were generally unsuccessful; conversely, there was no general pro-Viet Cong uprising in response to the Tet Offensive. The American pacification programme entailed a 'battle for hearts and minds', involving American-backed economic and political reforms. These reforms were difficult to implement, not only due to Viet Cong opposition and intimidation, and the effectiveness of their guerrilla and small-unit operations, but also because the South Vietnamese government was half-hearted, corrupt and weak, and thus unable to take advantage of military success.[96] The Americans could not find or create a popular alternative to the Viet Cong. As the Americans also brought much disruption, including high inflation, and devastation through the use of firepower, pacification faced additional problems. In addition, the culture-clash between the Americans and their South Vietnamese allies hindered co-operation.[97]

Mounting domestic financial and economic problems, as well as increasing political opposition, and his own growing disillusionment at continued signs of North Vietnamese vitality, had led Johnson to reject, in March 1968, Westmoreland's request for an additional 206,000 men in Vietnam. His views were confirmed by a policy review by a group of senior outside advisers, the 'Wise Men'. Instead, Johnson authorised only 13,500 more troops.[98] Military difficulties, combined with political pressures within the USA, resulted in an attempt to shift more of the burden back on the South Vietnamese army by improving its capability, and some success was achieved. Indeed, Vietnamese units fought better in response to the Tet offensive than had been anticipated. Yet, the context was very different to the use of large numbers of native troops in European imperial forces earlier in the century, for example the major contribution by Indian troops to British hegemony in South Asia.

Moreover, in what was reasonably described as the 'First Television War', domestic opposition in America to involvement in Vietnam rose, because of the duration of the conflict, because the goals seemed ill-defined, and, increasingly, as an aspect of the counter-cultural movement of these years which proved particularly attractive to the young. The latter opposition, which was very different to the situation during the Korean War, has attracted most attention in retrospect. However, it is important to remember also the wider-ranging basis of political criticism of the war. Their leadership divided on policy, the Americans had lost the strategic initiative, but there was already a lack of deep commitment. Dean Rusk, the Secretary of State, later commented:

> we never made any effort to create a war psychology in the United States during the Vietnam affair. We didn't have military parades through cities. We didn't have beautiful movie stars out selling war bonds in factories and things like that as we did during World War II. We felt that in a nuclear world it is just too dangerous for an entire people to get too angry and we deliberately played this down. We tried to do in cold blood perhaps what can only be done in hot blood.[99]

By denying the Americans victory in the field, and, instead, continuing to inflict casualties, the North Vietnamese and Viet Cong helped to create political pressures within America and to sap the will to fight; although their objectives were focused on success in South Vietnam: affecting American public opinion was only a side-issue. In the USA, the absence of victory resulted in many seeing the continuing casualties as futile, especially when the Tet Offensive led to the questioning of repeated optimistic Pentagon pronouncements about the course of the conflict. In contrast, North Vietnamese military strategy, and the political determination of its government, did not depend on popular support. The conscription necessary to sustain a large-scale American presence in an increasingly unpopular war played a major role in the growth of disenchantment. A majority of the Americans who went to Vietnam were volunteers, not draftees (conscripts). Nevertheless, in 1965–73, about two million Americans were drafted, and draftees accounted for a third of American deaths in Vietnam by 1969. The draft led to a massive increase in anti-war sentiment. Opposition was widely voiced and 'draft dodging' common, with many Americans taking refuge in Canada. The war was fought with soldiers who were, on average, younger and less educated than those who had taken part in World War Two. The education exemption and family '9' (fatherhood) exempted many citizens. Johnson abandoned his re-election bid on 31 March 1968 because he had failed to end the war and was facing a challenge from within the Democratic Party which was now very divided over the war. Once elected, his successor, Richard Nixon, the Republican candidate, who had promised peace with honour, pressed ahead with substituting Vietnamese for American troops, so that he could bring the troops back home, end the draft (conscription),[100] and reduce the political cost of the war while, he hoped, securing an acceptable outcome.

# The Middle East

The sense of failure in Vietnam contributed to a growing note of American alarm elsewhere. Far from the Soviet Union and Communism being contained, there were worrying signs in the late 1960s of their ability to act across much of the world. In particular, the situation in the Middle East became more threatening. Despite American aid, including wheat, to Egypt, Soviet influence in the Middle East rose from 1964. Crucially, President Nasser of Egypt, the impulsive leader of the pan-Arabist cause, decided that such an alignment would best serve his purposes. In part, this decision reflected the extent to which the Soviet Union was willing to back change and thus align with Arab nationalism and revisionist powers, whereas the USA served rather to support stability. In 1958, Syria joined Egypt as part of the United Arab Republic, the pro-Western regime in Iraq was overthrown in a bloody coup, and the USA sent 14,000 Marines to Beirut to protect the Lebanese government from what it claimed was the threat of international Communism, but what, in practice, was that of Nasserism. At the same time, Britain dispatched troops to protect Jordan. Both these interventions proved successful, as was 1961 British assistance to Kuwait against Iraqi territorial claims. In addition, although more cautiously, the USA, from 1963, backed Saudi Arabia in its support for the Royalist opposition to the Egyptian military that from 1962 had intervened in North Yemen to assist a coup by republican officers, led by General Abdullah al-Sallal, who had proclaimed the Yemen Arab Republic. American interests in Saudi stability and oil were countered by Egyptian calls for the overthrow of the Saudi regime, part of Nasser's demand for a more radical Arab world. The conflict in North Yemen proved an intractable, costly and unpopular commitment for Egypt, indeed its own Vietnam. Nasser ironically, but typically, took sides in the latter, backing Soviet support for 'wars of national liberation' in 1964 and inviting the Viet Cong to open an embassy in Egypt in 1965.

Unable to cope with inherent incompatibilities and with Syrian anger at direction from Egypt, the United Arab Republic had come to an end in 1961 when Syria seceded. However, tension increased in the Middle East in 1966 when Hafez al-Assad (father of the current President of Syria) and the Ba'ath party took control of Syria and reached an agreement with the Soviet Union which led to arms supplies. As a result, modern Soviet arms were now on Israel's northern border just as they were already found in Egypt. In November 1966, an Egyptian-Syrian defence treaty seemed to move Egypt closer to Syria's desire for war with Israel, and, thereby, also increasingly committed the Soviet Union. The provision of large quantities of modern arms had long helped to lend added danger to the regional conflict. In 1955, the Soviets, through Czechoslovakia, had agreed to provide 200 MIG-15 fighters, 50 Ilyushin-28 bombers and hundreds of tanks to Egypt. In 1956, an Egyptian-Soviet arms agreement led to the sending of 800

Soviet advisers. Similarly, a French-Israeli arms agreement in June 1956 had encouraged Israeli bellicosity; opposed to Nasser, the French armed Israel until 1967 and, in the late 1950s, jointly developed atomic weaponry.[101]

France's role was to be taken by the USA because, once out of Algeria in 1962, the French pursued improved Arab ties, while the USA changed policy. In 1957, in the aftermath of the Suez Crisis, Eisenhower's threat to impose economic sanctions had led Israel to withdraw its troops from the Sinai and Gaza which they had conquered from Egypt the previous year. However, as part of the agreement, the USA guaranteed Israel's right of passage, via the Straits of Tiran between the Sinai and Saudi Arabia, into the Red Sea, while the United Nations agreed to station observers along the Egyptian frontier. Part of the disengagement agreement was that the Egyptians would agree to letting Israeli ships go through the Suez Canal. This provision Nasser soon ignored. In the late 1950s, relations between Israel and the USA were not close, as Eisenhower then strove to improve relations with Nasser, a policy that continued under Kennedy. However, angered by Egyptian hostility and adventurism, as well as by deliberately provocative steps, such as the sacking of the offices of the American Information Agency in Cairo in December 1964, Johnson was less emollient than Kennedy towards Nasser. By 1966, Johnson saw Israel as a potential strategic support for the USA in the face of national liberation wars, while also being mindful of pro-Israeli feeling in Congress, notably among his Democratic colleagues. Having agreed to sell tanks to Israel in 1965, Johnson followed with aircraft in 1966.

Meanwhile, regional tensions had increased as a result of guerrilla attacks by al-Fatah and the Palestinian Liberation Organisation (PLO), founded in 1958 and 1964 respectively. These were followed, in 1966, by Israeli reprisal attacks on Palestinian bases in Jordan. The Soviet Union publicly backed what it termed the 'legitimate and inalienable rights of the Palestinian Arabs'. In 1967, Syrian artillery joined in, shelling Israel from the Golan Heights (which it had sporadically done for a number of years) as a sign of solidarity with the PLO. The Israeli air force acted to destroy the artillery batteries and shot down Syrian MIGs on 7 April 1966. In intelligence supplied to the Egyptians, that was possibly motivated by a wish to secure a naval base in Egypt, the Soviet Union exaggerated the possibility that Israel might attack the Golan, both vowing support and stirring up Nasser to help protect Syria.[102] Nasser was encouraged in his blustering by his desire to retain the leadership of the Arab cause, as the aggressive attitude of the new Syrian government towards Israel challenged his prestige. Nasser also felt under pressure from economic problems arising from his seriously misguided attempt to force-start the economy through state planning, a method that repeatedly failed. These failures were an important aspect of the geopolitics of the Cold War. They also need to be set against, or, at least, alongside the repeated criticisms of the neo-liberalism of the West in the 1980s, criticisms that imply that statist systems were better. Nasser's expulsion of the UN observers from the Sinai and Gaza frontier ordered on 16 May, and his closure of the Straits of Tiran to all Israeli shipping on 23 May 1967, provoked Israel. Nasser's steps also reflected a failure to appreciate the limitations of the Egyptian military, which, in turn, was greatly concerned about Yemen, where several of its leading units were deployed.

## The Six Day War

The closure of the Straits of Tiran was regarded by the Israeli government as an act of war. Keen to avoid a fresh international crisis, the Americans both urged Israel to avoid conflict and unsuccessfully pressed the Soviet Union to get Nasser to reopen the Straits. However, failure to produce a solution led Johnson to accept the idea of an attack on Egypt.[103] Israel attacked, to devastating effect, on 5 June, notably with the rapid destruction of the Egyptian air force in a surprise attack. Nasser inaccurately claimed that the USA had taken part in the attack. This destruction helped ensure the speedy victory of attacking Israeli forces in the Gaza Strip and the Sinai Peninsula. Nasser sought help from the Soviets and from other Arab states. Jordan provided the latter, resulting in the rapid Israeli conquest of East Jerusalem and the neighbouring West Bank, part of Palestine acquired/conquered (the choice of word can be debated) by Jordan in the 1948–9 Arab-Israeli war, the War of the Partition of Palestine. Responding to Soviet advice, the Syrians refused to provide assistance to Egypt, but there was some shelling of Israeli positions. On 9 June, with Egypt and Jordan defeated, Israel attacked. The Israeli government was keen to take advantage of an opportunity to occupy the Golan Heights from which Israel could be threatened and water obtained, and possibly to force a change in the Syrian government. Gaining the initiative, and using their aerial superiority for ground attack, the Israelis benefited from superior fighting quality and from a collapse in Syrian morale, and advanced to forty miles from the capital, Damascus.

Threatening to intervene, the Soviet Union made preparations to do so. Johnson responded with both conciliation and brinkmanship. Israel was urged to accept a UN-sanctioned ceasefire while, to pre-empt the possibility of a Soviet attack on Israel, the American Sixth Fleet was sent into the war zone. Both Israel and the Soviet Union backed down, Israel accepting the ceasefire. Israel was left with formidable gains: Sinai, the Gaza Strip, East Jerusalem, the West Bank (Jordan west of the River Jordan), and the Golan Heights; while Nasser and the cause of pan-Arabism were much weakened. However, the possibility that the regional crisis would continue to endanger super-power relations remained. Johnson swiftly offered a peace plan including Israeli withdrawal, and Arab commitment to a peace treaty and, therefore, recognition of Israel. This plan proved the basis for

UN Security Council Resolution 242; but implementation proved impossible not least because of Nasser's continued unwillingness to accept Israel. Soviet willingness to rearm Egypt and Syria, and with improved weaponry and advisers, contributed to the continuing crisis. On a quick trip to Cairo in the immediate aftermath of the war, Aleksei Kosygin, the Soviet Prime Minister, had stated that the Six Day War was an American attack on Soviet allies. He argued that American imperialism and its agent, Israel, were intent on throwing back Arab progressive forces and their supporter, the Soviet Union, and on maintaining – or even increasing – Western control ('imperialism') in the region. Kosygin promised resupply. Tension was also increased by the stepping up of PLO attacks on Israeli positions. More generally, the PLO played a major role in advancing the cause of liberation movements, which, in turn, provided the Soviet Union and China with means to extend their influence.[104] Aerial dogfights and artillery bombardments between Egypt and Israel in 'the War of Attrition' from late 1967 suggested that the situation might deteriorate. Moreover, the rapid build-up of the Soviet navy challenged the American position in the Mediterranean, not least as the American navy was stretched by its Vietnam commitment. In 1968, in response to Israeli requests, the USA decided to send Israel Phantom F4 jets, thus providing a cutting-edge capability. The Soviets in response deployed air and air defence units to Egypt, although these were also designed to improve the Soviet capacity to keep tabs on the American Sixth Fleet in the Mediterranean.[105]

# Eastern Europe

Continued Soviet strength and determination in Europe were demonstrated in August 1968 when about 250,000 Soviet troops, backed by Polish, Hungarian, Bulgarian and East German forces, suppressed a liberalising Communist regime in Czechoslovakia. Economic failure in Czechoslovakia in 1961 had contributed to a call for political reform, and Antonín Novotný, the President and First Secretary of the Party, a Stalinist, had been replaced in 1968 as First Secretary by Alexander Dubček who called for 'Socialism with a human face' and 'a new start to Socialism'. To the concern of the Soviet Union and other Communist states, this 'new start' involved a dilution of Communist control. In the Prague Spring, there was an abolition of censorship and increased freedom of speech. As far as the Soviet, East German, Polish and Hungarian leaderships' point of view was concerned, Dubček's loosening of the grip was tantamount to the Czech Communist Party losing its grip. From the Soviet perspective, the Czech failure to consult Moscow was as significant. Petro Shelest, the Ukrainian Party leader was concerned that, in the summer of 1968, Ukrainian dissidents (who were called nationalists in the Western Ukraine) were agitating for less repressiveness in Ukrainian cultural affairs. Yuri Andropov, the head of the KGB, Andrei Grechko, the new Minister of Defence, who was more militant towards the West than his predecessor in 1957–67 Rodion Malinovskii, and Kirill Mazurov, the Belorussian Party boss, were also displeased. The Soviet military was unhappy with the substandard performance of the Czech army during Warsaw Pact manoeuvres. This made the Soviet High Command feel that the Czech salient into southern Germany was vulnerable. The easternmost tip of Czechoslovakia touched Ukraine and was not far from Belorussia (Belarus). However, a division of opinion within the Politburo on what course of action to choose led to a sluggish Soviet response during the summer of 1968.

The Czech reformers had insisted that, unlike Hungary in 1956, Czechoslovakia would remain loyal to the Warsaw Pact and that the 'leading' role of the Communist Party would be retained, but, to the leadership of other Warsaw Pact states (bar independent Romania), the moves in Prague were signs of counter-revolution linked to the USA and West Germany, and threatened such a departure. On 18 August, in Moscow, the Soviet, East German, Hungarian, Polish and Bulgarian leaders met and agreed that an invasion was necessary to change the Czech Communist Party leadership and to insert a new regime that would be loyal to the Soviet Union. A group of hardliners in Czechoslovakia sent a 'letter of invitation' to the Soviet government claiming that 'the very existence of Socialism in our country is threatened' and pressing Brezhnev to use 'all means you have in your disposal, to help. Brezhnev explained the Warsaw Pact invasion by stating that it was intended to thwart the movement of Czechoslovakia out of the Pact. Thus, self-defence and 'fraternal assistance' in the cause of 'Socialist solidarity' was at stake. This was to become what was termed the Brezhnev doctrine, a justification of intervention to maintain 'Socialism', i.e. Communism. Some of the invading troops were told (totally inaccurately) that they were acting in response to a West German invasion of Czechoslovakia, which was a frontline Warsaw Pact state. Control was rapidly established. Dubček was flown to Moscow, allegedly in handcuffs. In the Soviet Union, workers were required to attend meetings to show their support for the invasion of Czechoslovakia. A small public demonstration in Moscow was brutally suppressed.

The official Western response to the invasion was muted. American forces had been drained from West Germany to Vietnam, which was one reason why the invasion of Czechoslovakia could be mounted so confidently. Far from deploying forces, as the Soviets claimed, NATO pulled some of them back. The USA at this time could have airlifted no more than 10,000 troops per day from North America to Europe, whereas the Warsaw Pact moved in 250,000 troops within 24 hours. The Soviets knew of this weakness. In early 1968, in the aftermath of French disengagement from NATO, from 1962 and, even more, 1966, there were press pieces, for example in *U.S. Business and News Report*, pondering the future of NATO as there no longer appeared a clear reason for its existence. The invasion of Czechoslovakia changed that. Non-violent protests in Czechoslovakia had a major impact on international opinion, and followed Hungary in 1956 in lessening Western support for the Soviet experiment. These protests, however, failed to dislodge the Soviets. Indeed, Czechoslovakia remained under firm Communist control until the fall of the Soviet bloc.

The suppression of the Czech reform movement was followed by the reimposition of a police state. 'Normalisation' entailed the purging of many members of the Communist Party, including Dubček in 1970, and the harassing of dissident groups. The nature of the Communist police state was different to the situation under Stalin, as European Communist regimes after the Stalin era did not routinely execute, still less slaughter, their citizens for political crimes. However, reliant on widespread surveillance, coercion, and the governmental control of the legal system, the state remained repressive across Eastern Europe and the Soviet Union. Those regarded as unacceptable were readily incarcerated, sentenced to internal exile, or, in the Soviet Union, committed to psychiatric clinics (*psikhushki*) where they were deliberately driven mad. Dissidents were increasingly sent to the Serbsky Institute and the Butyrskaya Prison Psychiatric hospital where they were diagnosed with sluggish schizophrenia and forcibly treated with psychotropic drugs. Work camps could be – in effect – a death sentence. The fate of dissidents tarnished Communist claims to political virtue and compromised or alienated Western European supporters. Moreover, the exposure of Communist policies made the international acceptance of the Communist bloc through normalisation sinister. In Poland, Jacek Kuron and Karol Modzelewski were sentenced in 1965 to three years in prison for writing an *Open Letter to the Party* in which they accused Communist authorities of stealing power from the workers and creating a dictatorship of the party bureaucracy. This led their students at Warsaw University to organise a campus group known as the Commandos for their tactic of asking party intellectuals difficult questions. Calls for democratic freedoms in March 1968 led to the brutal beating of students by police, as well as to a purge of universities and government. An intra-Party struggle played a key element, with Mieczystaw Moczar, an open anti-Semite, unsuccessfully seeking the post of Party Secretary occupied by Gomulka. Moczar used anti-Semitism as a means to purge those in the Party he castigated. Many Polish Jews found it expedient to emigrate. At the same time, and more profoundly, the Communist regimes experienced grave problems in their own capacity to govern, not least because much of the population proved adept at subverting the demands of the state, while its institutions did likewise. The regular manipulation of production targets and the evasion by individuals of internal passport and residence regulation requirements were the case even under Stalin, but became endemic during the 1960s and 1970s.

# Economic Challenges in the West

Alongside particular challenges for the West in the 1960s, there were problems posed by American economic and fiscal difficulties. This situation had seemed very promising in the 1950s. Thanks to the geopolitics of the Cold War, the Americans were then able to preside over, and organise, the most powerful part of the global economy, and to benefit from its growth, not least by disseminating the products, images and values of American consumer culture. There was a positive synergy, with the expansion of the global economy providing multiple investment and export opportunities for the USA, while the introduction of American technology and techniques, and the availability of the American market, provided opportunities for growth in Japan and Western Europe. The Marshall Plan contributed to this take-off. The economies of the non-Communist world benefited from the greater availability of capital and from a major increase in trade, which encouraged specialisation and economies of scale. Moreover, the efficiency of the international economic system was increased by structural reforms and by improved communications. Economic growth, in turn, helped provide the resources for a stronger military posture.

However, there was a major deterioration in the American position in the 1960s that gathered pace as the decade advanced. Growth rates then proved higher in Western Europe and Japan, in part as a consequence of their recovery from wartime damage and, in part, the possibility of making rapid advances by introducing American techniques and capital. Moreover, it proved difficult to sustain earlier rates of American innovation and productivity growth. As a result of rapid German and Japanese economic development, the USA faced increasing problems, first in some export markets and then in the domestic market. Part of the American economy was dominated by large corporations closely linked to major trade unions in a corporatist system in which the unions were bought off and increased costs passed to consumers. Innovation was stymied, not least because there was no wish to change working rules that would upset the unions. In contrast, the Japanese were far more innovative on the production line, notably in the prestigious field of car manufacture. By 1967–8, the USA was experiencing 2 per cent GNP growth, a rate that was increasingly regarded as evidence of a sick economy. The lacklustre competitiveness of certain categories of American goods within the American market, in relation to a growing popularity for better-made goods from Japan, West Germany and the Netherlands, began to affect the American economy.

In the USA, inflationary pressures also owed much to the decision to pay for both the Vietnam War and the 'Great Society' programme of social improvement by borrowing, rather than the increased taxation that consumerism made unwelcome. Public debt per capita rose from $1,585 in 1960 to $1,811 in 1970. Inflation rose and Johnson's 1966 sur-tax was not enough to deal with the problem. Loose money policies, notably in the USA, led to an inflation that spread through the global economy. Moreover, it was increasingly difficult to control financial flows in what had become a far larger world economy. Whereas liquidity had been largely restricted to the USA in 1945, and the American government had then in the late 1940s extended it to other governments, especially as Marshall Aid, by the late 1960s, liquidity was widely distributed and therefore difficult to control, while balance of payments deficits contributed to a fall in American gold reserves. At the same time as a crisis in Vietnam War policy and in presidential politics, dollars were abandoned for gold in March 1968 in a panic which led the American Treasury to restrict its willingness to exchange them.

# Conclusions

American problems looked toward a West that was less dominated by the USA, as was demonstrated in 1966 when Charles de Gaulle, a determined nationalist who disliked the idea of following an American lead or co-operating with Britain, took France out of the integrated NATO military command. Already, in 1962, de Gaulle had had the Americans remove their back-up supplies from France. He did not like the idea of European civilisation as dependent on the superpowers. NATO was left compromised by the changes of the late 1960s. French policy meant that a strategy of defence-in-depth for Western Europe was no longer viable. In addition, the invasion of Czechoslovakia put 80,000 Soviet troops in Western Czechoslovakia, in the bulge abutting the American forces in Bavaria.

Moreover, growing opposition to the Vietnam War compromised America's global reputation. This problem was exacerbated by the inability to end the conflict. This military and political intractability interacted with a sense, within America, of frustration, failure and, even, of redundancy in aspects of America's society, politics, culture, international stance and alliance system. Large-scale race-poverty riots in American cities, such as Detroit, in 1968, were seen by critics and opponents as a new battle-line for the American system. 'Black Power' demands were interpreted by some in terms of the Cold War. As an aspect of the criticism of the American system, academics and other commentators provided questioning, indeed hostile, accounts of American policy during the Cold War, both of government policy and that of American business.

Ironically, but far less prominently, a similar process of the weakening of the hegemonic power was in train in the Eastern Bloc. In part, the Soviet position in Eastern Europe was less solid than hitherto, with Romania, from which Soviet forces withdrew in 1958, in particular pursuing an independent course under Nicolae Ceauşescu, who became First Secretary

of the Communist Party in 1965, adding the Presidency of the State Council
in 1967. He was angry at the Soviet reorganisation of COMECON's
production and trade priorities in 1964. This had seemed to relegate
Bulgaria and Romania to the position of exporters of raw materials and
importers of finished goods, as if they were in the Third World. In response,
pursuing commercial and political benefits, Ceaușcescu sought to establish
better ties with West Germany and Yugoslavia. In 1975, Romania won
American Most-Favored-Nation trade status. Romanian policy irritated
the Soviet government which was also apprehensive that Ceaușcescu's
independent streak could set a bad example. However, the Soviets knew
that the Romanians, notably after liberalisation was abandoned in July
1971, were more repressive than they were and, therefore, did not bother
establishing security zones on the Romanian border as they did on the
Polish border. The Warsaw Pact achieved better force integration after
1968, and the Soviets, earlier, had not had much faith in the Czech army.
Nevertheless, the invasion of Czechoslovakia in 1968 also challenged the
capabilities and readiness of Warsaw Pact forces, as a lack of certainty
about the loyalty of national contingents weakened the alliance.

More seriously, growing rivalry between China and the Soviet Union
became acute. A longstanding Soviet failure to treat the Chinese Communists
as equals was exacerbated by Mao Zedong's anger at a failure of consultation over Soviet policy changes. Mao had been angered over Khrushchev's
1956 20th Party Congress speech attacking Stalin, by Khrushchev's unwillingness to meet Chinese requests for help in building a nuclear bomb,
and by his isolation of Mao at the March 1960 Bucharest International
Communist Party Congress. Khrushchev in a volatile manner denounced
the Chinese Communist Party for not embracing 'peaceful existence', for
deviating from the Soviet policy of heavy industrialisation, and for erratic
twists in policy. The Chinese likewise denounced the Soviet Communist
Party, accusing it of revisionism, trying to curry favour with Western
imperialists, and, in general, retreating from Stalin's line. Most of the
world Communist Parties had sent delegations to Bucharest, and both the
Soviets and the Chinese knew this in advance and were prepared to read
one another out of the international Communist movement. Claiming that
the real division was between North and South, not West and East, Mao
argued that the Soviet project was like that of the Western powers, and that
they both pursued imperialism. The Soviets knew by the late 1950s that
they could not count on the Chinese as reliable allies. The Soviets withdrew
their technical experts from China in the early 1960s, while China called
home its students from the Soviet Union. There was disagreement over
Khrushchev's handling of the 1962 Cuban Missile Crisis and over how to
support North Vietnam's struggle in South Vietnam. The Soviet government
regarded Mao as quixotic, and dangerously so. Mao's pursuit of allies
among the Communist powers in South-East Europe, notably Albania,
struck the Soviets as an incursion into their back yard. Under Enver Hoxha,

who remained a committed Stalinist, Albania had broken off diplomatic relations with the Soviet Union in 1961 and left the Warsaw Pact in 1968. Border disputes between the Soviet Union and China led to fighting in March 1969 over Damanskii/Zhenbao Island in the Ussuri/Ussuli River. The Soviet forces were able to use their massed artillery to drive back the Chinese, who could not maintain unit cohesion above the battalion level. The Chinese indulged in corpse-mutilation of the Soviet troops they ambushed. This fighting made the Sino-Soviet rift readily apparent. The rift thereby altered global geopolitics and greatly complicated the theme of civilisational struggle between the Communist and non-Communist worlds, at the same time as it underlined the range of Communist strategies on offer. There were also some small-scale border fights in 1966 between North Korea and China.

Alongside growing American problems, a sense of an international system in flux became more apparent in 1968. This sense was encouraged by the dissolution of the Western empires, a dissolution that accentuated a perception of volatility. The understanding of the Cold War at the time was affected by this volatility. Alongside uncertainty about developments, there was a growing lack of agreement about the purpose and intentions of both sides. This situation was to encourage new initiatives in the 1970s. These initiatives ranged from the American approach to China to the West German *Ostpolitik*. They were largely the result of the pressures of particular conjunctures, such as Nixon's need to negotiate an end to the Vietnam War. However, these initiatives both reflected a sense of greater fluidity and contributed greatly to it.

# CHAPTER FIVE

# 1968–79

On 17 July 1975, in orbit 120 miles above the Earth, American and Soviet astronauts shook hands in space, bringing the Apollo-Soyuz Test Project to fruition. This dramatic episode had been launched by Nixon in 1972 in order to further *détente*, while the Soviet Union supported it as it offered recognition as America's equal. The television images from space were vivid, but there was still intense competition between the powers. This was not a competition in which the Americans appeared to be doing well. Once lost, the impression of American military supremacy and political strength proved difficult to recreate. The years from 1968 to 1980 provided evidence of military failure, political crisis, fiscal problems and economic weakness. The ability to contain Communism seemed unclear; indeed, by the 1960s and 1970s, the USA appeared to have resigned itself to co-existence with Communism even if the latter advanced. This ability seemed further compromised as the Western colonial empires finally collapsed, with Britain retreating from east of Suez and Portugal abandoning its centuries' old empire. This collapse focused attention even more on the USA, which found itself manning the frontline and, as it saw it, resisting Communism, all round the world. Indeed, there was a Soviet offensive in several parts of the Third World. The 1971 Indo-Soviet treaty made India's victory over Pakistan in their war that year troubling for both the USA and China.[1] Rivalry between India and Pakistan was important to the Cold War, and indicated the two-way relationship of global and regional struggles.[2] From the late 1960s, Africa and the Middle East both came to be of greater importance for the USA which, to an extent, had left both hitherto to the care of Britain. Conversely, if America did not take an interest, then it could prove difficult to resist Communism or, at least, left-wing populism. At the same time, France's often bloody-minded determination to follow its own course, combined with the West German *Ostpolitik*, suggested that the Western bloc was increasingly lacking not only central direction but even cohesion. However, NATO still hung together.

The Soviet Union did not appear confronted by economic problems (although in practice it was), but it already faced serious political difficulties in the Communist bloc. Indeed, the latter were to ensure that the Vietnam War ended with a strategic result that was very different to the situation that had been feared when the Americans intervened in strength in the early 1960s. Thanks to this, the Vietnam period ironically eventually proved a strategic success for the USA, not that it felt like this at all at the time. Moreover, although the Vietnam War dominated attention at the outset of the period as the contested frontline in the Cold War, this commitment was to end, and was not to be replaced with anything similarly problematic for the USA.

## South-East Asia

American disengagement under President Nixon, which led to a fall in the American military commitment to Vietnam, from 536,000 men when he came to office at the start of 1969, to 156,000 by the end of 1971, and 60,000 by the autumn of 1972, was not to be an easy process. In 1969, knowledge that American withdrawal was beginning, and a sense that the conflict was pointless, led to a marked, cumulative, and escalating, decline in morale and discipline among the American troops, with a major impact on fighting quality and sense of purpose. Promising 'peace with honor', Nixon had only limited success in ensuring success in South Vietnam. With 'Vietnamization', he planned to move the burden of the ground war onto the South Vietnamese army, which was over a million strong at the close of 1971. However, there were to be more American casualties after 1968 than earlier in the conflict. Moreover, 1972 was to see a North Vietnamese offensive greater in scale than that in 1968, a conventional offensive with tanks and, even more, artillery.

Nixon and Dr Henry Kissinger, his National Security Advisor (1969–73, later Secretary of State, 1973–7), were seen as realists, developing negotiations with the North Vietnamese in Paris from January 1969. At the same time, because of the failure of the earlier Paris talks in 1968, they were stuck with Vietnam, indeed extending the war in order to defend the credibility of the USA and of the Nixon presidency. There was to be no parallel with the British bolt from Aden in 1967 or that of the Portuguese from their empire in 1973–4. Initially, Nixon relied on more intensive bombing, but, when that did not work, he turned to ground action. In April 1970, Nixon widened the scope of the conflict by launching an American-South Vietnamese ground invasion of neutral, neighbouring Cambodia to destroy Communist bases there, after heavy American bombing had failed to do so. This 'incursion' succeeded in the short term, helping to strengthen the Allied position in South Vietnam which had been attacked from these bases;

while, in Cambodia, the USA provided military aid and air support for the anti-Communist government of General Lon Nol which had seized power in March 1970. In turn, the North Vietnamese provided help to the Khmer Rouge, the Cambodian Communist movement led by Pol Pot. It benefited from the vacuum of power in the Cambodian countryside. However, the American 'incursion', which was of dubious legality to put it mildly, further lessened popular and Congressional support for the war in America, and helped the Communists to seize power in Cambodia in 1975; although the prime factor then was the situation on the ground.

In February–April 1971, LAM Son 719, a comparable invasion of Laos by the South Vietnamese without American support, other than air and logistical help, failed with heavy losses in fighting with North Vietnamese units. This operation was designed to cut the Ho Chi Minh Trail, to weaken the North Vietnamese army, and to buy time before the latter could launch fresh attacks in South Vietnam. It was as a test for Vietnamization, which the Nixon government had declared was already well advanced. American ground troops could not be deployed because of Congressional restrictions after the invasion of Cambodia. In practice, the South Vietnamese army, notably its commanders, were not sufficiently prepared in the face of strong resistance and a potent counter-offensive. This invasion indeed helped delay an invasion of South Vietnam for over a year, but made eventual Communist victory in the conflict within Laos far more likely, as, indeed, was to be the case. The South Vietnamese invasion of Laos upset the 1960 tripartite political agreement among the royalist, neutral and Communist factions in Laos, although this agreement was a dead letter because of the North Vietnamese presence in Laos.[3]

# Kissinger and Geopolitics

At the same time, the USA was moving toward a new stance in East and South-East Asia, one in which the Sino-Soviet rift was employed in order to strengthen the American position. This approach drew on American geopolitical thinking earlier in the decade. In a 1962 article in *Orbis*, 'The Sino-Soviet Tangle and U.S. Policy', Robert Strausz-Hupé, an influential Viennese-born American political scientist whose successful career reflected America's openness to talent, had argued that Marxist-Leninism was weakened by its failure to rate nationalism, and that this nationalism led to tensions in Sino-Soviet relations. This situation was seen as an opportunity for the USA which, he argued, should put aside ideological preferences and seek to ally with China as the weaker of the two Communist powers. Focused on Europe, Strausz-Hupé also regarded the Soviet Union as the key threat to the USA. After his defeat by Kennedy in 1960 and his loss of the 1962 gubernatorial (governership) race in California, Nixon, then a

failed Republican politician, was interested in the argument, and he drew
on it in his article 'Asia After Viet Nam', published in *Foreign Affairs* in
October 1967. Nixon saw the possibility of China taking an independent
role as useful to the USA. Winning the 1968 presidential election against
Johnson's Vice-President, Hubert Humphrey, Nixon moved self-proclaimed
pragmatic geopoliticians to the fore. Kissinger became National Security
Advisor in 1969, and Strausz-Hupé, who had wanted that job, began a
diplomatic career as an ambassador.

Kissinger, who was Secretary of State from 1973 to 1977, found
geopolitics a pertinent term in trying to conceptualise his view of international relations. This view was one in which the emphasis was on national
interests, rather than ideological drive, and the former interests were
traced to long-term geographical commitments within a multi-polar and
competitive international system. Thus, in an anticipation of the *détente* of
the 1970s, geopolitics was linked to *realpolitik*, indeed, in part, becoming
the assessment of the international consequences of the latter. For Kissinger,
such a view was important to the understanding both of American policy
and of that of the other great powers, although this position led him to
fail to appreciate the significant ideological charge in Soviet statecraft.[4]
Kissinger's deliberate discarding of Communist ideology as a factor in
Soviet foreign policy thinking was a fundamental error for there was a
revolutionary-realism dichotomy in Soviet thinking on foreign policy.[5] In
other respects, Kissinger was perceptive, although not entirely prescient.
In addition, he could be better as a negotiator than as strategist, a point
also true of John Foster Dulles, the Secretary of State from 1953 to 1959.
Moreover, in supporting disengagement from South-East Asia within a
context of continued adherence to a robust containment of the Soviet
Union, Kissinger had to provide a defence of what appeared militarily
necessary. *Realpolitik* provided context, content and tone for the explanation of American policy.

The policy context was made more difficult by pressure on American
interests elsewhere, particularly the Middle East, as well as by the consequences of serious economic and fiscal problems. Alongside these pressures,
came the crucial matter of political location. The Republican political and
rhetorical charge in the late 1940s, one then stated vociferously by Nixon,
had been that the Truman administration had 'lost' China to Communism,
and this charge had proved a way subsequently to berate the Democrats and
notably in California. In his successful 1950 California senatorial campaign
against Helen Gahagan Douglas, Nixon slandered her as the 'Pink Lady'
and a 'fellow traveller': she had served in the Roosevelt administration in
the 1930s, which turned the Republicans against her. Similarly, Kennedy
had run for President in 1960 in part on the claim that the Eisenhower
administration, in which Nixon was Vice-President for both terms, had
failed to be sufficiently robust, not least in maintaining American defences.
Nixon was well aware of the politics of policy. As President (1969–74),

Nixon was greatly helped by Democrat divisions and the leftward move of the Democratic Party, as well as by the extent to which the 1964 Civil Rights Act and the 1965 Voting Rights Act had weakened electoral support for the Democrats in their onetime heartland in the South. However, Nixon had to consider potential criticism from within the Republican Party and the pro-war movement. As a consequence, Kissinger's rationalisation of American policy has to be understood at least in part as a political defence, a point more generally true of other rationalisations of policy.[6]

In producing this defence, Kissinger had to argue not only that the USA could align with a Communist power, but also that such an alignment could be regarded as worthwhile (rather than a form of Communist deception of a duped USA) because China and the Soviet Union had clashing geopolitical interests. This approach built on Kissinger's own background as a distinguished Harvard scholar of European international relations in the nineteenth century, when powers of a similar political system nevertheless had been rivals. A refugee from the anti-Semitism of Nazi Germany, Kissinger associated ideology, emotionalism and ostentatious moralising in foreign policy with the destructive Germany he had fled. Instead, Kissinger favoured a statesmanship based on rational calculations of national self-interest in which the stress was on order and security.[7] Far more intellectually self-conscious than most politicians, Kissinger naturally looked for similarities between past and present, and found them in the concepts and language of national interests, balance of power, geopolitics, and the pressure of Russian/Soviet expansionism. Indeed, he provided a key instance of the historicised nature of geopolitics, as opposed to the tendency of ideologies to treat the world in terms of a gradient of ideological congruence or rivalry. Thus, the USA reaching out to China, a policy advocated by both Nixon and Kissinger, had a geopolitical logic directed against the Soviet Union, rather as Britain had allied with Japan in 1902 as a response to Russian expansionism and power.

The approach just offered emphasises American needs, notably due to the state of the Vietnam War, but China's shifting position can be regarded as the key issue. Soviet border clashes with China in the late 1960s underlined Mao's concern about Soviet policy. So also did Soviet support for Lin Piao, the Minister of Defence from 1959 and Mao's heir apparent from 1968. Lin Piao had played a key role as a leading Communist military figure, and in *Long Live the Victory of the People's War* (1965) proclaimed the invincible nature of the People's War as a means to defeat imperialism and the West. Backing Mao during the Cultural Revolution, Lin Piao used it to increase his power in the military and to remove his opponents. Concerned about the situation, the anxious Mao thwarted Lin Piao's drive to become Chairman of the Republic in 1970. In 1971, after an alleged coup attempt, Lin Piao was killed in an air crash while fleeing to the Soviet Union. It is not known if the plane was shot down by the Chinese or how far the Soviet Union was involved with Lin Piao's plans. Moreover, the coup story may have been fiction. Perhaps, the imprint of the earlier dynastic era came to play a role with the habitual instability represented by a successor. First, Liu Shaoqi, second in the political hierarchy from 1945 and President from 1966, fell by the wayside during the Cultural Revolution, and then Lin Piao.

These issues also suggested to the Soviets that China might be an unstable ally. Indeed, in 1969, Kissinger was sounded out first on joint action against China and then on the American attitude were the Soviets to launch a pre-emptive missile attack on the Chinese nuclear facilities at Lop Nor and perhaps a few other places, and to invade Manchuria.[8] The Soviets had an animalistic fear of the Chinese, and were concerned about being swamped. They also thought Maoism a parody of Soviet Communism. There was no American support for such moves. In response to China's stance, the Soviets redeployed many of their missiles to deter China.

Kissinger's theme was *realpolitik*. He sought to use Sino-American co-operation, which he pursued with negotiations via Pakistan, an ally of both powers, and with a secret trip to China in July 1971, to isolate and put pressure on the Soviet Union, in order to get the latter to persuade North Vietnam, which was seen as a Soviet client, to reach an accommodation with South Vietnam. China was troubled by the Indo-Soviet alliance of that year and by India's successful attack on Pakistan, an attack that resulted in independence for East Pakistan as Bangladesh. Kissinger had secretly pressed China to send forces to India's border to deter India from intervening in East Pakistan, although he knew that the Soviets might respond forcefully against China. Nixon and Kissinger reminded China that the American alliance with Japan would enable the USA to restrain Japan if its rapidly growing economy was to lead it back to expansionism, a key threat to China. To Kissinger, mutual interests were essentially variable, but the pursuit of interest was fixed, so that he advised Nixon in February 1972:

> I think in 20 years your successor, if he's as wise as you, will wind up leaning towards the Russians against the Chinese. For the next 15 years we have to lean towards the Chinese against the Russians. We have to play the balance of power game totally unemotionally. Right now, we need the Chinese to correct the Russians and to discipline the Russians.[9]

This was a policy based on the goal of managing, not ending, the Cold War. Such a policy instrumentally assumed that others would do as required, and may have been impossible anyway. It also proved too difficult for the post-Cold War presidents. As an instance of *realpolitik*, Nixon and Kissinger also favoured building up regimes they could influence, and giving them weaponry and other support, all because they were supposed anti-Communists who would stabilise their respective countries. This policy was followed with Jiang Jieshi in Taiwan, the Shah of Iran, the apartheid system in South Africa, and the Pinochet regime in Chile. The values of these states were antithetical to American values which shows how the Cold War put the USA on the wrong side of issues in many countries. Looked at differently, the Cold War confrontation affected situations that in reality had little to do with the Cold War.

## The Last Stages of the Vietnam War

On 30 March 1972, encouraged by increased Soviet military shipments inspired by a desire to limit Chinese influence, the North Vietnamese launched the Nguyen Hue campaign; to the Americans the Easter Offensive. A conventional invasion of South Vietnam across the Demilitarized Zone between the two states, this offensive led, on 1 May, to the fall of Quang Tri, a provincial capital, and to the siege of another, An Loc. The offensive also resulted in a heavy American air response, in the Linebacker I air campaign of May to October 1972, which hit the North Vietnamese supply system, cutting the movement of supplies to their forces. The conventional nature of the force that had invaded the South – 14 divisions including Soviet-supplied tanks and trucks that required fuel – made the air attacks more devastating than those directed against the Viet Cong had been, which had a major impact on the conflict on the ground. The enhanced effectiveness of American air power was due not only to North Vietnamese operational goals and methods, but also to a marked improvement in American air capability that reflected both the displacement of earlier doctrine, stemming from adjustment to the varied needs of the Vietnam war, and the use of laser-guided bombs. These precision weapons hit North Vietnamese logistics by destroying bridges, and were also very useful in close air support, for example against tanks. Furthermore, advances in ground-based radar technology helped in the direction of B-52 strikes.[10]

After initial North Vietnamese success in March, April and May 1972, that, in part, reflected the surprise nature of the attack and the strong forces deployed, the invading force was held off by the South Vietnamese, backed by the Americans, and territory was regained. The North Vietnamese suffered, in 1972, from their inability to master high-tempo manoeuvrist warfare. In particular, there was a failure to make the best use of tanks, which reflected both an operational inability to use them in a manoeuvrist capacity, in order to gain mobility and achieve particular objectives, and a tactical failure to achieve infantry-armour coordination. Instead, the tanks were employed as an assault force on South Vietnamese positions, indeed essentially as mobile artillery. The irrelevant dogmatism of Soviet armoured tactics was to be repeated by the Syrians in 1973 when they sought to recapture the Golan Heights from Israel.[11] Losing mobility meant squandering the initiative in operational terms, a fate to be repeated by the Iraqis when they invaded Iran in 1980 and defended conquered Kuwait in

1991. Losing mobility also meant for the North Vietnamese the tactical problem of providing ready targets for American airpower, and reflected a degree of inflexibility that suggested that determination was far less of an advantage for the North Vietnamese in conventional-style offensive operations than in guerrilla warfare.[12] The consequences remain to this day with the very extensive cemeteries between the Demilitarised Zone and Hué holding the remains of numerous North Vietnamese soldiers. Aside from possibly 100,000 deaths, there was also considerable disenchantment in the memoirs left by North Vietnamese soldiers.[13]

America, meanwhile, had greatly strengthened its diplomatic position by a *rapprochement* with China in 1972. Alongside the earlier American success in 1965–6 in aligning with the newly-dominant military in Indonesia, a success that gave the American's strategic depth in South-East Asia, this step made it less serious strategically to abandon South Vietnam. Using the pressure of further heavy air attacks on North Vietnam, the B-52 raids in the Linebacker II campaign from 18 December 1972 (the effectiveness of which, in the face of strong North Vietnamese air defences, has been doubted[14]), Nixon, who had been easily re-elected in November, was able to negotiate a settlement. Chinese pressure on North Vietnam also played a role. The Paris Peace Agreements were signed on 27 January 1973. With these, the Americans agreed that North Vietnamese troops could remain in the South, while the North Vietnamese dropped their demand for the removal of the South Vietnamese government. American troops were to leave in sixty days. That month, Nixon announced the end of all hostile acts by American forces in Vietnam. There were no commitments to the integrity of South Vietnam. Probably prefiguring the current situation in Afghanistan, the American withdrawal, completed in March 1973, left South Vietnam vulnerable, as Kissinger had anticipated in May 1972 in order to bait the peace,[15] the terms of which also reflected the skill of the North Vietnamese diplomats involved.

The war continued, with most ceasefire violations due to the Communist forces. There were heavy casualties on both sides. The South Vietnamese held their own in 1973 and early 1974, but came under increasing pressure in face of large-scale attacks in late 1974. Finally, in April 1975, South Vietnam was overrun, in the Ho Chi Minh campaign, by a renewed invasion from the North. Conventional North Vietnamese divisions achieved what both the Viet Cong fighting in more adverse conditions in 1968, and the earlier conventional attack in 1972, had failed to do. The North Vietnamese made good use of tanks in 1975, and ably integrated them with infantry and artillery. In contrast, when used against An Loc in 1972, they had fallen victim to American helicopter-fired wire-guided missiles and anti-tank weapons. The South Vietnamese showed in 1975 that, on their own, they were not a match for their opponents, which, in part, was an aspect of the failure of American intervention. Moreover, in 1975, the South Vietnamese followed an unwise strategy, with an abandonment of the

Central Highlands, where the North had launched its attack, and a focus on defending the south of Vietnam that gave their opponents a powerful impetus and gravely weakened South Vietnamese morale. Although some units fought bravely, resistance crumbled and, on 29 April, the government collapsed.[16]

In 1975, furthermore, the destructive civil war in Cambodia between the Khmer Rouge, the Cambodian Communist Party, and the pro-American Lon Nol government ended with the victory of the former. Moreover, the American abandonment of support for the Royal Lao armed forces was followed by the triumph of the Communists in the struggle for dominance of Laos, with the non-Communist leaders fleeing into Thailand in April, leaving the Pathet Lao in control. It is possible to argue that, had the Americans continued to provide the financial and military aid they had promised, but that Congress cut off under the 1973 War Powers Resolution (Kennedy-Cooper) Act, then the South Vietnamese and Cambodian forces would have gone on fighting successfully. Their morale would certainly have been strengthened.[17] American airpower could have made a major impact, as it had done in 1972, while the resupply of the South Vietnamese army with artillery, tanks and anti-tank weapons would have been significant. However, it was not only that America had abandoned its ally and thus the policy of a non-Communist, independent South Vietnam that had been pursued from 1954. In addition, South Vietnam was no South Korea: geographically, South Vietnam, and the areas within it held by the government, were far more exposed, while the regime was weaker, and its weaknesses were exacerbated by the poor military policy followed in 1975. It is instructive to see the stress on how continued American intervention might have altered the situation, as it is part of a longstanding American tendency to regard the conflict in American terms, and to underrate the extent to which the Vietnam War was in part an Asian civil war, one that began before the Americans arrived and ended after they left. In 1976, the two halves of Vietnam were reunited as the Socialist Republic of Vietnam, a state that has lasted to the present.

The Vietnamese War demonstrated that being the foremost world power did not mean that a state could beat, say, the fifteenth, because power existed in particular spheres and was conditioned by wider political circumstances;[18] especially, in this case for the Americans, the danger of a confrontation with other Communist powers. Growing opposition to the war in the USA was significant politically. The Americans themselves suffered more than 58,000 killed, while large numbers were wounded physically or mentally, the last leading to a considerable number of suicides. In addition, a sense of defeat and division had a major impact on American society. The legacy in the arts was very much seen in films such as *The Deer Hunter* (1978), *Apocalypse Now* (1979), *Platoon* (1986), and *Born on the Fourth of July* (1990). The personal traumas, collectively, were a major social issue, indeed crisis in the USA, although, of course, far, far less than the casualties and damage suffered by the Vietnamese. The Vietnam War also led in the USA to a major rethinking of the political context of force projection. The War Powers Resolution (Kennedy-Cooper) Act passed by a Democratic-dominated Congress, in November 1973, over Nixon's veto, stipulated consultation with Congress before American forces were sent into conflict and a system of regular presidential report and congressional authorisation thereafter. This law, which was an attempt to scale back the accretions stemming from the 1947 National Security Resolution, was to be evaded by successive presidents and was not to be enforced by Congress. Nevertheless, the law symbolised a post-Vietnam restraint that discouraged military interventionism in the 1970s. The percentage of GDP spent on the military not only fell after the Vietnam War, but was also lower in the late 1970s than it had been in the late 1950s.[19] Moreover, this restraint helped ensure that, in the 1980s, the more bellicose Reagan government did not commit ground forces in El Salvador or Nicaragua, let alone Angola, all of which were closer to the Continental USA than Vietnam. In March 1991, in the aftermath of the first American defeat of Iraq, President George H. W. Bush stated: 'By God, we've kicked the Vietnam syndrome once and for all'. However, the legacy of the conflict thereafter continued to influence not only civilian attitudes but also attitudes among military leaders. This led to a reluctance to get involved in counter-insurgency operations, and an emphasis on a clear mission, and an obvious exit-strategy that had to be abandoned after the Second Iraq War in 2003.

The American *rapprochement* with China ensured that the strategic consequences of defeat in Vietnam were tempered. Although Cambodia and Laos were 'lost', there was no advance of Communism into neighbouring Thailand, which would have provided an Indian Ocean coastline, nor into Malaysia or Indonesia, where Communism had been totally defeated in the 1950s and 1960s respectively. Nor was there a renewal of the successful Chinese pressure on India seen in 1962. China and Japan normalised their diplomatic relations. Instead, the multiple splintering of the Communist bloc altered the regional situation, leading in 1978–9 to warfare between China and Vietnam, which was pro-Soviet. Moreover, Vietnamese exhaustion also lessened the strategic consequences of American defeat. The Hanoi government had to consolidate its gains. This entailed staffing new admin-istrative offices in the South; farming out Party cadres to the South; linking up roads and the railway between North and South; clearing up war debris such as mines; conducting a hunt for real and make-believe hostile elements within South Vietnam; rounding up and sending senior and middle-ranking South Vietnamese civilian officials and military officers to 're-education camps' (concentration camps); and instituting the usual Communist policies of nationalisation and dispossession of property and assets. Mao had come to regard better relations with the USA as a way to secure China's status as a great power, and these relations were a major strategic advantage for both powers as they were seen as a deterrent to the Soviet Union; although both China and the USA were concerned about the determination and views of the other. The Soviets felt it necessary to devote more forces, both conventional and nuclear, to their frontier with a no-longer-isolated China, a China, moreover, that was now a nuclear power. From 1963, this need affected the launch plans of Soviet nuclear missiles, lessening the focus on Western Europe and the USA.

# Missiles

Deterrence was also practised in and as a consequence of the development of greater nuclear and thermo-nuclear capability. The American position in the 1970s was challenged by the Soviet response, part of the action-reaction cycle of the missile race. After 1962, and in response to their perceived weakness during the Cuban Missile Crisis, the Soviets had made major advances in comparative nuclear potency, especially in the development of land-based, intercontinental missiles. These advances produced a situation in which war was seen as likely to lead to MAD (mutually assured destruction), as both sides appeared to have a secure second-strike capability, ensuring that a surprise attack would not wipe out the opposition. Difficult to detect, submarines also provided a second-strike capability. They were intended to attack cities, which were regarded as soft targets. As a consequence, MAD-based strategies of deterrence and of graduated response were developed on the Western side, although it was never clear whether the Soviets agreed with the 'nuclear calculus' as it was called.[20] In particular, it was unclear whether it would be possible to use tactical nuclear weapons without risking escalation. The large number of nuclear weapons in Europe increased this risk, for, by 1967, the USA had over 7,000 nuclear weapons in Europe. Furthermore, the spread of any nuclear conflict and the value of attacking first with nuclear weapons led to the risk that a false warning of a conventional (let alone nuclear) attack would lead to a rapid resort to a nuclear first strike. Indeed, the superior capability of nuclear forces when used in a pre-emptive fashion weakened their value as a deterrent against success, but, in turn, pre-emption was threatened by limited accuracy and by the threat of a retaliatory attack. The lack of certainty about the responses and effectiveness not only of the rival power but also of one's own nuclear forces were issues, but so also was the risk that perceived threats and unwelcome policy initiatives might lead to the rival power resorting to the use of its nuclear forces.

The identity of any trigger for action was unclear for both sides, which again suggested that even the use of nuclear weapons only for deterrence posed problems. However, the weapons could not be wished out of existence, which ensured that they retained a major role in discussion of pre-emption, conflict and deterrence. If war between the leading powers had become too risky in terms of the devastation that would result for all, that did not mean that it could be ruled out as a possibility or an option. This conclusion also accorded with the need to display capability and to ensure national security and that of allies. Concern about both intelligence, and the command and control in any nuclear confrontation and conflict, led to attempts to gain real-time warnings of missile attacks and to provide a reliable communications network in order to retain central direction. Launch-on-warning was a response to the first issue and seems to have been in effect for the USA in the early 1970s, but it led to the danger of an accidental nuclear attack. There was also the particular issue posed by submarines with which there were communications problems and which were difficult for opponents to follow. It was possible to communicate with submarines from land, but this could only be done through long-wave radio transmissions. There was always the problem of salt water's opacity and thermal layers. There were also concerns about the reliability of anti-missile defences. A major reason why, in 1969, the Soviet Union and the USA agreed to hold the Strategic Arms Limitation Treaty (SALT) talks on nuclear armaments limitations was that the amount of guidance equipment that it was necessary to install on an anti-missile missile was too heavy and made the anti-missile missile ineffective.

In the 1970s, enhanced capability, notably the deployment of multiple independently-targetable re-entry vehicles (MIRVs) from individual missiles, was matched by attempts to lessen the possibility of nuclear war. The horrific prospects of any conflict, and the likelihood that there would be escalation, encouraged *détente*. The prospect of unparalleled devastation in the USA in the event of a nuclear war led to doubt whether the Americans would risk a nuclear response in the event of a Soviet attack in Europe, which troubled Western European policymakers, although the need to protect American forces in Europe was a significant element in American planning. At the same time, the Soviets assumed that, due to their weakness in conventional forces, the Western powers would use nuclear weapons first. Such an assumption encouraged interest in a number of courses, notably pre-emption, deterrence and negotiation. The American-Soviet Anti-Ballistic Missile Treaty of May 1972, which Nixon, seeking reputation as a peacemaker and keen to contain the Soviets, felt able to conclude thanks to the MIRV programme, limited the construction of defensive shields against missile attack. These shields were restricted to two anti-ballistic missile complexes, one around a concentration of intercontinental ballistic missiles and the other around the capital. By leaving the USA and the Soviet Union thereby vulnerable to damaging attack, the treaty was designed to discourage a first strike, as, in that event, there would be no effective defence against a counter-strike. Thus, atomic weaponry was to be used to prevent, not to further, war.

The agreement was part of the Interim Agreement of the Strategic Arms Limitation Treaty (SALT). This SALT I agreement, which limited the two powers' nuclear arsenals, also served as the basis for further negotia-tions which, after nearly reaching agreement in late 1975, were delayed by domestic political factors. The opposition of Donald Rumsfeld, the Secretary of Defense in the Ford administration, was particularly signif-icant in 1976. At this stage, arms control seemed an uncertain option and there were fears that it could be circumvented by new weapons and new strategies. Rumsfeld's support for enhanced American nuclear weaponry threatened the negotiation process. Moreover, Rumsfeld's predecessor, James Schlesinger, had expressed and, in part, stoked opposition to the SALT process. Schlesinger believed that the Americans had come out with a less than satisfactory deal on SALT I and had even more doubts about the ongoing SALT II negotiations. He also felt that, if the Americans were to short-change themselves with an unsatisfactory troop reduction plan in Western Europe, then they would lose military credibility. Eventually, after the Democratic Carter administration had replaced the Republican Ford one, following the 1976 presidential election, negotiations led to the SALT II treaty in 1979.[21]

Meanwhile, new military capabilities accentuated uncertainty and encouraged tension. In 1977, the Americans tested a neutron bomb, an 'Enhanced Radiation Weapon'. This bomb was intended to incapacitate Soviet tank crews and not, despite Soviet propaganda to the contrary, to be used against Soviet cities. The rationale for using the neutron bomb was a confession of weakness that not only could conventional arms alone not stop a Soviet armoured attack into West Germany, but that the Americans were afraid to use standard tactical nuclear weapons, knowing that the Soviets would retaliate with them (if they had not used them before), and that everything would escalate into the strategic domain. The Americans were trying to hammer out a new battlefield doctrine between conven-tional response (and conventional warfare including enormously lethal biological and chemical weapons) and standard tactical nuclear weaponry. At the combat-ready level, the first Soviet SS-20 missiles were deployed, These were more mobile and more accurate missiles, armed with nuclear warheads, that were designed to be used in conjunction with conventional forces in an invasion of Western Europe.

# Ostpolitik

Co-operation between West and East of a different type to the SALT treaties was to be attempted in Europe, and here a key element was the degree of initiative shown by European players. In part, this initiative reflected a decline in the relative influence of the USA. Both Britain under Harold Wilson (1964–70, 1974–6) and, even more, France, under the self-confident Charles de Gaulle (1958–69) who was determined to assert his own importance, had seen themselves as able to negotiate with the Soviet Union and had fitfully done so. However, the key impetus was provided by West Germany. Willy Brandt, the Social Democratic Party (SPD) leader, became West German Chancellor in 1969, when a Christian Democrat (CDU)-Social Democrat coalition was replaced by a Social Democrat-Free Democrat Coalition. Mayor of West Berlin from 1957 to 1966 and Foreign Minister in the 1966–9 coalition, Brandt wished to transform the inherited West German governmental hostility to East Germany and Eastern Europe into a more benign relationship. Brandt hoped that this would bring stability and also enable West Germany to take a more central role in Europe. The SPD was not politically linked to the aggrieved German refugees from Eastern Europe, as were its CDU rival, and even more the CDU's ally, the Bavarian-based Christian Social Union under Franz Josef Strauss. The SPD was readier than the CDU to renounce what it saw as outdated and unhelpful policies. This was 1960s politics in action.

Brandt's *Ostpolitik* (Eastern Policy) sought to address the tensions of the Cold War, not least the 1968 Czech crisis, as well as West Germany's refusal to recognise East Germany, and to accept the latter's border with Poland. This border represented massive losses of German territory as a result of World War Two and thus a major infringement of the German *Heimat* or homeland. Under the Hallstein Doctrine of 1955, West Germany had claimed to represent all Germans, which was a challenge to the legitimacy of East Germany. Under the CDU-dominated administrations that had governed prior to 1969, there had been a refusal to consider *détente* with the East until the division of Germany and frontier disputes with Poland had been addressed, but this policy had failed to deliver results. Moreover, the understandably passive NATO response to the Soviet invasion of Czechoslovakia in 1968 confirmed that it was prudent to reach a settlement in Central Europe, and necessary to do so by negotiating with the East. *Ostpolitik* also reflected a degree of assertion based on impressive West German economic growth, political stability, and, to a lesser extent, military strength. This assertion was reflected in an interest in a European destiny for Germany, an interest that expressed different values to those of the USA.[22] *Ostpolitik* was also a rejection of the nostrums of the previous generation. Indeed, as an aspect of the latter, *détente* in part was a reaction to the popular unrest in 1968. Furthermore, *Ostpolitik* was a key instance of the recurring European search for political alternatives to the military logic of the arms race, an alternative that was particularly pertinent for Germany as it would be the obvious nuclear battlefield. This search took different, sometimes contradictory, forms at particular times, and could lead to considerable criticism. However, the 1975 Helsinki Accords and *détente* were to confirm the worth of this strategy, as did the final stages of the Cold War in the late 1980s when the Americans took the strategy over. However, that remark can be qualified by asking how far the strategy was appropriate and viable for the early 1980s when international tensions rose. The vexed questions of why and how the Cold War was won for the West make it difficult to assess such questions with confidence. Brandt had a long-term strategy. He wished to use the leverage West Germany had not had in the early 1960s. In around 1964–5, West Germany had begun to trade on a moderate scale with the Communist bloc. This created economic and financial links that Brandt tried to use. Seeking a German solution for a German problem, Brandt was influenced by de Gaulle's conviction that Europe should settle its issues itself. American leadership of the West had become more qualified and conditional in the 1960s, and, notably, from 1968. Brandt also hoped that *Ostpolitik* could change Eastern Europe and the Soviet Union. There were attempts by some West German commentators to suggest that any settlement offered West Germany an opportunity to shift alignments and rediscover an 'Eastern vocation', but these ideas got nowhere. Despite longstanding Soviet hopes, West Germany was not to be neutralised like Austria and Finland, and remained an important partner in NATO with a large army.

Yet, American attitudes were also very important. Concerned about South-East Asia, and forced by its weakened circumstances to accept change, the American government was unwilling to focus on the former goal of German reunification, a measure anyway unacceptable to East Germany. Moreover, although sceptical about Brandt's policy, and even distrustful of Brandt, Nixon was willing, at least in public, to accept *Ostpolitik* as a means for stabilisation, while the West German government sought to ensure that American support was retained during the negotiations. The direction of American foreign policy towards the Soviet Union from 1963, a policy that picked up with the advent of Kissinger and Brandt, was broadly in step with the later *Ostpolitik*. A central tenet of this approach, most explicitly articulated by Kissinger, was that, through binding the Soviet Union into interlocking trade agreements with the West, it would deter the former from adventurism. The memory of the 1962 Cuban crisis remained strong in the USA. Ironically, these arrangements were to some extent lifting the Soviet Union out of its Leninist-Stalinist autarchy and into an international arena wherein the Soviet Union economically was acquiring the profile of a Third World county in relation to the economically advanced countries: exporting raw materials and importing finished goods.

*Détente* appealed to the Soviet Union which sought the acceptance of its dominant position in Eastern Europe as well as a stronger base from which to confront China. The prospect of cutting defence costs may have been significant for part of the Soviet leadership, and there was also interest in the benefits of expanded trade, not least importing Western technology. This interest was an admission of the serious failings of the Communist economic system. West Germany's *Osthandel* (East-trade policy) ensured that West Germany provided trade credits and the large-diameter steel pipe necessary for the building of oil and natural gas pipelines that provided both to Eastern and then Western Europe. As a result of the latter, the

Soviet Union became greatly dependent for its hard currency earnings on trade with Western Europe.[23] The CIA added faults to the software sold with the pipeline, causing much destruction.[24] The first deliveries of Soviet gas to Western Europe occurred in 1968, ten days after the Soviet invasion of Czechoslovakia, and Austria ignored calls to delay this trade as a protest against the invasion.[25] Soviet commitment to stability and peace in Europe was shown in 1971 in Brezhnev's speech to the Twenty-Fourth Party Congress in which he called for international security and devoted scant space to the cause of 'national liberation'. The Soviet focus was on Europe, and not on Vietnam, let alone Africa, although, later in the decade, the situation changed.

In 1970, West Germany signed treaties with the Soviet Union and Poland in effect recognising the existing borders, and thus accepting the verdict of defeat in World War Two. The Warsaw Treaty with Poland was most important as the Oder-Neisse Line meant recognition that Silesia and Eastern Pomerania were Polish, and thus a rejection of the call from expellee organisations for a 'Right to *Heimat*'.[26] The 1970 treaties were followed by the West German acceptance of East Germany as an independent state, thus ending the Hallstein Doctrine. The first inter-German governmental talks were held in March 1970. Brandt met Willi Stoph, as Chairman of the Council of Ministers the head of the East German government, at Erfurt and Kassel. There was to be one German nation and two German states, a development enshrined in the Basic Treaty with East Germany signed on 8 November 1972 and ratified by the West German Parliament in 1973. Brandt's victory over the Christian Democrats in the 1972 German elections made this certain.[27]

'Normalisation', however, meant recognising the legality of a totalitarian state that treated its citizens harshly, as any visit today to a *Stasi* prison will indicate, but that outcome was part of the burden of 'normalisation'; indeed, 'normalisation' meant acceptance of a regime that now put more of an effort into the *Stasi*. Another unpleasant aspect of the process were secret payments by the West German government in return for people allowed to leave East Germany, many for family reunification. Although it was common knowledge that such payments were made, it would have been counterproductive and provocative to give them a great deal of publicity. Meanwhile, the killing by East German border guards of refugees trying to flee across the border continued. Once diplomatic relations were established, the West Germans were willing not to react in the hostile way they had done in the early and mid-1960s over East German border shootings. Had Brandt not taken the lead in 'normalisation', other powers would probably have done so. At the same time, West German governmental and, to some degree, public complicity in the East German regime increased alongside engagement with it. This complicity was displayed both by Brandt's SPD successor, Helmut Schmidt, the Chancellor from 1974 to 1982, and by the latter's CDU replacement from 1982, Helmut Kohl.

Complicity, however, may be an inappropriate as well as harsh judgment, as little would have been achieved by upholding the Hallstein Doctrine and continuing to refuse to enter into dialogue with East Germany. Moreover, the change in policy brought real relief in the form of visiting rights and family reunifications, not to mention buying 'regime opponents' out of jail. The era of Schmidt and of his East German counterpart, Erich Honecker, Party Chief from 1971 and Chairman of the Council of State from 1976 to 1989, led to a sober, measured *rapprochement* and a resolution of relations between the two states. The West Germans sought to foster a German-German community of responsibility against the background of a reduction in international tension. Uneasiness in the early 1980s about the deployment of intermediate-range nuclear missiles in West Germany was a product of these attitudes. Nevertheless, as part of this community of responsibility, concern within West Germany about the plight of East Germans, let alone support for reunification, markedly declined, reflecting the extent to which the Germans had also been major players in creating the reality of two separate nations.[28] There was no real West German support for the citizens' rights movements in East Germany. Instead, stabilisation was more significant as a goal. The easing of relations thus entailed an acceptance of the governing system in Eastern Europe, for example of the suppression of the Czech Spring in 1968. East Germany, recognised for the first time as a state by much of the world in 1973, was admitted to the United Nations and other international bodies.

Thus, in Europe in the 1970s, there was to be no 'roll-back' of Communism, and, crucially, no equivalent to the transformative changes that were to occur in Greece, Portugal and Spain, as conservative dictatorships collapsed in 1973, 1974 and 1975 respectively. At the same time, there was also the assumption that the Soviet Union and its allies would not seek to 'roll forward' by destabilising these and other European countries. Although the coup in Portugal on 25 April 1974 by the 'Armed Forces Movement' was followed, until April 1976, by instability, social turbulence and low-level revolutionary strife, and by talk of Communists gaining power through a rebellion, the Communists lacked sufficient support in the army. A coup attempt failed in March 1975. Moreover, the coup attempted in November 1975 by elements of the army opposed to a rightward move of the government failed. The army and the Socialists held the Communists off. The Soviet Union did not intervene, which it would have been risky for it to do, and Portugal remained in NATO.[29] Kissinger had feared that Portugal would be lost to 'the enemy bloc'.[30] However, Portugal had no contiguous border with a Communist state, the Soviets had no direct overland connection to Portugal, and Soviet maritime connections to it were shaky.

The prospect of joining the European Economic Community (EEC, now European Union), as Portugal, Spain and Greece did in 1986, 1986 and 1991 respectively, helped stabilise them. The process of European integration was frequently affected by the Cold War. For example, French support for British entry into the EEC in 1973 owed something to concern about the German *Ostpolitik*.[31] More generally, the revolutions in Southern Europe, and the ability there to manage change without conflict, anticipated developments in Eastern Europe in 1989. An important example had been created but, more significantly, an element of volatility was introduced and that, in the case of Portugal and Spain, of states that had been dictatorships for longer than those established by the Communists in the 1940s.

The easing of relations in Europe in the 1970s was also an aspect of a growing conservatism in the Soviet bloc which owed much to the rejection of the adventurism associated with Khrushchev, who had fallen from power in 1964, and his replacement by a collective leadership in practice soon dominated by the more complacent Brezhnev. Fear was no longer the motivating force in Soviet government that it had been under Stalin. The old fear was still present to a degree under Khrushchev, but, after him, the ministries went their own way and what has been termed the era of Soviet feudalism began. The gerontocratic character of government there and elsewhere in the Soviet bloc was also important. Alongside the harrowing example of World War Two, this character suggests that using the Cold War to 'prove' that deterrence inherently works is unconvincing if applied to different circumstances, notably with bolder and less risk-averse leaders, as with North Korea today. The result of Soviet governmental attitudes was a less hostile stance in Europe, and an emphasis, instead, on stability, although interventionism or 'adventurism' was to be seen elsewhere in the 1970s, notably Angola, Ethiopia and Afghanistan. The stress on stability in Europe was encouraged by the invasion of Czechoslovakia in 1968, as the need to consider how best to respond to possible uprisings in the Warsaw Pact bloc affected Soviet military planning. In response to *Ostpolitik*, the Communist Party declared 'peaceful co-existence' with the West to be 'a form of class struggle', which was certainly squaring the circle, as well as ensuring a reduction in anti-Western propaganda. The West German ambition of 'change by closer relations' with the East was to prove more successful than Soviet policy, but only in the long term. Moreover, in the short term, the Western financial and economic aid provided as an aspect of *Ostpolitik*, and the growth of trade with Western Europe, stabilised the Communist regimes without bringing much liberalisation.

# Helsinki

*Ostpolitik* helped prepare the way for the Helsinki Accords of 1 August 1975 which were a European-wide process of stabilisation.[32] However, as proof of the necessity to use NATO in order to act as a counterweight to the Soviet Union, both the USA and Canada were also represented among the 35 states that signed the Accords. This number included both West and East

Germany, and was thus an aspect of *Ostpolitik*. The American presence clashed with the Soviet strategy, once Brandt had replaced Kurt Kiesinger as German Chancellor in 1969, of decoupling the USA from Western Europe. However, the Soviets also wished to ensure that a German-dominated Europe did not arise. If American disengagement led to a powerful West Germany with nuclear arms, that would be totally unacceptable to the Soviet Union, and, indeed, to France. While flowing from the settlement of the German question, Helsinki, a step agreed upon by NATO ministers in December 1971, also owed much to an American policy of *détente* as seen in Nixon's visit to China in 1972. Indeed, *détente* in Europe was more than a product of American weakness and European stabilisation, as the American-Chinese *rapprochement* helped strengthen the American position. The Americans therefore became more relaxed about the Soviet Union. The Americans were confident that they had a winning card with China, that Brezhnev was not Khrushchev, and that the Soviets sought accommodation with the West over Berlin and with West Germany. The *rapprochement* with China gave the Americans the problem of deterring any Soviet attack on China, and encouraged the Soviet leadership to improve relations with the West so as to lessen the possibility, and risks, of American-Chinese co-operation. Thus, the American-Chinese *rapprochement* created uncertainties for all three powers. Uncertainty carried with it the risk of conflict, which made *détente* more attractive. The preparatory talks for what led to the Helsinki Accords began in November 1972 and the final summit was on 30 July 1975.

The Helsinki Accords accepted existing borders (Principle III), and non-intervention in the internal affairs of other states (Principle VI), thus meeting Soviet objectives. Although linked, in Principle VII, to remarks about human rights and fundamental liberties, the Soviet Union, like other Communist regimes, was sufficiently adept in preaching rights while practicing autocracy, for this linkage to appear to pose no problem to it. These glosses on Principle VII reflected the differing meanings of *détente*, but that they became normative in an international treaty covering all of Europe was important. Furthermore, the combination of stabilisation, rights, and a European common space, provided a window of opportunity for dissidents in Eastern Europe who cited the Helsinki Accords as a cover for their activities and notably as a reason for external support.[33] This window also owed much to the changing nature of government in Eastern Europe, not least the abandonment of Stalinist repression. Indeed, both in East and West, *détente* in part reflected changes in state and society, notably a decline in the power and authority of the former and of deference in the latter. Thus, *détente*, in part, was a product of the changes of 1968, as well as showing that the Cold War was not incompatible with resolving conflicts through negotiations. However, although Poland and, to a lesser extent, Hungary were relative islands of freedom in terms of what could be printed in comparison with the other Warsaw Pact states, they scarcely compared with Western countries, and the others certainly did not.

*Détente* found little favour with those who saw themselves as realists. As an aspect of the tension between American policy and *Ostpolitik*, Kissinger scorned the Helsinki Accords; so also did Yuri Andropov, the powerful head of the KGB and the party chiefs of Belarus and Ukraine. In 1974, Alexander Solzhenitsyn, who had won the Nobel Prize for Literature in 1970, was arrested and exiled for his description of Stalinist terror in *The Gulag Archipelago* (1973). In Czechoslovakia, the 'normalisation' regime of Gustàv Husàk sought to renew the Communist Party in order to thwart the 'dissidents', such as Václav Havel, and their human rights organisation, Charter 77, which used the Helsinki Accords as a way to castigate the regime. In the very different context of Yugoslavia, there was also a strengthening of Communist authoritarianism as Tito suppressed the liberal Communists of both Croatia and Serbia.[34] In East Germany, the continuing determination to control culture was demonstrated in 1976. The Palace of the Republic opened that year in East Berlin housed not only the Parliament but also leisure facilities and works of art commissioned under the rubric 'Are Communists allowed to dream', notably Hans Vent's painting *People on the Beach*. The same year, Wolf Biermann, a prominent satirical balladeer, was expelled from East Germany.

In recognising the position and interests of the Eastern bloc, the Helsinki process appeared to stabilise the Cold War, although the Accords called for follow-up conferences which offered the possibility of additional changes. Another aspect of stabilisation occurred in 1975 with an agreement under which American grain was exported to the Soviet Union to counter the impact of its poor harvests and agricultural mismanagement. These exports created an unexpected constituency of interest in continued good relations, one that included such Republican states as Kansas, a key grain producer. This interest affected Robert Dole, one of the leading Republican politicians in Congress and a Senator for Kansas.

# Middle East

Far from marking any triumph of the West, the stabilisation of Europe in the early and mid-1970s suggested that both East and West still had all to play for in a world adapting to the end of the Western European colonial empires. The situation outside Europe appeared particularly threatening to Western commentators in the early 1970s, and notably in the Middle East, Africa and South-East Asia. In the Middle East, Nixon and Kissinger had made little effort to resolve the Israeli-Arab impasse. In 1971 and 1972, Anwar Sadat, Nasser's successor as the Egyptian President in 1970, had approached Nixon to ask him to act as an intermediary with Israel. Once the Soviet Union had rearmed Egypt, Sadat had expelled Soviet advisors in 1972.[35] Golda Meir, the Israeli Prime Minister, however, rejected this approach, insisting on direct negotiations with Egypt.

Instead, in the 1973 Arab-Israeli War (the Yom Kippur War to Israelis and the October to Ramadan War to Arabs), Egypt and Syria launched a surprise attack on Israeli forces on 6 October. The war was a serious blow to Israeli prestige and to the Israeli reputation for invulnerability. Soviet planners had helped the Soviet-trained Egyptians prepare their attack, and Soviet SAM ground-to-air missiles greatly limited the effectiveness of Israeli air attacks on Egyptian forces that, in the initial attack, had successfully crossed the Suez Canal. The portable, infantry ground-to-tank missiles and the armoured personnel carrier mounted ground-to-tank and ground-to-air missiles were an unwelcome surprise to the Israelis and to NATO. The inventory had been kept secret. However, in a striking illustration of the difficulties of assessing relative capability, claims varied (and still vary) over the respective effectiveness of tanks and missiles in this conflict.[36] The Syrians had two new tanks, the T-62 and the T-64; both had infrared night sights, which the Israelis did not possess. In addition, the T-62 was the first Soviet tank with an automatic shell extractor. Nevertheless, very poor armoured tactics by the Syrians prevented them from breaking through the Golan Heights,[37] and the Israeli counter-attack drove the Syrians back on nearby Damascus. Moreover, in response to this, the Egyptians unwisely advanced their tank force into the Sinai beyond the cover of the SAM batteries and took heavy casualties.

As the conflict developed, the Soviets flew in state-of-the-art weaponry without affecting their garrison forces. By contrast, the Americans came close to denuding their forces in southern Germany of artillery, so much of it was sent to Israel. The Americans also rushed supplies to the Israelis from the USA by air during the war, via their air base in the (Portuguese) Azores. This base had been originally developed during World War Two to close the mid-Atlantic gap in air support against German submarines. In geopolitical and military terms, the Cold War after 1945, like its earlier stage from 1917, was greatly affected by the overhang from the previous world war. Nixon ignored pressure from the heads of American oil companies to stop the delivery of military aid to Israel.

As the conflict turned against the Egyptians in 1973, the Soviet Union faced the threat that the crisis would lead to pressure for Soviet intervention. To avoid this, the Soviets urged the Americans to agree to joint mediation. Talks in Moscow led to agreement for a United Nations Security Council Resolution for an immediate ceasefire followed by peace negotiations, but, whereas Egypt agreed, Israel fought on in order to pursue its battlefield advantages. Sure they had been cheated, the Soviet government, on 24 October, threatened unilateral action against Israel, which led the Americans, next morning, to issue a DEFCON III alert, ordering military readiness just short of war. American pressure forced Israel to stop fighting.

Like Cuba in 1962, this serious confrontation showed the capacity of

Third World crises to cause superpower conflict. Unlike Cuba, there was also a crippling economic consequence in the shape of an Arab oil embargo that quadrupled the price of oil with serious short and long-term economic consequences. Subsequently, American diplomacy led to a disengagement agreement between Egypt and Israel, which angered the Soviets as they felt excluded.[38] This anger helped lead to the Soviets being less co-operative, both in the Middle East and elsewhere, notably in Angola. However, the Soviet Union discovered anew that its ideological affinity with Arab nationalists was limited.

## Africa

Decolonisation was closely linked to the Cold War across much of Africa. The last of the European colonial empires, Portugal, faced a left-wing coup in April 1974, a revolution that owed much to dissatisfaction, both military and civilian, with the intractable conflict with guerrilla movements in Portugal's colonies. Indeed, the war effort cost close to half of public spending and the percentage of the total population involved in the conflict was greater than that of the Americans in Vietnam.[39] The change of government of Portugal led to the granting of independence to the colonies the following year. The consequences became a key instance of the southward move of the Cold War, one that provided the Communist powers with significant opportunities, and that involved much conflict.

In Angola, the most significant colony, the Portuguese tried in early 1975 to transfer power to a coalition government willing to oversee free elections, but conflict began on 1 February when the two leading independence movements, the MPLA (*Movimento Popular de Libertação de Angola*) and UNITA (*União Nacional para a Independência Total de Angola*), clashed in the capital, Luanda. Their rivalry included a powerful tribal and regional dimension as was also true of Cold War antagonisms elsewhere in Africa, for example between Soviet and Chinese-backed guerrilla movements against white rule in Southern Rhodesia (Zimbabwe). Within six months, the MPLA had defeated its opponents and seized control of the government, but this did not prevent a lengthy civil war. The clash between UNITA and the MPLA was also closely intertwined with the Cold War, as the MPLA government looked to the Soviet Union and Cuba, while UNITA received American backing. The conflict was also linked with the continuing anti-colonial struggle against white rule in Southern Africa, as South Africa, ruled by an apartheid regime and backed by the USA, provided money, weaponry and advisers to UNITA, as well as bases in its neighbouring colony, South-West Africa (now Namibia), and more direct military intervention, including a large force sent into Angola in 1975 and air cover for UNITA. Similarly, after the end of Portuguese power in

Mozambique, South Africa supported the RENAMO rebels against the FRELIMO government. This support also affected the war in Southern Rhodesia, which, like South Africa, bordered Mozambique. Cuban forces (up to 50,000 troops), and Soviet money, arms and advisers, were sent to Angola to help thwart the South Africans, whose advance on Luanda in 1975 was blocked by the Cubans and left in the lurch by the USA. The Ford government was distracted and weakened by the fall of South Vietnam and the aftermath of the Watergate affair, and could not afford to be seen openly supporting the apartheid regime. The South Africans had to withdraw, but their support for UNITA continued, and, in helping UNITA to consolidate its position in southern Angola, covered the South African position in South-West Africa, a South African possession from World War One. Angola was scarcely *détente* in action, as the Soviet Union successfully pursued a unilateral advantage there to counter what it saw as the one gained by the USA in the Middle East through negotiating better relations between Egypt and Israel.[40]

The Cubans, moreover, played a significant role in war in East Africa where a secessionist dispute became a violent part of the Cold War, as Somalia's support for secession from Ethiopia by the large Somali-populated Ogaden region ensured that the rebellion involving the Western Somali Liberation Front became a war between two states. When Soviet-armed Somalia (where the Soviets had an Indian Ocean naval base at Berbera that also threatened the entrance to the Red Sea) attacked Ethiopia in August 1977 with weapons including MIG fighters and Iluyshin-28 bombers, the Soviet Union offered arms to Ethiopia if it abandoned its American alliance, which it did. As a result, the Soviets changed ally and, by March 1978, 11,000 Cuban and 4,000 South Yemeni soldiers had arrived to help Ethiopia. East German troops were also sent. The Cubans were necessary in order to man the tanks, armoured personnel carriers and artillery provided by the Soviets. Backing Ethiopia against their former Somali allies, the Soviets also provided air reconnaissance, airlift, signal intercepts, and an innovative tank commander, General Petrov, who adapted cutting-edge weaponry and operational systems devised for war in Europe to the exigencies of Africa. Assaults spearheaded by tanks and rocket-launchers and supported by air attacks, parachutists and helicopter troops, conquered the Ogaden in early 1978. The war enabled the Soviets to test out tactics and equipment. The American response was divided, in part because Zbigniew Brzezinski, the National Security Advisor, who sought a hostile approach, found that Carter backed the Secretary of State, Cyrus Vance, who argued that the Soviet Union was supporting an ally under attack. Moreover, Vance did not wish to jeopardise the SALT talks. As a result, the Americans pursued a negotiated outcome when the matter in practice had already been settled on the ground.[41] Carter also distanced American policy over Angola from South Africa.

The Soviet willingness to overlook the bloody reign of terror of Haile

Mengistu, the dictator of Ethiopia from 1977 to 1991, indicated the degree to which the attitudes associated with Stalinism continued thereafter, not least if circumstances contributed to the Soviet Union gaining traction outside Europe. As a reminder of the longstanding tendency for Soviet commentators to interpret developments in terms of Soviet history and ideology, the Soviet envoy, Anatolii Ratanov, saw a similarity between the brutal activities of Mengistu's supporters within the *Derg* (Coordinating Committee) and the early revolutionary experience in Russia. There was certainly a parallel with the War Communism and Terror of the Russian Civil War. Far from being marginal, success in Africa in the 1970s and early 1980s gave many Soviets a renewed sense of pride in their own achievements, and a conviction that the Soviet Union could contribute decisively to breakthroughs for Communism elsewhere. The American (and French) willingness, in response, to support Sese Soko Mobuto, the corrupt, brutal and dictatorial President of Zaire from 1965 to 1997, revealed a more general preparedness to overlook multiple faults in order to ensure that 'our bastard' was in charge, a policy long followed by the Americans in Latin America.

There was an *ad hoc* and opportunistic character to Soviet geopolitical strategy, and it is unclear that the Soviet state really possessed the resources to become involved in so many areas and conflicts. The use of Cuban forces in Africa reflected some success in linking up the disparate areas of Soviet strength, but the wider Soviet bloc did not cohere in economic terms nor develop mutual, self-reinforcing bonds. The International Department of the Central Committee of the Soviet Communist Party provided ideological arguments, but the different elements of the Soviet world did not really add up. More specifically, the Soviet Union was involved, outside Eastern Europe, in unprofitable economic situations and difficult political scenarios. There was a failure to operate interventionism, or even informal imperialism, successfully, as well as a Soviet concept of profit and loss that, in practice, offered limited political and economic gains.

## Naval Capability

The Soviet ability to operate at a distance was enhanced by their greater naval strength, which also challenged the traditional Western dominance of the oceans with its apparent ability to restrict Communism to the Eurasian 'heartland', the theme of much geopolitical discussion. The conventional doctrine of Soviet naval power, looking back to the reign of Peter the Great (1689–1725), had emphasised the support of Russian land forces in the Baltic and Black Seas and the quest for naval superiority in these areas. However, Soviet forces based in these seas could only gain access to the oceans through straits, the Bosporus, Dardanelles and Kattegat, and shallow waters, where they were vulnerable. A similar problem affected the Soviet Far East naval base of Vladivostok, and Japan's contribution to American naval strategy was that of providing submarine support against Soviet ships trying to reach the Pacific, as well as anti-submarine capability. Japanese submarines became very skilled in shadowing submarines leaving Soviet bases.

As a result of this problem of access to the oceans, the Soviet navy developed their Northern Fleet based at Murmansk and nearby Severomorsk. Indeed, the rise of Soviet naval capability was intricately linked with the foundation of submarine bases that gave the Soviets access to the Atlantic. As a result, by 1980, the Kola Peninsula contained the greatest concentration of naval power in the world. This concentration owed much to the Gulf Stream which ensured that the water off the Peninsula remained relatively warm and did not freeze. The Northern Fleet became the largest Soviet fleet, with a particularly important submarine component. The supply effort required to keep these facilities in operation was immense, including multiple railway tracks and large amounts of rolling stock able to move oil. Over three quarters of Soviet naval expenditure was on the submarine force and the Soviets deployed nuclear-armed missiles and torpedoes on the submarines in order to attack American carriers.

This threat obliged NATO powers to develop patrol areas for their submarines and to locate underwater listening devices near the Soviet bases, and also to establish similar capabilities in the Denmark Strait between Iceland and Greenland and in the waters between Iceland and Britain through which Soviet submarines would have to travel en route to the Atlantic. To the anger of the Americans, the Canadians encountered problems in detecting Soviet submarines sailing from under the Arctic polar ice pack into the Davis Strait dividing Greenland from Baffin Island and Labrador, and from there into the North Atlantic where they could maintain a station off the eastern coast of the USA.[42] Fishing boats were also used for keeping tabs on Soviet submarine movements. The significance of submarine warfare led to a major expansion in financial support for marine sciences. The NATO framework included a Science Committee. Oceanography as a subject and institutional structure grew significantly from the 1960s, although influential oceanographers, such as George Deacon and Henry Stommel, were troubled about the consequences of military links.[43]

As a result of the emphasis on maritime dominance and a balanced fleet, the Soviet Union also built up an important surface fleet, especially, from the 1960s, a fleet which included missile cruisers firing sea-to-sea missiles. In both his policy and his publications, Admiral Gorshkov, the head of the navy, pressed the case for sea power.[44] In 1971, the Soviet Union supplanted Britain as the world's number two naval power, although the geographical range of its navy was less than that of Britain had been, and the Soviets lacked a big aircraft carrier until 1985. In 1967 and 1973, the Soviet navy was able to make substantial deployments in the eastern Mediterranean in order to advance Soviet views during Middle Eastern crises and to threaten Israel, thus putting considerable pressure on the USA.[45] In the 1970s, the Soviets developed naval bases in Vietnam (Danang), Somalia (Berbera) and Syria (Latakia and Tartus), to add to the facilities they already had in Cuba. These offered significant power projection and the visits of Soviet warships were intended to demonstrate the effectiveness of Soviet technology.

Soviet naval development led the Americans from 1969 to focus on planning for naval conflict with the Soviets, rather than, as hitherto, on amphibious operations, such as acting against coastal positions in East Asia. Naval Force Atlantic was established as a standing NATO force in 1967. The emphasis, which became stronger after the Vietnam War ended, was on being able to destroy Soviet naval power in battle and in its home waters, before Soviet warships, and notably submarines, could depart for the oceans.[46] NATO's CONMAROPS (Concept of Maritime Operations) proposed a forward attack on Soviet submarines near their bases in order to secure the North Atlantic sea-lines of communication for the supply and resupply of NATO forces in Europe. This stress led to an American focus on big aircraft carriers and large submarines, both intended to attack the Soviet fleet, whether surface or submarine. For example, the American blue water re-orientation in 1986, part of the Reagan arms build-up, saw calls for a Maritime Strategy, and a 600-ship navy with fifteen carrier groups. There was also a focus on anti-submarine warships, such that the British Type 22 *Broadsword*-class frigates of the 1980s lacked a main gun armament as this was seen as irrelevant for their anti-submarine duties. In contrast to the American emphasis on carriers, the Soviet Union relied on land-based long-range bombers and reconnaissance planes and had only one big carrier, the *Admiral Kuznetsov*, launched in 1985.

## Western Economic Weakness

Conflict in Africa suggested that, as far as the Soviet Union and the USA were concerned, *détente* was only a truce between rivals. *Détente*, indeed, arose from the particular circumstances of the mid-1970s and also from the military stalemate in Europe that was the product of nuclear confrontation, a stalemate that encouraged a truce and permitted a registration of shifts of political alignment, as well as a measure of accommodation. The West, meanwhile, appeared in a parlous position, both economically and politically. Its economic strength seemed compromised. First, it was compromised by inflationary pressures that owed much to the American decision to pay for the 1960s, both social policy and war, by borrowing rather than taxation and that led, from 1971, to the collapse of the Bretton Woods system. Secondly, there were the difficulties of sustaining earlier rates of innovation and productivity growth. Thirdly, there were the serious economic strains following the oil price hike after the 1973 Arab-Israeli War, from $2.50 per barrel in 1972 to $12 at the close of 1974. This was an increase introduced by OPEC (the Organisation of Petroleum Exporting Countries) in order to put pressure on the Western supporters of Israel, and it did so. This rise hit oil importers and fuelled inflation, hitting consumption and living standards, and damaging economic confidence and investment.

A fall in American oil production contributed to the crisis. Until the early 1970s, America was the world's largest oil producer. By deciding how much the state's producers could extract, the Texas Railroad Commission stabilised world prices. Moreover, it had acted to do so in difficult political circumstances, as in 1967 when an oil embargo was imposed by the Arab states. A large production boost was permitted by the Texas Railroad Commission. However, falling production and rising consumption in the USA hit this ability, and in 1972 the Texas Railroad Commission called for no restrictions on production. Now, lacking the margin to respond to crises, it proved impossible for the USA to stabilise prices in 1973. Instead, OPEC was the new arbiter. Moreover, American protectionism, banning crude-oil exports in 1975 in order to ensure supplies and restrain prices, made the situation more difficult elsewhere and both encouraged reliance on the Middle East and led Western European powers to look to the Soviet Union for energy. The OPEC oil-price hike caused inflation to shoot up in the USA. The stock markets took a real hit, causing considerable nervousness, while there was some serious supply and demand confusion within American industry. However, there was no collapse of the stock markets or the currency or the banking system. Under the chairmanship of Arthur Burns from 1970 to 1978, the Federal Reserve, which followed aggressive deflationary policies, proved robust and, although demand remained lower for a while, manufacturing had improved by mid-1974.

## The Soviet Economy

As the Soviet Union was a major oil producer, the rise in the price of oil helped Soviet finances. This enabled the Soviets to invest more heavily in exporting their brand of Communism to Africa, notably to Angola and Ethiopia. However, the financial improvement encouraged a complacent failure to address serious structural problems in the Soviet economy, let alone to modernise it. In part, this was because the benefits of oil prices came on top of the improvement in Soviet economic performance in the late 1960s. Indeed, there appears to have been significant improvement in the economic lot of Soviet citizens during the Brezhnev period (1964–82), notably in housing and the provision of goods. Moreover, much of the Brezhnev period was a time of moving forward, of progress, in which Soviet society as a whole, keeping in mind the basic constraints of its being run by a police-state, was becoming less closed-off and more open. The Brezhnev years saw a significant improvement in investment into the Soviet social welfare system. Wages increased by 50 per cent between 1967 and 1977, and a five-day working week was introduced. The rise in wages permitted only a modest standard of living, but it represented a major switch from the harsh memories of the 1930s and 1940s. The wages of collective and state farm workers rose above the average wage. Moreover, although the Soviet cult of statistics incorporated major problems with manipulation and accuracy, production figures suggested a range of improvements.

## Western Political Problems

The lengthy Watergate Scandal, which eventually led to the fall of Nixon in 1974, helped cause a crisis of confidence in American leadership. Moreover, Western disunity was seen in Western European unwillingness to respond in NATO to America's global commitments[47] as well as growing French alienation from the USA. Edward Heath, British Prime Minister from 1970 to 1974, was determined not to be branded as the American spokesman in Europe, was not eager for close co-operation with Nixon, and argued that membership in the European Community represented a welcome alternative to the USA.[48] Britain was also faced from 1974 by a political upheaval stemming from a coalminers' strike, and then by a more general crisis as high inflation and trade union power contributed to an acute sense of malaise and weakness. The idea of Britain playing a role in resisting Communist expansion and activity outside Western Europe and the North Atlantic appeared increasingly incredible. Nationalist violence in Northern Ireland placed a new strain on the British military. In part drawing on the examples of the Vietnam War and of Maoist Red Guards, West Germany and Italy were affected by violent radical movements, the Baadar-Meinhof Gang and the Red Brigade respectively, creating an impression of current instability and future deterioration. Western weakness seemed clear and varied. Apparent nuclear parity left the Soviet superiority in conventional forces a threat to Europe, while Congress limited American intervention in Angola. American annual inflation rose at a rate of 15 per cent in early 1974, the economy went into recession, and stagflation (stagnation combined with inflation) posed a threat to the social fabric, notably creating uncertainty and a sensation that the current standard of living could fall. In America, stagflation was linked to rising crime rates in the cities, while the terrorist Weather Underground movement aroused alarm. Stagflation was also a serious issue in Britain.

# The Late 1970s

Yet, alongside Western weaknesses, there were also serious problems for the Soviet system, while the American position was less bleak, in both absolute and relative terms, than the successive electoral defeats of presidents Gerald Ford and Jimmy Carter in presidential elections in 1976 and 1980 might suggest. Moreover, the failure of the Communists to benefit substantially from the changes in Portugal, Spain and Greece was matched by Communist weakness elsewhere in Western Europe. Valéry Giscard d'Estaing, French President from 1974 to 1981, and Helmut Schmidt, German Chancellor from 1974 to 1982, combined to act as a very strong stabilising force and to relaunch the EEC project. Within the Socialist International, the so-called Socialist Triangle of Willy Brandt, Olof Palme, Swedish Prime Minister, and Bruno Kreisky, Austrian Chancellor, was dominant. In Italy, the Communist Party, the most powerful in Western Europe, adopted a 'Euro-Communism' that was opposed to Soviet direction. Enrico Berlinguer, who became Party Secretary in 1973, a key figure, was committed to the existing democratic system and pursued what was termed the 'historic compromise' with the established Christian Democrat-dominated political system. A pact was negotiated in 1976, with the Communist Party agreeing not to try to overthrow the Christian Democratic government. Euro-Communism was a term coined in 1975 by Western European Communist leaders keen to demonstrate their democratic credentials. More generally in Western Europe, the declining position of heavy industries was a challenge to the trade unions that were central to left-wing political parties, and notably to the Communists.

The Communist economies were hit by the economic downturn of the mid-1970s, and the Brezhnev government lacked an effective response. Heavy investment in armaments, which continued despite *détente*, was distorting for these economies. More generally, they suffered from the role of state planning, particularly by Gosplan, the State Planning Commission in the Soviet Union, and from the failure to develop the consumer spending that was so important to economic activity and growth in the USA and Western Europe. This was a political decision, lest consumerism lead to the fetish of things and to bourgeois attitudes. Politburo member Mikhail Suslov was the key figure. An ideologue of the Stalinist school, he had played a major role in overthrowing Khrushchev, and continued in office until his death in 1982. Conventional Communist ideology was underlined in 1977 with the new Soviet constitution which essentially confirmed that of 1936 produced under Stalin, and asserted without hesitation the role of the Party. It was declared both the leading and guiding force of Soviet society and the force that determined the course of Soviet domestic and foreign policy.

In 1965, Prime Minister Aleksei Kosygin had tried to push through a modest move back from centralisation that would have enabled factory managers on the spot to determine within limits the amount of production they wished to pursue. This move, however, had been blocked by middle-ranking administrators in many of the industrial-production ministries. Moreover, the output figures for the five year plans showed a clear decline over the decades, and more than could be explained by the base gradually becoming larger. From 1950 to 1965, the annual rate of increase in GDP varied between 4.5 per cent and 5.5 per cent followed by:

| Five Year Plan | Years | Annual Rate of Increase in GDP |
| --- | --- | --- |
| 8 | 1966–70 | 4.8 |
| 9 | 1971–5 | 2.9 |
| 10 | 1976–80 | 1.8 |
| 11 | 1981–5 | 1.7 |
| 12 | 1986–90 | 1.3 |

The productivity of Soviet workers was not really increasing and Soviet machinery was ageing and not being replaced adequately. The Soviets regarded industrial machinery as a wasting asset to be used until it wore out, whereas other industrial societies had a time-and-profit-based, techno-logically sensitive, approach towards depreciation. In the mid-1960s, machine tools in the USA could be totally depreciated in tax terms after seven years, which acted as a stimulus for technological innovation. In contrast, Soviet machine tools, the foundation for any kind of industrial sophistication, were being fully depreciated over a thirty year period. More generally, the resources, cheap and plentiful labour, and government confi-dence that were all available in the Soviet Union in the 1950s, were no longer there by the 1970s, although the product mix was far greater than it had been in the 1930s.

America benefited from an economic rebound after the crisis of 1974–5. Problems continued, notably with inflation, from 1977, and a lack of export-led growth. Whereas the Federal Reserve under Burns had helped reduce inflation to 4.9 per cent by December 1976, Bill Miller, his replacement under Jimmy Carter, President from 1977 to 1981, relaxed the borrowing rates and inflation took off again, unofficially reaching 20 per cent by mid-1979: it was already nearly 15 per cent at the start of March 1979, before the OPEC oil hike of that year. Nevertheless, the general revival of world growth helped the American economy. Moreover, issues of investment opportunity and confidence ensured that much of the OPEC money was recycled back into the USA, notably the greater profits enjoyed by Saudi Arabia, the leading oil-exporting state. Much of the OPEC money was recycled to South America by American banks and caused financial chaos there.

Carter wished to downplay the Cold War and to move from a West–East to a North–South orientation, as well as to emphasise human rights. However, the Soviet Union and China disagreed. The Americans benefited from some major foreign policy successes. As a result of considerable effort, the Carter administration helped to arrange a peace settlement between Egypt and Israel, with the Camp David Accords of 17 September 1978 followed by the Egypt-Israel treaty of 26 March 1979. The Camp David Accords focused on 'peace for land', Israel withdrawing from its Sinai (although not Gaza) gains of 1967, and Egypt, in return, signing a formal peace treaty with Israel, and thereby giving recognition.

Nasser's successor, Anwar Sadat, the Egyptian President, who had expelled Soviet advisers in 1972, wanted to include the Palestinians in the treaty, but Menachem Begin, the Israeli Prime Minister, was willing only to agree to an informal link to a temporary halt on new Israeli settlements on the West Bank. The peace process was condemned by the Soviet Union and the PLO (Palestine Liberation Organisation). Nevertheless, the peace agreement helped lessen tensions in the Middle East (not least by isolating Syria and the PLO), which was important as, from 1979, the Cold War was to become far more difficult in South Asia.

More significant than developments in the Middle East, the death of Mao Zedong in September 1976 was not followed by any abandonment of China's American alignment. As so often during the Cold War, rivalries within Communist parties played a major role in international developments. The attempt by the radical 'Gang of Four', including Mao's widow, to gain power was thwarted by Hua Guofeng, the Premier, who became Chairman of the Central Committee. He, in turn, became less powerful as his rival, Deng Xiaoping, rose. Deng had been dismissed as Vice-Premier of the State Council earlier in 1976 as a result of the influence of the Gang of Four. Deng was reinstated in July 1977 and, while supporting control by the Communist Party, outmanoeuvred the more ideological Hua by emphasising pragmatism. Deng's leadership was confirmed in December 1978 at the Third Plenum of the 11th CCP Congress. He remained in power until 1997. Deng Xiaoping favoured not only the alignment with America, but also a re-evaluation in terms of economic liberalisation rather than a revolution focused on Marxist purity. The modernisation of Taiwan, South Korea and Singapore convinced Deng that capitalist modernisation worked. Formal diplomatic relations with America were established on 1 January 1979 and, later that year, Deng became the first Chinese Communist leader to pay an official visit to the USA. On this, Deng visited the NASA facilities in Houston and the Boeing headquarters in Seattle. He appreciated the significance of American technology and the need for modernisation were China to match this.[49] One of the desired outcomes of this visit was to inaugurate what would become a massive influx of Chinese students that became an astounding transfer of human and technological skills. In 1978, moreover, a treaty of friendship with Japan helped foster stability in East Asia and marked China's willingness to ease relations with the Western bloc. In 1979, the Americans ended the Taiwan Patrol Force, which, from 1950, had policed the waters between China and Taiwan, protecting the latter.

War, when it came, was not with the Western bloc. In the event, the Chinese attack on Vietnam in February-March 1979, launched in support of the Khmer Rouge in Cambodia and in response to Vietnamese pressure on Laos, was largely unsuccessful and did not force Vietnam to withdraw from Cambodia. Nevertheless, the attack showed China's readiness not to be deterred by Soviet-Vietnamese links. The Chinese eventually sent about 120,000 troops to confront an equal number of Vietnamese. The Chinese captured three provincial capitals, but were knocked off balance by the Vietnamese decision to turn to guerrilla tactics. Affected by poor logistics, inadequate equipment, and failures in command and control, the Chinese withdrew, having suffered maybe 63,000 casualties.[50] The war demonstrated the strength of rivalry within the Communist bloc, which very much served Western interests, not least by making it clear that the consequences of this rivalry were unpredictable. Zbigniew Brzezinski, Carter's National Security Adviser, referred to the 'proxy war' between the Soviet Union and China. Ideologically, there was a clear challenge, as the armies of Communist states should not fight each other if Communist societies were supposedly lacking in the contradictions bringing about strife that non-Communist societies in theory contained. Although the Chinese withdrew their troops from Vietnam in 1979, hostility between the two powers continued during the 1980s, helping to deepen the Sino-Soviet split and thus to maintain good relations between China and the USA.[51] The Soviet invasion of Afghanistan had similar consequences.

American moves away from Taiwan, notably a lessening of military co-operation, were an aspect of better relations with China. In contrast to growing limits on its military relationship with Taiwan, America in 1980 agreed to sell arms to China. Already, in the late 1970s, China had co-operated with the Americans in setting up listening posts in north-west China abutting Soviet Kazakhstan and Soviet Kirghizia (now Kyrgyzstan), with the provision that the Americans would share their intelligence data obtained there with China. This was a significant *de facto* alliance that was important to defence against possible Soviet attack.

At the same time, Kissinger, Carter and *détente* were condemned as weakening the West by a group of conservative Democrats led by Henry (Scoop) Jackson, a critic of SALT, as well as by key Republicans who were influential in the Ford administration (1974–7), notably his Chief of Staff, Richard (Dick) Cheney, and the Secretary of Defense, Donald Rumsfeld. They drew on advice from commentators such as Richard Perle, Richard Pipes and Paul Wolfowitz who warned about Soviet intentions. The continuity of this group, through 1990s' opposition to Clintonian liberal internationalism, to the neo-conservative activism of the early 2000s, especially against Iraq, is notable.

A situation in Asia that was not without considerable promise for the USA was to become far more threatening in 1979. The overthrow, in the face of mass-demonstrations, of the Shah of Iran, who left Tehran on 16 January 1979, and his replacement by a theocratic state hostile to the USA, combined with the Soviet invasion of Afghanistan at the end of 1979 to create a highly volatile situation that posed problems for analysts.[52] There was the prospect, first, that the USA might lose the struggle for regional hegemony and, secondly, that this might have wider consequences across Asia. Although authoritarian and prone to initiatives that were not always welcome, Iran was America's leading ally in South Asia, an opponent to Arab radicalism, and a block to Soviet expansionism and that of Iraq, a key Soviet ally. The USA had used Iran to support the Kurds against Iraq, and, in 1973, to send troops to help the Sultan of Oman overcome left-wing rebels based in the region of Dhofar, rebels backed by Communist powers. Iran was also a major purchaser of American arms, and a key oil exporter. Under the Shah, it had long played a central role in the forward containment of the Soviet Union, not least by providing important radar bases to screen the southern Soviet Union. After the collapse of Iran, the Americans fell back upon Israel.

In practice, opposition by the new Iranian regime to the Americans did not necessarily extend to support for the Soviet Union. Two days after the Soviet invasion of Afghanistan, the Soviet envoy in Iran promised Ayatollah Khomeini, the leader of the Islamic Revolution and Guardian of the Islamic Republic, assistance in any conflict with the USA; only to be told that there could be no mutual understanding between a Muslim nation and a non-Muslim government. Nevertheless, as a result of American backing for the Shah and for Israel (with whom the Shah had co-operated), and its identification with liberalism and consumerism, Khomeini saw America as 'the Great Satan'. He instigated the seizure of the American embassy in Tehran by student radicals on 4 November 1979, an act that created a hostage crisis lasting until 20 January 1981. This crisis, and the failed American attempt to rescue the hostages in April 1980, discredited Carter[53] and helped Khomeini sustain a highly-charged atmosphere in Iran. It was clear that America's loss of a strategic partner had altered the Cold War even if Iran had not joined the Soviet Union, which Khomeini described as 'the other Great Satan'. Thus, there was no equivalent for the Soviet Union to the now-closer relations between the USA and both China and Egypt.

American concern about Soviet intentions rose, and ranged widely in 1979, with Nicaragua in Central America seen as a threat when the Cuban-backed Sandinista National Liberation Front overthrew the dictatorship of Anastasio Somoza in June 1979. As in Iran, Nicaragua proved an instance of the problem of managing reform. In Iran, the USA had wanted a liberalisation of the Shah's autocratic regime, a regime reliant on a brutal secret police; only to end up with a vicious and far more brutal and oppressive theocracy. In Nicaragua, Carter had sought to ensure human rights and democratic government and, to those ends, had wanted Somoza to yield power to a moderate government able to hold fair elections. An unwilling Somoza argued that the only choice was him or the radical Sandinistas, whom he presented as Communists, and he was certain that this argument would ensure American support. An upsurge of Sandinista activity in 1978 was matched by Somoza's obdurate refusal to accept American pressure to yield. However, in 1979, the end of American aid was followed by the Americans beginning negotiations with the Sandinistas, and then by Somoza's fall. The Sandinistas were not to fulfil Carter's hopes. Instead, Nicaragua was linked to Cuba in practice as well as by Americans concerned to demonstrate a strategic threat in Central America.

The situation in South-West Asia was more serious, as America's strategic and military interests there were intertwined with economic concerns. The Iranian Revolution led to another major hike in oil prices, notably in March 1979 when it rose from $10 to $30 a barrel. This rise contributed to inflation levels and to a global economic crisis. A sense of America as being passed by the Soviet Union, or at least vulnerable to it, was scarcely new, and had, in particular, been exploited by Kennedy in the 1960 election. Yet, in 1979 the economic and strategic contexts appeared far more threatening than they had been in 1960. Concern about the general strategic situation was shown by Carter, but was exploited more successfully politically by Ronald Reagan when he challenged Carter for the presidency in 1980.

# CHAPTER SIX

# 1979–85

On 26 September 1983, the Cold War nearly resulted in nuclear catastrophe. The Soviet early-warning system reported first the launch of an American missile from Montana and, subsequently, a large-scale attack. Fortunately, the reports were treated as false alarms by Stanislav Petrov, the deputy chief for combat algorithms, and the Soviets did not launch their own missiles.[1] There was, however, a marked intensification of the Cold War in the early 1980s.

## Afghanistan and Iran

Afghanistan and Iran were key sites of international activity and concern at the outset of the period, and also contributed greatly to a hardening of the international mood, indeed a revival of Cold War animosities and tensions. The resort to violence in one area led to anxiety about it everywhere. The Soviets, who had sought to woo Afghanistan as an ally against Britain prior to World War Two, had been major aid donors to Afghanistan from the 1950s, taking its side in a frontier dispute with US-backed Pakistan. In 1973, the Afghan monarchy was overthrown in a coup and an authoritarian strongman, Mohammed Daoud Khan, a cousin and the brother-in-law of King Zahir Shah (r. 1933–73), who was also a former Prime Minister, took power. Backed by a group of Soviet-trained officers, Khan was willing to accommodate the Soviet Union. The coup was seen as an extension of Soviet influence, which certainly increased; but Khan was a nationalist, not a Communist. In turn, in the Saur Revolution on 27–8 April 1978, Daoud was overthrown and killed in a coup mounted by the Soviet-backed People's Democratic Party of Afghanistan. The presidential palace fell to a tank assault assisted by air strikes.

Bitterly divided between the Khalq (Masses) and Parcham (Banner) factions, the new government responded to opposition with repression. Its attempts to reform a largely conservative Islamic society, particularly with land reform and equality for women, both staples of the Communist prospectus for supposedly backward societies, led to rebellions from late 1978. The government met these with considerable brutality, including the bombing of recalcitrant cities, notably Herat. After a coup from within the regime, on 16 September 1979, did nothing to stem the tide of chaos, the Soviets militarily intervened in Afghanistan from 25 December 1979, violently overthrowing the government of Hafizullah Amin (who was killed), and installing Babrak Karmal as a client president.

The Soviet intervention appears to have resulted from a number of factors. Concern about the stability of their position in neighbouring Central Asia was a factor, notably anxiety that Afghanistan's problems could spill over into Soviet Tajikistan. There was an unwillingness to see a client state collapse. There was also anxiety that the Amin government might turn to China, thus extending the threat to Soviet borderlands. Chinese delegations were travelling to Afghanistan in 1978. Contemporary Western suggestions that the Soviet Union was seeking to advance to the Indian Ocean appear overstated, although the Soviets were interested in developing a major air base of Shindand near Kandahar from which the entrance to the Gulf could be rapidly over-flown. The takeover of Afghanistan offered a way to follow up the eviction of the Americans from neighbouring Iran and also to put pressure on neighbouring Pakistan, which was seen as a Chinese ally and as an enemy of India, the Soviet Union's largest South Asian ally. There was also an opportunity to hit American prestige.

The Soviet intervention in Afghanistan helped lead not only to Western alarmism, but also to pressure for an active response, both there and elsewhere. The Soviet invasion was regarded not as a frontier policing operation designed to ensure a pliant government, but as an act of aggression that needed to be countered. This view drew on a tendency, seen throughout the Cold War, to exaggerate Soviet political ambitions and military capability. It was, however, difficult for the Americans to acquire accurate information. The Soviet Union was a closed society with little in the way of open information or of possibilities for Western journalists and politicians to talk to members of the Central Committee and even the Politburo. Nothing of substance was offered to the American Senatorial delegations that visited Moscow. In his State of the Union address to Congress in January 1980, Carter warned that the Afghan invasion 'could pose the most serious threat to peace since the Second World War'.

The overthrow of the ineffectively authoritarian Shah in January 1979 had already led to greater American anxiety about the Gulf and the broader region. Manifested in the Carter Doctrine in January 1980, this concern resulted in the establishment, two months later, of a Rapid Deployment Task Force supposedly able to provide a rapid response across the world. However, Carter's earlier cuts in military expenditure, in response to the fiscal and economic problems of the late 1970s and as part of a *détente* 'peace dividend', helped ensure that the Carter Doctrine could not have been fulfilled if necessary. Moreover, the humiliation of the inability to free the American hostages held captive by Iranian radicals in the Tehran embassy, particularly the unsuccessful rescue mission of April 1980, combined with other factors, including high inflation, to associate Carter with repeated failure. On the heels of Vietnam, the trauma arising from the lengthy and public hostage crisis fuelled a sense of decline and a desire for rejuvenation. Ronald Reagan, the Republican candidate, understood and exploited this mood to beat Carter in the presidential election that year, although, late into the campaign, polls during the election were closer than people remember. The landslide in the Electoral College (489 to 49) did not match that in the popular vote (43.9 million to 35.5).

## Reagan and Cold War Escalation

A determined opponent of Communism, as well as an improviser at the level of implementation, Reagan was happy to be associated with a marked intensification of the Cold War. However, Carter had already adopted a moral approach to the Soviet Union that differed from Nixonian *realpolitik* and that, from 1977, took him increasingly away from *détente*. Carter's stance owed much to concern about harsh Soviet human rights policies. This stance was also a product of the Soviet modernisation of their nuclear missiles, specifically the deployment of the SS-20 missile, as well as of opposition to Soviet expansionism in the Third World. Mobile, accurate, and armed with nuclear warheads, the SS-20s were designed to be used in conjunction with conventional forces in an invasion of Western Europe. Carter's criticism angered the Soviet leadership, leading them not to negotiate seriously on a number of contentious issues, which provided Reagan with a further rationale for his anti-Soviet attitudes.[2] Although he backed down in 1978, in the face of a Soviet propaganda blitz, from deploying the enhanced radiation neutron bomb,[3] Carter began the military build-up that Reagan continued and for which he received at the time most of the credit. Moreover, Carter adopted a more active regional stance after the Soviet invasion of Afghanistan, for example pressing Somalia to provide access to the Indian Ocean port of Berbera.

Ironically, although Reagan regarded Carter as hopelessly idealistic, he was equally ideologically motivated in foreign policy and, indeed, rejected *realpolitik*. Reagan's earlier political career, notably his right-wing stance in the 1960s, in his successful 1966 campaign to be Governor of California and in his unsuccessful campaigns for the Republican nomination in 1968 and 1976, had made his views clear. Reagan restated these views during the election campaign, declaring in June 1980 that 'the Soviet Union underlies all the unrest that is going on'.[4] Reagan was encouraged in his anti-Communist resolve by Margaret Thatcher, Britain's resolute

Conservative Prime Minister from 1979 to 1990, who had seen Carter as insufficiently firm,[5] and by Karol Wojtyla, John Paul II, Pope from 1978 to 2005. However, there was no comparable drive from elsewhere in Western Europe. Relations with Thatcher were eased by American logistical support and diplomatic forbearance during Britain's 1982 war with Argentina over the Falkland Islands. There was no repetition of the undermining of Britain seen in the 1956 Suez Crisis.[6] At the same time, the possibility that key NATO anti-submarine naval assets would be sunk served as a reminder of the dependence of the Cold War on other agendas.

Reagan was not prepared to accept that the Cold War should, or could, end in a draw enforced by a threatening nuclear peace and the related arithmetic of deterrence. Instead, Reagan, Thatcher and John Paul II were determined to defeat what they each saw as an immoral and dangerous ideology. Reagan referred to the Soviet Union as an 'evil empire' in a speech on 8 March 1983. This remark provoked a very hostile media reaction. It is rarely wise to invoke theological judgments when discussing foreign policy. At the same time, Reagan's remark was mild compared with the gross cartoons and inflammatory and inaccurate articles that were a staple of the Soviet newspaper *Pravda*.

Already, on 2 September 1981, Reagan had warned that the USA was prepared to pursue a nuclear arms-race with the Soviet Union. Visiting Britain in June 1982, Reagan addressed British parliamentarians in the Royal Gallery in the Palace of Westminster, calling for a 'crusade for freedom' and for discarding Marxist-Leninism on the 'ash-heap of history'. Europe was the centre of his concern: 'From Stettin on the Baltic to Varna on the Black Sea', there had been no free elections for three decades, while Poland, where the independent trade union movement Solidarity was under assault, was, he declared, 'at the center of European civilisation'. This approach did not accept the idea that Poland should be securely located in the Communist bloc. Reagan also provided encouragement and support for the Afghan resistance to Soviet occupation, notably, from 1985–6, shoulder-fired ground-to-air missiles. This support strengthened the resistance, as well as providing the Soviets with a factor to blame when explaining continued opposition there. There has, however, been considerable controversy over whether Reagan had a grand strategy for the confronting and weakening of Communism, as argued, for example, by John Lewis Gaddis.[7] Alternatively, it has been claimed that there was no such strategy but, rather, a set of beliefs, notably the clashing aspirations of destroying Communism, and ending the risk of war: a 'crusade for freedom' alongside 'peace through strength'.[8]

Far from being cowed by Soviet military developments and deployments in the 1980s, not least the creation of a major naval capability and the deployment of intermediate-range missiles, the American government and military responded with higher expenditure and a vigorous determination to develop doctrines that would enable an aggressive response, on land, sea and air, to any Soviet attack. The former brought profit to the military-industrial complex which, in turn, helped ensure that particular localities, and thus politicians, had an incentive to support military expenditure.[9] This build-up was accomplished without conscription. On the part of the American military, there was a focus on how war with the Soviet Union could be won without a massive nuclear exchange. The example of Israeli success in the Yom Kippur War of 1973, and the doctrine of AirLand Battle, led to a stress on the integration of firepower with mobility in order to thwart the Soviet concept of Deep Battle. Proposing an effective synergy between land and air, and an intermediate level between the tactical and the strategic, this doctrine was designed to permit the engagement and destruction of the second and third echelon Warsaw Pact forces, at the same time that the main ground battle was taking place along the front; which suggested that NATO would be better placed than had been argued to repel a Soviet conventional attack in Europe. This doctrine led to an emphasis on the modernisation of conventional weaponry. New weapon systems included the Blackhawk helicopter introduced in 1979; the M1A1 Abrams tank, deployed from 1980; the Bradley Fighting Vehicle, designed to carry a squad of infantry and armed with a TOW (tube-launched, optically tracked, wire command data link) missile system, introduced in 1981; and the Apache attack helicopter, equipped with radar and Hellfire missiles, introduced in 1986.[10] Looked at more critically, the Americans were over-reliant on the capabilities of what airpower could achieve. This was also seen at sea. In 1982, in the Northern Wedding naval exercise, American carrier battle groups approached close enough to the Kola Peninsula to be able to launch planes carrying a full load to attack the Severomorsk naval base and then return.

There were also attempts to expand the range of American capability. These focused on the deployment of tactical nuclear weapons carried on Cruise and Pershing intermediate-range missiles. This deployment proved divisive in Western Europe, with particular concern about their deployment in West Germany. Both Reagan and Thatcher devoted considerable effort to winning support in Western Europe. The zero option was offered of no deployment if all Soviet intermediate-range missiles were removed from Europe, with Reagan keen on it as a first step for getting rid of all nuclear weapons. In contrast, Thatcher supported the measure only because she believed the Soviets would not agree: she wanted the American missiles deployed in order to counter Soviet conventional superiority, a reprise of the general strategy of nuclear deterrence.

Separately, there was an American commitment to the development of new space-mounted weaponry. The 'Star Wars' programme or Strategic Defense Initiative (SDI), outlined by Reagan in a speech on 23 March 1983, was designed to enable the USA to dominate space, using space-mounted weapons to destroy Soviet satellites and missiles.[11] It was not clear that the technology would work, in part because of the possible Soviet use of devices and techniques to confuse interceptor missiles. Indeed, Gorbachev was to support the Soviet army in claiming that the SDI could be countered.[12] However, the programme was also a product of the financial, technological and economic capabilities of the USA, and thus highlighted the contrast in each respect with the Soviet Union. The Soviets were not capable of matching the American effort, in part because they proved far less successful in developing electronics and computing and in applying them in challenging environments. Effective in heavy industry, although the many tanks produced had pretty crude driving mechanisms by Western standards, the Soviet Union failed to match such advances in electronics. Moreover, the shift in weaponry from traditional engineering to electronics, alongside the development of control systems dependent on the latter, saw a clear correlation between technology, industrial capacity, and military capability. It was in the 1980s that the Soviet Union fell behind notably. In 1986, an American interceptor rocket fired from Guam hit a mock missile warhead dead-on. This test encouraged the Soviets to negotiate.

In response to the Reaganite military build-up, the Soviet Union, with its anxious leadership fed intelligence reports about a hostile USA by the influential KGB, also adopted an aggressive pose. With the KGB providing inaccurate reports of American plans for a surprise nuclear first strike, the Soviets deployed more weaponry. Six *Typhoon*-class ballistic missile submarines entered Soviet service from 1980, as did their most impressive surface warships, including, in 1985, the *Admiral Kuznetsov*, their only big aircraft carrier. The *Typhoon*-class competed against the American *Ohio*-class, as the submarine evolved into an underwater capital ship as large as World War One *Dreadnought*-class battleships, and with a destructive capacity never seen before (or since) in any other type of warship. The USS *Ohio* and its sister submarines were 170.7 metres long with 18,700 tons submerged displacement. The Soviet *Typhoon*-class was 171.5 metres long with 25,000 tons submerged displacement. In each case, the submerged displacement was somewhat greater than the surface displacement. By comparison, the British *Dreadnought* of 1906 was 161 metres long and displaced 18,420 tons. These submarines were in a completely different league to the German U-boats of World War Two. Since the *Typhoons* carried newer, long-range missiles, they could remain under the sanctuary of the Arctic ice cap and then surface just at the edge of it, fire their missiles, and then retreat to under the ice cap. The *Typhoons* looked monstrous because they were triple-hulled, possibly because the Soviets did not trust the quality of their welding of the second hull. The titanium used for the pressure hull required more sophisticated welding than regular welding: the welding temperature is much higher and must be done in a vacuum. The Soviets were aware of the shortcomings, or feared that they had shortcomings, in their ability to construct minutely calibrated, pure micro-environments for difficult product fabrication, whether it be computer chips or titanium parts.

More secretly, as an interview, published in the *New York Times* of 25 February 1998, with Kanatjan Alibekov, formerly an official in the programme, revealed, the Soviet Union prepared anthrax, smallpox and plague virus cultures that would have been delivered by intercontinental ballistic missiles. This would truly have been anti-societal warfare. Nixon had abjured further American research and development of bacteriological and chemical weapons in 1969, a move that was not reciprocated by the Soviets. The Americans even began destroying their stores of these weapons. If the Soviets, into the early 1960s, had pursued bacteriological and chemical weapons as the 'poor man's' alternative to tactical nuclear weapons, they still continued with the research when their tactical and strategic nuclear disadvantage had disappeared.[13]

The role of the KGB and the military helped ensure that foreign policy was scarcely under the control of Soviet diplomats. This role also contributed to the nature of Soviet foreign policy. The Ministry of Defence and its industrial ministry allies in the Council of Ministers, as well as the representatives of major industrial concerns in the Central Committee, directly and indirectly, were a major factor in Soviet foreign policy, which was reactive, hostile and defensive, rather than attempting to seek international co-operation. Soviet diplomats were expected to respond to policies determined not by the Foreign Ministry but by a wide spectrum of office-holders. Party unity was a key element. It reinforced the institutional conformity seen in the Soviet Union, with the General Secretary of the Communist Party determining policy on what were presented as Party lines. Conformity and cohesion ensured that information was prepared, presented and analysed accordingly.

There were alternative sources of information for foreign policy, notably regional institutes associated with the Soviet Academy of Sciences that were established for Latin America (1961), Africa (1962), Asia (1966) and North America (1967). The Maurice Thorez Institute of Foreign Languages was an outstanding and highly prestigious institution that provided superlative training in foreign languages and cultures for those destined to serve in the Soviet foreign service. This proved particularly valuable in Latin America. However, although the regional institutes had access to information about the outside world, their ability to influence the decision-making process was limited. Moreover, there was no Soviet equivalent to the often politicised and frequently open debate about policy options seen in the USA, nor to the alteration of power there (and in Britain, France and West Germany) between the political parties. The Cold War thus saw a significant qualitative difference between the diplomatic systems in the two states, and a difference that was very much in favour of the USA and its major allies. There was a parallel difference in the intelligence services, with the KGB less ready to entertain debate than its Western counterparts. The Soviets proved better at descriptive intelligence gathering than at its analytic intelligence counterpart. The information from foreign agents was not synthesised in the manner seen in the West. Instead, the data entered depicted ever increasing corroborations of what 'Centre' expected to hear in relation to its orders to gather information on specific phenomena. Thus, the data served to buttress a priori assumptions. It was frequently not integrated and analysed with respect to new analytic frameworks that the data might point to. This defect emerged glaringly during Able Archer in 1983 (see p. 182) when the Soviets over-reacted, although this was not always the case. The KGB was divided into numerous sections or directorates, each of which was entrusted with specific responsibilities with respect to domestic and foreign intelligence gathering and operations. Although individual directorates could perform well, integrating the information provided (and thus the integration already performed) by different directorates was often below the standard of American and British counterparts. The Soviets found it difficult to put together the empirical pieces. Whereas case officers who processed data could be accurate, it was often interpreted differently by their seniors.

## Competing Regions

Europe came to the forefront in the early 1980s in part because the opportunistic and unsuccessful attack of Saddam Hussein of Iraq on Iran in 1980 began a major war that lasted until 1988. This conflict continued after the Iraqi forces were driven out of Iran in 1982. The decision was taken by the Iranians to invade Iraq in an attempt to overthrow Saddam Hussein. This commitment ensured that Iran seemed a far less serious threat to America's allies in the Gulf, especially Saudi Arabia. During the war, the West provided indirect support to Iraq, not least by sending warships to protect tanker traffic in the Gulf from Iranian attack. This deployment led to clashes between American and Iranian forces, clashes in which the latter were defeated. Although largely armed by the Soviet Union, Iraq was also provided with Western weaponry. However, in contrast to the situation from 1990, South-West Asia in the 1980s required only a relatively modest outlay of American resources, which ensured that attention could be devoted elsewhere.

## Poland

As a demonstration that the Cold War involved actions and initiatives by many players, and, linked to this, involved a high level of unpredictability, developments in Poland in the early 1980s were very important. They focused Soviet concerns about the stability of the Communist bloc and Western anxieties about the nature of Communist power. The background was the gradual unfolding economic crisis of Poland during the 1970s. The increase in the price of food in 1970 led to widespread riots, notably in the

Baltic seaports, especially Gdańsk. Wladyslaw Gomulka lost his position as First Secretary of the Polish Communist Party, being replaced by Edward Gierek. To buy off the population, Gierek borrowed billions of dollars from the West in order to finance major economic improvements, but, in reality, to keep an inefficient economic system going. Borrowing in hard currency created problems in repayment. Indebtedness, which reached $40 billion by 1977, forced the government to export its meat production for hard currency, and also, increasingly, other food as well. By 1979, food shortages in Poland had become intolerable.

Poland proved a lightning rod for the unpopularity of Communist regimes, with the added ingredients of traditional hostility to Russia and a strong national Christian commitment. This was shown in 1979 when John Paul II, the Polish Pope elected in 1978, drew millions on his 'pilgrimage' to the country. John Paul was at once theologically highly conservative and determined to challenge Communism as an unwelcome excrescence, especially in Poland. While a Cardinal there, he had met opposition leaders in 1976, and his stance was important in a major shift from the earlier position of the Catholic hierarchy there. In the 1960s, this hierarchy had sought better relations with the regime, but now, under John Paul, there was to be no compromise with Marxism and, instead, an affirmation of the authority of the Church. The strength of Catholic devotion in Poland was shown in public religious services. In turn, via Bulgarian intermediaries, the KGB may have been involved in the attempted assassination of the Pope in Rome in 1981. Although far from on the same scale or as public, Christian commitment and activity was also seen elsewhere in the Communist Bloc. Indeed, in this period, the Council for Religious Affairs in the Soviet Union received frequent complaints on this head from local agents.[14]

Large-scale strikes in Poland in 1976 led to repression but also to the organisation of KOR, a Workers' Defence Committee that was the first open opposition organisation in the Communist bloc. Information on repression was communicated to foreign journalists, which brought a measure of protection. Dissidents created the Flying University, which enabled students to sidestep government propaganda. Moreover, dissident publications spread works critical of totalitarianism, such as those of Hannah Arendt and George Orwell. This was an attempt to use intellectual energy to create a joint movement of intelligentsia and workers, thus wresting the population from a Communist Party that did not deserve to represent either.[15]

The crisis in Poland was precipitated in July 1980, with an increase in the price of meat, leading to large-scale strikes that were particularly prominent in the Lenin shipyard of Gdańsk (pre-war Danzig) where, organised by a KOR activist, Bogdan Borusewicz, the workers went on strike on 14 August. *Solidarność* (Solidarity), an unofficial trade union, was established under the leadership of an electrician, Lech Wałesa. After intimidation had failed, the government accepted the right to establish and join free unions, those independent of state authority. Solidarity became a nationwide trade union with about ten million members, the largest opposition movement in the world, and it was a key part of a newly-organised civic society outside the structure of the Communist state. Gierek, meanwhile, was replaced in September by Stanislaw Kania, another longstanding Communist bureaucrat. However, he failed to stabilise the situation.

Caution on the part of Solidarity's leaders prevented a breakdown in their uneasy relations with the Communist government, and the Soviet Union did not send in the tanks, as it had done in Hungary in 1956 and in Czechoslovakia in 1968. However, the Polish economy, already weak, deteriorated, while the Soviet government was concerned about the impact of the crisis on other Communist regimes and on the geopolitics of the Cold War. As the link between the Soviet Union and its forces on the Iron Curtain frontline in East Germany, Poland was strategically far more significant than the Communist mavericks in South-East Europe: Romania, Albania and Yugoslavia. Strikes in Poland threatened the links, notably rail routes, particularly that from Brest Litovsk in the Soviet Union via Warsaw to East Berlin. This threat led the Soviets to devote attention to maritime routes to East Germany across the southern Baltic and to develop infrastructure accordingly. In 1976, responding to price rises, rioting Polish workers at the Ursus tractor factory west of Warsaw tore up a section of the main railway line, much to the annoyance of the Soviets. Strikes also compromised Warsaw Pact defence in depth in the event of any confrontation with the West.

In 1980, the Soviets were pressed to act against Poland by the Communist leaders in East Germany and Czechoslovakia, who were concerned about the example being created, while they were also fearful that Solidarity would lead Poland to become another Yugoslavia. In October, the East German government imposed travel restrictions with Poland and stepped up *Stasi* activity. The Soviet Defence Minister, Dmitriy Ustinov, supported intervention; but his colleagues were reluctant to do so and the Soviet Union was warned not to by Reagan. Poland was probably too big to invade easily and doing so would have destroyed whatever remained of *détente*. There was also anxiety that the Poles would fight, unlike the Czechs in 1968, and concern about the effect that an invasion of Poland would have on Soviet troops, especially on the morale of men from Western Ukraine and Belarus. By not intervening with its own forces, the Soviet Union ensured that the Polish crisis did not become more serious, and this in the context of superpower hostility over NATO's plans to introduce intermediate-range nuclear weapons in Western Europe. This decision not to intervene also prefigured Mikhail Gorbachev's unwillingness to act in 1989 to preserve Communist control in Eastern Europe: the official creed of 'Socialist Internationalism' only meant so much.

General Wojciech Jaruzelski, the Minister of Defence since 1968 and thus a major Warsaw Pact figure, became Prime Minister in February 1981 and

First Secretary of the Polish Communist Party in October 1981. Jaruzelski had taken part in operations against anti-Communist resistance fighters in the late 1940s, had led Poland's contribution to the invasion of Czechoslovakia in 1968, and had been in command when Polish troops shot striking shipyard workers in 1970. Jaruzelski claimed he had opposed the last operation and he sought a peaceful settlement with Solidarity, but serious economic problems continued to create discontent in Poland and to lead to criticism of the government. Meanwhile, the Soviet Union pressed Jaruzelski to come out in defence of Communism. This pressure indicated that any meaningful change in the Soviet bloc would have to come from Moscow, and thus underlined the subsequent importance of Gorbachev's stance.

In 1996, Jaruzelski was to comment 'I always considered myself a Polish soldier and a Polish patriot first'.[16] He possibly thought of himself as another Józef Piłsudski, who had taken over the Polish government in 1926 and instituted a benign, quasi-military dictatorship. As Prime Minister, Jaruzelski downgraded the role of the highly unpopular Polish Communist Party and sought to play off Solidarity against the Soviet Union in order to gain concessions from each – stability and aid respectively. However, temperamentally, Jaruzelski found uncertainty difficult. In an effort to end political unrest and strikes, he declared martial law on 13 December 1981, arresting Solidarity's leaders and thousands of others without trial (scores were killed), and appointing a military council to govern Poland. On that day, with American attention riveted on Poland, Menachem Begin, the Israeli Prime Minister, annexed the occupied Golan Heights. Martial law remained in place in Poland until July 1983 and indicated the strength and weakness of the Communist system: it could maintain order, but could not provide the economic growth or popular support that made order much more than a matter of coercion and indoctrination. Opposition in Poland remained at a far greater scale and was far more popular than the left-wing terrorist movements in the West such as November 17 in Greece, FP-25 in Portugal, and the *Cellules Communistes Combattantes* in Belgium.

In response to martial law in Poland, Reagan, who feared direct Soviet intervention in Poland, introduced sanctions and provided covert aid to Solidarity. Reagan also sought to stop the building of the Yamal oil-gas pipeline from Siberia to Western Europe. This pipeline threatened to increase energy-dependence on the Soviet Union, especially in West Germany, a dependence seen as likely to have serious military and political consequences. Moreover, NATO and the European Community warned of the threat martial law in Poland posed to *détente*. However, the response in Western Europe to developments in Poland was largely pusillanimous, although Hungary in 1956 and Czechoslovakia in 1968 scarcely suggested that anything could or would be done. The French and West German governments sought stability and were ready to recognise Soviet dominance of Eastern Europe. If much public opinion, encouraged by the earlier reporting of Solidarity's activities, took a supportive view, the Left did not mobilise much of its vigour on behalf of the Polish workers. Indeed, in West Germany the Left was to be more vocal against the deployment of Cruise and Pershing missiles in 1983 than on behalf of the Poles, and similar priorities could repeatedly be seen in Britain. Western European governments, including the British under Thatcher, refused American pressure to stop the sale of equipment necessary for the completion of the Yamal pipeline.

## Cold War Tensions, 1983–4

Cold War international tensions rose to a peak in 1983, with the deployment of Cruise and Pershing missiles in Western Europe exciting Soviet concern and anger, and the Soviets fearing attack under the cover of Able Archer, a NATO military exercise held from 2 to 11 November. Reagan going aloft in his command plane during the exercise worried the Soviets. Moreover, the unrepentant Soviet shooting down on 1 September 1983, over Soviet airspace, of Korean Airlines flight 007, suspected of espionage, increased tension. Two hundred and sixty-nine people, including an American congressman, were on the plane.

Decided on by NATO ministers on 12 December 1979, in response to the deployment of Soviet SS-20 intermediate range ballistic missiles in Eastern Europe, and despite considerable West German division and reluctance[17], the Cruise and Pershing missiles arrived from November 1983. Their deployment demonstrated the continued strength and effectiveness of the Western alliance. In addition, American rhetoric, notably Reagan's 'evil empire' speech, which in some respects matched a longstanding Soviet pattern in rhetoric, rankled the Soviet leaders. Moreover, the American invasion of the unstable, left-wing Caribbean island of Grenada in October 1983 accentuated Soviet concern about American actions and intentions. Yuri Andropov, the Soviet leader from 1982 to 1984, interpreted these actions to support his suspicions of the USA, and he suspended Soviet participation in the arms-control talks in Geneva. Andropov came out of *Gosbes* (State Security) and was a genuine ideologue. He believed in the inherent mendacity of Western imperialist leaders and society, and in imperialists' treachery and willingness to wage war against the Soviet Union. However, there was no precipitant to conflict, in part due to Soviet caution and in part because the Soviet Union could not afford war.

The situation was different in Central America and the Caribbean. In these areas, like the Soviet Union in Poland, the USA faced problems in a traditional sphere of influence. This helped explain the American invasion of Grenada in 1983. A more sustained issue was posed by Nicaragua, where the Americans had intervened militarily against radicals in the 1920s. The left-wing Sandinistas who gained control of Nicaragua drew inspiration and support from Cuba, and also provided support for left-wing rebels in neighbouring El Salvador. Concerned about the risk of instability throughout Central America, and the wider regional challenge, and determined to mount a robust response, the Reagan administration applied economic, political and military pressure on the Sandinistas, providing funds from 1981 to train and equip the Contras, a counter-revolutionary force that was based in neighbouring Honduras. Although the Contras helped to destabilise Nicaragua, inflicting considerable damage, they could not overthrow the Sandinistas. The Contra threat increased the bellicosity of the Sandinista state. In contrast to indirect pressure on Nicaragua, the USA successfully used its military in October 1983 in Operation Urgent Fury against the Caribbean island of Grenada, a former British colony. This operation was motivated by concern about Grenada's leftward move, and the possibility that this would lead to a Cuban and Soviet military presence. There was a tendency to see Grenada as another Cuba. The island was seized and the government changed.

In El Salvador, where civil war had broken out in 1981, Reagan sought to protect, not overthrow, a government. Advisors, arms, including helicopter gunships, and massive funds were provided to help the right-wing junta resist the Farabundo Marti National Liberation Front (FMLN). However, the commitment of numerous American advisers was not followed by ground troops, which enabled the USA to define the struggle as low-intensity conflict; and, thus, compatible with a definition of the Cold War centred on war-avoidance. The conflict did not appear in this light to the population of El Salvador as they were caught between guerrillas and brutal counter-insurgency action which frequently took the form of terror. As with limited warfare, low-intensity conflict proved anything but for the civilians involved. The American hope that the election of the moderate José Napoleon Duarte as President in 1984 would lead to peace proved abortive.

Tensions in the Middle East were accentuated by the crisis in Lebanon where Israel hit the Syrians hard in 1982 when invading southern Lebanon. American Sidewinder missiles gave Israeli aircraft a vital capability. The dispatch of a multi-national Western force the same year, designed to try and bolster Lebanon's stability in the face of pressure from the PLO, competing militias and Syria, was unwelcome to the Soviet Union which provided support to both the PLO and Syria. In a demonstration of legitimation, the PLO was given diplomatic status. For example, the PLO had offices in Prague from 1976 and was officially recognised by the Czech government in 1983. Successful suicide attacks on the Western force in Beirut in 1983 led to its withdrawal.

The replacement of the dead Andropov, an adroit Cold War warrior who ran the country from a dialysis machine in his hospital room, by Brezhnev's protégé and former valet, the insipid and unimaginative Konstantin Chernenko, in February 1984, had scant effect in easing tension. Suspicious of Reagan, the Soviet leadership ignored his approaches for better relations.

# Afghanistan

In Afghanistan, the war did not go well, as the Soviets found it impossible to crush guerrilla resistance. As a result, the Soviets and their Afghan allies held little more than the cities. They had to confront an intractable military environment and faced obdurate opponents, harsh terrain, disease, and the difficulty of translating operational success into lasting advantage. Soviet soldiers were concerned about capture. Castration and the *rubashka* (the shirt: making an incision around the entire waistline and then lifting off the skin above it) were but two of the grisly tortures inflicted on captured troops. The Soviets also failed to understand both their opponents and the fragmented and bellicose nature of Afghan politics and society. Moreover, the mistaken Soviet belief that insurrectionary movements were the characteristic of progressive forces, and that conservative systems lacked real popularity, an ideological analysis shared by much of the Left, ensured that they did not have the necessary military doctrine to confront the Afghan resistance, nor an understanding of the relationship between military moves and political outcomes in Afghanistan. Prepared instead for high-tech conflict with NATO in Europe, the Soviets suffered from the lack of effective counter-insurgency doctrine, strategy and tactics, repeating the problems the Americans had faced in the Vietnam War.[18]

The Soviets were unable to force large-scale battle on their opponents, who generally proved able to avoid Soviet advances; and, although the Soviet airborne special forces were able to carry the fight to opposing Afghans, they were not employed with sufficient frequency. Sweeps or operations were followed by a return to base that brought no permanent benefit. When the Red Army tried 'hearts and minds' policies, they did not work. Driving the population off land that could not be controlled did not win support, and was further compromised by Soviet indiscipline and atrocities. About five million refugees from a population of fifteen million fled the country. Third World solidarity was scarcely on display on the part of the Soviet Army, and this situation, and the inability to win popular support, contributed to the sense that the war was without meaning on the part of the Soviets. A perception of the conflict as absurd and pointless contributed to discontent in the Soviet Union. However, there was nothing in terms of discontent that stood in the way of the Soviet government or General Staff in implementing their wishes, and certainly nothing even remotely comparable to the American protests during the Vietnam War.

# Economic Developments

In Central America and Afghanistan, the great powers might appear to have been operating in similar fashions, but their circumstances were very different. The revival of world economic growth after the 1970s crisis, especially in countries, such as Japan, Taiwan and West Germany, that were able to contain labour inflation, raise productivity, and move into new areas of demand, greatly helped the American economy in the 1980s. Coupled with the ability to borrow, economic recovery, and a sense of forthcoming further recovery, underwrote a more assertive American stance in international relations; although the role of attitudes and policies, specifically those of the Reagan presidency, was also highly important. The financial situation was significant, and the marked expansion of capital availability in the USA and abroad proved particularly valuable for the USA, both for the American economy and for its public finances. Domestic borrowing was stepped up to cover an ever-widening federal deficit. Aside from issuing a very large number of bonds, the government was paying 14 per cent interest on them by 1984. The reinvestment of oil revenues in the USA ensured that petrodollars became a measure of American influence and, in turn, meant that it was necessary for the USA to maintain its position in the Middle East. Similarly, the beneficiaries of East Asian economic growth, particularly Japan which had become the world's second largest economy, invested in the USA, thus helping the Americans to finance imports from East Asia and strengthening its stake in American success. Indeed, one reason why America won the Cold War was that it was able to ally with East Asia and, in particular, with the economic growth of Japan and the strategic asset of China. Moreover, under the American umbrella, there were no serious issues in dispute between China and Japan. The Soviet refusal to make any concession over returning the Kurile Islands, seized in 1945, to Japan, ensured that the Soviets passed up the possibility of massive Japanese investment in the Soviet Far East, which therefore remained underdeveloped and unable to threaten China or to offset the American-Chinese *rapprochement*.

The inflow of foreign capital into the USA was encouraged with the ending in 1984 by the Reagan government of the withholding tax on interest on income paid to non-residents. This inflow led to the large-scale foreign purchase of Treasury bonds, a purchase which reduced bond yields and ensured that the federal government could readily borrow large amounts in order to cover expenditure, including rising military expenditure. Bond yields also fell due to the reduction in the inflation rate from 1980 thanks to the Federal Reserve Board keeping bank-borrowing rates higher than in the late 1970s when inflation had dramatically increased. In 1984, the USA became a debtor instead of a creditor nation. Moreover, attractive American interest rates in the 1980s kept the demand for the dollar in foreign-exchange markets strong; and this demand ensured that global capital flows focused on the USA. In turn, this focus put enormous pressure on states that had borrowed heavily in the 1970s, such as those in Eastern Europe, notably Poland and Hungary, and Latin America. This pressure weakened the economic fundamentals of Communist rule in Eastern Europe. For

Latin American and other free-market states that had borrowed heavily, the resulting need for fiscal adjustment, and the dependence on American finance and on American-influenced global financial institutions, helped ensure the dissemination of the remedies of American neo-liberalism. In turn, these remedies directed capital flows, ranging from debt interest to private money seeking a safe haven, towards the USA.

In a sense, the 1980s helped bring further to fruition American hopes in the mid-1940s that economic liberalism would spread American influence, although the Bretton Woods generation of the 1940s had not intended regional major indebtedness. The spread of American influence was to be taken further in the 1990s after the fall of Eastern European and Soviet Communism. Free market economies also provided a major incentive for countries to look to the USA, the largest market in the world. The reduction of tariffs made the USA a more attractive commercial partner. In another light, this was a question of the outsourcing of American manufacturing jobs, a process that owed much to the quest for cheap labour, greatly encouraged by Western investment in parts of the Third World. The free market ideology of the West, and notably of Reagan and Thatcher, and the willingness to encourage structural adjustment, helped create an economic affinity, both within the West and in the Third World, that was not matched by the Soviet Union. In particular, Chinese economic links with the USA developed rapidly.[19]

Much of the regulatory looseness of the Reagan years built up serious problems for the future. This was notably so with the abandonment of economic guardianship for the American manufacturing base, notably but not only protectionism; and, with the Savings and Loans scandals that cost maybe $150 billion, discredited the George H. W. Bush administration (1989–93), and prefigured the financial crisis of the late 2000s. However, at the time, America's development proved a prime instance of the way in which the West adjusted to economic challenges with far less difficulty than did the Communist states, and shaped the resulting opportunities far more successfully.

In the 1930s, the crisis of the capitalist model had helped produce a new authoritarianism, notably in Germany, but also elsewhere, an authoritarianism characterised by autarky, populism and corporatism. In contrast, in the 1970s and 1980s, widespread fiscal and economic difficulties, many linked to globalist pressures, led either to the panacea of social welfare or to democratic conservative governments, especially in the USA and Britain, that sought to 'roll back the state' and that pursued liberal economic policies. These governments opened their markets and freed currency movements and credit from most restrictions. The economic crises in the West in the 1980s did not lead either to authoritarian regimes or to governmental direction of national resources on the Soviet model, even if the Left, notably in Britain in 1974–9 and in France in 1981–3, increased such direction. Economic difficulties encouraged the rise of far-Right political parties, as in France, West Germany, Belgium, Italy and Austria, but neither they, nor the radical Left, were able to seize power, nor even to exercise much influence on political or economic policies in West Germany and France. However, in Italy, the far-Right came into coalition government and it also became a key political player in Austria.

In Britain, Thatcher was comfortably re-elected in 1983 and 1987, and the radical left-wing challenge of a coal miners' strike designed in effect to bring down the government was defeated in 1984–5. This strike had its own dynamic very much located in British industrial and labour politics, but can also be placed within the Cold War. The leadership of the British NUM (National Union of Mineworkers), was very left-wing and was ready to take money from both the Soviet Union and Libya. Faced by a national dock strike in support of the miners, the government, in July 1984, drew up plans for troops to move coal and food around the country. Thatcher's closest aides saw the struggle as one to maintain effective government. In the end, the dock strike petered out in 1984. As another link with Cold War tensions, Thatcher survived an IRA bomb attack in 1984. The provision of arms to the IRA in part came from American sympathisers of Irish origin, but Eastern Bloc supplies were also significant, notably from Libya and Czechoslovakia. The IRA endorsed radical Marxist positions.

In Western Europe as a whole, the extremes proved weaker than had been the case in the 1930s. In part, this reflected greater prosperity and social welfare, but the role of international bodies, notably NATO, the IMF and the European Community (later European Union), were all significant. So also was the ability, on instantaneous notice, to transfer funds electronically to beleaguered banks and other financial institutions.

## Communist Stagnation

The Soviet failure to fulfil the goal of agricultural self-sufficiency ensured that grain had to be imported, notably from the USA, which was a striking instance of economic and political failure, as the free market remedied the failings of the command economy. In large part, the Soviet failure was due to the inability of collective forms of management (that in practice represented central state direction) to realise the potential of Soviet agriculture. This was a problem repeated across Eastern Europe. Managerial quality and peasant motivation were greatly lacking on the collective farms. By the late 1970s, the Soviet Union had easily out produced the Americans in the amount of farm machinery, and in the black-soil region of Ukraine they had a rich arable resource, but American agriculture was more productive. Collectivisation was a harmful legacy in the Soviet Union: there was a lack of private agriculture and little incentive on the part of collective farm members to work hard on public farmland. Moreover, due to central planning, there was an acute shortage of spare parts which meant that much farm machinery was not usable. In addition, there was a very high spoilage rate for Soviet agricultural products. A lot of produce rotted in rural warehouses or at train stations where it would not be picked up in time, and that was after substantial damage from the farms as the lorries bounced along ill-maintained dirt roads. From 1963, the Soviet Union imported grain from several Western countries, first Canada and, later, the USA. The Soviet government in the late 1950s had committed themselves to sharply increasing meat production, giving rise to Khrushchev's 1958 remark that the Soviets would overtake the Americans in meat production by 1960. To increase the numbers of livestock meant a significant rise in the amount of feed grain, which affected the availability of grain. Thanks to production problems, two-thirds of the revenue from the oil exported by the Soviets was being used by 1982 to purchase grain from the West, which was not the profile of a balanced industrial economy.

Moreover, some of the biggest planning disasters in the world occurred in Soviet agriculture, notably with cotton production in Soviet Central Asia, a sphere in which rampant corruption, and the serious misreporting of production statistics, vied with fundamental environmental degradation not least due to excessive irrigation that caused the exhaustion of the Aral Sea. These problems were a major issue for Mikhail Gorbachev who, in the early 1980s, was the Politburo member responsible for agriculture. Environmental issues included the whisking into the air, as injurious dust, of dried out soil contaminated by chemical fertilisers. This led to an increase of birth defects among Uzbek and Turkmen children. The children living in eastern Kazakhstan were afflicted with such horrors due to the aftermath of nuclear bomb tests.

Given problems with agricultural production, it is not surprising that both life expectancy and infant mortality were unsatisfactory in the Soviet Union. In turn, this situation discredited claims about the superiority of the Soviet system and also fed through into economic problems, for a decline in population growth hit the increase in the labour force in the 1970s and, even more, in the 1980s. Soviet labour needs had, in part, been met by high employment rates among women, but, by the 1980s, there was less new female labour that could be added to the workforce. Labour issues, moreover, were seriously compounded by the scale of under-employment that resulted from a failure to allocate resources in accordance with market mechanisms including the properly-costed use of resources. The Soviets were trapped into under-employment for that was the only means of fulfilling the ideologically-driven nostrum of full employment. In the late 1970s, Huta Stalowa Wola, the Polish steel plant outside Warsaw, employed 20,000 workers, although 8,000 would have done the job. A failure to accept the reality of unemployment in the Soviet bloc helped exacerbate the problems of economic management.

The Soviet bloc was in a very difficult situation by the mid-1980s.

Economic downturns interacted with already pronounced systemic faults. In particular, there was a failure to ensure adequate mechanisms for incentive, which reflected the lack of entrepreneurship and capitalism in the bloc. With bright people unable to follow the Western pattern of raising money for investment and, moreover, generally excluded from state monopolies governed by timeserving and unimaginative bureaucrats, it was not surprising that the Soviet system could not engage adequately with change. This inability to engage with change was seen dramatically in the failure to produce sufficient computers, which was indicative of an unwillingness to put an accurate cost on the use of human time, as well as an unhappiness about departing from paper mechanisms of recording and deploying information. This unwillingness was a symptom of a more systemic management incompetence and planning failure that helped ensure that the commitment of resources and effort did not yield qualitative improvements in the economic system. The focus solely on output, or rather on claims of output, proved greatly misconceived. Communist economics entailed scant concern with the free market, and this situation led to numerous instances of the supply of only part of the process: shaving cream without shaving implements, for example.

Economic and other statistics from the Soviet era are unreliable. Nevertheless, there is little doubt that measures of economic growth show a fall in the Brezhnev era (1964–82); with earlier rates of increase, in national income, production, productivity and return on investment, not being sustained. This fall also represented a serious failure in the planning set out under the five-year plans, and the mismatch between these plans and the reality of often lacklustre outcomes helped discredit Communism as a system of economic analysis, a guide to planning, and a means for social progress. The conceptual problems were serious. Alongside state bureaucratic control, there was a difficulty in understanding time and value in economics, as well as the energy and labour inadequacies and insufficiencies of Eastern Bloc manufacturing, the growing impracticality of the centralised monitoring of the ever-escalating product mix, and the general realisation that the implications of opportunity costs arising from technological innovation conferred economic benefits that were not the same as those connected with the maintenance of wasting, depreciated capital assets. The Soviets appeared unable to visualise economic reform other than Kosygin's 1965 attempt to provide factory managers with some leeway in determining output capacity, an attempt that was squashed. The economic impasse of the Soviet Union was reflected in the lack of alternative plans. There was no longer any lived business experience. When these aggregate failures were combined with a lack of economic transformation toward innovation and new product ranges, then the situation was indeed serious. The command economy, with its micromanagement in planning and execution from the centre, was failing. Limited growth, moreover, intensified competition for resources, and the state lacked an adequate mechanism to cope with this

competition which, anyway, it did not understand fully. The nostrums of
Marxist-Leninism offered no help and decreasingly little inspiration.

In Eastern Europe, there was a degree of greater flexibility than in the
Soviet Union. This was especially so in Hungary and Poland, where the
availability of consumer goods was regarded as part of a silent bargain
to secure popular compliance with the Communist dictatorship, and thus
to avoid a recurrence of the 1956 risings. Consumerism and leisure, in
place of the earlier focus on work and production, were also stressed
in East Germany by the 1970s. Poorly-balanced from the outset, the
Communist command economies, however, were in serious difficulties by
the mid-1980s. Hamstrung by ideological management, earlier attempts
to reform them had proved flawed. In particular, the 1970s *détente* had
led to substantial Western loans, particularly, but not only, as a result of
West German *Ostpolitik*. There was a willingness on the part of Western
European governments to provide export guarantees and credits. However,
due both to the nature of Communist economic management and to the
indiscriminate distribution of loan money, these loans had not been translated into effective investment and economic take-off, and had, instead,
enabled a postponement of necessary economic reforms while increasing
indebtedness. These substantial debts greatly reduced the options for
Eastern European governments, creating, with their creditors, a shared
dependency on *détente*, at the same time as they exposed the major
weaknesses of the Eastern European economies. Economic limitations and
financial problems made it difficult to import Western technology; and this
difficulty accentuated the political pressure to turn to low-efficiency Soviet
products. Economic integration in the Communist bloc all too frequently
entailed what in practice was the bartering of shoddy goods without any
real concern with quality or the necessary understanding of how best to
establish value or to improve the system. Barter trade was to be expected
since the values of the Eastern Bloc currencies were manipulated by the
respective governments. No one really understood what their value was in
relation to one another unless one went by black market rates. Moreover,
using Western currencies for current accounts was out of the question.

Economic problems, notably low productivity and massive under-
employment, meant that per capita GNP was very low compared to the
West. Combined with the high rate of military expenditure, these economic
problems limited the funds available for social investment and consumer
spending. Unlike in the West, economic growth in the Soviet bloc did not
lead to personal prosperity, and certainly not by the conspicuous standards
of the West. This limitation increasingly compromised popular support
for the system, especially because television made the public notably in
East Germany, thanks to the heavy exposure to West German television,
aware of better times elsewhere. Furthermore, viewers in northern Estonia
could watch Finnish television. Television 'soaps', soap-operas of family
life, proved particularly seductive as they apparently showed how families

lived in the West. This awareness of a better life elsewhere encouraged the attempt in Eastern Europe not only to provide consumer goods but also to block Western television transmissions. Travel also challenged Communist suppositions and claims, which helped explain why travel outside the Communist Bloc was limited to those judged safe, and was closely scrutinised by the secret police. Poland was the exception, as the government there, beginning in 1970, allowed large numbers of its citizens to travel abroad to work and to visit Western countries. Across the Bloc, foreign travellers were regulated and placed under surveillance.

Communist governments pushed 'Socialist social policies' as they sought to reconcile economic with social policies and to use social welfarism to enhance labour productivity. Instead, this welfarism, designed to create the 'guaranteed tomorrow', proved a potent drain on the economy, while also failing to satisfy rising popular expectations, and, indeed, undermining the incentive to work.

Despite the presence of plentiful lignite ('brown coal'), which itself was used with no concern for the human or natural environment, the East German economy was affected by a lack of natural resources. Like most of Eastern Europe, it was dependent on Soviet assistance, not least in the form of cheap oil. In some respects, the transition from a coal to an oil economy proved one of the major handicaps for Eastern Europe. The provision of Soviet economic assistance had helped ensure an ability to cope with structural weaknesses, but, in the 1970s, Soviet assistance to Eastern European states declined. This decline led in Eastern Europe, notably in Poland, to the build-up of very large external debts to the West, as well as big internal deficits within the Communist bloc and individual states. Such debts and deficits did not permit the capital accumulation necessary for the industrial modernisation that was required in the 1980s if the Communist economies were to compete, if only to service their heavy debts, by means of earning export income and by import substitution. More than financial factors were at stake, however. Economic rationality was not possible due to the political structure and ideology of Communist states. This lack of rationality was particularly true of the ideological commitment to heavy industry, especially steel production, and to the political, social and gender narratives bound up in this commitment. Nor was it possible to provide productivity increases that could sustain the relatively high wages that workers, especially industrial, received, nor indeed produce the goods for them to buy. One clear sign of failure in East Germany and the Soviet Union was that workers had a high saving ratio, as they could not find sufficient things to buy. This was not the case, however, in Poland where the cost of living had outpaced regular wages by the mid-1970s.

Visiting East Germany in 1980 in order to carry out archival research, I was repeatedly struck not so much by the limited nature of goods available for personal consumption, which I had expected, as by the poor state of public provision in terms of such criteria as street lighting, pavements, and the frequency of postal collections and rail services. The use of lignite, 'brown coal', with singularly little concern for the environmental consequences, also resulted in a serious deterioration of air quality that was readily noticeable, while rivers were badly polluted as a result of the drive for industrial output. The regulation enforced on personal opinions scarcely extended to factory chimneys or outflows, a Bloc-wide phenomenon. Lignite was also burned in western Czechoslovakia and in south-western Poland.

The second oil price hike, that of March 1979 due to the overthrow of the Shah in Iran, had helped precipitate a global economic shock that posed a major problem for the weaker economies. This was particularly true of the Eastern European states. However, due to their political system and ideology, their inability to service their debts did not lead to the economic transformation necessary for them to modernise. Fiscal pressures and discipline were to have different effects in Eastern Europe to those experienced in Western Europe and, differently, Latin America.

Falling life expectancy, which owed much to pollution, was a clear symptom of the social failure of the Communist economies and challenged their legitimacy, which Communist governments based on social progress including good universal health provision. Moreover, political failure was seen in the prominence of corruption, not only for personal profit but simply in order to get economic processes to work. Unreported and illegal production and trades were necessary for the economy to function, not least through a large-scale barter system which encompassed industry, agriculture, the bureaucracy, services and individuals. This production and these trades also led to the development of a parallel world of personal gain regulated by bribery. These practices made a mockery of Communism, not least as this parallel world included public institutions. The ability of Party officials to gain special privileges, notably in housing, the purchase of goods, travel, education and preference for relatives, further helped to discredit the Communist system and to make it unpopular. The manner of economic functioning was pre-capitalist and a regression from Marx's third stage of economic development, which followed what he called slave and feudal societies. Thus, the Communist Bloc's economic performance by the 1970s invalidated Marx's argument about a superior, fourth stage of history, socialism.

# The Crisis of the Soviet Bloc

With time, the sham character of Communist progress became more apparent: to the peoples of the Soviet Union and Eastern Europe, and to foreign commentators. The failure to match Western European improvements in living standards helped cause widespread apathy, cynicism and disillusionment among the population. The inherent weaknesses of the Communist system, and notably its economics, were increasingly brought to fruition and understood in Eastern Europe.[20] However, in a serious failure of knowledge, analysis and assumptions, Western intelligence agencies were to be surprised by the speed of the eventual collapse of the Communist regimes. Practically no one in the Russian history field in 1985 predicted that the Soviet Union would fall apart. The seeming durability of dictatorships proved an imposing idea and image for Western observers. More predictably, Left-wing sympathisers continued to publish articles praising Communist states and, at the least, putting them on an equivalent with the USA.

The Brezhnev regime (1964–82) was increasingly characterised by incompetence, corruption and sloth. The sluggish and complacent Brezhnev, who failed to see the need for change, neglected warnings of problems and proved particularly negligent in economic management.[21] Subsequently, the disastrous explosion at the Chernobyl nuclear plant in Ukraine in April 1986, and the dishonest and inefficient response of the Soviet government, helped to suggest that the entire Soviet system was weak and negligent. The Chernobyl episode indicated sub-optimal Soviet management. The plant managers decided to run a safety test by withdrawing all primary and secondary safety back-up measures, including lifting the lead rods from the old-fashioned water containment cylinders. As a result, the air pressure inside the dome increased 1,400 times within four seconds and the dome exploded. The Soviets waited two weeks before reporting the accident, ensuring that the necessary precautions against radioactivity could not be taken.

Nevertheless, despite serious economic problems, the Brezhnev regime retained control, in large part because of the strength of the Soviet dictatorship. This strength was not simply a matter of coercion, although that was important. Much activity was devoted by the KGB to spying on dissidents and to persecuting them by methods such as imprisonment, internal exile, and consigning sane people to psychiatric hospitals in order to drive them mad. The Soviet ambassador to the USA, Dobrynin, claimed that Brezhnev kept 800,000 political prisoners in prison or mental hospitals. There was similar activity across the Communist bloc. In East Germany, in the 1980s, the ubiquitous Ministry for State Security, the *Stasi*, read 90,000 letters and 2,810 telegrams daily, they also tapped telephones on a large scale, activities that required a huge personnel. It was not enough to act against those judged dissidents. Instead, the entire population was under surveillance, with informers in every workplace and apartment block, and family members and lovers encouraged to spy on each other.

Inertia, however, was more potent than coercion across the Communist bloc. There was a fatalist sense among the public that there was no alternative to Communist rule. This sense encouraged widespread despair and high rates of drunkenness, in turn affecting health and life expectancy.

Alongside inertia and coercion, the state's ability to seem to offer some improvement or benefits was also useful with particular constituencies of support, notably the bureaucracy and the military. Enthusiasm, however, was limited and, across the bloc, the Communist Party, which did not succeed in inspiring, was pushed to the back by state bureaucracies that did not seek to inspire. In addition to a rise in political opposition to the Communist regimes, especially the Solidarity movement in Poland, there was a widespread privatisation of commitment on the individual and household level, and a focus on getting by, and on the shifts and expedients of life under Communism. These shifts and expedients involved bartering, persuasive corruption, and often shoddy compromises. Personal integrity and the sense of self-worth were repeatedly bargained away, both to obtain benefits and in reporting on others. Suicide rates among the young were particularly high. This situation did not mean or lead to significant active opposition, but it left government and the Communist Party in a vacuum, with Party members largely cut off from the working class they were supposed to represent. There was also a disconnect from the peasantry and intelligentsia. As a consequence, political opposition, where it existed, could hope to win a measure of public acceptance, possibly support, even if it was denied the means of political expression employed in the West. The Solidarity movement in Poland suggested what this could lead to, and was therefore a disruptive example for the rest of the Communist bloc.

## Shuffling the Deckchairs

Dying on 10 November 1982, Brezhnev was succeeded as General Secretary of the Communist Party by the 68-year old Yuri Andropov, Soviet ambassador in Hungary in 1956, and the head of the KGB from 1967. He appeared to offer the possibility of a new start because he did not share Brezhnev's complacency and, instead, appreciated the need for improvement. However, Andropov had scant concept of improvement other than better social and work discipline. He had little in the way of any notion of improving qualitative industrial output, or making radical changes. Policies included the dispatch of agents into cinemas in the early afternoon in order to check viewers' identities so as to establish whether they were absentee workers, and the decree that liquor stores had to open later in the day, rather than in the morning, so as to prevent workers from leaving their jobs to buy vodka. As was true for many Soviet propaganda campaigns, after a short period of time, matters continued on their usual course and nothing substantive was done. Andropov was anyway increasingly ill with kidney disease. On 17 January 1983, Reagan had approved National Security Decision Directive 75, which included the goal of promoting 'the process of change in the Soviet Union toward a more pluralistic political and economic system in which the power of the privileged ruling elite is gradually reduced'. There was scant sign of such a prospect under Andropov, and the Directive was correct in pointing out that 'Soviet aggressiveness has deep roots in the internal system'. Dying on 9 February 1984, Andropov was replaced by Konstantin Chernenko, another member of Brezhnev's gerontocracy and, like Andropov, in poor health when appointed. Chernenko lacked even Andropov's energy and had none of his intellect, and this contributed greatly to the sense of policy deadlock.

Andrey Gromyko, a key senior member of the Politburo, who had been Foreign Minister since 1957, maintained continuity in foreign policy. An expert on relations with the USA, where he served at Washington from 1939, before becoming Delegate to the United Nations from 1946 to 1949, Gromyko saw the world almost exclusively through the prism of Soviet-American relations. He did not seek a breakthrough with the USA. Instead, under Gromyko, Soviet foreign policy was nearly as rigid as he was unsmiling. Certainly, there was no bold initiative comparable to Nixon's approach to China, nor, subsequently, any Soviet ability to retrieve the situation in China. At the same time, there were changes and openings before the rise of Gorbachev. In September 1984, Gromyko travelled to Washington to meet Reagan, and in January 1985 the Politburo decided to engage again in arms negotiations with the USA.

A staleness was particularly apparent in the early 1980s, and notably under Chernenko, who died on 10 March 1985. An impression of stagnation, if not decay, became more insistent and was commented on both within and outside the Soviet Union. 'The patient had died already on the operating table' by 1985, although few of the top Soviet leaders under-stood that. Yet, underlying later counterfactuals about whether different outcomes were possible, very few commentators proved willing to predict that the Soviet bloc would soon collapse. There was an awareness in the West of its economic problems, but not of their consequences. The ability to suppress dissent in Poland in 1981 encouraged a sense that force would help deal with problems.[22] However, the combination of Soviet economic difficulties, Soviet political sluggishness, and a much broader and better educated Soviet citizenry, indicated that the country in 1985 was very different to what had been called for and anticipated during the 1917 Revolution. Moreover, the citizenry was aware of this contrast.

# CHAPTER SEVEN

# 1985–92

## War Planning

At the beginning of 1985, conflict linked, albeit in part indirectly, to the struggle for primacy between the USA and the Soviet Union continued in several areas of the world, notably in Afghanistan, Angola and Central America. Moreover, although the Soviet government agreed in January 1985 to re-open talks on arms limitations, confrontation remained serious along the Inner-German Frontier between West and East Germany, as both sides game-planned for war. The crisis year of 1983 had passed, but there was no guarantee that it would not recur. Soviet fears, notably at the time of the NATO exercise Able Archer in November 1983, that NATO would launch a surprise attack were misplaced. Nevertheless, the USA was increasingly confident that it could win a sub-nuclear war. In particular, the Americans were emboldened by the Israeli success against the Syrian air force over Lebanon in 1982. This justified the superiority, in American eyes, of American avionics and air weaponry over their Soviet counterparts. The competition for defence funding contributed to this belief, as did the need for a new military doctrine to deal with the reality that the Americans no longer had conscription and therefore could not maintain an army of the size that had met commitments in the 1960s. A group of defence politicians, intellectuals and opportunists, notably Casper Weinberger, the Secretary for Defense, Richard Perle and Paul Wolfowitz, all found the AirLand Doctrine useful. As there was no war, the likely sustainability of this doctrine in prolonged combat is unclear. The assumption that a sub-nuclear war could be fought, that containment in that fashion was possible, presumed a congruence in Soviet thinking that was unproven. Moreover, this assumption ignored all the Rand and other Think Tank studies of the 1960s and 1970s claiming the unavoidability of escalation once fighting had broken out between the USA and the Soviet Union. At the level of American weaponry, there were also questions of effectiveness, and notably if the weaponry had been used against a genuinely hard opponent like the Warsaw Pact forces, and not against soft opponents like Syria and, in the 1990s, Iraq and Serbia. In 1986, East Germany deployed a frigate with a radar believed capable of tracking the American stealth (radar-evading) aircraft. American 'Star Wars' weaponry failed to live up to its billing.

American planning in the 1980s sought to benefit from major developments in the capability of airpower, especially the advances stemming from more powerful air-to-air radars, the enhancement of air combat resulting from heat-seeking short-range air-to-air missiles and their radar-guided, long-range counterparts, and the use of AWACS (Airborne Warning and Control System) aircraft. In the event of war, the USA planned to employ stealth attack aircraft and 'smart' laser-guided weapons fired from stand-off platforms. The capabilities of precision-guided munitions were to be exploited. Laser-guided projectiles and programmed Cruise missiles would inflict heavy damage on Soviet armour, supplementing the anti-tank ordnance on the A-10 Warthog jet; while advanced aircraft, such as the F-15 and F-16, would win air superiority and also attack Soviet ground forces as well as providing cover for helicopter attacks. Stealth technology, it was believed, would permit the penetration of Soviet air defences, obliging the Soviets to retain more aircraft at home, and would also threaten their nuclear deterrent. Co-ordination would be made possible by computer networking, a new generation of spy satellites with six-inch resolution, AWACS aircraft, and the Global Positioning System.[1] The emphasis, for Britain and West Germany as well as the USA, was on manoeuvrism in the shape of a flexible defence, and counter-attacks. Greater British engagement with this approach owed much to the role of Sir Nigel Bagnall, successively commander of the 1st British Corps in Germany (1981–3) and of NATO's Northern Army Group (1983–5), and Chief of the General Staff (1985–8).

At sea, the *US Maritime Strategy* published in 1986 pressed for a forward, attacking deployment of warships in north-east Atlantic and north-west Pacific waters in order to protect allies and communications, threaten Soviet nuclear missile submarines and bases, and force battle on the Soviet navy. This was seen as a way to offset Soviet strength on land in Europe.[2]

# Conflicts

In the event, there was no conflict on the European frontline. In part, the Soviets and the Americans had developed restraint, predictability, and a certain honesty in handling nuclear-fraught situations. A small-scale demonstration of American capability was provided when Libya was bombed by American planes from British airbases on 15 April 1986, in response to its large-scale sponsorship of terrorism against American interests.[3] By spending over £20 billion on Soviet arms, Colonel Qaddafi, the oil-rich dictator of Libya since 1969, had, by the mid-1980s, built up a military that included 535 combat planes and over 2,800 tanks. However, repeated and effective French air action, notably in 1983 and 1986, against Libyan forces unsuccessfully intervening in neighbouring Chad, a former French colony, indicated the serious deficiencies of this force, as well as the extent to which the Cold War comprehended distant battlefields and varied struggles. In Afghanistan, the anti-Soviet guerrillas benefited from 1985–6 from the supply of American ground-to-air Stinger missiles, which brought down Soviet helicopter gunships. This forced them and Soviet aircraft to fly higher, which cut the effectiveness both of their ground support and of their bombing.

## Gorbachev

Yet, although the Cold War continued to be registered on battlefields and in espionage round the world, a dramatic shift in policy was already underway in the Soviet Union, a shift that was to bring the Cold War and, inadvertently, the Soviet bloc to an end. A recognition of Soviet weakness was central to the change in policies introduced by Mikhail Gorbachev. The youngest member of the Politburo (of which he became a full member only in 1980), he became leader, as General Secretary of the Central Committee of the Communist Party of the Soviet Union, on 11 March 1985, at the age of 54. The first Soviet leader who was really a post-Stalinist, Gorbachev had joined the Communist Party in 1952 and had benefited from the Khrushchev thaw.[4]

His main rival for power in 1985, Grigori Romanov, a hardliner, would probably not have taken reform so far.[5] Internal security in Leningrad, where he was the Party boss, was tight, as the city had the reputation of being the Westernising city. Romanov was affected by a scandal involving his commanding the Hermitage Museum to send valuable china to a family wedding in which it was broken by the drunken guests. Rumour spread the news which served to discredit Romanov as extravagant.

Gorbachev's key policy changes were domestic, as he sought to modernise Communism by introducing reforms; but there was also a drive for a less combative and confrontational international stance. Aware that the Soviet Union and the Communist cause faced difficulties, Gorbachev put them in a Marxist context in which the strains of global capitalism instead appeared apparent. The notion of progressive crises in the capitalist order remained strong among Communist thinkers, and Gorbachev was confident that these economic and social crises would lead to political rivalry within the West, weakening the USA, and helping the Soviet Union. Moreover, Gorbachev initially pressed for a more coordinated and successful approach to the

Third World, based not on the withdrawal of Soviet commitment but rather on appropriate policies by allies, combined with prioritisation by the Soviet Union. This approach meant stricter budgeting as the Soviet government could no longer afford all its overseas commitments. This prioritisation was partly responsible for the decision to withdraw from Afghanistan. It would be mistaken, therefore, to use this (eventual) withdrawal in order to suggest that Gorbachev was unwilling to defend overseas Soviet interests and allies. Thus, in 1985, in response to an American trade embargo of Nicaragua, Gorbachev both increased economic assistance to Nicaragua and promised Cuba help if it backed Nicaragua against an American military attack. In addition, Soviet planes flew into Pakistani airspace soon after he came to power.

The reform policies of the Gorbachev government were, in effect, its own attempt to create what had been termed, with reference to Dubcek and Czechoslovakia in 1968, 'Socialism with a human face'. The sham propaganda of Communist progress, however, helped ensure that these policies inadvertently destroyed Communism in Eastern Europe and the Soviet Union, as well as the Soviet state. It proved impossible, in yet another stage of the attempt at uplifting the Soviet standard of living, and thus promoting the efficacy of Soviet ideology, to introduce a market responsiveness in a planned economy. Consumerism was a Western bourgeois concept to the Soviet government but, nevertheless, there was a wish to win popular support through economic means. Efforts from 1985 to achieve economic and political reform, however, faced the structural economic and fiscal weakness of the Soviet system, not least the preference for control as opposed to any price system that reflected cost and availability. Moreover, the post-Communist dismantling of the old command economy was to expose the uncompetitive nature of much Soviet-era industry, both of individual enterprises and of the economy as a whole. By 1985, it took the Soviet Union three times as much electricity to produce one ton of steel as in the case of the West Germans, and at least twice as much time (i.e. labour) as in the West German and American cases. Soviet economic inefficiency and costs led to the moment of truth that Gorbachev faced in the mid-1980s

Assessing the Soviet economy, and indeed the Cold War as a whole, faces the challenge of teleology: making the outcome appear inevitable. Ironically, such an approach was a characteristic of Communist thought. However, this characteristic was accompanied, in practice, by a total failure to predict eventual outcomes or to understand processes at work and changes that were occurring. All of this proved the case with the collapse of the Communist bloc. However, whatever the confidence of assessment stemming from eventual collapse, there are problems with any argument that the Soviet Union could not sustain its position as a great power because its economy was illiberal. Indeed, although the economy was not capitalist, it managed to produce sufficient material to underpin Soviet military strength to the degree necessary to make the Soviet Union a great power. Their opponents *might* have been effective in the event of war, but the sheer size of the Soviet forces induced grave strategic concern in the West. More generally, the amount of Soviet production (not the means or efficiency of obtaining it) was significant; and the Soviet focus on the strength of the state, and not on the wealth nor well-being of the individual, was not inherently inefficient. An emphasis on per-capita GNP, which reflects both the quantity of goods brought to market and liberal economic views of the superiority of comparative advantage, is not invariably valid, as per-capita GNP does not determine power. Russia, indeed, had demonstrated that in the nineteenth century.

These points about the amount of production, however, seem more valid for the 1930s than for the 1980s when the pace and nature of techno-logical change suggested that the character of economic development was moving very clearly away from a situation in which the process could be readily directed by government. Moreover, the fall in the price of oil and natural gas in the 1980s hit Soviet finances as the economy had become heavily dependent on exports of them. The price of oil fell by nearly 80 per cent between 1980 and 1986. But linking the respective significance of these points to the more general fashion in, and after, the 1980s for liberal economics remains unclear and, in part, reflects different interpretative approaches. Aside from the economic situation, the international political and military environment was not auspicious: the Soviet Union was on unfriendly terms in the 1980s with the USA, much of Western Europe, China and Japan.

The serious intellectual crisis of Marxism was not the reason for the collapse of the Communist states. However, the failure of what the Soviet Communists under Lenin and Stalin had fashioned and presented as the Marxist model for an economic system joined its political to its intellectual crisis. The Soviet Communist Party labelled Marxist-Leninist theory a 'science'. Marxist-Leninist theory could, allegedly, predict outcomes but science cannot do so for human society. The contrast created a problem for Marxist-Leninist thinkers that was philosophical, methodological, epistemological and psychological. The sterility of intellectual thought surrounding Soviet Marxist-Leninism was profound. There was no infusion into Soviet Marxism from the Frankfurt School, or the relatively liberal Italian Communist Party, or the British Marxist School, or Latin American Liberation Theology, or Chinese developments towards a more liberal economic order. Soviet Marxist-Leninism remained ideologically autarkic until the late 1980s and, when it no longer chose to do so, it fell apart and Soviet Party members by the millions discarded their Party cards. Nevertheless, the collapse of Communism was largely due not to this intel-lectual failure, but to the specific political and economic circumstances of the 1980s. Moreover, the possibility of a different trajectory, and thus the value of counterfactual speculations that probe such possibilities, was exemplified by developments in China. There, the introduction of capitalism proved compatible with the Communist rule that was maintained by the availability of force and, in 1989, by the willingness to use it. As a further reminder that ideological issues should be set in context, the problems of Soviet Communism were to be matched in post-Communist Russia. The situation then, now capitalist (of a type) and democratic (of a form), was, in practice, like the earlier Communist system. There was a reliance on informal networks, personalised loyalty notably to Putin, and the exchange of favours, all of which sapped institutional effectiveness.[6] As under Communism, assets were not properly costed, while private property was at risk.[7]

As far as the intellectual crisis of Marxism was concerned, the commitment of much of the population in Communist countries to Marxism as the basis for understanding themselves and their world was, anyway limited; and debate among intellectuals was of scant relevance to them. Polish, Hungarian and Yugoslavian journals were the only ones in Eastern Europe that attempted to rise above total dogmatic sterility, but not enough people paid them attention. For the Yugoslavs in the late 1960s and the Hungarians in the late 1960s and early 1970s, there were some broader flickerings of public interest in the contents of some of these journals, such as *Praxis* in Yugoslavia, but it was transitory. There was no such stimulation in the Soviet Union, not until the late 1980s. Furthermore, the relevance of intellectuals, if critical, was limited, as the political authorities were in control of the educational process. Moreover, the crisis of Marxism as a viable theory was not of great relevance for the Soviet government nor for other Communist governments. Instead, their sense of change as necessary owed far more to pragmatic considerations.

Linked to this was the modest impact of the dissidents, especially in the Russian Federation, the major part of the Soviet Union. Although of considerable interest to foreign commentators, dissent there did not gather pace to become opposition. This failure was a reflection of the nature of Russian public culture, the dominant role of the Communist Party in education and among workers, the effectiveness of repression, and a marked degree of anti-intellectualism. The last included persistent and strong anti-Semitism: many dissidents were Jews. The Soviet government began selectively adopting anti-Semitism during World War Two, before becoming more persistent in the late 1940s and the early 1960s, and very much so after Israel's victory in the Six Days' War in 1967. There was certainly no comparison in Russia to the major impact of the opposition intelligentsia in Czechoslovakia, let alone in Poland. In each case, the intelligentsia expressed a degree of nationalism that was compatible with their calls for reformed Communism.

Among the Soviet élite there was a sense by the mid-1980s that change was necessary, which helps explain why Gorbachev was not removed by an indignant Politburo, as had happened in 1964 to Khrushchev, and as might, otherwise, have been expected. He did not come from the KGB, had few links with the military, and was not closely allied with the remaining members of previous generations of policymakers. Nevertheless, critics of Gorbachev's changes were sidelined. Thus, in 1985, Gorbachev dismissed Nikolai Baibakov, a Stalinist who had headed Gosplan from 1965, and had earlier served Stalin as minister for the oil industry, a crucial ministry. Baibakov's generation, which had dominated the ministries from the 1940s, was now superseded and was unable to move beyond a measure of criticism of Gorbachev. Unused to attacks from the leadership, Party ideologues were pushed onto the defensive, and this was important both to a fundamental split within the Communist Party and to the loss of its legitimacy.

This leads to the question of whether a leader with views different to Gorbachev's could have kept the Soviet system in place as suggested by some commentators.[8] In China, popular disturbances were brutally suppressed. Gorbachev, however, saw liberalism as essential for a stronger Soviet Union, and he was willing to argue the case publicly, pressing for a 'Socialist pluralism' in 1987, and persuading the Party conference the following year to support truly contested elections for a legislature independent of the executive. These elections entailed Communists able to compete with each other, and to do so pushing different policies, which was a rejection of the Leninist idea of democratic centralism in favour of what Gorbachev called, in 1990, 'political pluralism'. His public rejection of Party infallibility in February 1990 meant that the Soviet Communist Party had now become a Menshevik or parliamentary Marxist Party, like (earlier) the German SPD (Social Democratic Party). Gorbachev's support for real checks and balances and his backing for the rule of law both broke with the authoritarian legacy of Communist rule. So did his sweeping relaxation of censorship, which made it far easier to question Marxist-Leninism, a process which rapidly had consequences that neither he nor most others anticipated.

Supporting *glasnost* (openness), Gorbachev was confident that the Soviet Union and the Communist Party would not only be able to survive these challenges, but would also be mutually strengthened by them. He was to be proved completely wrong. Instead, economic reform, in particular *perestroika* (restructuring), the loosening of much of the command economy, led, unexpectedly, to economic problems. These included inflation, which caused much popular unease, as well as hitting economic activity. There was also a major rise in the budget deficit. Shortages resulted in the stockpiling of goods by individuals and factories, and contributed to a breakdown in economic integration within the Soviet Union, including in the confidence on which systems of barter were based. There was nothing to buy. *Perestroika* also created pressure for political change. Indeed, Gorbachev's economic and political reforms helped cause economic confusion and a marked increase in criticism that delegitimated the Communist Party and affected the cohesion of the Soviet Union. Opposition to Gorbachev was not only mounted by Party ideologues unhappy with, and worried about, the content and direction of change, but also came from reformers within the Party who were dissatisfied with the pace of change. Boris Yeltsin, like Gorbachev born in 1931, a reformer brought into the Central Committee of the Soviet Communist Party in 1981, was promoted under Gorbachev, becoming, in 1986, First Secretary of the Moscow City Party Committee and a Candidate Member of the Politburo, both important roles. However, Yeltsin fell foul of Yegor Ligachev, who supervised Party organs from within the Central Committee secretariat. Yeltsin attacked Ligachev, and also, in effect, Gorbachev, at the 70th anniversary of the October Revolution in 1987. Yeltsin was removed from his posts, and clashed with Ligachev and Gorbachev when he pressed for political rehabilitation at the Party conference in 1988.

Gorbachev was far more successful in external affairs than in domestic policy,[9] and notably in easing relations with the USA and ending the Afghan commitment. His commitment to good relations abroad greatly defused tension, although he was clear on the need to maintain the fundamentals of the Soviet position. Thus, the Warsaw Pact, then thirty years old, was renewed for twenty years in April 1985. However, willing to challenge the confrontational world-view outlined in KGB reports, Gorbachev was convinced that American policy on arms control was not motivated by a hidden agenda of weakening the Soviet Union, and this conviction encouraged him to negotiate. A one-time protégé of Andropov, Gorbachev had been described by Thatcher in December 1984, when he visited London, as 'a man with whom I can do business'. Her opinion was influential with Reagan. Gorbachev was also prepared to abandon an approach to foreign policy suffused with the rhetoric of class, as well as to reject the vested interests of the powerful, but costly, military-industrial complex. His openness on policy helped ensure that his first summit with Reagan, at Geneva in November 1985, went well. In December 1987, the Soviet government accepted the Intermediate Nuclear Forces Treaty, which, in ending land-based missiles with ranges of between 500 and 5,000 kilometres, forced heavier cuts on the Soviets, while also setting up a system of verification through on-site inspection. These confidence-building measures reflected the extent to which Gorbachev and Reagan disliked a reliance on nuclear weaponry. This agreement pushed the German question to the fore as West Germany was the base and target for short-range missiles, American and Soviet respectively. The entire range of arms limitation was now open to negotiation, and agreements followed. In 1990, NATO and the Warsaw Pact were able to agree a limitation of conventional forces in Europe. Moreover, in July 1991, START 1 led to a major fall in the number of American and Soviet strategic nuclear warheads.[10]

# Afghanistan

Although the Soviets could afford their manpower losses in Afghanistan, and indeed the unpopularity of the struggle, Gorbachev, nevertheless, decided to end the commitment. He correctly regarded the Afghanistan commitment as detrimental to the Soviet Union's international position, particularly his wish to improve relations with the West and China; as well as domestically unpopular. Having warned the Afghan leader, Babrak Karmal, in March 1985, that Soviet forces would not stay for ever, Gorbachev decided that autumn that the Afghan regime would have to be able to defend itself by the summer of 1986. Nevertheless, prior to that, as with Nixon and Indochina, although on a far smaller scale, Gorbachev supported fresh military activity, including more attacks on *Mujahedin* bases in Pakistan, so as to leave as favourable a situation as possible in Afghanistan. In a clear breach from traditional Soviet policies, Karmal was urged in October 1985 to rely on traditional elements, including Islam, in order to strengthen the regime. Withdrawal from Afghanistan, however, took longer than anticipated. Implementation, as so often, proved far more difficult than devising policy and strategy. In part, this was because, as with other militaries in their time, the Soviet Army did not wish to appear to have lost the war, and, in part, because it proved difficult to arrange an international settlement that would cover the retreat. The risk of spreading disorder, a Domino Effect in reverse, was seen in April 1987 when a Pakistani-backed *Mujahedin* group launched a deadly attack in the Soviet republic of Uzbekistan, which bordered Afghanistan. This attack led to a Soviet threat to attack Pakistan. Such activity encouraged those in the Soviet Union who urged caution before withdrawing from Afghanistan.

Backed by Gorbachev, the UN-brokered Geneva Accords of 14 April 1988 led to a phased Soviet withdrawal, completed by 15 February 1989, although Soviet military and financial aid to the Afghan government continued. As in South Vietnam, the departure of the supporting outsiders did not lead to the fall of the regime at once. However, as also in South Vietnam, the regime finally collapsed: in the Afghan case, in April 1992. Bordering the Soviet Union and, in part, sharing the ethnic and religious configuration of its Central Asian republics, Afghanistan was a more challenging defeat for the Soviet Union than South Vietnam had been for the USA. Failure in Afghanistan, moreover, in the sole war it fought after 1945 hit the morale of the Soviet military. This had an impact on the army's uncertain response to the crises caused by the collapse, from 1989, of Soviet and Communist dominance in the Soviet bloc.

# Angola and Central America

There was also Soviet disengagement from Angola, where the war had become too costly for the Soviet Union, its ally, Cuba, and their opponent, South Africa. When, in 1987, Cuba increased its involvement in order to defeat the South Africans for good, it was against the wishes of Gorbachev. A ceasefire, agreed in 1988, was followed by South African withdrawal, while the Cubans finally left in 1991.[11] Having rejected the results of the 1992 election, UNITA resumed its conflict with the government, which was now weakened by the withdrawal of the Cuban and Soviet assistance that had greatly helped it in the late 1970s and 1980s. Defeated by the scale of the country, neither side was able to win. The operational effectiveness of the government's conventional forces declined in the wet season, which favoured UNITA guerrilla tactics. Both sides mounted attacks on the supply-systems of the other, but without lasting effect, other than to cause large numbers of civilian casualties, and even larger numbers of refugees. These were a silent testimony to the heavy cost of the Cold War. International pressure and a failure to win led Jonas Savimbi, the UNITA leader, to negotiate anew in 1994. This negotiation resulted in a *de facto* partition of the country that lasted until 1997 when the government attacked UNITA. UNITA now suffered from both the loss of its supply route through Congo and from divisions, with Savimbi's leadership under challenge. In 1999, Jamba, where Savimbi had established his capital in 1984, and which the government had failed to take in the 1980s, finally fell. UNITA forces were in a poor position by 2001 and the government used its oil wealth to enhance its military capability. It did not need to rely on Soviet or Cuban assistance, for this was a Cold War struggle that had been transformed after the fall of the Soviet Union. However, a lasting settlement had to await Savimbi's death in conflict of 22 February 2002. The peace agreement was signed on 4 April.

There was also in the late 1980s a reduction of Cold War tensions in Central America. Diplomatic pressure from the international community led, in 1989, to free elections in Nicaragua that resulted in the replacement of the pro-Soviet Sandinista government. In El Salvador, however, Cold War conflict continued in the late 1980s both to be acute and to reveal the weaknesses of guerrilla and counter-insurgency strategies. The guerrillas faced the difficulties of moving from rural power and harassing attacks, which they could achieve, to dominance and control of the towns and an ability to achieve overall victory, which they could not achieve, while the government conversely could not overcome the problems of using, and seeking to use, military strength, especially air attacks, to ensure civil peace. In November 1989, while Communist hegemony in Eastern Europe collapsed, there was a large-scale FMLN offensive in El Salvador, with part of the capital, San Salvador, taken over for a week. However, the FMLN could not incite a popular uprising. At the same time, the failure of the government to prevent the offensive led its American sponsors to press for negotiations. These pressures eventually resulted, in 1992, in a settlement under which the FMLN translated its activism to civilian politics.

Such an agreement reflected the extent to which defiance of the USA appeared less plausible after the fall of the Soviet Union. This was particularly so in Central America, as Cuba, the principal means of Soviet action there, was greatly weakened by the end of Soviet economic assistance, including of supplies of oil. In 1990, Cuba declared a 'Special Period in Time of Peace' in order to deal with a national economic emergency.

## The Fall of the Soviet Bloc

Developments in Afghanistan, Angola and Central America in 1988–9 were each regionally highly significant. In combination, these developments contributed greatly to a reduction in international tension. At the same time, they had far less of an impact on global attention than developments in the heartlands of the Communist bloc. These developments revealed two different tendencies. The brutal suppression in 1989 of pressure in China for political liberalisation, notably with the massacre of student protesters in Tiananmen Square in Beijing in April (but not only there), was central to the maintenance of a Communist bloc in East Asia. The decision to act followed tension within the leadership, with Zhao Ziyang, the General Secretary of the Party, being sympathetic to the protesters, whereas the Premier, Li Peng, wanted to use force against them. Ultimately, Deng Xiaoping backed Li. The *People's Daily* referred to the pro-democracy movement as an 'anti-Party and anti-Socialist upheaval'. It was seen as a challenge to the position and legitimacy of the Party leadership.

Communism already meant very different situations in China, North Korea and South-East Asia (Vietnam, Cambodia, Laos). In particular, the authoritarian *juche* (self-reliance) of North Korea was similar to a Stalinism China had dispensed with when rejecting the brutal legacy of Mao from 1976. Although clearly malign, corrupt, economically inefficient, and consigning much of its population to semi-starvation, and some of it to murderous slave labour conditions in prison camps, this system was still in control of North Korea in 2015. The legacy of Confucianism in China was significant there for attitudes towards authority and for a lack of social rebelliousness.

In the very different circumstances and culture of Eastern Europe, in contrast, Communist regimes successively collapsed in 1989. The end of the Cold War had been long envisaged,[12] but largely through negotiations between states. That was not to be the key element in 1989. Instead, Gorbachev unintentionally provoked the fall of the Soviet bloc. His attempts to push through modernisation in Eastern Europe (which totally surprised the East German leadership who argued that there was no need for reform or openness) left the regimes weak in the face of popular demand for reform and for more change. Moreover, Gorbachev was unwilling to use the Soviet Army to maintain these regimes. Visiting Prague in April 1987, Gorbachev repudiated the Brezhnev Doctrine of intervention in order to uphold Communism ('the defence of the Socialist Commonwealth' in Soviet terms), intervention which had been used in Czechoslovakia in 1968. Instead, Gorbachev claimed that 'fraternal parties determine their political line with a view to national conditions'. On 7 December 1988, he announced, significantly at the United Nations in New York rather than at a Communist gathering, that Eastern European states should be free to choose their own political path. This was a clear signal for change, and for a reduction in international tension. In his speech, Gorbachev also declared that the Soviet armed forces would be cut.

A change in policy reflected a sense of failure. The Communist regimes had failed, in part because they lacked the necessary flexibility to respond to problems, although there were important differences between the regimes, with Hungary proving the most flexible economically. Janos Kádár, its dictator, had been responsible for the decision to build the labour camp at Recsk, the most secret Hungarian one, which was opened in 1950,[13] had played a major role in the brutal repression that closed the 1956 rising, and had ordered the execution of Nagy. However, from the late 1960s, still under his control, Hungary, which became known as the home of 'Goulash Socialism', adopted a less rigid approach, offering its people small economic freedoms and in 1982 becoming a member of the International Monetary Fund and the World Bank. Nevertheless, in the face of growing pressure for reform, these freedoms were insufficient by the late 1980s, and Kádár was replaced as General Secretary of the Communist Party in May 1988.

Poland was the driver to what was to happen in Eastern Europe in 1989, first in Hungary, then in East Germany, and then elsewhere. Despite the suppression of Solidarity in 1981, Poland after 1956 was a relative island of freedom in Eastern Europe and, indirectly, was the inspiration for what would happen by the late 1980s. The weakness of the Eastern European regimes was demonstrated anew in Poland, both by the activities of underground Solidarity and by the serious strikes that began in April 1988. The government had grudgingly sought to widen its support by negotiating with other elements, but it wished to exclude Solidarity. The Catholic Church, however, refused to create a co-operative Christian labour movement as the government wanted, preferring to leave the more intransigent Solidarity as the key body for negotiations. The Communists were opposed to trade union pluralism, but, as a sign of movement on the government's part, the amnesty of 1986 had freed political prisoners. The 1988 strikes discouraged the Party leadership and demonstrated its failure to find a solution to Poland's problems. Combined with Gorbachev's renunciation of intervention on behalf of Communism, this failure encouraged the leadership to move toward yielding its monopoly of power. On 30 November 1988, there was a televised debate between Lech Walesa and Alfred Miodowicz, the head of the official trade union federation and a member of the Politburo. This was a highly significant step as the television served as a means of controlling the dissemination of opinion. On 6 February 1989, Round Table talks between government and the technically illegal opposition began, with the Church, an institution of great prestige in Poland, playing an important mediatory role. Under an agreement, signed on 5 April 1989, reached against a background of widespread strikes, elections were held in Poland on 4 June. Only 35 per cent of the seats in the lower house, the *Sejm*, were awarded on the basis of the free vote, the remainder going to the Communists and their allies, but all of these seats were won by Solidarity. This expression of the public will was a dramatic blow to the old order. Communist cohesion collapsed, not least with the Communist Party being abandoned by its hitherto pliant allies. Strikes and other protests meanwhile continued. The new government was headed by Tadeusz Mazowiecki, a member of Solidarity and a Catholic intellectual. He became the first non-Communist Prime Minister behind the Iron Curtain. There was, however, to be a major division between those who endorsed the 'Round Table' political settlement of 1989 as a way to avoid bloodshed, and those who criticised it as, allegedly, a compromise providing subsequent cover for ex-Communists to pillage the state.[14]

East Germany, apparently the most successful Communist regime, although with its economy wrecked by ideological mismanagement, was on the edge of bankruptcy in the autumn of 1989. It had only been able to continue that long thanks to large loans from the West, notably West Germany. As a sign of good relations, Erich Honecker paid an official visit to West Germany in 1987. However, the East German government could no longer finance its social programmes. Gorbachev's *glasnost* and *perestroika*, to which Honecker reacted critically, intensified the regime's loss of legitimacy and, by September, East German society was dissolving as people, especially the younger generation, left in large numbers. Hungary's opening of its Austrian border on 2 May had permitted substantial numbers of East Germans to leave for West Germany via Hungary and Austria. They abandoned not only economic failure but also the lack of modern civilisation in the shape of free expression, tolerance, opportunity and cultural vitality. Hungary refused to heed pressure from East Germany to stem the tide of departures, and Gorbachev was unwilling to help. In the first nine months of the year, 110,000 East Germans resettled in West Germany. Others took part in mass demonstrations in East Germany, notably in the major city of Leipzig from 4 September, with steadily larger numbers demonstrating. A sense of failure and emptiness demoralised supporters of the regime, while West German consumerist democracy, and what had been pejoratively termed the fetishism of 'things', proved far more attractive to the bulk of the population. The repressive state, moreover, no longer terrified. Indeed, it had suffered a massive failure of intelligence, with a serious inability to understand developments, let alone to anticipate them. All its intercepted letters and spying availed the *Stasi* naught.[15] In addition, the situation was very different to that when East Germany had faced disturbances in 1953 and 1961: unwilling to compromise its domestic and international reputation, the regime did not wish to rely on force. The old ruthlessness was no longer there: the Leninist instinct for survival had been lost. The East German army anyway was unwilling to act. Moreover, the nature of the demonstrations – both peaceful and without central leadership – lessened the opportunity for repression; not that that had stopped the Chinese authorities earlier in the year.

Honecker was deposed by his colleagues on 16 October 1989, but, under pressure from popular action, they could not gain control of the situation, nor even, more significantly, produce an impression of control. The entire government and Politburo resigned on 7–8 November, and, on 9 November, the Berlin Wall was opened. An occasion and symbol of freedom, the Fall of the Wall became a totemic act, like that of the Bastille in Paris in 1789 at the outset of the French Revolution. However, whereas only a few insignificant prisoners were freed from the Bastille, large numbers of East Berliners poured over the now open border. The significance of the popular action in East Germany in 1989 was picked out in March 2014 when President Park Geun-hye of South Korea spoke in Dresden setting out proposals to ease reunification with North Korea. Developments in East Germany invite counterfactuals including, 'What if the Hungarians had not opened their Austrian border, permitting a mass exodus of East Germans that destabilised the state?', as well as the question whether the East German system could have been stabilised by removing Honecker earlier, and giving reform Communism a greater chance.[16]

From the opening of the Wall, pressure for reform in East Germany was increasingly supplemented by demands for German unity, although the majority in the citizens' movement wanted a liberal East Germany, not unification. Meanwhile, with Gorbachev not changing policy[17] in order to pursue repression, as Khrushchev had done toward Hungary in 1956, government authority in East Germany collapsed. Honecker's successors, Egon Krenz, Chairman of the Council of State from October to December 1989, and Gregor Gysi, his successor, could not provide the reform from above they sought to ensure stability, while the *Stasi* headquarters in Berlin were occupied by demonstrators on 15 January 1990. Communist one-party rule was followed by multi-party politics; while constitutional change gathered pace. On 1 February 1990, Hans Modrow, the new East German Premier, unveiled a plan for a German-German confederation as part of a United Fatherland. Gorbachev responded to Modrow that a unified Germany was acceptable only if it was demilitarised and neutral, but the Americans were unwilling to accept the Soviet proposal for the mutual withdrawal of troops

from Germany. Free elections, held in East Germany on 18 March, demonstrated the lack of support for Communism: the East German CDU under
Lothar de Mazière won 48.1 per cent of the vote and the SPD 21.8 per cent.
Once democratised, Communism had become redundant, and the same
process affected the very state of East Germany.[18] Currency union with West
Germany took effect on 1 July, East Germany came to an end as a separate
state on 3 October, and all-German elections followed on 2 December 1990.

Thatcher was unhappy about German re-unification,[19] while President
Mitterrand of France wanted two democratic Germanys and not the speedy
creation of an over mighty Germany. However, in response to the victory of
the pro-unification parties in the East German election in March 1990, he
proved more accommodating, not least because of a promise from Helmut
Kohl, the German Chancellor, that French companies would be allowed to
acquire East German state-owned companies in the rapid privatisation that
was pushed through.[20] Kohl traded subsequently on his role in securing
unification, and this helped him win re-election, as Chancellor of the united
Germany, in 1994.

East Germany had been seen as the leading and most successful Soviet
client state, and the fall of Communism there was followed by its unravelling
elsewhere in Eastern Europe. In popular protest and in shifts in government
policy toward reform, developments in Poland and Hungary had been
a prelude to those in East Germany, but, in each case, the crisis in East
Germany helped encourage the move to free elections. In Czechoslovakia,
which had remained more authoritarian than Hungary, there were mass
demonstrations, and an end to Communist rule, in the Velvet Revolution of
November 1989, the term being indicative of the peaceful nature of change.
The end to Communist rule was followed in December by the creation of a
largely non-Communist government and the choice of the dissident Václav
Havel as President. In April 1990, a new constitution was adopted, and
free elections were held on 8–9 June. The escalating pace of the change
that seemed graspable was indicated by a slogan of the Velvet Revolution:
'Poland – ten years, Hungary – ten months, German Democratic Republic
– ten weeks, Czechoslovakia – ten days'. The public nature of the pressure
for change was important as it could be captured by a domestic media no
longer under state control, as well as by the international media. Scenes of
East Germans travelling West were followed by those of the demolition of
the Berlin Wall. In December 1989, in turn, they were succeeded by demonstrators in the capital Bucharest booing Nicolae Ceauşescu, the Romanian
dictator, when he spoke in public. Abetted by the vicious Secret Police, he
sought to resist reform by the use of force against demonstrators. However,
Ceauşescu was overthrown after mass demonstrations. The army, which
played a key role, providing force sufficient to overawe the Secret Police,
was responsible for his execution on Christmas Day.

In Bulgaria, the key development was not people power, but rather a crisis
in the Communist Party as the elderly leader (he was born in 1911), Todor

Zhivkov, First Secretary of the Bulgarian Communist Party since 1954, no longer enjoyed the confidence of many of his colleagues, and did not have that of Gorbachev. Zhivkov had been completely slavish to the internal policies of the Soviet Union. As was true in all of the Eastern Bloc countries, standards of living, industrialisation, urbanisation, education, medical care and longevity went up in Bulgaria, from the early 1950s into the mid-1980s; having a southerly location helped considerably in encouraging a healthy diet. However, no dissent was tolerated. The intellectual discontent that ebbed and waned in Poland would never have been tolerated in Bulgaria. The *Derzhava Sigurnost*, Bulgaria's KGB, were heavily repressive. From the mid-1980s, Zhivkov had expelled ethnic Turks from Bulgaria, forcing some 200,000–300,000 of them to flee to Turkey. Zhivkov did not have the mentality of a reformer although in the last month or so of his rule he introduced pseudo-reforms. However, in November 1989, opposition by Politburo colleagues led to his resignation. A pro-Gorbachev group took power in Bulgaria only to find itself under pressure from public expectations. Elections, held in June 1990, led to the former Communists winning power. Nevertheless, their inability to deal with the serious economic crisis and with strikes resulted in the formation in December of a coalition. The new constitution, promulgated in July 1991, was that of a democratic state.

By then, the Soviet Union was dissolving. In theory, a federation, the Soviet state had sought to develop a nationalism separate to that of its constituent republics, an idea expressed in the 1970s song 'My address is not a house or a street / My address is the Soviet Union'. However, the state rested on a powerful degree of Russian as well as ideological imperialism. As a result, in some of the non-Russian republics, nationalism had long provided a popular and inclusive language and form for dissent, not least about the role of Russians. In contrast, dissent within the Russian Federation lacked such focus. Russian nationalism was not the theme of dissent there, in part because the Soviet system acted as the protector of Russian interests. From mid-1988, the growing weakness of the Soviet state, and the division and confusion of the government's response to nationalism, was accentuated by the strength of nationalist sentiment, especially in the Baltic republics, the Caucasus republics, and the western Ukraine. This sentiment had been manifested from the mid-1980s in increased opposition to Communist rule. The waving of national flags and singing of national songs became more frequent. On 23 August 1989, two million people formed a human chain between the capitals of the Baltic Republics. The Soviet idea of a limited flowering of national cultures as part of a wider concept of a unified Soviet people, a policy adopted in 1923, had proved a total failure, although, during the late Soviet period, some Russians resented the 'internationalism' of the Soviet Union wherein resources, money and technical know-how were handed over by Moscow to the non-Russian sectors. There was also resentment over the foreign accents that the non-Russians had when speaking Russian in the army and elsewhere. Moreover, an explicitly conveyed sense of Russian identity had emerged by the late 1960s with the *derevenshchiki* (ruralists): Russian writers such as Valentin Rasputin. Without tackling the censorship head-on, what the *derevenshchiki* tended to do was to decry the baneful effects of Soviet Communist modernisation upon the older rural way of life and its values. By the later 1970s, different strands of Russian national identity, expressed in the form of resentment over the perceived shunning of Russian cultural values, emerged with other writers.

While separatist nationalisms developed and were increasingly expressed, there was no protracted attempt to use the extensive military resources of the Soviet state to prevent the collapse of the Soviet Union. Already, in 1986–7, the government had refused to employ force to support party leaders in the Baltic Republics. When the crisis rose to a height, counter-reform attempts by the Soviet military, keen to preserve the integrity of the state, led to action against nationalists in Georgia (1989), Azerbaijan (1990), Lithuania (1991), Latvia (1991), and Moldova (1992). However, these steps were small-scale, and there was no significant violent supporting action by the 25 million Russians living within the Soviet Union but outside Russia, those, for example, who played a key role in crises in Crimea and eastern Ukraine in 2014.

Gorbachev, the Sorcerer's Apprentice of Marxism without there being, as in the story, any Sorcerer to restore order, had never sought the disruption he created. Article six of the Soviet constitution, which guaranteed the Communist Party a monopoly of power, was abolished in February 1990. However, the Party proved unable to compete effectively in the new political situation. Moreover, Gorbachev wanted to preserve the Soviet Union, if necessary only as a loose confederation. Thus, when the republics declared their independence, Gorbachev supported the attempt to maintain the authority of the Soviet Union by sending troops into them in January 1991. This policy led to clashes in Riga and Vilnius, the capitals of Latvia and Lithuania respectively. Fourteen unarmed people protecting the television tower in Vilnius were killed and five civilians in the seizure of the Interior Ministry in Riga. These steps did not intimidate the nationalists but led to the building of barricades in both cities. Iconic moments and locations were provided both for the nationalist movement and for post-independence memorialisation, notably in Vilnius.

A very different demonstration of military power was provided in February 1991 when Iraq was driven from Kuwait in a swift campaign by an American-led coalition. In this conflict, the Americans used their post-Vietnam weapon systems, including the Blackhawk helicopter introduced in 1979; the M1A1 Abrams tank, deployed from 1980; the Bradley Fighting Vehicle, designed to carry a squad of infantry and armed with a TOW (tube-launched, optically tracked, wire command data link) missile system, introduced in 1981; and the Apache attack helicopter, equipped with radar and Hellfire missiles, introduced in 1986. The Americans also employed airplane stealth technology. The use of Cold War assets involved the new grasp and employment of the operational dimension of war, a grasp that had developed with the doctrine, planning and training of the 1980s as the Americans enhanced their capability to fight the Soviets without having to make an automatic resort to atomic weaponry. About half the Iraqi army was rapidly destroyed.

Nationalism in the Soviet Union meanwhile culminated when Yeltsin, in effect, successfully launched a Russian nationalist movement against the remaining structures of the Soviet Union. While Russians did not feel the core-periphery tug of war in the same way that Ukrainians or Estonians did, since most of the Russians lived inside the core, in the end the Russian Federation was itself to secede from the Soviet Union. In 1988, the Party conference had decided that there should be competitive elections both for Party posts and for the Congress of People's Deputies, the new-style Soviet legislature. The latter elections, held in March 1989, enabled Yeltsin to show his popularity in Moscow by easily winning a seat there, that put him not only on the Congress but also on the Supreme Soviet. The problems of Soviet society were bluntly outlined from a populist perspective in Yeltsin's election manifesto in which he attacked the unjustified stratification of the population and the privileges of the *nomenklatura*. Yeltsin won nearly 90 per cent of the vote in Moscow. Prominent in the Inter-Regional Group of Deputies, Yeltsin pressed for economic and political reform. In 1990, competitive elections were held for the first time for the legislatures of the republics in the Soviet Union, and Yeltsin was elected to the Congress of People's Deputies of the Russian Soviet Federal Socialist Republic, becoming, by May, Chairman of the Supreme Soviet of the Republic. In an instructive parallel to the relationship between England and Britain, the Russian Republic had had no real institutions of its own until 1990, being, instead, conflated with the Soviet Union. To Yeltsin, this was unacceptable. Russian dissent contained explicit secessionist aspirations, while Russian sovereignty was in effect declared in June 1990 when Yeltsin announced that Russian legislation would prevail over Soviet legislation if the two clashed. As an indication of how changes in Russia interacted with those in some of the other republics, this was an approach also taken by the Baltic Republics. The greater Soviet Russia which protected Russians living in the other republics was thus replaced by a post-imperial Russian nation-state,[21] a development about which President Putin was to complain publicly in 2014.

As so often in history, personalities played a major role in the developing crisis, in this case Yeltsin's unwillingness to co-operate with Gorbachev. So also did the staples of, first, the pressure of international competition, in the form of the strains arising from the Cold War and, secondly and more specifically, nationalism. Both undermined the Soviet Union as they had earlier done the Austro-Hungarian empire in the 1910s, and the British empire after the two world wars. Whereas, the Austro-Hungarian empire had been willing to grant a degree of autonomy to its various areas in the nineteenth century, in the Soviet Union the nationalist forces came to the fore abruptly. Neither the Austro-Hungarian empire nor the Soviet Union had a Western-style political party capable of transcending ethnic lines. The Emperor in the one and the Communist Party in the other were the transnational symbols and reality that worked well for a long period, but, in the end, neither was capable of adapting sufficiently. The same was true of the British empire in the case of Ireland and India respectively after World War One and World War Two. Challenges themselves were not new. As a reminder of continuities, such as that of Russian/Soviet expansionism, Russian nationalism was in part another version of the Slavophile attitudes seen in the nineteenth century. Nevertheless, as a political force during the Soviet period, this nationalism was new.

Yeltsin clashed with Gorbachev and Party conservatives, and, in July 1990, announced that he was leaving the Communist Party, a course followed by other prominent figures in Russia, and one opened up by the Party no longer having a monopoly of power. In the late summer of 1990, Yeltsin and Gorbachev sank their differences to establish a committee to establish measures necessary for the transition to a market economy, but the 500 Days Programme it produced, which included privatisation and decentralisation, proved too radical for much of the government. Gorbachev backed away from his original support, harming his relations with Yeltsin. The two negotiated anew in 1991 over a new Union Treaty intended to preserve most of the Soviet Union. Elected President of Russia in June 1991, Yeltsin pressed for more rights for the republics than Gorbachev wanted. However, the latter was willing to go farther than many of his governmental colleagues, a difference that triggered an attempted coup.

Hardline Communists, organised as the State Committee for the State of Emergency in the USSR, or the Gang of Eight, attempted a coup in Moscow on 19 August 1991. Motivated by loyalty to the Party and the state, they were also anxious to preserve their position and the Soviet Union. However, like the attempted right-wing coup in Spain in February 1981, this coup proved an abject failure that also greatly helped advance the change it had sought to stop. Thus, the coup encouraged opposition in the republics to the Soviet Union. More immediately, the coup boosted the prestige of Yeltsin, who played a prominent public role in opposing it, leading the protestors in Moscow's streets from the Russian Parliament, and thereby providing a clear and effective symbol of popular constitutionalism. In street-fighting not seen in Moscow since 1917, three protesters were killed by the army, which was itself divided.[22] Soviet citizens were no longer the supposedly supine creatures and docile masses that the Party leadership had taken for granted in decades past. Gorbachev, a prisoner in his summer retreat in Crimea, did not play a role comparable to Yeltsin and, indeed, was regarded as displaying a degree of ambivalence about the attempted coup.

The coup's failure was followed by Yeltsin deciding to sweep aside the old system, and by the marginalisation of hardline Communists and their power-centres: the KGB was abolished on 11 October 1991. Moreover, Soviet Cold War foreign policy was abandoned. The previous month, Gorbachev and Yeltsin had yielded to American pressure to stop sending aid to Afghanistan and to withdraw all Soviet troops from Cuba. In addition, the Soviet Foreign Ministry largely abandoned Communist ideology.

In late 1991, nationalism in the republics led to their independence. Soviet federalism did not distinguish between the republics, which ensured that disintegration proved cumulative.[23] The Ukrainian referendum of 1 December, which saw a 90 per cent vote for independence, was decisive and, thanks to the failed coup, a major shift from the situation in Ukraine earlier in the year. A week later, Yeltsin, as President of Russia, and his Belarus and Ukrainian counterparts, announced at Minsk, the capital of Belarus, that they were forming a Commonwealth of Independent States, in place of the Soviet Union, and invited the other republics to join. Gorbachev protested the next day, but he was now without consequence. On 21 December, at Alma Alta, the capital of Kazakhstan, the heads of all the republics, bar Georgia, Estonia, Latvia and Lithuania which sought a more complete independence, endorsed the step taken on 8 December, joined the Commonwealth of Independent States, and declared that the Soviet Union had ceased to exist. Gorbachev resigned on 25 December as President of the Soviet Union.

The new system was seen by Yeltsin as truly federal, but this was not the case as far as, most crucially, Ukraine was concerned. Most other republics followed its example of independence in action. Russia under Yeltsin accepted this situation. In 1994, Russia signed a treaty guaranteeing the borders of Ukraine which, in turn, gave up its nuclear weapons.[24] The influence of the former Soviet Union, however, created serious tensions in the 2000s and 2010s as Vladimir Putin, as President of Russia, then Prime Minister, then President again, sought to drive through political and economic coordination for at least part of the former Soviet Union under Russian leadership,[25] and to limit links with the West, notably the accession of Georgia and Ukraine to NATO, and of Ukraine to the European Union.

# Conclusion

The collapse of the Soviet Union is usually explained with reference to four elements. An economic explanation focuses on long-term economic difficulties, notably an autarkic economic system that did not adequately understand time and value. A military-economic explanation centres on the impact of Soviet military expenditure being far greater than that of the USA. A sociological explanation suggests that, three or four generations after 1917, the élite groups had lost their elan for the cause, while other population sectors had become disillusioned and apathetic. The political explanation emphasises the degree to which Gorbachev's opportunistic and poorly-planned strategies precipitated a series of crises for the governing élites of Eastern Europe and the Soviet Union that otherwise might have been avoided.

The account of Soviet collapse offered in this chapter does not put the Cold War foremost. It is possible to focus on the degree to which the arms race that was a central element in the Cold War inflicted economic penalties on the Soviet Union as it sought to match American defence spending,[26] caused a sense of Soviet weakness, and resulted in a pressure for change there. This approach produces a top-down account that has value. However, it directs attention away from the view of the populace in the maintenance or otherwise of the Soviet system, and the related question of consent and opposition. Of course, to write of the populace and consent can imply a democratic aspect. This, however, requires qualification as all consenters were not equal. Indeed, even more significant than the absence of popular support for the regimes of Eastern Europe and the Soviet Union, important as that absence was, was the disengagement of Communist Party members, particularly those in their thirties and forties who had grown up in Party-controlled systems. They decided, correctly, that these systems were not working and that they could do better without existing governmental, political and economic arrangements. Their attempt to create a modified or 'reformed' Communist system of control helped cause the collapse of the system. This was similar to the rapid end of the right-wing authoritarian Francoist regime in Spain in 1975 after the death of the dictator: in both cases, the willingness of ostensible supporters to conceive of different arrangements, and to adjust accordingly, was crucial to the fall of an authoritarian system.

These specific factors in the fall of Soviet Communism are crucial in explaining the crises of 1989–91, but it is also important to consider long-term problems. These problems ranged from grave economic misman-agement to stultifying military expenditure. Totalitarian regimes, such as the Soviet Union and Nazi Germany, were command systems that were inherently prone to impose inefficient direction, rather than to respond to independent advice and to independent popular demand. Nazi Germany was greatly weakened by this characteristic during World War Two and, had that regime survived that conflict, would have been harmed by it subsequently in the confrontations to which its ideology inherently gave rise. This outcome was, indeed, the fate of the Soviet Union. As such, although by then there was no comparison with the methods or ethos of Nazi Germany or Stalinism, 1989–91 saw a crisis of totalitarianism, a crisis that fortunately did not lead to war, civil, international or both. Gorbachev deserves praise for responding to the crisis and disintegration of the Soviet Union without recourse to international war.

Alongside discussion of the collapse of the Soviet bloc in terms of the failure of totalitarianism can come consideration of this collapse with reference to the fall of empires.[27] Here, there is an interesting parallel with the end of the British empire, as, in a different context and on a different timetable, that end involved the loss not only of 'external' possessions, but also of the territorial integrity and cohesion of the British Isles. Eastern Europe, the Soviet Union and Russia scarcely offer a precise comparison with Britain's trans-oceanic colonies, the United Kingdom, and England; but each transition captures the extent to which change can be rapid and total. There is also the debate, in each case, about the respective role of changes in the metropole and those in the colonies. Yeltsin can be seen as a key instance of the former, as he sought to abandon empire, whereas Gorbachev wished to preserve it, albeit in a different form. In the British case, the closest analogy to the latter goal would be the Commonwealth.

The Western powers were observers of the changes in Eastern Europe and the Soviet Union, rather than principals. Indeed, there was a measure of reluctance about welcoming the changes in practice, whatever the willingness to acclaim greater freedom. Happy with the fall of Communism in Poland, Thatcher was concerned that its end in East Germany would result in a unification that left Germany too powerful. This view was shared by Mitterrand, although he proved better able than Thatcher to accommodate himself to Kohl's support for unification, as, indeed, did George H. W. Bush. Once Saddam Hussein invaded Kuwait in 1990, the focus of international attention, notably that of Bush and Thatcher, shifted to the Gulf, which left greater opportunities for change, or resistance to change, in the Communist bloc. Concerned about international stability, and notably control over nuclear weapons, Bush was reluctant to see the Soviet Union collapse in 1991 beyond the loss of the Baltic Republics which he did welcome.

The rapid collapse, without direct external pressure, of the Soviet bloc would have surprised commentators earlier in the Cold War, indeed as late as the mid-1980s. Thus, this collapse serves as an instance of the unexpected character of history, the play of contingency, and the role of individuals in a roller-coaster decade that began with full-scale Soviet intervention in Afghanistan and ended with crises in the centres of Communist power, both European and Asian.

# POSTSCRIPT

In its various versions, the Cold War dominated the military history of the second half of the twentieth century. Moreover, military factors played a major role in its course, notably from 'hot' war, particularly in 1919–20 (Russian Civil War) and 1946–53 (Chinese Civil War; Korean War), to confrontation, and then eventually to negotiation and resolution. The Russian Civil War was the key formative experience, but the conflicts of the 1940s were also crucial in transforming the geopolitics of the Cold War. The destruction of an independent Poland in 1939 and the defeat and partition of Germany in 1944–5 left the Soviet Union dominant in Eastern Europe and not facing any serious threat on land there. The defeat and surrender of Japan and the overthrow of its empire in 1945 left the Soviet Union dominant in East Asia. This process was brought to fruition when Communist victory in the Chinese Civil War in 1946–9 destroyed the prospect of a Chinese-American alliance. War thereby appeared to vindicate Soviet confidence in the inevitability of Marxist victory, an inevitability allegedly owing much to the inherent weakness of its opponents. Indeed, the exhaustion of Britain and France in World War Two thrust the USA to the fore.

As with other conflicts, the Cold War should not be detached from its political contexts, and this is far more the case for the Cold War as this was a conflict in which full-scale war did not break out. Western intervention in the Russian Civil War was small-scale while the Korean and Vietnam Wars, although deadly for many, were limited conflicts. Indeed, as a war of limited action and infinite potential, the Cold War was a struggle in which politics within, and between, the rival systems were particularly to the fore. These politics centrally affected the course and content of the struggle. There is a parallel with the struggle between Christendom and Islam or, in a more limited fashion, the Habsburg and Ottoman empires. Protagonists with different civilisational values competed, with long periods of limited conflict alternating with shorter ones of warfare, all the while laid over with constant doctrinal and military alertness.

The Soviet Union was a military super-power that had an international mission but also lacked a solid basis of support for this mission, both domestically and internationally. The popular domestic support and international backing available to fight a defensive struggle against Germany in 1941–5 were less apparent thereafter. Commitment to militarism in part was a product of competition with the West, but also owed much to the particular political and ideological character of the Soviet system. There was a strong sense of vulnerability. In part, this sense reflected real threats. These included serious challenges to territorial integrity and interests, notably from Japan in 1918–22 and 1931–41. There were threats to the very existence of the Soviet regime, particularly in the Russian Civil War of 1918–20, and then again from Germany in 1941–5. There was also a paranoid concern about threats that were non-existent or greatly overplayed. This sense of vulnerability can be traced back certainly to the early seventeenth century, but owed much to foreign intervention in the Russian Civil War, to the working of the Leninist-Stalinist political system predating World War Two, to the experience of unexpected German attack in 1941, and to the American deployment of the atom bomb. This sense of vulnerability encouraged a major stress on military expenditure.

Nearly a quarter of state expenditure went to military purposes in 1952, when the Soviet Union was not at war, and the amount increased as greater nuclear capability was added to the arsenal. The Soviet Union sought an all-round capability to match that of the USA, developing for example the world's second largest navy even though that was marginal to its focus on land, air and rocket power. By the early 1980s, defence expenditure was 15–25 per cent of the GDP of a significantly larger economy, and may even have been higher. Like Khrushchev before him, Gorbachev and his generation correctly felt that any meaningful economic reform demanded cuts in this expenditure. The USA also had a tradition of concern and rational fear, as well as irrational fear or paranoia.[1] Like the Soviet Union, there was also excessive military expenditure. However, America's stronger economy, more liberal fiscal system, and alliance with states that provided massive liquidity, notably the oil-producing states, made it easier to manage this expenditure.

The weight of Soviet and American defence expenditure serves as a reminder that the military dimension was not simply some add-on to the ideological confrontation. Particularly under Stalin, but not only under him, industrialisation and military security were seen as so intertwined in the USA and the Soviet Union as to be generally inseparable. Moreover, in the Soviet Union, the themes of mobilisation and conflict were central to an ideology that did not rate peaceful change. This point was also true of Mao's China. The USA, in turn, allied, often to its discredit, with a number of autocratic regimes across the world. Moreover, the USA, on occasion, supported the overthrow of democratic governments. This was notably, but not only, the case in Latin America, as with Guatemala in 1953, Brazil in 1965 and Chile in 1973. Nevertheless, America's alliance system centred on democracies, particularly Japan, Britain, France[2] and West Germany, and the modernisation it advocated was that of a democratic liberal capitalism.[3]

The themes of military preparedness and ideological confrontation underline the importance of the Cold War ending without large-scale conflict. A focus on peaceful change highlights the significance of Gorbachev's attitudes and policies, a point also valid for the Deng reforms in China. This assessment suggests that a revived Soviet Union, had it been possible, might have been very troubling under less accommodating leadership. Whether that will be the case for China, a partly-capitalist system under an authoritarian Communist government spending increasing amounts on armaments, remains unclear. In the event, the Gorbachev changes were followed by a collapse that resulted in a marked decline in Russian military readiness. Alongside continued American capability, this decline dramatically rewrote the military balance, both in Europe and globally. In 2014, the West was concerned about Soviet military moves against an independent Ukraine, a situation that would have been regarded as remarkable in 1988. Indeed, Ukraine's independence had, in a fashion, been guaranteed in 1994. The Western response in 2014 would also have appeared remarkable in 1988. It included defensive precautions on behalf of Poland and the Baltic Republics, formerly part of the Communist bloc, but now NATO members.

The Soviet collapse led not only to a transformation in geopolitics, but also to a rewriting of Cold War history. The emphasis in the literature was increasingly on Soviet weaknesses, and on the related suggestion that the West had exaggerated Soviet capability and the Soviet threat, either mistakenly or for political reasons of its own. The latter approach encouraged the argument that the Cold War had been unnecessary and a cost to all. Arguing that the Soviet threat had been exaggerated led to a focus on the Cold War away from the military dimension and, instead, on the Cold War as in large part a clash between ideological camps. Moreover, in this account, the West was not seen solely in terms of liberal democracy. Instead, due weight was given to anti-Communism and its domestic and international consequences.

A number of strands were identified in this anti-Communism. One was that of the Catholic Church and its supporters, a strand that can be widely traced, not least with the career of Eugenio Pacelli, a prominent Papal diplomat, Secretary of State of the Holy See, and, finally Pope Pius XII (r. 1939–58).[4] In the USA, anti-communism was seen with Catholic influence on President John F. Kennedy, especially in support of the authoritarian Diem regime in South Vietnam.[5] In a preponderantly Buddhist country, this regime, and the South Vietnamese officer corps, were heavily Catholic, not least because a large number of Catholics, about a million strong, had fled from North Vietnam. Opposition to Communism in Latin America in the 1950s and 1960s can also in part be linked with Catholic concerns. In Europe, there was the part played by attitudes toward the Church during the Spanish Civil War (1936–9) and, later, the important role of Pope John

Paul II in encouraging the rejection of Communism, particularly in Poland. Catholic leaders frequently opposed Communism, possibly most bluntly the Archbishop of Braga in Portugal in 1975 when he declared that the struggle against Communism should be seen 'not in terms of man against man, but Christ against Satan'.

Scholarly re-examination of the Cold War has proved less significant than the changing nature of public remembrance. Here, the end of the Cold War in Europe in 1989–91 led both to abrupt shifts in governmental accounts of the recent past, and to a totally different environment for the expression of public and private views. Eastern Europeans regarded themselves, sometimes misleadingly, as victims of Communist rule who had played no role in the regime, and Communism was presented as a foreign ideology. This tendency was part of a new Eastern Europe that wished to see Communism as finished; and this widespread desire contributed greatly to the idea of a fundamental turning point in 1989–91. Moreover, as a result of Soviet collapse, there was a dramatic change, amounting to a rupture, in the international situation. The Western powers, led by the USA, were able to intervene decisively against states that earlier would have looked for Soviet support, notably Iraq in 1991, in the First Gulf War, and Serbia in 1995 and 1999 in the Bosnia and Kosovo crises respectively. Indeed, when welcoming the annexation of Crimea in 2014 after a plebiscite of dubious legality, President Putin complained on this head, particularly about the Kosovo crisis. In addition, in the 2000s, as an aspect of the problems facing the former allies of the Communist bloc, Libya found it helpful to seek reconciliation with the West. In contrast, North Korea, Iran and Syria sought safety in developing their own nuclear capability, not that a far more critical interpretation of their decisions is not also pertinent.[6] Colonel Qaddafi of Libya, formerly a Soviet ally, was overthrown with the help of NATO intervention in 2011.

The combination of Soviet collapse in 1991 and Iraqi defeat in 2003 led to talk of a 'new world order' and of the 'end of history'. These triumphalist claims, which encompassed arguments on the cause, course and outcome of the Cold War,[7] rested on the belief that Soviet collapse represented a triumph for American-led democratic capitalism, and that there would be no future clash of ideologies to destabilise the world. However, while global politics were indeed reshaped in the early 1990s, Russia was mishandled, while the conviction that American-led global multilateralism would work appeared far less obvious by 2014 than had been the case in the early 1990s. In part, this development reflected the problems America faced (as Britain had done in 1919–38) in the Islamic world. In 1979–80, there had been an American 'pivot' to the Middle East in response to the overthrow of the Shah in Iran and the resulting threat to American interests, notably in the Gulf. This was a new point of departure in American policy, even if the revival of confrontation in Europe and Central America in the final decade of the Cold War obscured it at the time. This point of departure ultimately led into the 'War on Terror' that began in 2001, which reflected the ability of non-state actors to defy a super-power. This was a situation already seen, at a variety of scales, with the Cold War, notably with the successful opposition to Soviet forces in Afghanistan in 1979–88. It was seen anew with the problems the Americans encountered in Iraq and Afghanistan in the 2000s and 2010s.

At the same time, this was a problem faced by the USA in the international order that succeeded the Cold War. Despite the understandable queries and caveats of scholars and critics, who pointed to the very heavy economic, political and social costs involved, the West indeed won the Cold War as President George H. W. Bush pointed out. This was a victory that transformed the lives of many millions, notably in Eastern Europe and the Soviet Union, but not only there. Nevertheless, the triumph proved less fruitful than had initially appeared probable. Russian ambitions and actions in recent years, notably in the Caucasus, where Georgia was successfully attacked in 2008, and, more particularly, in Ukraine in 2014, have reawakened echoes of the Cold War and led to questions of whether it is really over, or whether there is a new one in process. It is easy to understand such suggestions. Moreover, policy during these crises was debated in terms of the supposed lessons of the Cold War, whether, for example, it had been won by force or by the West's political and economic example.[8]

Yet, despite talk of a new Cold War in 2014, the end of the Soviet Union and the fall of its Communism had brought major changes. This could be readily seen in the ideology of foreign policy. For example, because of their blood-and-soil connotations with 'bourgeois nationalism' and Fascism, ideas of the interrelationship, or inter-determination, of geography and politics had had scant purchase in the Soviet Union. However, these ideas came to enjoy widespread credence and popularity in post-Soviet Russia as a new territoriality was developed. This was in particular true of Aleksander Dugin, a polemical, nationalistic commentator who offered an assertive account of national space and the supposed biological imperatives of the nation.[9] The nationalism was and is anti-Western, which encourages talk of a new Cold War launched by Russia. However, this nationalism is not linked to an account of global progress and strife, as had been the case with the Soviet implementation of Marxist ideas.

The expansion of Chinese influence in South Asia and Africa is also a major challenge to the USA, as also, from 2013, were signs of Chinese bellicosity toward Japan in the East China Sea and, in 2014, Chinese expansionism in the South China Sea. Indeed, the years 1989–91 did not represent the rupture in Asia seen in Europe; and the same was true of the longer period that began with the death of Mao in 1976. China today is scarcely Mao's China, and there is much criticism of the government on the Internet in China. Yet, this criticism is still controlled, while China is a state where the Communist Party remains dominant and democracy absent. Moreover, China aims to match the USA in military capability and, on current trends, appears closer to doing so eventually than the Soviet Union ever was, whatever American fears in the late 1950s. Communist dominance and bellicosity are even more the case with North Korea. Yet, if a cold war thus continues, it is difficult, walking round a former *Stasi* prison in onetime East Germany to feel anything less than a sense of joy that such tyranny has lost part of its sway.

# SELECTED FURTHER READING

The best recent introduction is provided by the essays in *The Cambridge History of the Cold War* (2010). Edited by Melvyn Leffler and Odd Arne Westad, this is a three-volume collection that ranges widely. Effective shorter introductions are provided by John Lewis Gaddis' *The Cold War* (2007) and Westad's *The Global Cold War: Third World Interventions and the Making of Our Times* (2005). The bibliographies and notes of these books offer far more titles than can be cited here. *Cold War History* is an important journal. The following is only a brief introduction to a few relevant titles.

Andrew, C. and V. Mitrokhin, *The Mitrokhin Archive: The KGB in Europe and the West* (1999).

Bacon E. and Sandle M. (eds), *Brezhnev Reconsidered* (2002).

Ball, S. J., *The Cold War: An International History* (1998).

Breslauer, G. W., *Gorbachev and Yeltsin as Leaders* (2002).

Carafano, J. J., *Waltzing into the Cold War: The Struggle for Occupied Austria* (2002).

Castle, M., *Triggering Communism's Collapse: Perceptions and Power in Poland's Transition* (2003).

Chen, J., *Mao's China and the Cold War* (2001).

Craig, C. and Longevall, F., *America's Cold War: The Politics of Insecurity* (2009).

Cronin, J. E., *The World the Cold War Made: Order, Chaos and the Return of History* (1996).

Dennis, M., *The Stasi: Myth and Reality* (2003).

Ellwood, D., *The Shock of America. Europe and the Challenge of the Century* (2012).

Fontaine, A., *La Guerre Froide, 1917–1991* (2006).

Frankel, M., *High Noon in the Cold War: Kennedy, Khruschev and the Cuban Missile Crisis* (2004).

Gaddis, J. L., *What We Now Know: Rethinking the Cold War* (1997).

—*The Cold War* (2007).

Gambone, M. D., *Capturing the Revolution: The United States, Central America and Nicaragua, 1961–1972* (2001).

Gleijses, P., *Conflicting Missions: Havana, Washington, and South Africa, 1959–1976* (2002).

Grogin, R. C., *Natural Enemies. The United States and the Soviet Union in the Cold War, 1917–1991* (2000).

Grose, P., *Operation Rollback: America's Secret War Behind the Iron Curtain* (2000).

Halberstam, D., *War in a Time of Peace* (2001).

Hanhimaki, J., *The Rise and Fall of Détente: American Foreign Policy and the Transformation of the Cold War* (2013).

Haslam, J., *Russia's Cold War: from the October Revolution to the Fall of the Wall* (2011).

Hogan, M. J., *A Cross of Iron: Harry S. Truman and the Origins of the National Security State, 1945–1954* (1998).

Holloway, D., *Stalin and the Bomb* (1994).

House, J. M., *A Military History of the Cold War, 1944–1962* (2012).

Isaacs, J. and Bell, D. (eds), *Uncertain Empire: American History and the Idea of the Cold War* (2012).

Isaacs, J. and Downing, T., *The Cold War* (2008).

Joppke, C., *East German Dissidents and the Revolution of 1989: Social Movement in a Leninist Regime* (1995).

Judt, T., *Postwar: A History of Europe since 1945* (2005).

Kaiser, D., *American Tragedy: Kennedy, Johnson, and the Origins of The Vietnam War* (2000).

Leffler, M. P., *For the Soul of Mankind: the United States, the Soviet Union, and the Cold War* (2007).

Leffler, M. P. and Westad, O. A. (eds), *The Cambridge History of the Cold War* (3 vols, 2010).

Lévesque, J., *The Enigma of 1989: The USSR and the Liberation of Eastern Europe* (1997).

Lowell, S., *The Shadow of War: Russia and the USSR, 1941 to the Present* (2010).

McCauley, M., *Russia, America and the Cold War 1949–1991* (2008).

McMahon, R. J., *The Limits of Empire: The United States and Asia since World War II* (1999).

Marples, D. R., *The Collapse of the Soviet Union, 1985–1991* (2004).

Mastny, V., *The Cold War and Soviet Insecurity: The Stalin Years* (1996).

Okey, R., *The Demise of Communist Eastern Europe: 1989 in Context* (2004).

Prados, J., *Presidents' Secret Wars: CIA and Pentagon Covert Operations from World War II through Iranscam* (1985).

Schrecker, E. (ed.), *Cold War Triumphalism: the Misuse of History after the Fall of Communism* (2004).

Soutou, G.-H., *La Guerre Froide, 1943–1992* (2011).

Stone, D. (ed.), *The Oxford Handbook of Postwar European History* (2012).

Stöver, B., *Der Kalte Krieg* (2007).

Stueck, W., *Rethinking the Korean War: A New Diplomatic and Strategic History* (2002).

Trachtenberg, M., *Between Empire and Alliance: America and Europe During the Cold War* (2003).

Tse-tung, M., *Selected Military Writings of Mao Tse-tung* (1963).

Westad, O. A. (ed.), *Reviewing the Cold War: Approaches, Interpretations, Theory* (2000).

—*Decisive Encounters: The Chinese Civil War, 1946–1950* (2003).

White, M. J., *The Cuban Missile Crisis* (1995).

Young, J. W. and Kent, J., *International Relations since 1945: A Global History* (2nd edn, 2013).

Zubok, V. M. and Pleshakov, C., *Inside the Kremlin's Cold War: from Stalin to Khrushchev* (1996).

# NOTES

## Preface

1   P. Albanese, *Mothers of the Nation. Women, Families and Nationalism in Twentieth-Century Europe* (Toronto, 2006).

2   For a critical view, H. Nehring, 'What was the Cold War?', *English Historical Review*, 127 (2012), pp. 920–49, esp. p. 924.

3   K. Jarausch and T. Lindenberger (eds), *Conflicted Memories. Europeanising Contemporary Histories* (Oxford, 2007), p. 117.

4   J. Isaac and D. Bell (eds), *Uncertain Empire: American History and the Idea of the Cold War* (New York, 2012).

## Chapter One: 1917–39

1   P. Gatrell, *Russia's First World War: A Social and Economic History* (Harlow, 2005). For the pre-war situation, W. Dowler, *Russia in 1913* (DeKalb, IL, 2010).

2   T. G. Otte, '"A Very Internecine Policy": Anglo-Russian Cold Wars before the Cold War', in C. Baxter, M. L. Dockrill and K. Hamilton (eds), *Britain in Global Politics I. From Gladstone to Churchill* (Basingstoke, 2013), pp. 17–49.

3   B. W. Blouet, *Halford Mackinder* (College Station, TX, 1987), p. 174.

4   A. Rieber, 'The Origins of the Cold War in Eurasia: A Borderland Perspective', in K. H. Jarausch and T. Lindenberger (eds), *Conflicted Memories. Europeanising Contemporary Histories* (Oxford, 2007), p. 117.

5   J. P. LeDonne, *The Grand Strategy of the Russian Empire, 1650–1831* (Oxford, 2004), p. 233.

6   C. S. Leonard, *Agrarian Reform in Russia: The Road from Serfdom* (Cambridge, 2011).

7   C. Kinvig, *Churchill's Crusade: The British Invasion of Russia, 1918–1920* (London, 2006).

8   The correct term is Bolshevik and not all Communists supported Lenin. However, for the sake of clarity, Communist is the term used.

9   P. Brown to Black, email, 2014.

10    D. J. Raleigh, *Experiencing Russia's Civil War: Politics, Society and Revolutionary Culture in Saratov, 1917–1922* (Princeton, NJ, 2002), p. 410; D. Schlapentokh, *The French Revolution in Russian Intellectual Life* (Westport, CT, 1996) and *The French Revolution and the Russian Anti-Democratic Tradition: a Case of False Consciousness* (New Brunswick, NJ, 1997).

11    H. H. Nolte, 'Stalinism as Total Social War', in R. Chickering and S. Förster (eds), *The Shadows of Total War: Europe, East Asia, and the United States, 1919–1939* (Cambridge, 2003), pp. 295–311.

12    G. Leggett, *The Cheka: Lenin's Political Police* (2nd edn, Oxford, 1986), p. 17.

13    V. N. Brovkin, *Behind the Front Lines of the Civil War. Political Parties and Social Movements in Russia, 1918–1922* (Princeton, NJ, 1994).

14    British War Office Report, July 1919, NA. WO. 106/6238, p. 19.

15    C. J. Richard, *When the United States Invaded Russia: Woodrow Wilson's Siberian Disaster* (Lanham, MD, 2013).

16    T. Stovall, *Paris and the Spirit of 1919: Consumer Struggles, Transnationalism, and Revolution* (Cambridge, 2012).

17    General Staff report, 22 July 1919, NA. CAB. 24/84 fol. 284.

18    G. Swain, *Russia's Civil War* (Stroud, 2000).

19    War Office report on military situation, revised up to 19 January 1921, NA. CAB. 24/120 fol. 56.

20    A. Kocho-Williams, *Russian and Soviet Diplomacy, 1900–1939* (Basingstoke, 2011), p. 45.

21    A. Zamoyski, *Warsaw 1920: Lenin's Failed Conquest of Europe* (Basingstoke, 2008).

22    J. Borzecki, *The Soviet-Polish Peace of 1921 and the Creation of Interwar Europe* (New Haven, CT, 2008).

23    J. L. Gaddis, *The United States and the Origins of the Cold War, 1941–1947* (New York, 1972), p. 360.

24    D. Schlapentokh, *The Proto-Totalitarian State: Punishment and Control in Absolutist Regimes* (New Brunswick, NJ, 2007).

25    M. Ádám, *The Versailles System and Central Europe* (Aldershot, 2004).

26    K. Neilson, *Britain, Soviet Russia and the Collapse of the Versailles Order, 1919–1939* (Cambridge, 2006).

27    P. Holquist, *Making War, Forging Revolution: Russia's Continuum of Crisis, 1914–1921* (Cambridge, MA, 2002).

28    J. Borzecki, *The Soviet-Polish Peace of 1921 and the Creation of Interwar Europe* (New Haven, CT, 2008).

29    Lord Beaverbrook, *The Decline and Fall of Lloyd George* (London, 1963), p. 292.

30    H. L. Dyck, *Weimar Germany and Soviet Russia 1926–1933* (1966).

31    D. R. Stone, 'The Prospect of War? Lev Trotskii, the Soviet Army, and the

German Revolution in 1923', *International History Review*, 25 (2003), pp. 799–817, esp. pp. 801–2.

32   G. Bennett, '*A most Extraordinary and Mysterious Business': The Zinoviev Letter of 1924* (London, 1999).

33   S. T. Ross, *American War Plans 1890–1939* (London, 2002), pp. 121–6.

34   V. Madeira, *Britannia and the Bear. The Anglo-Russian Intelligence Wars, 1917–1929* (Woodbridge, 2014).

35   M. Kellogg, *The Russian Roots of Nazism: White Émigrés and the Making of National Socialism, 1917–1945* (Cambridge, 2005).

36   Z. Steiner, 'The Soviet Commissariat of Foreign Affairs and the Czechoslovakian Crisis in 1938: New Material from the Soviet Archives', *Historical Journal*, 42 (1999), pp. 777–9.

37   J. Frémeaux, *Les Empires Coloniaux. Une Histoire-Monde* (Paris, 2012), p. 399.

38   C. Andrew, 'British Intelligence and the Breach with Russia in 1927', *Historical Journal*, 25 (1982), pp. 457–64; J. Haslam, 'Comintern and Soviet Foreign Policy, 1919–41', in R. G. Suny (ed.), *The Cambridge History of Russia, III: The Twentieth Century* (Cambridge, 2006), pp. 637–42.

39   Haslam, 'Comintern and Soviet Foreign Policy', pp. 648–9.

40   N. E. Saul, *Friends or Foes? The United States and Soviet Russia, 1921–1941* (Lawrence, Kansas, 2006).

41   O. H. Bullitt (ed.), *For the President. Personal and Secret. Correspondence Between Franklin D. Roosevelt and William C. Bullitt* (London, 1973), p. 135. The reference was to an Edward Lear limerick.

42   A. Dirlik, *The Origins of Chinese Communism* (Oxford, 1989); E. J. Perry, *Shanghai on Strike: The Politics of Chinese Labor* (Cambridge, 1995); B. G. Martin, *The Shanghai Green Gang: Politics and Organised Crime, 1919–1937* (Berkeley, California, 1996).

43   S. Roskill, *Admiral of the Fleet Earl Beatty* (London, 1980), p. 299.

44   J. Fisher, 'Major Norman Bray and Eastern Unrest in the British Empire in the aftermath of World War I', *Archives*, 27 (2002), p. 5.

45   M. Broxup, 'The Last *Chazawat*: The 1920–1921 Uprising', and A. Avtorkhanov, 'The Chechens and Inguish during the Soviet Period', in M. Broxup (ed.), *The North Caucasus Barrier* (London, 1992), pp. 112–45, 157–61, 183.

46   A. Khalid, 'The Soviet Union as an Imperial Formation. A View from Central Asia', in A. L. Stoler et al. (eds), *Imperial Formations* (Santa Fé, NM, 2007), pp. 121–2.

47   P. Holquist, '"Information Is the Alpha and Omega of Our Work": Bolshevik Surveillance in its Pan-European Context', *Journal of Modern History*, 69 (1997), p. 448.

48   D. Shearer, 'Elements Near and Alien: Passportization, Policing, and Identity in the Stalinist State, 1932–1952', *Journal of Modern History*, 76 (2004), pp. 835–81.

49    C. Merridale, 'The 1937 Census and the Limits of Stalinist Rule', *Historical Journal*, 39 (1990), pp. 225–40.

50    M. von Hogen, *Soldiers in the Proletarian Dictatorship: The Red Army and the Soviet Socialist State, 1917–1930* (Ithaca, NY, 1990).

51    J. Jacobson, *When the Soviet Union Entered World Politics* (Berkeley, CA, 1994).

52    K. E. Bailes, *Technology and Society Under Lenin and Stalin. Origins of the Soviet Technical Intelligentsia, 1917–1945* (Princeton, NJ, 1978); D. Brandenburger, *Propaganda State in Crisis: Soviet Ideology, Indoctrination, and Terror under Stalin, 1927–1941* (Stanford, CA, 2011).

53    D. Priestland, *Stalinism and the Politics of Mobilisation: Ideas, Power, and Terror in Inter-War Russia* (Oxford, 2007).

54    In the case of China, this is a reference to the Nationalist success against the warlords and not to conflict with the Communists.

55    L. Young, *Japan's Total Empire: Manchuria and the Culture of Wartime Imperialism* (Berkeley, CA, 1997); Y. T. Matsusaka, *The Making of Japanese Manchuria, 1904–1932* (Cambridge, Massachusetts, 2001).

56    D. R. Stone, *Hammer and Rifle: The Militarisation of the Soviet Union, 1926–1933* (Lawrence, KA, 2000).

57    D. R. Stone, 'The First Five-Year Plan and the Geography of the Soviet Defence Industry', *Europe-Asia Studies*, 57 (2005), pp. 1047–63.

58    T. R. Maddux, 'United States-Soviet Naval Relations in the 1930s. The Soviet Union's Efforts to Purchase Naval Vessels', in D. J. Stoker and J. A. Grant (eds), *Girding for Battle. The Arms Trade in a Global Perspective, 1815–1940* (Westport, CT, 2003), p. 207.

59    I. Lükes, 'The Tukhachevsky Affair and President Edvard Benes: Solutions and Open Questions', *Diplomacy and Statecraft*, 7 (1996), pp. 505–29.

60    J. A. Getty and O. V. Maumov, *The Road to Terror: Stalin and the Self-Destruction of the Bolsheviks, 1932–1939* (New Haven, CT, 1999), p. 446.

61    J. Rohwer and M. S. Monakov, *Stalin's Ocean-Going Fleet: Soviet Naval Strategy and Shipbuilding Programmes, 1935–1953* (London, 2001); S. McLaughlin, 'USSR', in V. P. O'Hara, W. D. Dickson and R. Worth (eds), *On Seas Contested. The Seven Great Navies of the Second World War* (Annapolis, MD, 2010), p. 260.

62    S. C. M. Paine, *The Wars for Asia, 1911–1949* (Cambridge, 2012).

63    J. Haslam, *The Soviet Union and the Threat from the East 1933–1941: Moscow, Tokyo and the Prelude to the Pacific War* (Basingstoke, 1992).

64    A. Coox, *Nomonhan: Japan Against Russia 1939* (Stanford, CA, 1985).

# Chapter Two: 1939–45

1    J. A. Maiolo, 'Anglo-Soviet Naval Arms Diplomacy Before the Second World War', *English Historical Review*, 123 (2008), p. 352.

2    Z. Steiner, *The Triumph of the Dark: European International History, 1933–1939* (Oxford, 2011).

3    S. Fitzpatrick and M. Geyer (eds), *Beyond Totalitarianism: Stalinism and Nazism Compared* (Cambridge, 2009); T. Snyder, *Bloodlands: Europe Between Hitler and Stalin* (London, 2010).

4    I. Lukes, 'Did Stalin Desire War in 1938? A New Look at Soviet Behaviour during the May and September Crises', *Diplomacy and Statecraft*, 2 (1991), esp. pp. 36, 41–2.

5    K. R. Jolluck, *Exile and Identity: Polish Women in the Soviet Union during World War II* (Pittsburgh, PN, 2003).

6    R. Moorhouse, *The Devils' Alliance. Hitler's Pact with Stalin, 1939–41* (London, 2014), pp. 67–70.

7    T. R. Philbin, *The Lure of Neptune. German-Soviet Naval Collaboration and Ambitions, 1919–1941* (Columbia, SC, 1994).

8    T. Snyder, *Bloodlands: Europe Between Hitler and Stalin* (London, 2010).

9    R. C. Raack, *Stalin's Drive to the West: 1938–1945* (Stanford, CA, 1995).

10   C. Hartmann, *Operation Barbarossa: Nazi Germany's War in the East, 1941–1945* (Oxford, 2013).

11   C. Johnson, *An Instance of Treason: Ozaki Hotsumi and the Sorge Spy Ring* (2nd edn, Stanford, CA, 1990).

12   D. Culbert, 'Our Awkward Ally: *Mission to Moscow*', in J. E. O'Connor and M. A. Jackson (eds), *American Cinema/American History* (New York, 1979).

13   K. Berkhoff, *Motherland in Danger: Soviet Propaganda during World War II* (Cambridge, MA, 2012); D. Stafford (ed.), *Flight from Reality: Rudolf Hess and his Mission to Scotland 1941* (London, 2002).

14   J. Haslam, 'Stalin's Fears of a Separate Peace, 1942', *Intelligence and National Security*, 84 (1993), pp. 97–9.

15   D. Watson, *Molotov. A Biography* (Basingstoke, 2005).

16   J. E. Haynes, H. Klehr and A. Vassiliev, *Spies: The Rise and Fall of the KGB in America* (New Haven, CT, 2009).

17   M. Broekmeyer, *Stalin, the Russians, and Their War, 1941–45* (Madison, WI, 2004).

18   S. M. Miner, *Stalin's Holy War: Religion, Nationalism, and Alliance Politics, 1941–1945* (Chapel Hill, NC, 2003).

19   D. Dilks, *Churchill and Company: Allies and Rivals in War and Peace* (London, 2012), p. 172.

20   Reporting about visit to MacArthur's headquarters in Manila, Major-General William Penney, Director of Intelligence, HQ Supreme Allied Commander, SE Asia, to Major-General John Sinclair, Director of Military Intelligence, War Office, 2 May 1945, London, King's College, Liddell Hart Archive, Penney Papers, 5/1.

21   J. Lewis, *Changing Direction: British Military Planning for Post-War Strategic Defence, 1942–47* (2nd edn, London, 2003).

22 M. E. Glantz, *FDR and the Soviet Union: The President's Battles over Foreign Policy* (Lawrence, KA, 2005).

23 F. J. Harbutt, *Yalta 1945. Europe and America at the Crossroads* (Cambridge, 2009); S. Plokhy, *Yalta. The Price of Peace* (New York, 2010). For a willingness to accede to Soviet demands over Finland, H. P. Evans, *Diplomatic Deceptions: Anglo-Soviet Relations and the Fate of Finland, 1944–1948* (Helsinki, 2011).

24 M. Edele, *Soviet Veterans of World War II* (Oxford, 2008); R. Reese, *Why Stalin's Soldiers Fought* (Lawrence, KA, 2011).

25 V. Mastny, *The Cold War and Soviet Insecurity: The Stalin Years* (New York, 1996); G. Roberts, *Stalin's Wars: from World War to Cold War, 1939–1953* (New Haven, CT, 2008).

# Chapter Three: 1945–53

1 Roberts to Ernest Bevin, Foreign Secretary, NA. FO. 371/56763 fols 37–8.

2 A. J. Rieber, 'The Crack in the Plaster: Crisis in Romania and the Origins of the Cold War', *Journal of Modern History*, 76 (2004), pp. 62–106.

3 B. J. Bernstein, 'The Uneasy Alliance: Roosevelt, Churchill, and the Atomic Bomb, 1940–1945', *Western Political Quarterly*, 29 (1976), pp. 214–16; J. Rose, 'Winston Churchill and the Literary History of Politics', *Historically Speaking*, 14/5 (November 2013), p. 6.

4 *Foreign Relations of the United States. The Conferences at Malta and Yalta 1945* (Washington, 1955), pp. 450–1.

5 L. Briedis, *Vilnius: City of Strangers* (Vilnius, 2008); W. J. Risch, *The Ukrainian West: Culture and the Fate of Empire in Soviet Lviv* (Cambridge, MA, 2011); G. Thum, *Uprooted: How Breslau became Wroclaw during the Century of Expulsions* (Princeton, NJ, 2011); M. Mazower, J. Reinisch and D. Feldman (eds), *Post-war Reconstruction in Europe: International Perspectives, 1945–1949* (Oxford, 2011); R. M. Douglas, *Orderly and Humane: The Expulsion of the Germans after the Second World War* (New Haven, CT, 2012). The title is angrily ironic.

6 R. J. McMahon, *Dean Acheson and the Creation of an American World Order* (Dulles, VI, 2009).

7 NA. FO. 371/56763 fol. 26.

8 T. T. Hammond, *The Anatomy of Communist Takeovers* (New Haven, CT, 1975).

9 M. P. Leffler, 'The American Conception of National Security and the Beginnings of the Cold War, 1945–48', *American Historical Review*, 89 (1984), pp. 346–81.

10 C. S. Gray, 'Mission Improbable, Fear, Culture, and Interest: Peacemaking 1943–49', in W. Murray and J. Lacey (eds), *The Making of Peace: Rulers, States, and the Aftermath of War* (Cambridge, 2009), pp. 265–91.

11  *Foreign Relations of the United States 1947*, vol I (Washington, 1973), p. 80.

12  R. Ginat, 'Soviet Policy towards the Arab World, 1945–48', *Middle Eastern Studies*, 32 (1996), pp. 321–35.

13  G. Lenczowski, *Russia and the West in Iran, 1918–1948: A Study in Big-Power Rivalry* (New York, 1949).

14  T. H. Etzold and J. L. Gaddis (eds), *Containment: Documents on American Policy and Strategy, 1945–1950* (New York, 1978), pp. 84–90; Gaddis, *The United States and the Origins of the Cold War, 1941–1947* (New York, 1972) and *George F. Kennan: An American Life* (New York, 2011).

15  M. Schain (ed.), *The Marshall Plan: Fifty Years After* (Basingstoke, 2001).

16  R. Cockett (ed.), *My Dear Max. The letters of Brendan Bracken to Lord Beaverbrook, 1925–1958* (London, 1990), p. 112.

17  P. Steege, *Black Market, Cold War: Everyday Life in Berlin, 1946–1949* (Cambridge, 2007).

18  M. P. Leffler, *A Preponderance of Power: National Security, the Truman Administration and the Cold War* (Stanford, CA, 1992).

19  C. J. M. Goulter, 'The Greek Civil War: A National Army's Counter-insurgency Triumph', *Journal of Military History*, 78 (2014), pp. 1017–55.

20  C. M. Woodhouse, *The Struggle for Greece, 1941–1949* (St Albans, 1976); H. Jones, *'A New Kind of War': America's Global Strategy and the Truman Doctrine in Greece* (Oxford, 1989); T. Jones, 'The British Army, and Counter-Guerrilla Warfare in Greece, 1944–1949', *Small Wars and Insurgencies*, 8 (1997), pp. 80–106; C. R. Shrader, *The Withered Vine: Logistics and the Communist Insurgency in Greece, 1945–1949* (Westport, CT, 1999).

21  A. Statiev, *The Soviet Counterinsurgency in the Western Borderlands* (Cambridge, 2010).

22  P. Grose, *Operation Rollback: America's Secret War Behind the Iron Curtain* (New York, 2000).

23  V. Mastny, *The Cold War and Soviet Insecurity* (Oxford, 1996).

24  A. J. Prazmowska, *Civil War in Poland, 1942–1948* (Basingstoke, 2004), pp. 143–67.

25  G. Bruce, *The Firm: The Inside Story of the Stasi* (Oxford, 2010).

26  M. Schoenhals, *Spying for the People: Mao's Secret Agents, 1949–1967* (Cambridge, 2013).

27  NA. FO. 371/56763 fol. 24.

28  Y. Gorlizki and O. Khlevniuk, *Cold Peace: Stalin and the Soviet Ruling Circle, 1945–1953* (Oxford, 2004); J. Rubenstein and V. Naumov (eds), *Stalin's Secret Pogrom: The Postwar Inquisition of the Jewish Anti-Fascist Committee* (New Haven, CT, 2002).

29  G. Jones, *Science, Politics and the Cold War* (London, 1988).

30  A. J. Falk, *Upstaging the Cold War: American Dissent and Cultural*

*Diplomacy, 1940–1960* (Amherst, MA, 2010); M. Stokes, *American History through Hollywood Film. From the Revolution to the 1960s* (London, 2013), pp. 191–2.

31   J. J. Gladchuk, *Hollywood and Anti-Communism. HUAC and the Evolution of the Red Menace, 1935–1950* (New York, 2007).

32   L. Mary, *The Big Tomorrow: Hollywood and the Politics of the American Way* (Chicago, IL, 2000); D. Noble, *The Death of a Nation: American Culture and the End of Exceptionalism* (Minneapolis, MN, 2002); W. Wall, *Inventing the 'American Way': The Politics of Consensus from the New Deal to the Civil Rights Movement* (New York, 2008).

33   P. Mandler, *Return from the Natives: How Margaret Mead Won the Second World War and Lost the Cold War* (New Haven, CT, 2013).

34   T. W. Devine, *Henry Wallace's 1948 Presidential Campaign and the Future of Postwar Liberalism* (Chapel Hill, NC, 2013).

35   V. A. Wilson, 'Elizabeth Bentley and Cold War Representation: Some Masks Not Dropped', *Intelligence and National Security*, 14 (1999), p. 52.

36   E. Latham, *The Communist Controversy in Washington from the New Deal to McCarthy* (Cambridge, MA, 1966).

37   K. Osgood, *Total Cold War: Eisenhower's Secret Propaganda Battle at Home and Abroad* (Lawrence, KA, 2008).

38   M. Sherry, *In the Shadow of War: The United States since 1930* (New Haven, CO, 1995); A. Bacevich, *New American Militarism: How Americans are Seduced by War* (New York, 2006).

39   NA. CAB. 130/37. For the problems of managing the BBC, A. Webb, *London Calling: Britain, the BBC World Service and the Cold War* (London, 2014).

40   A. J. Nicholls, *Freedom with Responsibility. The Social Market Economy in Germany 1918–1963* (Oxford, 1994).

41   W. Wei, *Counterrevolution in China: The Nationalists in Jiangxi during the Soviet Period* (Ann Arbor, MI, 1985).

42   *Selected Military Writings of Mao Tse-tung* (Beijing, 1963).

43   B. Yang, *From Revolution to Politics: Chinese Communists on the Long March* (Boulder, CO, 1990).

44   G. Benton, *New Fourth Army: Communist Resistance along the Yangtze and the Nuai, 1939–1941* (Richmond, 1999).

45   O. A. Westad, *Decisive Encounters: The Chinese Civil War, 1946–1949* (Stanford, CA, 2003).

46   G. N. Nash, *The American West Transformed: The Impact of the Second World War* (Bloomington, IN, 1985).

47   S. I. Levine, *Anvil of Victory: The Communist Revolution in Manchuria, 1945–1948* (New York, 1987).

48   T. Tsou, *America's Failure in China, 1941–1950* (Chicago, IL, 1963); O. Y. K. Wou, *Mobilizing the Masses: Building Revolution in Henan* (Stanford, California, 1994); J. K. S. Yick, *Making Urban Revolution in*

*China: The CCP-GHD Struggle for Beiping-Tianjin, 1945–1949* (Armonk, NY, 1995).

49    R. J. McMahon, *Colonialism and Cold War: the United States and the Struggle for Indonesian Independence, 1945–49* (London, 1981).

50    K. M. Boylan, 'No "Technical Knockout": Giap's Artillery at Dien Bien Phu', *Journal of Military History*, 78 (2014), pp. 1349–83.

51    G. Lockhart, 'In Lieu of the *Levée-en-mass*. Mass Mobilization in Modern Vietnam', in D. Moran and A. Waldron (eds), *The People in Arms. Military Myth and National Mobilization since the French Revolution* (Cambridge, 2003), pp. 227–31; F. Longevall, *Embers of War: The Fall of an Empire and the Makers of America's Vietnam* (New York, 2012).

52    S. W. Duke and W. Krieger (eds), *US Military Forces in Europe: The Early Years, 1945–1970* (Boulder, CO, 1993).

53    J. A. Huston, *Outposts and Allies: US Army Logistics in the Cold War, 1945–1953* (Selinsgrove, PN, 1988).

54    G. Schmidt (ed.), *NATO. The First Fifty Years: From 'Security of the West' towards 'Securing Peace in Europe'* (London, 2000).

55    A. R. Millett, *The War for Korea* (2 vols, Lawrence, KA, 2005–10). For a critical view of American policy, B. Cumings, *The Korean War: A History* (New York, 2010), but see review in *Proceedings of the U.S. Naval Institute*, 136, 12 (December 2010), pp. 73–4.

56    Chancery to American Department, Foreign Office, 2 August 1950, NA. FO. 37/81655.

57    Ibid.

58    M. W. Cagle and F. A. Manson, *The Sea War in Korea* (Annapolis, MD, 2000).

59    X. Zhang, *Red Wings Over the Yalu: China, the Soviet Union, and the Air War in Korea* (College Station, TX, 2002).

60    J. W. Spanner, *The Truman-MacArthur Controversy and the Korean War* (New York, 1965); D. Herspring, *The Pentagon and the Presidency: Civil-Military Relations from FDR to George W. Bush* (Lawrence, KA, 2005).

61    D. C. James, 'Command Crisis: MacArthur and the Korean War', in H. R. Borowski (ed.), *The Harmon Memorial Lectures in Military History, 1959–1987* (Washington, 1988), pp. 218–19.

62    *Foreign Relations of the United States 1950* vol. VII (Washington, 1976), pp. 1296–7.

63    C. C. Crane, *American Airpower Strategy in Korea, 1950–1953* (Lawrence, Kansas, 2000).

64    The extensive literature includes W. Stueck, *Rethinking the Korean War: A New Diplomatic and Strategic History* (Princeton, NJ, 2002).

65    C. K. Armstrong, *Tyranny of the Weak: North Korea and the World, 1950–1992* (Ithaca, NY, 2013).

66    S. H. Lee, *Outposts of Empire. Korea, Vietnam and the Origins of the Cold*

*War in Asia, 1949–1958* (Liverpool, 1995), p. 85; A. Roland, *The Military-Industrial Complex* (Washington, 2001).

67    R. E. Herzstein, *Henry R. Luce, 'Time', and the American Crusade in Asia* (Cambridge, 2005).

68    *Executive Sessions of the Senate Foreign Relations Committee,* vol. 5: 1953 (Washington, 1977), p. 450.

69    E. Abrahamian, *The Coup: 1953, the CIA and the Roots of Modern U.S.-Iranian Relations* (New York, 2013).

70    R. L. Benson and M. Warner (eds), *Venona: Soviet Espionage and the American Response, 1939–1957* (Laguna Hills, CA, 1996).

71    Among the vast literature on this subject, J. Prados, *Presidents' Secret Wars: CIA and Pentagon Covert Operations from World War II through Iranscam* (New York, 1985); P. Lashmar, *Spy Flights of the Cold War* (Stroud, 1996); C. Andrew and V. Mitrokhin, *The Mitrokhin Archive: The KGB in Europe and the West* (London, 1999); S. Dorril, *MI6; Fifty Years of Special Operations* (London, 2000); R. Aldrich, *The Hidden Hand: Britain, America and Cold War Secret Intelligence* (London, 2001); K. Conboy, *The Cambodian Wars. Clashing Armies and CIA Covert Operations* (Lawrence, KA, 2013); H. Dylan, *Defence Intelligence and the Cold War. Britain's Joint Intelligence Bureau 1945–1964* (Oxford, 2014). For criticism of the CIA, M. Goodman, 'Espionage and Covert Action', in C. Eisendrath (ed.), *National Insecurity: US. Intelligence after the Cold War* (Washington, 1999), pp. 23–43, and R. Jeffrey-Jones, *Cloak and Dollar. A History of American Secret Intelligence* (New Haven, CT, 2002).

72    C. Walton, *Empire of Secrets: British Intelligence, the Cold War, and the Twilight of Empire* (London, 2013).

73    M. Grant (ed.), *The British Way in Cold Warfare: Diplomacy, Intelligence and the Bomb, 1945–1975* (London, 2009).

74    J. M. Diefendorf, A. Frohn and H. J. Rupieper (eds), *American Policy and the Reconstruction of West Germany, 1945–1955* (Cambridge, 1993); N. Wiggerhaus and R. G. Foerster (eds), *The Western Security Community: Common Problems and Conflicting National Interests during the Foundation Phase of the North Atlantic Alliance* (Oxford, 1993); S. Mawby, *Containing Germany: Britain and the Arming of the Federal Republic* (London, 1999).

75    R. Markwick, 'The Great Patriotic War in Soviet and Post-Soviet Collective Memory', in D. Stone (ed.), *The Oxford Handbook of Postwar European History* (Oxford, 2012), pp. 692–3.

76    J. L. Gaddis, *Strategies of Containment: A Critical Appraisal of Postwar American National Security* (New York, 1982).

77    M. J. Hogan, *A Cross of Iron: Harry S. Truman and the Origins of the National Security State, 1945–1954* (Cambridge, 1998).

78    H. Zimmermann, *Money and Security: Troops, Monetary Policy, and West Germany's Relations with the United States and Britain, 1950–1971* (Washington, 2002).

79    M. Connelly, 'Taking off the Cold War Lens: Visions of North-South Conflict during the Algerian War of Independence', *American Historical Review*, 105 (2000), pp. 739–69.

80    M. E. Latham, *The Right Kind of Revolution: Modernization, Development, and US Foreign Policy from the Cold War to the Present* (Ithaca, NY, 2011).

81    S. Mawby, 'Mr Smith goes to Vienna: Britain's Cold War in the Caribbean, 1951–1954', *Cold War History*, 13 (2013), pp. 541–61.

82    G. R. Sloan, *Geopolitics in United States Strategic Policy, 1890–1987* (Brighton, 1988).

# Chapter Four: 1953–68

1     J. Maiolo, *Cry Havoc: How the Arms Race Drove the World to War, 1931–1941* (New York, 2010).

2     D. G. Muller, *China as a Maritime Power* (Boulder, CO, 1983), pp. 18–19, 29, 38.

3     For concerns about the revived possibility of a German-Soviet alignment, T. H. Tetens, *Germany Plots with the Kremlin* (New York, 1953).

4     *Foreign Relations of the United States 1946*, vol. I (Washington, 1972), pp. 1198–9.

5     M. S. Goodman, *Spying on the Bear: Anglo-American Intelligence and the Soviet Bomb* (Palo Alto, CA, 2007).

6     D. Holloway, *Stalin and the Bomb* (Oxford, 1994).

7     G. Herken, *The Winning Weapon: The Atomic Bomb in the Cold War, 1945–1950* (New York, 1990); H. R. Borowski, *A Hollow Threat. Strategic Air Power and Containment Before Korea* (Westport, CI, 1982); G. H. Quester, *Nuclear Monopoly* (New Brunswick, NJ, 2000).

8     M. Trachtenberg, 'The Making of a Political System: The German Question in International Politics, 1945–1963', in P. Kennedy and W. I. Hitchcock (eds.), *From War to Peace: Altered Strategic Landscapes in the Twentieth Century* (New Haven, CT, 2000), pp. 118–19.

9     R. Rhodes, *Dark Sun: The Making of the Hydrogen Bomb* (New York, 1995).

10    U. Bar-Nori, 'The Soviet Union and Churchill's Appeals for High-Level Talks, 1953–54: New Evidence from the Russian Archives', *Diplomacy and Statecraft*, 9 (1998), pp. 110–33; K. Larres, *Churchill's Cold War* (London, 2002).

11    S. T. Ross, *American War Plans, 1945–1950* (New York, 1988).

12    R. E. McClendon, *Autonomy for the Air Arm* (Washington, DC, 1996); H. S. Wolk, *Towards Independence: The Emergence of the US Air Force, 1945–1947* (Washington, DC, 1996); W. S. Borgiasz, *The Strategic Air Command: Evolution and Consolidation of Nuclear Forces 1945–55* (New York, 1996); C. H. Builder, *The Icarus Syndrome: The Role of Air Power*

*Theory in the Evolution and Fate of the U.S. Air Force* (New Brunswick, NJ, 1998); B. Yenne, *SAC: A Primer in Modern Strategic Air Power* (Novato, CA, 1985).

13  S. J. Ball, *The Bomber in British Strategy: Doctrine, Strategy and Britain's World Role 1945–60* (Boulder, CO, 1995).

14  T. A. Hughes, *Over Lord: General Pete Quesada and the Triumph of Tactical Air Power in World War II* (New York, 1995).

15  H. York, *Race to Oblivion: A Participant's View of the Arms Race* (New York, 1970).

16  R. Buhite and C. Hamel, 'War for Peace: The Question of an American Preventive War against the Soviet Union, 1945–1955', *Diplomatic History* (1990), pp. 367–84.

17  H. Strachan, *The Direction of War. Contemporary Strategy in Historical Perspective* (Cambridge, 2013), p. 41.

18  C. C. Crane, 'To Avert Impending Disaster: American Military Plans to use Atomic Weapons during the Korean War', *Journal of Strategic Studies*, 23 (2000), pp. 2–88.

19  T. H. Thomason, *US Naval Air Superiority: Development of Shipborne Jet Fighters 1943–1962* (North Branch, MN, 2007).

20  *Executive Sessions of the Senate Foreign Relations Committee*, vol. 9 (Washington, DC, 1979), p. 488.

21  S. Dockrill, *Eisenhower's New-Look Security Policy, 1953–61* (London, 1996).

22  A. J. Bacevich, *The Pentomic Era: The US Army between Korea and Vietnam* (Washington, 1986).

23  A. J. Bacevich, 'The Paradox of Professionalism: Eisenhower, Ridgway, and the Challenge to Civilian Control, 1953–1955', *Journal of Military History*, 61 (1997), pp. 303–33.

24  D. Redford and P. D. Grove, *The Royal Navy. A History Since 1900* (London, 2014), p. 237.

25  Southampton, University Library, MBI/I149. For a distinctive approach, R. Maguire, 'The use of weapons: mass killing and the United Kingdom government's nuclear weapons programme', *Journal of Genocide Research*, 9 (2007), pp. 394–401.

26  M. Y. Tokarev, 'Kamikazes. The Soviet Legacy', *Naval War College Review*, 67, 1 (winter 2014), p. 70.

27  J. Abbate, *Inventing the Internet* (Cambridge, MA, 1999).

28  P. Major and J. Osmond (eds), *The Writers' and Peasants' State: Communism and Society in East Germany under Ulbricht, 1945–1971* (Manchester, 2002).

29  M. E. Latham, *Modernisation as Ideology: American Social Science and 'Nation Building' in the Kennedy Era* (Chapel Hill, NC, 2000) and *The Right Kind of Revolution: Modernisation, Development, and U.S. foreign Policy from the Cold War to the Present* (Ithaca, NY, 2011); N. Gilman,

*Mandarins of the Future: Modernization Theory in Cold War America* (Baltimore, MD, 2003). J. Rohde, *Armed with Expertise: The Militarization of American Social Research during the Cold War* (Ithaca, NY, 2013).

30    M. Farish, *The Contours of America's Cold War* (Minneapolis, MN), pp. 147–92.

31    S. Gerovitch, *From Newspeak to Cyberspeak: A History of Soviet Cybernetics* (Cambridge, MA, 2002).

32    J. Rettie, 'How Khrushchev Leaked his Secret Speech to the World', *History Workshop Journal*, 62 (2006), pp. 187–93.

33    K. P. Benziger, *Imre Nagy, Martyr of the Nation: Contested Memory, Legitimacy, and Popular Memory in Hungary* (Lanham, MD, 2008).

34    *Executive Sessions of the Senate Foreign Relations Committee*, vol. 8: 1956 (Washington, 1978), pp. 657–8.

35    D. L. Snead, *The Gaither Committee, Eisenhower, and the Cold War* (Columbus, OH, 1999).

36    M. Phythian, 'CND's Cold War', *Contemporary British History*, 15 (2001), pp. 133–56; T. Shaw, 'The BBC, the state and Cold War culture: the case of television's *The War Game* (1965)', *English Historical Review*, 121 (2006), pp. 1351–84.

37    A. E. Gorsuch, *All This Is Your World: Soviet Tourism at Home and Abroad After Stalin* (Oxford, 2011).

38    W. Taubman, *Khruschev: the Man and His Era* (New York, 2003).

39    F. Spufford, *Red Plenty* (London, 2010).

40    M. David-Fox, *Showcasing the Great Experiment: Cultural Diplomacy and Western Visitors to the Soviet Union, 1921–1941* (Oxford, 2012). Not all the visitors were taken in.

41    M.-L. Djelic, *Exporting the American Model: The Postwar Transformation of European Business* (Oxford, 1998); V. de Grazia, *Irresistible Empire: America's Advance through Twentieth-Century Europe* (Cambridge, MA, 2005); R. Kuisel, *The French Way: How France Embraced and Rejected American Power and Values* (Princeton, NJ, 2011); D. Ellwood, *The Shock of America: Europe and the Challenge of the Century* (Oxford, 2012).

42    J. A. Delton, *Rethinking the 1950s. How Anticommunism and the Cold War Made America Liberal* (Cambridge, 2013), p. 156.

43    C. Craig, *Destroying the Village: Eisenhower and Thermonuclear War* (New York, 1998).

44    G. Heefner, *The Missile Next Door: The Minuteman in the American Heartland* (Cambridge, MA, 2012).

45    K. Brown, *Plutopia: Nuclear Families, Atomic Cities, and the Great Soviet and American Plutonium Disasters* (New York, 2013).

46    K. Frederickson, *Cold War Dixie: Militarization and Modernization in the American South* (Athens, GE, 2013); A. Friedman, *Covert Capital: Landscapes of Denial and the Making of U.S. Empire in the suburbs of Northern Virginia.* (Berkeley, CA, 2013).

47 *Executive Sessions of the Senate Foreign Relations Committee*, vol. 12, 1960 (Washington, DC, 1982), p. 7.

48 P. J. Ling, *John F. Kennedy* (London, 2013), p. 54.

49 J. M. Logsdon, *John F. Kennedy and the Race to the Moon* (Basingstoke, 2011).

50 M. Uhl, 'Storming on to Paris: The 1961 *Buria* Exercise and the Planned Solution to the Berlin Crisis', in V. Mastny, S. G. Holtsmark and A. Wenger (eds), *War Plans and Alliances in the Cold War: Threat Perceptions East and West* (London, 2006), pp. 46–71.

51 F. Kempe, *Berlin 1961: Kennedy, Khrushchev and the Most Dangerous Place on Earth* (New York, 2011).

52 P. Broadbent and S. Hake (eds), *Berlin: Divided City, 1945–1989* (New York, 2010).

53 A. W. Daum, *Kennedy in Berlin* (Cambridge, 2008).

54 I have benefited from listening to an unpublished lecture by James Mark, 'Che in Budapest: Decolonisation, Globalisation, and the Socialist World, 1950s–1990s', given in Exeter 2014.

55 J. Ferris, 'Soviet Support for Egypt's Intervention in Yemen, 1962–1963', *Journal of Cold War Studies*, 10 (2008), pp. 5–36.

56 P. Nash, *The Other Missiles of October: Eisenhower, Kennedy and the Jupiters, 1957–1963* (Chapel Hill, NC, 1997).

57 J. G. Hershberg, 'Before "The Missiles of October": Did Kennedy Plan a Military Strike against Cuba', *Diplomatic History*, 14 (1990), p. 198.

58 T. Greenwood, *Making the MIRV: A Study in Defence Decision Making* (Cambridge, MA, 1975).

59 D. K. Stumpf, *Titan II: A History of a Cold War Missile Program* (Fayetteville, CO, 2000).

60 *Executive Sessions of the Senate Foreign Relations Committee*, vol. 7: 1955 (Washington, 1978), p. 390.

61 R. T. Bobal, '"A Puppet, Even Though He Probably Doesn't Know So": Racial Identity and the Eisenhower Administration's Encounter with Gamal Abdel Nasser and the Arab Nationalist Movement', *International History Review*, 35 (2013), pp. 943–74.

62 B. Palmer, *Intervention in the Caribbean: The Dominican Crisis of 1965* (Lexington, KT, 1989).

63 M. Thomas, *Fight or Flight. Britain, France, and their Roads from Empire* (Oxford, 2014), p. 351.

64 R. B. Rakove, *Kennedy, Johnson, and the Non-aligned World* (Cambridge, 2013).

65 O. M. Ulus, *The Army and the Radical Left in Turkey. Military Coups, Socialist Revolution and Kemalism* (London, 2011).

66 G. Brazinsky, *Nation Building in South Korea: Koreans, Americans and the Making of a Democracy* (Chapel Hill, NC, 2007).

67   B. Simpson, *Economists with Guns: Authoritarian Development and US-Indonesian Relations, 1960–1968* (Stanford, CA, 2008).

68   T. C. Field, 'Ideology as Strategy: Military-Led Modernization and the Origins of the Alliance for Progress in Bolivia', *Diplomatic History*, 36 (2012), pp. 147–83; S. G. Rabe, *US Intervention in British Guiana: A Cold War Story* (Chapel Hill, NC, 1999).

69   J. Kuzmarov, 'Modernizing repression: Police training, political violence, and nation-building in the "American century"', *Diplomatic History*, 33 (2009), pp. 191–221.

70   E. Miller, *Misalliance: Ngo Dinh Diem, the United States, and the Fate of South Vietnam* (Cambridge, MA, 2013).

71   L-H. T. Nguyen, *Hanoi's War: An International History of the War for Peace in Vietnam* (Chapel Hill, NC, 2012).

72   R. H. Whitlow, *U.S. Marines in Vietnam: The Advisory and Combat Assistance Era, 1954–1964* (Washington, DC, 1977); R. H. Spector, *Advice and Support: The Early Years, 1941–1960, United States Army in Vietnam* (Washington, DC, 1983); D. Toczek, *The Battle of Ap Bac, Vietnam: They Did Everything but Learn from It* (Westport, CT, 2001); F. Logevall, *Choosing War: The Last Chance for Peace and the Escalation of War in Vietnam* (Berkeley, CA, 2001); W. J. Rust, *So Much to Lose: John F. Kennedy and American Policy in Laos* (Lexington, KY, 2014).

73   P. Asselin, *Hanoi's Road to the Vietnam War, 1954–1965* (Berkeley, CA, 2013).

74   J. Carter, *Inventing Vietnam: The United States and State Building, 1954–1968* (Cambridge, 2008).

75   D. Kaiser, *American Tragedy: Kennedy, Johnson, and the Origins of The Vietnam War* (Cambridge, MA, 2000).

76   N. E. Sarantakes, 'In the Service of Pharaoh? The United States and the Deployment of Korean Troops in Vietnam, 1965–1968', *Pacific Historical Review*, 68 (1999), pp. 425–49.

77   W. J. Duiker, *Sacred War: Nationalism and Revolution in a Divided Vietnam* (New York, 1995); R. E. Ford, *Tet 1968. Understanding the Surprise* (London, 1995); R. Brown, 'Limited War', in C. McInnes and G. D. Sheffield (eds), *Warfare in the Twentieth Century: Theory and Practice* (1988), pp. 177–84.

78   D. T. Zabecki, 'Artillery Fire Doctrine', in S. C. Tucker (ed.), *Encyclopedia of the Vietnam War* (3 vols, Santa Barbara, CA, 1998), pp. i, 49.

79   P. Roberts (ed.), *Behind the Bamboo Curtain. China, Vietnam and the World beyond Asia* (Palo Alto, CA, 2006).

80   L. M. Lüthi, 'Reading and Warning the Likely Enemy – a Commentary: Signalling Across Four Continents', *International History Review*, 35 (2013), pp. 807–16.

81   R. Steininger, '"The Americans are in a Hopeless Position": Great Britain and the War in Vietnam, 1964–65', *Diplomacy and Statecraft*, 8 (1997), pp. 273–4.

82  J. Hanhimaki, 'Selling the "Decent Internal": Kissinger, Triangular Diplomacy, and the End of the Vietnam War, 1971–73', *Diplomacy and Statecraft*, 14 (2003), pp. 164–5.

83  A. Preston, *The War Council: McGeorge Bundy, the NSC, and Vietnam* (Cambridge, MA, 2010).

84  F. G. Hoffman, 'The Real "Forever War"', *Orbis*, 58 (2014), pp. 299–300.

85  M. L. Pribbenow, 'The –Ology War: Technology and Ideology in the Vietnamese Defense of Hanoi, 1967', *Journal of Military History*, 67 (2003), pp. 175–200.

86  D. J. Mrozek, *Air Power and the Ground War in Vietnam: Ideas and Actions* (Maxwell Air Force Base, AL, 1988).

87  C. D. Walton, *The Myth of Inevitable U.S. Defeat in Vietnam* (Portland, OR, 2002).

88  T. C. Shelling, *Arms and Influence* (New Haven, CT, 1966).

89  London, King's College, Liddell Hart Archive, Fuller Papers 4/6/24/2.

90  S. W. Wilson, 'Taking Clodfetter One Step Further: Mass, Surprise, Concentration and the Failure of Operation Rolling Thunder', *Air Power History*, 48 (2001), pp. 40–7.

91  *Executive Sessions of the Senate Foreign Relations Committee* vol. 11, 1959 (Washington, DC, 1982), p. 125.

92  J. A. Nagl, *Counterinsurgency Lessons from Malaya and Vietnam: Learning to Eat Soup with a Knife* (Westport, CT, 2002).

93  M. Elliott, *RAND in Southeast Asia: A History of the Vietnam War Era* (Arlington, VA, 2010).

94  L. Baritz, *Backfire: A History of How American Culture Led us into Vietnam and Made Us Fight the Way We Did* (New York, 1985); J. J. Clarke, *Advice and Support: The Final Years, 1965–1973, United States Army in Vietnam* (Washington, DC, 1988); G. Gaddis, *No Sure Victory: Measuring US Army Effectiveness and Progress in the Vietnam War* (Oxford, 2011).

95  S. P. Mackenzie, *Revolutionary Armies in the Modern Era. A revisionist approach* (London, 1997), pp. 172–3.

96  R. A. Hunt, *Pacification. The American Struggle for Vietnam's Hearts and Minds* (Boulder, CO, 1995); E. M. Bergerud, *The Dynamics of Defeat. The Vietnam War in Hau Nghia Province* (Boulder, CO, 1990).

97  G. Herring, 'People's Quite Apart: Americans, South Vietnamese and the War in Vietnam', *Diplomatic History*, 14 (1990), pp. 1–23.

98  R. H. Collins, 'The Economic Crisis of 1968 and the Waning of the "American Century"', *American Historical Review*, 101 (1996), pp. 413, 417; J. Chace, *Acheson* (New York, 1998), pp. 424–8.

99  M. Charlton and A. Moncrieff, *Many Reasons Why: The American Involvement in Vietnam* (London, 1978), p. 115.

100  G. Q. Flynn, *The Draft, 1940–1973* (Lawrence, Kansas, 1993).

101  Z. Levey, *Israel and the Western Powers, 1952–1960* (Chapel Hill, NC, 1997).

102    E. Primakov, *Russia and the Arabs: Behind the Scenes from the Cold War to the Present* (New York, 2009); G. Laron, 'Playing with fire: The Soviet-Syrian-Israeli Triangle, 1965–1967', *Cold War History*, 10 (2010), pp. 163–84; J. Ferris, 'Guns for Cotton? Aid, Trade, and the Soviet Quest for Base Rights in Egypt, 1964–1966', *Journal of Cold War Studies*, 13 (2011), pp. 35–7.

103    M. Gat, 'Let Someone Else do the Job: American Policy on the Eve of the Six Day War', *Diplomacy and Statecraft*, 14 (2003), p. 154.

104    P. T. Chamberlain, *The Global Offensive: The United States, the Palestine Liberation Organisation, and the Making of the Post-Cold War Order* (Oxford, 2012).

105    D. Adamsky, '"Zero-Hour for the Bears": Inquiring into the Soviet Decision to Intervene in the Egyptian-Israeli War of Attrition, 1969–70', *Cold War History*, 6 (2006), pp. 119–29.

# Chapter Five: 1968–79

1    S. Raghavan, *1971: A Global History of the Creation of Bangladesh* (Cambridge, MA, 1971).

2    R. J. McMahon, *The Cold War on the Periphery: the United States, India and Pakistan* (New York, 1994).

3    J. H. Willbanks, *A Raid Too Far: Operation Lam Son 719 and Vietnamization in Laos* (College Station, TX, 2014).

4    R. Weitz, 'Henry Kissinger's Philosophy of International Relations', *Diplomacy and Statecraft*, 2 (1991), pp. 124–5.

5    A. Dobrybin, *In Confidence: Moscow's Ambassador to America's Six Cold War Presidents* (New York, 1995).

6    S. Scanlon, *The Pro-War Movement: Domestic Support for the Vietnam War and the Making of Modern American Conservatism* (Amherst, MA, 2013).

7    E. Kurz, *The Kissinger Saga: Walter and Henry Kissinger – Two Brothers From Germany* (London, 2009). For an historical dimension, H. Kissinger, *A World Restored: Metternich, Castlereagh, and the Problems of Peace, 1812–1822* (London, 1957).

8    Kissinger, *White House Years* (Boston, MA, 1979), p. 183 and after-dinner speech to New York conference of Social Affairs Unit and Foreign Policy Institute, October 2013.

9    M. Jones, 'Between the Bear and the Dragon: Nixon, Kissinger and U.S. Foreign Policy in the Era of Détente', *English Historical Review*, 123 (2008), p. 1283; J. Suri, *Henry Kissinger and the American Century* (Cambridge, MA, 2007).

10    W. Thompson, *To Hanoi and Back: The U.S. Air Force and North Vietnam, 1966–1973* (Washington, DC, 2000).

11    J. L. Young, 'The Heights of Ineptitude: The Syrian Army's Assault on the
      Golan Heights', *Journal of Military History*, 74 (2010), pp. 852–70.

12    D. Andrade, *America's Last Vietnam Battle: Halting Hanoi's 1972 Easter
      Offensive* (Lawrence, KA, 2001).

13    Ex inf. Richard Connell.

14    M. L. Michel, *The 11 Days of Christmas: America's Last Vietnam Battle*
      (San Francisco, CA, 2002).

15    J. Hahhimaki, 'Selling the "Decent Interval": Kissinger, Triangular
      Diplomacy, and the End of the Vietnam War, 1971–73', *Diplomacy and
      Statecraft*, 14 (2003), p. 176.

16    N. V. Long, 'Post-Paris Agreement Struggles and the Fall of Saigon', in
      J. S. Werner and D. H. Luu (eds.), *The Vietnam War: Vietnamese and
      American Perspectives* (Armonk, NY, 1992), pp. 203–15; J. Willbanks,
      *Abandoning Vietnam: how America left and South Vietnam lost its War*
      (Lawrence, KA, 2004).

17    I. A. Hunt, *Losing Vietnam: How America Abandoned Southeast Asia*
      (Lexington, KT, 2013).

18    Amidst the extensive literature, H. G. Summers, *On Strategy: A Critical
      Analysis of the Vietnam War* (Novato, CA, 1982); L. J. Matthews and D. E.
      Brown (eds), *Assessing the Vietnam War* (Washington, 1987); M. J. Gilbert
      (ed.), *Why the North Won the Vietnam War* (New York, 2002).

19    H. Rockoff, *America's Economic Way of War. War and the US Economy
      from the Spanish-American War to the Persian Gulf War* (Cambridge,
      2012), p. 273.

20    T. Terriff, *The Nixon Administration and the Making of U. S. Nuclear
      Strategy* (Ithaca, 1995); B. Heuser, *NATO, Britain, France and the FRG:
      Nuclear Strategies and Forces for Europe, 1949–2000* (1997).

21    G. Smith, *Doubletalk: The Story of the First Strategic Arms Limitation
      Talks* (New York, 1980); M. Mandelbaum, *The Nuclear Question: The
      United States and Nuclear Weapons, 1946–1976* (Cambridge, 1979);
      F. Kaplan, *The Wizards of Armageddon* (New York, 1983).

22    J. L. Logermann, *Trams or Tailfins: Public and Private Prosperity in Postwar
      West Germany and the United States* (Chicago, IL, 2012); M. Nolan, *The
      Transatlantic Century: Europe and America, 1890–2010* (Cambridge, 2012).

23    W. D. Lippert, *The Economic Diplomacy of Ostpolitik: Origins of NATO's
      Energy Dilemma* (New York, 2011).

24    T. C. Reed, *At the Abyss: An Insider's History of the Cold War* (New York,
      2004), p. 269.

25    P. Högselius, *Red Gas: Russia and the Origins of German Energy
      Dependence* (New York, 2013).

26    A. Demshuk, *The Lost German East: Forced Migration and the Politics of
      Memory, 1945–1970* (Cambridge, 2012).

27    M. E. Sarotte, *Dealing with the Devil: East Germany, Détente and
      Ostpolitik, 1969–1973* (Chapel Hill, NC, 2001).

28 E. Scheffer, *Burned Bridge: How East and West Germans Made the Iron Curtain* (Oxford, 2011).

29 K. Maxwell, *The Making of Portuguese Democracy* (Cambridge, 1995).

30 J. M. Sardica, *Twentieth Century Portugal* (Lisbon, 2008), pp. 85–9, quote, p. 87.

31 N. P. Ludlow (ed.), *European Integration and the Cold War: Ostpolitik-Westpolitik, 1965–1973* (London, 2009).

32 P. Villaume and O. A. Westad (eds), *Perforating the Iron Curtain: European Détente, Transatlantic Relations, and the Cold War, 1965–1985* (Copenhagen, 2010).

33 D. C. Thomas, *The Helsinki Effect: International Norms, Human Rights, and the Demise of Communism* (Princeton, NJ, 2001).

34 H. K. Haug, *Creating a Socialist Yugoslavia: Tito, Communist Leadership and the National Question* (London, 2012).

35 A. Vitan, 'The Soviet Military Presence in Egypt, 1967–1972: A New Perspective', *Journal of Slavic Military Studies*, 8 (1995), pp. 547–65.

36 S. Bronfeld, 'Fighting Outnumbered: The Impact of the Yom Kippur War on the U.S. Army', *Journal of Military History*, 71 (2007), pp. 477–8.

37 J. L. Young, 'The Heights of Ineptitude: The Syrian Army's Assault on the Golan Heights', *Journal of Military History*, 74 (2010), pp. 852–70.

38 A. Siniver (ed.), *The October War: Politics, Diplomacy, Legacy* (London, 2013).

39 A. Barreto, 'Social Change in Portugal: 1960–2000', in A. C. Pinto (ed.), *Contemporary Portugal* (New York, 2003), p. 160.

40 N. MacQueen, *The Decolonization of Portuguese Africa. Metropolitan Revolution and the Dissolution of Empire* (Harlow, 1997); P. Gleijses, *Conflicting Missions: Havana, Washington, and Africa, 1959–1976* (Chapel Hill, NC, 2002).

41 D. Jackson, *Jimmy Carter and the Horn of Africa: Cold War Policy in Ethiopia and Somalia* (Jefferson, NC, 2007).

42 I owe this point to Peter Brown.

43 J. D. Hamblin, *Oceanographers and the Cold War: Disciples of Marine Science* (Seattle, WA, 2005).

44 S. Gorshkov, *Navies in War and Peace* (Annapolis, MD, 1974) and *The Sea Power of the State* (Oxford, 1979).

45 G. E. Hudson, 'Soviet Naval Doctrine and Soviet Politics, 1953–1975', *World Politics*, 29 (1976), pp. 90–113; B. Ranft and G. Till, *The Sea in Soviet Strategy* (London, 1983).

46 P. Nitze et al., *Securing the Seas: The Soviet Naval Challenge and Western Alliance Options* (Boulder, CO, 1979); J. D. Watkins, *The Maritime Strategy* (Annapolis, 1986); E. Rhodes, '"… From the Sea" and Back Again. Naval Power in the Second American Century', *Naval War College Review*, 52, no. 2 (1999), pp. 22–3; D. Winkler, *Cold War at Sea: High Seas*

*Confrontation between the United States and the Soviet Union* (Annapolis, MD, 2000).

47    R. S. Jordan, *An Unsung Soldier: The Life of Gen. Andrew J. Goodpaster* (Annapolis, MD, 2013), p. 125. Goodpaster was NATO's Supreme Allied Commander, Europe from 1969 to 1975.

48    A. Spelling, 'Edward Heath and Anglo-American Relations 1970–1974: A Reappraisal', *Diplomacy and Statecraft*, 20 (2009), pp. 638–58.

49    E. F. Vogel, *Deng Xiaoping and the Transformation of China* (Cambridge, MA, 2011).

50    K. C. Chen, *China's War against Vietnam: a Military Analysis* (Baltimore, MD, 1983) and *China's War with Vietnam, 1979: Issues, Decisions, and Implications* (Stanford, California, 1987); S. J. Hood, *Dragons Entangled: Indochina and the China-Vietnam War* (Armond, NY, 1992).

51    K. C. Chen, *China's War with Vietnam, 1979: Issues, Decisions, and Implications* (Stanford, CA, 1987).

52    U. Bar-Joseph, 'Forecasting a Hurricane: Israeli and American Estimations of the Khomeini Revolution', *Journal of Strategic Studies*, 36 (2013), pp. 718–42.

53    C. G. Cogan, 'Desert One and Its Disorders', *Journal of Military History*, 67 (2003), pp. 201–16.

# Chapter Six: 1979–85

1     D. Hoffman, *The Dead Hand: The Untold Story of the Cold War Arms Race and Its Dangerous Legacy* (New York 2009), pp. 6–11.

2     T. M. Nichols, 'Carter and the Soviets: The Origins of the US Return to a Strategy of Confrontation', *Diplomacy and Statecraft*, 13 (2002), pp. 39–40.

3     K. S. Readman, 'Germany and the Politics of the Neutron Bomb, 1975–1979', *Diplomacy and Statecraft*, 21 (2010), pp. 259–85.

4     *Wall Street Journal*, 3 June 1980; R. Perlstein, *The Invisible Bridge: The Fall of Nixon and the Rise of Reagan* (New York, 2014).

5     C. Moore, *Margaret Thatcher. The Authorised Biography. I, Not For Turning* (London, 2013), p. 553.

6     A. Chiampian, 'Running with the Hare, Hunting with the Hounds: The Special Relationship, Reagan's Cold War and the Falklands Conflict', *Diplomacy and Statecraft*, 24 (2013), pp. 640–60.

7     J. L. Gaddis, *The Cold War: A New History* (London, 2005).

8     J. G. Wilson, 'How Grand was Reagan's Strategy, 1976–1984?', *Diplomacy and Statecraft*, 18 (2007), pp. 773–803.

9     R. Higgs, 'The Cold War Economy: Opportunity Costs, Ideology, and the Politics of Crisis', *Explorations in Economic History*, 31 (1994).

10 S. Bronfeld, 'Fighting Outnumbered: The Impact of the Yom Kippur War on the U.S. Army', *Journal of Military History*, 71 (2007), pp. 465–98; I. Trauschweizer, *The Cold War U.S. Army: Building Deterrence for Limited War* (Lawrence, KA, 2008).

11 F. Fitzgerald, *Way Out There in the Blue* (New York, 2000).

12 J. Haslam, *Russia's Cold War* (New Haven, CT, 2011), pp. 353–4.

13 D. E. Hoffman, *The Dead Hand: Reagan, Gorbachev and the Untold Story of the Cold War Arms Race* (London, 2011).

14 C. Wanner (ed.), *State Secularism and Lived Religion in Soviet Russia and Ukraine* (Washington, DC, 2013).

15 S. Sierakowski, 'Poland's forgotten dissident', *International New York Times*, 30 May 2014, p. 7.

16 D. R. Herspring, 'A Conversation with General Jaruzelski', *Diplomacy and Statecraft*, 8 (1997), p. 205.

17 D. L. Bark and D. R. Gress, *Democracy and its Discontents* (Oxford, 1992), pp. 313–16.

18 L. W. Grau and M. A. Gress (eds), *The Russian General Staff: The Soviet Afghan War: How a Superpower Fought and Lost* (Lawrence, KA, 2002).

19 D. Harvey, *A Brief History of Neoliberalism* (Oxford, 2005).

20 A. Applebaum, *Iron Curtain. The Crushing of Eastern Europe 1944–1956* (London, 2012), p. 465.

21 E. Bacon and M. Sandle (eds), *Brezhnev Reconsidered* (Basingstoke, 2002).

22 S. Kotkin, *Armageddon Averted. The Soviet Collapse 1970–2000* (Oxford, 2001).

# Chapter Seven: 1985–92

1 B. Heuser, 'Victory in a Nuclear War? A Comparison of NATO and WTO War Aims and Strategies', *Contemporary European History*, 7 (1998), pp. 311–27.

2 'The Maritime Strategy 1986', in J. B. Hattendorf and P. M. Swartz (eds), *US Maritime Strategy in the 1980s. Selected Documents* (Newport, RI, 2008), pp. 203–25.

3 J. T. Stanik, *El Dorado Canyon: Reagan's Undeclared War with Qaddafi* (Annapolis, MD, 2003).

4 Gorbachev, *Memoirs* (London, 1996).

5 M. Almond, '1989 Without Gorbachev: What if Communism had not Collapsed?', in N. Ferguson (ed.), *Virtual History* (London, 1997), pp. 392–415.

6 S. Handelman, *Comrade Criminal. Russia's New Mafiya* (New Haven, CT, 1995); A. V. Ledeneva, *Can Russia Modernize? Sistema, Power Networks, and Informal Governance* (Cambridge, 2013); H. Goscilo (ed.), *Putin. Celebrity and Cultural Icon* (London, 2014).

7    P. Reddaway and D. Glinski, *The Tragedy of Russia's Reforms. Market Bolshevism Against Democracy* (1999); V. Shlapentokh, *Freedom, Repression, and Private Property in Russia* (Cambridge, 2013).

8    F. L. Pryor, 'The Rise and Fall of Marxist Regimes: An Economic Overview', *Orbis*, 49 (2005), p. 137; M. Almond, '1989 Without Gorbachev: What if Communism had not Collapsed?', in N. Ferguson (ed.), *Virtual History* (London, 1997), pp. 392–415.

9    M. McCauley, *Gorbachev* (Harlow, 1998), p. 271.

10   A. Grachev, *Gorbachev's Gamble: Soviet Foreign Policy and the End of the Cold War* (Cambridge, 2008). J. G. Wilson, *The Triumph of Improvisation: Gorbachev's Adaptability, Reagan's Engagement, and the End of the Cold War* (Ithaca, NY, 2014).

11   P. Gleijeses, *Visions of Freedom: Havana, Washington, Pretoria, and the Struggle for Southern Africa, 1976–1991* (Chapel Hill, NC, 2013).

12   F. Bozo, M. P. Rey, N. P. Ludlow and B. Rother (eds), *Visions of the End of the Cold War in Europe, 1945–1990* (Oxford, 2012).

13   A. Applebaum, *Iron Curtain: The Crushing of Eastern Europe 1944–1956* (London, 2012), p. 279.

14   M. Castle, *Triggering Communism's Collapse: Perceptions and Power in Poland's Transition* (Lenham, MD, 2003).

15   M. Dennis, *The Stasi: Myth and Reality* (Harlow, 2003).

16   A. J. McAdams, *Germany Divided. From the Wall to Reunification* (Princeton, NJ, 1993), p. 194.

17   J. Lévesque, *The Enigma of 1989: The USSR and the Liberation of Eastern Europe* (Berkeley, CA, 1997); T. G. Ash, *The Magic Lantern: the Revolution of '89 Witnessed in Warsaw, Budapest, Berlin, and Prague* (New York, 1990); P. Kenney, *A Carnival of Revolution: Central Europe 1989* (Princeton, NJ, 2002); R. Okey, *The Demise of Communism in Eastern Europe: 1989 in Context* (London, 2004); O. Sebestyen, *Revolution 1989: The Fall of the Soviet Empire* (New York, 2009); S. Savranskaia, T. S. Blanton and V. M. Zubok, *Masterpieces of History: the Peaceful End of the Cold War, 1989* (Budapest, 2010).

18   C. Joppke, *East German Dissidents and the Revolution of 1989: Social Movement in a Leninist Regime* (New York, 1995).

19   Hugh Trevor-Roper to Max Perutz, 15 Aug. 1990, in A. Palmer (ed.), 'The letters of Hugh Trevor-Roper', *Standpoint*, 59 (January/February 2014), pp. 82–3.

20   F. Bozo, *Mitterrand, the End of the Cold War, and German Unification* (New York, 2009).

21   S. Lovell, *The Shadow of War: Russia and the USSR, 1941 to the Present* (Oxford, 2010).

22   T. J. Colton, *Yeltsin: a Life* (New York, 2008).

23   S. Plokhy, *The Last Empire. The Final Days of the Soviet Union* (New York, 2014), p. 403.

24    G. W. Breslauer, *Gorbachev and Yeltsin as Leaders* (Cambridge, 2002);
      D. R. Marples, *The Collapse of the Soviet Union, 1985–1991* (Harlow,
      2004).

25    H. Strachan, *The Direction of War. Contemporary Strategy in Historical
      Perspective* (Cambridge, 2013), p. 236.

26    J. L. Black, *Vladimir Putin and the New World Order: Looking East,
      Looking West?* (Lanham, MD, 2004).

27    V. M. Zubok, *A Failed Empire: the Soviet Union in the Cold War from
      Stalin to Gorbachev* (Chapel Hill, NC, 2007).

# Postscript

1     R. Hofstadter, *The Paranoid Style in American Politics* (New York, 1965);
      D. B. Davis, *The Fear of Conspiracy: Images of Un-American Subversion
      from the Revolution to the Present* (Ithaca, NY, 1971); F. Donner,
      *Protectors of Privilege: Red Squads and Political Repression in Urban
      America* (Berkeley, CA, 1990); I. Katznelson, *Fear Itself: The New Deal and
      the Origin of Our Time* (London, 2013).

2     Britain and France were not democracies as far as their empires were
      concerned.

3     M. E. Latham, *The Right Kind of Revolution: Modernisation, Development,
      and US Foreign Policy from the Cold War to the Present* (Ithaca, NY,
      2011).

4     P. Kent, *The Lonely Cold War of Pope Pius XII: The Roman Catholic
      Church and the Division of Europe, 1943–1950* (Montreal, 2002);
      M. Phayer, *Pius XII, the Holocaust, and the Cold War* (Bloomington,
      IN, 2008); R. A. Ventresca, *Soldier of Christ: the Life of Pope Pius XII*
      (Cambridge, 2013).

5     S. Jacobs, *America's Miracle Man in Vietnam: Ngo Dinh Diem. Religion,
      Race and US Intervention in Southeast Asia* (Durham, NC, 2005).

6     M. Klare, *Rogue States and Nuclear Outlaws: America's Search for a New
      Foreign Policy* (New York, 1995).

7     F. Fukuyama, *The End of History and the Last Man* (New York, 1992);
      E. Schrecker (ed.), *Cold War Triumphalism: The Misuse of History after the
      Fall of Communism* (New York, 2004).

8     *The Week*, 29 March 2014, p. 4.

9     M. Bassin, 'Classical Euroasianism and the Geopolitics of Russian Identity',
      *Ab Imperio*, 4 (2003), pp. 257–67; W. Laqueur, 'The Russian enigma: is the
      bear turning east?', *Standpoint*, 60 (March 2014), pp. 31–3.

# INDEX

Able Archer (NATO exercise) 182, 197
Abrams, Creighton 123
Acheson, Dean 64
Adenauer, Konrad 84
Afghanistan 171–2, 174, 199, 200
    Soviet Union and 171–2, 184, 205
Africa 158–60
air conflict
    Korean War and 68
    Vietnam War and 120–2
air power 86–7, 89, 91–2 see also
        Soviet Union, air force; USA, air
        force
AirLand Doctrine 197
Albania 49, 134–5
Algeria 78
Alibekov, Kanatjan 176
All-Russian Extraordinary
        Commission for Struggle
        Against Sabotage and Counter-
        Revolution (Cheka) 6
Allied forces
    Germany and 31–2
    Soviet Union and 31–4
American-Soviet Anti-Ballistic Missile
        Treaty (1972) 148
Americanisation 101
Amin, Hafizullah 172
Andropov, Yuri 130, 156, 182, 183, 194–5
Angleton, James 75–6
Angola 158–9, 206
anti-imperialism 16–19
Appeasement 29
Arab-Israeli War (1973) 157–8
arms control 148–9, 204
arms race 81–2, 174
Assad, Hafez al- 126

atom bombs 38, 47, 83, 89 see also
        nuclear weapons
Auchinleck, Claude 43
Australia 116
Austria State Treaty (1955) 82

B-29 bomber 86
B-36 bomber 86
B-47 bomber 86
B-50 bomber 86
B-52 bomber 86, 92–3
bacteriological weapons 177
Baghdad Pact 91
Bagnall, Nigel 198
Baibakov, Nikolai 203
Baltic States 31
Barff, Strafford 65
Battle of Warsaw (1920) 10
Bay of Pigs invasion 105
Begin, Menachem 167
Belgrade Declaration (1955) 95
Beria, Lavrentii 94
Berlin Crisis (1961) 47–8, 103–5
Berlin Wall 210
Berlinguer, Enrico 165
Biermann, Wolf 156
Big Four, The (1927) (Christie) 14
Bismarck, Otto von 29
Bohlen, Charles 90
Bolivia 112
Bolshevism 1, 2
Bond, James 55, 91–2, 98, 101
Borusewicz, Bogdan 179
Bracken, Brendan 48
Brandt, Willy 150–1, 152, 165
Brazil 112
Breslau 40
Brezhnev, Leonid 108, 130, 152, 193, 194

Brezhnev doctrine 130
Britain xi, 3, 164, 187 *see also* Allied
   forces
   air force 87
   American alliance and 42
   American military stations and
      47–8
   Baghdad Pact and 91
   Bagnall, Nigel 198
   Communism and 14, 55–6
   empire and 42–3, 91, 218
   intelligence and 75
   Korea and 65
   militarisation and 72–3
   nuclear weapons and 56, 87, 91
   Russia and 2
   Soviet Union and 2, 12–13, 15,
      17–18
   Stalin, Joseph and 27–8
   strikes and 187
   submarines and 176
Brzezinski, Zbigniew 159, 168
Buchan, John 14
Bucharest International Communist
      Party Progress (1956) 134
Bukharin, Nikolai 21
Bulgaria 95, 211–12
Bullitt, William C. 16
Bush, George H. W. 218

Cambodia 138–9, 145, 168
Camp David Accords (1978) 167
Carter, James 'Jimmy' 159, 166–7,
      172–3
Carter Doctrine, the 172
Casablanca Conference (1943) 32
*Casino Royale* (1953) (Fleming) 55
Catholic Church 221–2
Ceauşescu, Nicolae 88, 133–4, 211
Central Intelligence Agency (CIA) 75
Cheka (All-Russian Extraordinary
      Commission for Struggle
      Against Sabotage and Counter-
      Revolution) 6
Chemical weapons 177
Cheney, Richard (Dick) 168
Chernenko, Konstantin 183, 195
Chernobyl 193
Chervenkov, Vulko 95

*Children of Glory* (2008) 97
China 82–3, 167, 221, 223–4
   air force 68
   civil war 57–60
   Communism and 57–60, 114, 202,
      207
   India and 106
   Japan and 22–3
   Korean War and 66–71, 117
   Manchuria and 22–3
   radicalisation and 72
   Sino-Soviet War 1929 18
   Soviet Union and 15, 16–18, 25,
      50, 104, 134–5 *see also* Lin
      Piao
   Tiananmen Square 207
   Tibet and 34
   USA and 59, 139–42, 146–7, 155,
      167–8
   Vietnam and 117, 168
Christie, Agatha: *Big Four, The* (1927)
      14
Churchill, Winston 3, 12, 32
   atom bombs and 38
   empire and 42–3
   'Iron Curtain' speech and 41
   nuclear deterrence and 85
   Soviet expansion and 33–4
CIA (Central Intelligence Agency) 75
Civil Rights movement 101
Cold War, definition of ix–xi, 2
Combined Bomber Offensive 32
Cominform, the 46
Comintern, the 9, 12, 32
Commonwealth of Independent States
      216
Communism 2–3, 11–16 *see also*
      containment
   anti-Communist movements 49–50,
      52–8, 131, 179–800, 221–2 *see
      also* Solidarity
   Brezhnev doctrine and 130
   Britain and 14, 55–6
   Bucharest International Communist
      Party Progress (1956) 134
   Catholic Church and 179, 221–2
   China and 57–60, 114, 202, 207
   Czechoslovakia and 129–31
   Domino Theory of 74, 113, 115

East Asia and 207
economy and 165, 190–2
Europe and 153, 165, 222
expansion and 9–10
fall of 200–2, 207–17, 223
fiction and 14–15
Germany and 9, 56–7
Gorbachev, Mikhail and 208
Greece and 48–9
Hitler, Adolf and 28
Hungary and 96–8
incarceration and 131
Indonesia and 116
Italy and 56
Korea and 207 *see also* Korean
    War (1951–3)
Latin America and 112
life expectancy and 192
Philippines, and the 73
Poland and 131, 179–82, 208–9
Russian Civil War and 3–4, 6–7
South-East Asia and 146 *see also*
    Vietnam
Soviet Union and 11–16, 46–7,
    165, 215
Stalinism, reaction against 93–6
television and 190–1
Third World and the 110–12
threat of 14–15
USA and 14, 32, 52–5, 137
use of terror and 6–7, 131
Vietnam and *see* Vietnam
weaknesses of 192–5
Western Europe and 55
Yugoslavia and 46–7, 49
Communist International 9 *see also*
    Comintern
Congo 111
consumerism 100–1
containment 11–12, 45, 48, 77–9, 111
Crabb, Lionel 98
Cuba 159, 206, 207
Cuban Missile Crisis (1962) 105–9
cybernetics 93–4
Czechoslovakia 28, 29, 42, 129–31,
    211
    Helsinki Accords (1975) and 156

Daoud Khan, Mohammed 171

DARPA (Defense Advanced Research
    Projects Agency) 92
Davies, Jospeh E.: *Mission to Moscow*
    (1943) 32
de Gaulle, Charles 91, 133
Defense Advanced Research Projects
    Agency (DARPA) 92
Deighton, Len: *Funeral in Berlin*
    (1965) 105
Deng Xiaoping 167, 207
*derevenshchiki* 213
*détente* 150, 151, 155–6, 162, 168
    loans and 190
Diem, Ngo Dinh 112, 113
displacement 40
Dole, Robert 156
Domino Theory 74, 113, 115
Donovan, 'Wild Bill' 55
Douglas, Helen Gahagan 140
*Dr No* (1958) (Fleming) 101
Dubček, Alexander 129, 130, 131
Dugin, Aleksander 223
Dulles, Allen 103
Dulles, John Foster 61, 110–11, 140
Dzerzhinskii, Felix 6

early-warning systems 92, 171
East Asia 24–5
East Germany 152–3, 156 *see also*
    Berlin Crisis (1961); Germany
    Communism and 57, 209–11
    dissidents and 193
    economy and 191–2, 209
    fall of Communism and 209–11
    pollution and 192
    Warsaw Pact and 77
Eastern Europe 129–31, 222
economy 93, 132–3, 162–5, 184–7
EEC (European Economic
    Community) 153–4, 165
Egypt 110–11, 126–9, 156–7 *see also*
    Arab-Israeli War (1973)
    Camp David Accords (1978) 167
Egypt-Israel treaty (1979) 167
Eisenhower, Dwight 63, 71, 75, 140
    nuclear deterrent and 85, 89–90
El Salvador 183, 206–7
espionage 53, 55, 76, 98
    Korean Airlines flight 007 and 182

Estonia 10–11
Ethiopia 159–60
ethnic cleansing 40
European Economic Community
    (EEC) 153–4, 165
European Payments Union 45

Finland 10–11, 30–1
Fleming, Ian 55–6
    Casino Royale (1953) 55
    Dr No (1958) 101
    Live and Let Die (1954) 92
    Moonraker (1955) 98
Flexible Response strategy 109
France
    empire and 43
    Germany and 211
    Middle East and 127
    NATO and 133
    nuclear weapons and 91
    Soviet Union and 15
    Vietnam and 61–2
Frankfurt Declaration (1951) 57
Fuch, Klaus 53
Funeral in Berlin (1965) (Deighton)
    105

Gaither Committee 99
Gaitskell, Hugh 55–6
Geneva Accords (1988) 205
Geneva Summit (1955) 82
geopolitics 140
Germany 44, 217 see also East
    Germany; West Germany
    Allied forces and 31–2
    Berlin Crisis (1961) 47–8, 103–5
    Communism and 9, 56–7
    rearmament and 76–7
    Soviet Union and 13, 15, 27–35, 44
    Stasi 50
    unification and 210–11, 218
    USA and 31, 151
'Germany First' policy 31
Giap, Vo Nguyen 120
Gierek, Edward 179
Giscard d'Estaing, Valéry 165
Godesberg Programme (1959) 57
Goldwater, Barry 115
Golitsyn, Anatoly 75

Gomulka, Wladyslaw 96, 179
Gorbachev, Mikhail 180–1, 199–200,
    202–4, 221
    Afghanistan and 205
    agriculture and 188
    Soviet fall and 207–8, 213, 215–16,
        218
Grapes of Wrath, The (1940) 51
Grecho, Andrei 130
Greece 38, 48–9
Grenada 182–3
Gromyko, Andrey 195
Groves, Leslie 83
Guevara, Che 105
Gulag Archipelago, The (1973)
    (Solzhenitsyn) 156
gulags 30, 31
Gysi, Gregor 210

Harriman, Averell 39
Havel, Václav 156, 211
Heath, Edward 164
helicopters 118–19, 122, 175, 213
Helsinki Accords (1975) 154–6
Hess, Rudolf 32
Hiss, Alger 53
Hitler, Adolf
    Britain and 27–8
    Communism and 28
    Stalin, Joseph and 27–33
Ho Chi Minh 61, 108
Ho Chi Minh Trail 118, 119, 122
Holodomor [The Famine Epidemic] 19
Honecker, Eric 153, 209, 210
Hoxha, Enver 134–5
Hua Guofeng 167
Hué 120
Hungary 9, 85, 96–8, 190, 208
Husàk, Gustàv 156
Hussein, Saddam 178
hydrogen bombs 71, 84 see also
    nuclear weapons

I Was a Communist for the FBI (1951)
    52
ideology 41, 51–7, 100–1
India 42–3, 106, 137
Indochina 43, 61, 74, 114
Indonesia 116

intelligence 75–6, 177–8 *see also*
    espionage
intercontinental missiles 89, 98–9,
    102–3, 109–10, 147 *see also*
    missiles
Intermediate Nuclear Forces Treaty
    204
IRA (Irish Republican Army) 187
Iran 74, 169, 172–3, 178
Iraq 178, 213–14
Iron Curtain, the 41
Israel 43, 127–9, 156 *see also*
    Arab-Israeli War (1973)
    Camp David Accords (1978) 167
    Egypt-Israel treaty (1979) 167
Italy 56, 164, 165

Jackson, Henry (Scoop) 168
Japan 22–3, 25, 31, 185
    economy 132
    nuclear technology and 84
Jaruzelski, Wojciech 180–1
Jiang Jieshi 17, 57, 60
John Paul II (Pope) 174, 179, 221–2
Johnson, Lyndon B. 114, 115, 124,
    125
    Middle East and 128
Johnstone, Eric 52
Jordan 128

Kádár, Janos 208
Kaganovich, Lazar 94, 100
Kalinin, Mikhail 40
Kaliningrad 40
Kania, Stanislaw 180
Karelia 31
Karmal, Babrak 172, 205
Kennan, George 45
Kennedy, John F. 103, 140, 221
    assassination 108–9
    Berlin and 104
    Cuban Missile Crisis (1962) and
        105–9
Kennedy, Robert 54
KGB 178
Khanh, Nguyen 115
Khomeini, Ruhollah (Ayatollah) 169
Khrushchev, Nikita 30, 82, 94–5,
    100–1

Berlin and 104, 105
China and 134
Cuban Missile Crisis (1962) and
    105–9
foreign policy and 105
Kim Il-Sung 64
Kissinger, Henry 138, 140–2
    *Ostpolitik* and 156
Kohl, Helmut 152, 211
Königsberg 40
Korean War (1950–3) 54–5, 63–71,
    82, 87–9
    impact of 72–5, 79
Kosygin, Aleksei 129, 166
Kreisky, Bruno 165
Krenz, Ego 210
Kuchek Khan 18
Kuron, Jacek 131

Latvia 10–11, 213
Le Duan 113
Lebanon 183
LeMay, Curtis 106
Li Peng 207
Libya 198–9
Ligachev, Yegor 204
Limited War theory 116–17
Lin Pao 141–2
    *Long Live the Victory of the
        People's War* (1965) 141
Lithuainia 11, 213
Litvinov, Maxim 33
Liu Shaoqi 142
*Live and Let Die* (1954) (Fleming) 92
Lloyd George, David 12
*Long Live the Victory of the People's
    War* (1965) (Lin Piao) 141
Lumumba, Patrice 111
Lysenko, Trofim 51, 108
Lysenkoism 51–2

MacArthur, Douglas 64, 65, 66–7, 69
McCarren Internal Security Act (1950)
    54
McCarren-Walter Act (1952) 54
McCarthy, Joseph 53–4
McCarthyism 53–4
Mackinder, Halford 2
McNamara, Robert 109

MAD (mutually assured destruction) 81, 147–9
Malenkov, Georgy 85, 94, 100
Malinovskii, Rodion 130
Manchuria 22–3
Mao Zedong 57, 60, 72, 134
    Korean War and 66–7, 71
    Lin Piao and 141–2
Marshall Plan Aid 45–6, 132
Marx, Karl 9
Marxism 201, 202
Marxist-Leninism 201
Maurice Thorez Institute of Foreign Languages 177
Mazowiecki, Tadeusz 209
Mazurov, Kirill 130
Meir, Golda 157
Mengistu, Haile 159–60
Middle East, the 126–9, 156–8
militarisation 72–5
    Germany and 76–7
    Soviet Union and 76
military, importance of the 112
Miodowicz, Alfred 209
MIRVs (multiple independently-targeted re-entry vehicles) 110, 148
missiles 98–9, 101–3, 110, 147–9, 173, 175–7 see also nuclear weapons
    Arab-Israeli War and 157
    Cuban Missile Crisis (1962) 105–9
    deployment of 182
    early-warning systems 92, 171
    Immediate Nuclear Forces Treaty 204
    intercontinental 89, 98–9, 102–3, 109–10, 147
    Polaris missiles 110
    SAGE (Semi-Automatic-Ground Environment) Air Defense system 92
    Vietnam War and 121
Mission to Moscow (1943) (Davies) 32
Mitterand, François 211, 218
Mobuto, Joseph 111
Mobuto, Sese Soko 160
Moczar, Mieczystaw 131

Modrow, Hans 210
Modzelewski, Karol 131
Molotov, Vyacheslav 33, 94, 100
Mongolia 17
Moonraker (1955) (Fleming) 98
Moscow Declaration on General Security (1943) 39
Mozambique 159
multiple independently-targeted re-entry vehicles (MIRVs) 110, 148
Munich agreement (1938) 29
mutually assured destruction (MAD) 81, 147

Nagy, Imre 97
Narkomindel (People's Commissariat for Foreign Affairs) 12
Nasser, Gamal Abdel 110–11, 126, 127–8
national liberation struggles 18
National Security Act (1947) 75
nationalism 110–12, 212–13, 214–15, 216, 223
NATO (North Atlantic Treaty Organisation) 45, 62–3, 130–1
    Czechoslovakia and 130–1
    France and 133
    Hungary and 98
    naval forces and 161–2
    nuclear weapons and 87–8
    strategy 78, 87–8
Naval Force Atlantic 162
neutron bombs 149, 173 see also nuclear weapons
'New Look' policy 88–9, 90–1
Ngo Dinh Diem 112, 113
Nguyen Khanh 115
Nicaragua 169–70, 182–3, 200, 206
Nixon, Richard 103, 141
    China and 139–40, 142
    Communism and 53
    consumerism and 101
    nuclear weapons and 148
    Vietnam and 125, 138, 144
North American Air Defense Command 92
North Atlantic Treaty Organisation (NATO) see NATO

North Korea 71, 207 *see also* Korean
    War
North Yemen 126
Northern Expedition 17
Nosenko, Yuri 76
November Revolution 1917 xi, 1, 4
Novotný, Antonín 129
nuclear confrontation 83–93, 171,
    197–8
nuclear deterrence 67, 85, 109–10 *see
    also* MAD (mutually assured
    destruction)
    Korean War and 71
    USA and 88–9, 109–10
nuclear retaliation 101–3
nuclear weapons 56, 89–93, 101–3 *see
    also* missiles; nuclear deterrence
    arms control and 99, 108, 148–9,
        204
    atom bombs 38, 47, 83, 89
    Britain and 56, 87, 91
    Cuban Missile Crisis (1962) and
        106–9
    delivery systems of 85–6
    early-warning systems and 92, 171
    France and 91
    hydrogen bombs 71, 84
    Intermediate Nuclear Forces Treaty
        204
    launches of 171
    neutron bombs 149, 173
    Partial Test-Ban Treaty (1963) 108
    SALT (Strategic Arms Limitation
        Treaty) 148–9
    Soviet Union and 83, 173, 176 *see
        also* MAD (mutually assured
        destruction)
    USA and 83–6, 88–93, 102–3,
        109–10, 174–5 *see also* MAD
        (mutually assured destruction)

oceanography 161
Ochakov Crisis 2
oil 9, 74, 158, 163, 170
Operation Barbarossa 31
Operation Chromite 66
Operation Mongoose 105
Operation Rolling Thunder 121–2, 124
Operation Whirlwind 97

Orwell, George: 'You and the Atomic
    Bomb' (1945) ix
*Ostpolitik* (Eastern Policy) 150–6
Oswald, Lee Harvey 108–9

Pacelli, Eugenio 221
Pahlavi, Reza 74
Pakistan 137, 205
Palestine Liberation Organisation
    (PLO) 127, 129, 183
Palme, Olaf 165
Partial Test-Ban Treaty (1963) 108
P'eng The-huai 70
*People on the Beach* (1976) (Vent) 156
People's Commissariat for Foreign
    Affairs (*Narkomindel*) 12
*perestroika* 203
Persia (Iran) 18
Petrov, Vasily 159
Philby, Kim 49, 75
Philippines, the 73
Pilsudski, Józef 181
Pius XII (Pope) 221
PLO *see* Palestine Liberation Authority
Poland 10, 11, 171, 178–82
    anti-Communist movements and
        131, 208
    economy and 190, 191
    fall of Communism and 208–9
    militarisation and 76
    rebellion and 95–6
    Russia and 1–2
    Soviet Union and 10–11, 29–30,
        34–5, 96, 180
    travel and 191
Polaris missiles 110
pollution 192
popular culture 53 *see also* television
population movements 40
Portugal 78, 153, 158
Powers, Gary 75
*Pravda* 174
propaganda 12, 19, 51–7, 100
Putin, Vladimir 216

Qaddafi, Muammar 199, 222

radicalisation 72
radio 95

Reagan, Ronald 52, 170, 173–8
    Poland and 181
*realpolitik* 13, 140, 142–3
Red Army 7, 38
*Red Menace, The* (1949) 52
religion 11–12
Ribbentrop-Molotov (Nazi-Soviet)
    Pact (1939) 28–9, 30
Ridgway, Matthew 69
Roberts, Frank 41
Rokossovsky, Konstantin 76
Romania 31, 88, 133–4, 211
Romanov, Grigori 199
Roosevelt, Franklin Delano 16, 34
Rosenberg, Ethel 53
Rosenberg, Julius 53
Rosselli, Carlo 56
Rumsfeld, Donald 149, 168
Russia 1–2, 202, 216, 223 *see also*
        Russian Civil War; Soviet Union
    army 7, 38
    Britain and 2
    nationalism and 212–13, 214
    November Revolution 1917 xi, 1, 4
    religion and 11
Russian Civil War 3–11
    foreign intervention and 4–5, 8–9
    use of terror and 6–7

Sadat, Anwar 156, 167
SAGE (Semi-Automatic-Ground
    Environment) Air Defense
    system 92
Sallal, Abdullah al- 126
SALT (Strategic Arms Limitation
    Treaty) 148–9
Saudi Arabia 126
Savimbi, Jonas 206
Schlesinger, James 149
Schmidt, Helmut 152, 165
SDI (Strategic Defense Initiative) 175
SEATO (South-East Asia Treaty
    Organisation) 91
Shelest, Petro 129
Siberia 23
Six Day War 128–9
Smith, Walter Bedell 42
social welfarism 191
Solidarity 174, 179–81, 208–9

Solzhenitsyn, Alexander 156
    *Gulag Archipelago, The* (1973) 156
Somalia 159
Somoza, Anastasio 169–70
Sorge, Richard 31
South Africa 158–9
South-East Asia 61–2
South-East Asia Treaty Organisation
    (SEATO) 91
South Korea 49–50, 71 *see also*
    Korean War
    Vietnam and 115
Southern Rhodesia 158–9
Soviet Union xi, 1, 9, 12, 219–20 *see
    also* Russia; Stalin, Josef
    Afghanistan and 171–2, 184, 205
    Africa and 159–60
    agriculture and 108, 187–88
    air force 23, 68, 91–2, 121
    Allied forces and 31–3
    Angola and 206
    Arab-Israeli War (1973) and 157
    army 38
    bacteriological weapons and 177
    Baltic States and 31
    Berlin Crisis (1961) and 47–8,
        103–5
    Britain and 2, 12–13, 15, 17–18
    chemical weapons and 177
    Chernobyl 193
    China and 15, 16–18, 25, 50, 104,
        134–5 *see also* Lin Piao
    collectivisation and 187–8
    Cominform and 46
    Comintern and 9, 12, 32
    Communism and 11–16, 46–7,
        165, 215 *see also* Communism
    conservatism and 154
    consumerism and 100–1
    Cuban Missile Crisis (1962) and
        105–9
    cybernetics and 94
    Czechoslovakia and 129–31
    data fabrication in 21–2
    *détente* and 151
    diplomacy and 13–16
    dissidents and 193, 202
    economic stagnation and 187–90
    economy and 19, 21–2, 93–4,

99–101, 163–6, 200–1 *see also*
*perestroika*
employment and 188
expansion and 9–10, 33–5, 39–42
fall of 193, 199, 200–1, 207–17,
221–3
famine and 19, 21
Finland and 30–1
foreign policy 39–42, 81–2, 177,
195, 204 *see also* Cuban Missile
Crisis (1962)
France and 15
Germany and 13, 15, 27–35, 44
ideology 35, 51–2, 100
industry and 23, 73
intelligence and 177–8
Iran and 169
Jews and 51, 202
KGB 178
Korean Airlines flight 007 and 182
Korean War and 68, 72
Lysenkoism and 51–2
Middle East and 126–7, 128–9
militarisation and 76
military equipment 23–4, 38–9, 87,
176
military expenditure 217, 220
military industrialization and 20–4
military purges 24
nationalism and 212–13, 214–15,
216
navy 23–4, 160–2, 176, 220
nuclear weapons and 83–92, 171,
173, 176, 197–8 *see also* MAD
(mutually assured destruction)
opposition and 88
Persia (Iran) and 18
Poland and 10–11, 29–30, 34–5,
96, 180
propaganda and 12, 19, 51–2, 54,
100
reform and 199–200, 203–4, 214
Romania and 31, 133–4
Sputnik I and 98, 99–100
Stalinism, reaction against 93–5
state control and 19–20, 21–2
surveillance and 50
technology and 176
territories of 39–41

threats to 220
trade and 151–2, 156
USA and 15–16, 17, 151, 156, 174,
182
use of terror and 6–7, 21–2, 50,
131
Vietnam and 117, 122
weaknesses 192–5, 221
Western targets of 16–19
World War Two and 27–35
Yugoslavia and 46–7
space programmes 137
Sputnik I 98, 99–100
USA and 101, 103, 137
Spain 78
Spanish Civil War (1936–9) 28, 221
spies 193 *see also* espionage
Sputnik I 98, 99–100
stagflation 164
Stalin, Joseph 3, 13–14, 15
Britain and 27–8, 32
expansion and 33–4
foreign policy and 81
Germany and 32–3
Hitler, Adolf and 27–33
Korea and 64, 67
military industrialization and 20–1
Stalinism, reaction against 93–6
*Stasi* 50
State Committee for the State of
Emergency in the USSR 215
Stoph, Willi 152
Strategic Arms Limitation Treaty
(SALT) 148–9
Strategic Defense Initiative (SDI) 175
Strauss, Franz Josef 84
Strausz-Hupé, Robert 139–40
submarines 102–3, 107, 109–10,
147–8, 161–2, 176
Suez Canal 110–11, 127
Suez Crisis (1956) 110–11
Sun Yat-sen 16
surveillance 50
Suslov, Mikhail 165
Syria 126, 128, 157 *see also*
Arab-Israeli War (1973)

Taiwan 64, 74, 168
TB-3 bomber 23

television 190–1, 209
Tet offensive (1968) 119–20, 124
Texas Railroad Commission 163
Thailand 42
Thatcher, Margaret 173–4, 187, 218
Third World 110–12
Tibet 60
Titan II missile 110
Tito, Josip 46, 95
Tonkin Gulf Resolution (1964) 114
totalitarianism 217
trade unions 43, 55–6, 187 *see also*
    Solidarity
Treaty of Brest Litovsk (1918) 4
Treaty of Dunkirk (1947) 42
Treaty of Friendship (1925) 18
Treaty of Moscow (1940) 30–1
Treaty of Non-Aggression (1939) 28
    *see also* Ribbentrop-Molotov
    (Nazi-Soviet) Pact (1939)
Treaty of Rapallo (1922) 13
Treaty of Riga (1921) 10
Trotsky, Leon 13–14
Truman, Harry 31, 67, 69
Truman doctrine 48
Tucker, Francis 42–3
Tukhachevsky, Mikhail 25
Turkey 22

Ukraine 19, 129–30, 216, 221
UNITA (*União Nacional para a
    Independência Total de Angola*)
    158–9, 206
United Arab Republic 126
United Nations 35, 39
Urals 23
USA *see also* Allied forces
    Africa and 159–60
    air force 68, 86–7, 91–3, 120–2,
        198 *see also* helicopters
    Arab-Israeli War (1973) 157
    Berlin Crisis (1961) 47–8, 103–5
    China and 59, 139–42, 146–7, 155,
        167–8
    Civil Rights movement 101, 133
    Communism and 14, 32, 52–5, 137
    consumerism and 100–1
    containment and 45, 48
    conventional weapons and 175

Cuban Missile Crisis (1962) 105–9
*détente* and 168 *see also détente*
    economy and 132–3, 164,
        166–7, 185–6
    El Salvador and 183
    foreign policy 220–1
    Germany and 31, 151
    Greece and 48–9
    Grenada and 182–3
    Hollywood blacklists 52
    Hungary and 98
    ideology and 52
    Indochina and 74
    intelligence 75–6
    Iran and 74, 169
    Iraq and 213–14
    Korean War and 64–9
    Marshall Plan Aid and 45–6, 132
    McCarthyism and 53–4
    Middle East and 127–9, 222–3
    military equipment 175, 198, 213
    military expenditure and 72–3, 90,
        103, 146, 173–5, 197
    military stations in Britain and
        47–8
    NATO and 62–3
    navy 68, 89–90, 102–3, 162, 176,
        198
    Nicaragua and 170, 182–3
    nuclear weapons and 102–3,
        109–10, 174–5 *see also* MAD
        (mutually assured destruction);
        nuclear confrontation
    Philippines and 73
    political campaigns 140–1
    propaganda 52–3
    *realpolitik* and 140, 142–3
    Soviet Union and 15–16, 17, 151,
        156, 174, 182
    space programmes 101, 103, 137,
        175–6
    strategies of 77–9, 85, 87–9, 109
        *see also* Limited War theory
    Taiwan and 74
    Vietnam and 61–2, 138 *see also*
        Vietnam
    war powers and 146
USS *Ethan Allen* 102
USS *Forrestal* 89

USS *George Washington* 102
USS *Maddox* 113
USS *Nautilus* 103

Vance, Cyrus 159
Vent, Hans: *People on the Beach* (1976) 156
Viet Cong 112–13, 117, 119–20, 122–4
Vietnam 61–2, 90, 112–25, 133, 138–9, 143–6
  China and 117, 168
  religion in 221
Vo Nguyen Giap 120

Walesa, Lech 179, 209
Wallace, Henry 52
'War on Terror' 223
War Powers Resolution (Kennedy–Cooper) Act (1973) 146
Warsaw Pact 77
  Czechoslovakia and 130, 134
Warsaw Treaty (1970) 152
Watergate Scandal 164
West Germany *see also* Berlin Crisis (1961); Germany
  Communism and 56–7
  defence of 78
  East Germany and 152–3
  militarisation and 76–7

normalization and 152–3
nuclear technology and 84
*Ostpolitik* (Eastern Policy) and 150–5
radical movements in 164
trade and 151
Warsaw Treaty (1970) and 152
Westmoreland, William 115, 118–19, 123
Whampoa Military Academy 17
Wilson, Harold 56, 116
Wojtyla, Karol 174
World War One 4
World War Three 34
World War Two 27–35, 37–8
Wroclaw 40

Yeltsin, Boris 204, 214–16, 218
'You and the Atomic Bomb' (1945) (Orwell) ix
Yugoslavia 46–7, 49, 88, 95, 202
  Helsinki Accords (1975) and 156

Zaire 160
Zhao Ziyang 207
Zhivkov, Todor 211–12
Zhukov, Georgi 94, 100
Zimbabwe *see* Southern Rhodesia
Zinoviev, Grigory 14